The Second
Handbook on
Parent Education

Educational Psychology

Allen J. Edwards, Series Editor
Department of Psychology
Southwest Missouri State University
Springfield, Missouri

The Second Handbook on Parent Education

Contemporary Perspectives

Edited by

Marvin J. Fine

Department of Educational Psychology and Research
School of Education
University of Kansas
Lawrence, Kansas

Academic Press, Inc.
Harcourt Brace Jovanovich, Publishers
San Diego   New York   Berkeley   Boston
London   Sydney   Tokyo   Toronto

ACADEMIC PRESS, INC.
San Diego, California 92101

United Kingdom Edition published by
ACADEMIC PRESS, INC. (LONDON) LTD.
24-28 Oval Road, London NW1 7DX

ISBN 0-12-256482-0 (alk. paper)
Library of Congress Catalog Card Number: 88-45803

PRINTED IN THE UNITED STATES OF AMERICA
88 89 90 91   9 8 7 6 5 4 3 2 1

Contents

v

Part II. Delivery Systems of Parenting Education

Part III. Training and Research

Part IV. Trends and Directions

Contributors

Numbers in parentheses indicate the pages on which the authors' contributions begin.

BARBARA L. BORDEN (279), 440 Dell Lane, Highland Park, Illinois 60035

DIANE G. BRAGE (347), University of Nebraska Medical Center, College of Nursing, Lincoln Division, Lincoln, Nebraska 68588

BRIDGET CANNON-NIFOUSSI (305), Cooperative Health Education Program, Lincoln, Nebraska 68510

HELEN K. CLEMINSHAW (257), Center for Family Studies, University of Akron, Akron, Ohio 44304

CAROLYN S. COOPER (197), Department of Special Education, Eastern Illinois University, Charleston, Illinois 61920

JOHN DEFRAIN (53), Department of Human Development and the Family, College of Home Economics, University of Nebraska-Lincoln, Lincoln, Nebraska 68583

CRAIG R. FIEDLER (145), Department of Special Education, College of Education and Human Services, University of Wisconsin-Oshkosh, Oshkosh, Wisconsin 54901

MARVIN J. FINE (3), Department of Educational Psychology and Research, School of Education, University of Kansas, Lawrence, Kansas 66045

BRYNA GAMSON (279), Program and Financial Development, Alfred Adler Institute of Chicago, Chicago, Illinois 60605

JOHN GUIDUBALDI (257), Department of Educational Psychology, Kent State University, Kent, Ohio 44240

STEPHAN A. HENRY (3),   Topeka Public Schools, Topeka, Kansas 66611

HOPE HORNSTEIN (279),   Ravenswood Community Mental Health Center, Chicago, Illinois 60625

HELGA E. KAPLAN (21),   Honors College, Kent State University, Kent, Ohio 44242

MARVIN S. KAPLAN (21),   Department of Educational Psychology and Policy Studies, College of Education, Kent State University, Kent, Ohio 44242

ROGER KROTH (119),   Department of Special Education, Manzanita Center, College of Education, University of New Mexico, Albuquerque, New Mexico 87131

PAUL A. LEE (347),   Department of Human Development and the Family, University of Nebraska-Lincoln, Lincoln, Nebraska 68583

FREDERIC J. MEDWAY (237),   Department of Psychology, University of South Carolina, Columbia, South Carolina 29208

MARLENE A. MERRILL (173),   Topeka Public Schools, Topeka, Kansas 66611

BARBARA A. NYE (325),   Tennessee State University and Education Corporation of America, Nashville, Tennessee 37203

NANCY L. PETERSON (197),   Department of Special Education, University of Kansas, Lawrence, Kansas 66045

MICHAEL H. POPKIN (77),   Active Parenting Inc., Atlanta, Georgia 30342

RICHARD L. SIMPSON (145),   Department of Special Education, University of Kansas Medical Center, Kansas City, Kansas 66103

NICK STINNETT (53),   Department of Human Development and the Family, College of Human Environmental Sciences, University of Alabama, Tuscaloosa, Alabama 35487

SALLY VAN ZANDT (305),   Department of Human Development and the Family, University of Nebraska-Lincoln, Lincoln, Nebraska 68583

SUE VARTULI (99),   Department of Curriculum and Instruction, School of Education, University of Missouri-Kansas City, Kansas City, Missouri 64110

MILDRED WINTER (99), Parents as Teachers: The National Center, Missouri Department of Elementary & Secondary Education at the University of Missouri-St. Louis, St. Louis, Missouri 63121

Preface

The statement was recently made that "child care and parent education are the instruments most readily available to increase the nation's capacity to achieve its human development aspiration and fulfill its human development needs" (Hobbs, Dokecki, Hoover-Dempsey, Moroney, Shayne, & Weeks, 1984, p. 2). Data on divorce rates, the incidence of children being raised in single-parent, step-parent, and blended families, the number of employed mothers, and the continued economic and social pressures on families all argue for a full range of parent and family education and support programs.

A multifaceted concept of parent education envisions programs and services being offered through the private and public sectors, to parents of varying educational and economic levels, for normal and exceptional children. Furthermore, narrowly defined programs on child care and parenting skills extend quite naturally into the broader picture of healthy family functioning. This progression projects to a parent–family support and education model that is not age related and can apply via a complex of available sources to parents and families at all age levels. The services can be of an educative and preparatory nature as well as in response to crisis.

The forerunner of this book, the *Handbook on Parent Education* (Fine, 1980), examined some popular models of parent education and the application of parent education to diverse populations. The preparation of this book was substantially encouraged by the favorable response to the earlier book. The study of the American family and concern with the development and welfare of children continue as keen interests of both scholars and practitioners. Much is left to learn about families and the parenting of children, and perhaps even more is needed in terms of dissemination of information and educating parents.

Despite the commonly used term "handbook," it is unrealistic to expect any volume to capture the total state of the art in a given area. This book is considered both as an extension of and as a companion volume to the *Handbook on Parent Education*. The contributors were selected as persons actively involved in a particular area of parenting education and able to write not only from a scholarly position but from an awareness of issues related to the application and dissemination of knowledge and skills.

The book reveals a broad range of topics, beginning with the chapter in Part I by Fine and Henry on professional issues facing those who conduct formal parent education programs. The chapter on national policy by the Kaplans is a comprehensive, thoughtful exposition on federal philosophy and activities related to family policy. The third chapter, by Stinnett and DeFrain, summarizes the landmark efforts by Stinnett and his associates in investigating the characteristics of healthy families.

The second part of the book considers delivery systems and various focuses of parenting education. Popkin's chapter on "Active Parenting" highlights the utilization of and educational potential of a video-based program. The pioneering efforts in the state of Missouri to implement Burton White's ideas on early parenting experiences are described in the chapter by Vartuli and Winter. The effective and comprehensive parenting programs discussed by Kroth were developed as a collaborative effort between the public schools and a university. A central requirement in the education of exceptional children is the inclusion of parents in an individual educational program conference. The chapter by Simpson and Fiedler addresses the needs of parents in terms of active participation in such conferences as well as issues related to parent involvement in the education of handicapped children.

The figures on teenage pregnancies are frightening in their implications for the futures of the children and mothers in those circumstances. The chapter by Merrill provides an overview of this problem and examines a number of programs related to the needs of pregnant mothers. The last chapter in the part on delivery systems, by Peterson and Cooper, looks into the special needs of parents of young handicapped and developmentally delayed children. This is an underserved population that is just beginning to receive the attention it deserves.

The third part, concerned with training and research, begins with a chapter by Medway on measuring the effectiveness of parent education. The parent satisfaction scale as developed and described by Guidubaldi and Cleminshaw represents a significant contribution to our ability to measure important aspects of family functioning. The chapter by Gamson, Hornstein, and Borden presents a formalized instruction training program. While the program depicts one specific model, Adlerian in nature, this chapter was selected because it describes a comprehensive and extended training program that incorporates high standards.

The fourth and last part of the book deals with trends and directions. It includes a chapter by Van Zandt and Cannon-Nifoussi, focusing on the issues that adult children face with their aging parents. In her chapter, Nye describes a range of parent education and involvement programs and contemporary strategies for school implementation. The last chapter, by Lee and Brage, is a comprehensive examination of several important shifts in the focus on family life education. This chapter helps to further broaden and extend the view of parenting education into the larger and perhaps more meaningful picture of family life education.

In sum, this book should enhance the reader's understanding of the contemporary scene in parenting education, including effective programming, important issues, and future trends.

Marvin J. Fine

REFERENCES

Fine, M. (Ed.). (1980). *Handbook on parent education*. New York: Academic Press.
Hobbs, N., Dokecki, P., Hoover-Dempsey, K., Moroney, R., Shayne, M., & Weeks, K. (1984). *Strengthening families*. San Francisco: Jossey-Bass.

I

Introduction

1

Professional Issues in Parent Education

Marvin J. Fine
Stephan A. Henry

Introduction

Although the contemporary interest in parent education suggests its novelty, the concept is hardly new. Croake and Glover (1977) have provided an excellent history of parent education, dating the first serious activities in 1806. During the 1930s thousands of adults participated in parent education groups and several volumes of research on the topic were published (Davis & McGinnis, 1939; Hattendorf et al., 1932; Ojemann et al., 1932).

Two important contributions to the contemporary interest in parenting education are the national, federally subsidized movement to educate preschoolers and their families, Head Start, and the Parent Effectiveness Training Program (PET) (Gordon, 1970). The latter program had not only reached over 250,000 parents by 1976, but had also formally trained 8,000 instructors (Brown, 1976). Behind the scenes, however, were several conditions that prompted national attention to the needs of parents (Clarke-Stewart, 1981); (1) parents were increasingly seen as the most important influence on children's development; (2) schools were not seen as effective in changing children; (3) families were under greater societal stress; (4) there was evidence that many parents were not effective; and (5) new scientific knowledge on childrearing was available.

A recent survey of parents' attitudes and beliefs reported that 75% of the 30,000 respondents believed that it is harder to be a parent today than in the past (Greer, 1986). Certainly recognition of the magnitude of drug use by children and youth, adolescent suicide rates, and the generally

Note: Both writers share equally in authorship of the chapter.

precocious development of many children have created a need in many
parents to obtain information, support, and more effective parenting
skills.

The proliferation of parenting education programs has raised a number
of important questions for the involved professionals. There has been a
confluence of applied, academic, and commercial interests. A rather
varied group of persons have staked out claims to the parenting field, and
the issues that have arisen range from ethical problems to concerns with
the knowledge base of programs.

The Effects of Parenting Styles

Parent programs are developed on implicit, if not explicit, assumptions
about the effects of parenting or family styles on child behavior and
development. Is there an adequate empirical and conceptual basis for
those assumptions? A substantial amount of research has attempted to
relate specific parental behaviors and attitudes to the development of
particular personality characteristics of children. To this end a number of
studies have isolated some basic dimensions of parenting styles and
produced remarkably consistent findings (Baldwin, Kalhorn, & Breese,
1945, 1949; Baumrind, 1967, 1971, 1972; Becker, 1964; Kagan & Moss,
1962; McClelland, Constantian, Regalado, & Stone, 1978; Schaefer, 1961;
Sears, Maccoby, & Levin, 1957). Two basic dimensions—"control
versus autonomy" and "love and hostility"—were identified as characterizing parental interaction with and attitudes toward their children.
Baumrind (1967, 1971, 1972) reported as two additional dimensions
"degree of maturity demands" and "clarity of communication."

Baumrind's studies are particularly of interest because her work
contains a rich description of the impact of various parenting styles.
Baumrind was able to identify three basic styles of child rearing which she
labeled "authoritarian," "permissive," and "authoritative." The authoritarian parents were described as being highly controlling of their
children, less warm, and more punitive than other parents. They tended
to produce children who were withdrawn, discontented, and distrustful.
The permissive parents were warm, supportive, and nurturant, but tended
to be overprotective and lax in discipline. They did not particularly
encourage independence and made few demands on their children. These
parents tended to produce children who were lacking in self-control and
self-reliance.

The third and most effective group of parents was labeled by Baumrind
as authoritative. They were found to make frequent use of parental

control and maturity demands but were also warm in their interaction with their children and used clear communications with them. The authoritative parents tended to produce the most self-reliant, competent, and mature children.

The unevenness of authority in parent–child relationships was underscored by Baumrind. She proposed that it is reasonable and desirable for parents to be more in charge when the children are young, with the gradual shift of more autonomy to children as they mature. Family counselors are familiar with problem family situations in which children are allowed more authority than is appropriate and where there is a blurring of the line between parent and child subsystems.

The work of Baumrind and others suggests that the authoritative parenting style may serve as a useful model for developing parent education programs and evaluating the adequacy of existing programs. The descriptions of parenting styles and their associated outcomes are somewhat limited in scope, but they appear to be reliable and represent a valuable contribution to our understanding of child rearing. The evidence which has accrued on child-rearing styles, however, seems to suggest that the global impact of various techniques is likely to be mediated by variables such as the child's sex, age, and socioeconomic status (Kagan & Moss, 1962). Moreover, the impace of general patterns of child rearing appears to be determined by the nature of the total constellation of behavioral and attitudinal factors operating in the particular family environment in which they are used.

A Broadened Family Perspective

Early efforts to relate parenting styles to child behavior were often linear in nature and narrow in scope. The forgotten variable was the family. The chapter in this book by Stinnett and DeFrain on "healthy families" delineates several key characteristics of healthy families and depicts the child developing within and as an interactive part of the family.

Stinnett and DeFrain discussed six major factors within a family that seem to represent the basis of healthy child development: commitment, appreciation, communication, time together, spiritual wellness, and the ability to cope with stress and crisis. Appropriate parent control and guidance are evident, as well as, most important, parental modeling of healthy behavior. There is a strong sense of inclusion and involvement in the family by all members.

Other models of healthy family functioning have been described in the literature (Lewis, Beavers, Gossett, & Phillips, 1976; Olson et al., 1983).

Baumrind's description of the authoritative parent model seems consistent with those descriptions of parent behavior within a healthy family. The healthy family models, however, expand the picture of the reciprocity of the child in interaction with other family members and within a value context that supports a sense of well being on the part of the child. The descriptions of open family communication, mutual support, and appropriate generational boundaries add more pieces to the picture of settings in which it is highly probable that healthy child development will occur.

Relating Theory to Specific Programs

Many contemporary parent programs such as Parent Effectiveness Training (Gordon, 1970, Systematic Training for Effective Parenting (STEP) (Dinkmeyer & McKay, 1976), and Active Parenting (Popkin, 1983) seem to identify with an authoritative parenting model. These and similar programs offer parents important communication tools, stress the importance of a nurturing relationship, and support the parent in assuming an appropriately authoritative as opposed to authoritarian role. More narrowly defined behavioral programs with their dominant focus on the tools of behavior management and control would seem to be susceptible to the charge that they are training parents to be authoritarian. These observations are somewhat simplistic but ought to be considered by parent educators who are attempting to assume a long-term, human development approach to parent education. The situational needs of parents to bring "disobedient" children back under control by assuming a more directing and accountability oriented approach can be effectively met through behavioral intervention.

One could argue that an exclusively behavioral approach to parent–child relationships would produce an "exchange" orientation to relationships. As such, affectional bonds and the give and take of authoritative relationships could be replaced with an "I'll do this if you do that" or "I'll do this if you don't do that" style of interaction. The behaviorally valued elements of consistency and accountability can help parent and child deal in a more predictable and less limit-testing way with each other. Consistency and accountability also are important aspects of an authoritative approach to parenting. A key question of styles of parenting is whether they represent a broad parenting philosophy concerned with the quality of relationships over time or whether they represent a more tightly aimed problem-solving strategy.

In summary, there is a growing body of knowledge about the impact of child-rearing styles which can be utilized in designing and conducting parent education. Many current parent education programs seem to be based on the developer's bias rather than on child-development data; yet the models of parenting frequently advocated do seem to approximate Baumrind's description of the authoritative parent. Overall family functioning has been studied less in relation to impact on specific child behavior, but there are some models of healthy family functioning that should broaden the base of parent education programs.

Goals and Activities for Parent Education

Goals and activites for planned parenting sessions may cover a broad spectrum of content areas, including everything from child health care to how to survive emotionally when children "leave the nest." An examination of parent education programs reveals a focus on one or more of the following areas; information sharing, skill building, improving self-awareness, and problem solving (Fine & Brownstein, 1983). Figure 1.1, modified from Fine (in press), depicts these areas as overlapping entities. Any parent education leader is faced with the need to make decisions regarding the relative weight given to these four areas. The consideration of specific goals, such as delineated, also raises questions regarding group composition and the nature of values being transmitted. It is reasonable to expect a parent program to articulate its focus and emphasis and to relate its objectives to group composition and value considerations.

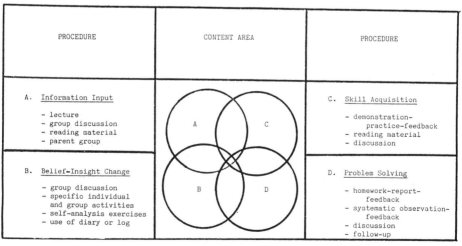

Figure 1.1. Program emphasis.

Information Sharing

The leader may engage in information sharing, presenting factual and theoretical information about child health care, developmental tasks and milestones, peer interaction, or disciplinary techniques. Goals in this area relate mainly to imparting concepts and facts which are deemed to be helpful for parents. There are a multitude of books, pamphlets, and cassettes that allow the easy dissemination of information on aspects of parenting and child development. The availability appears to be considerably higher than the use of such materials.

Skill Building

Information sharing is often insufficient to bring about behavioral changes in parents, so it is not surprising that another function, skill building, is almost routinely incorporated into parent education groups. Just telling people what to do has never prove to be an effective educative vehicle. Role-playing, modeling, and behavioral rehearsals are frequently used to teach specific child-rearing skills to parents and to back up information sharing. Parents have been taught how to use "I messages," reflective listening, modeling, praise, encouragement, and how to hold family meetings, negotiate, set limits, use time out, and "shape" the behavior of their children. These skill-building goals have the common attribute that they can be stated in terms of observable behaviors. Skill building is an important component of many commercially produced parent education programs including Parent Effectiveness Training, (Gordon, 1970), Active Parenting (Popkin, 1983), Responsive Parenting (Clark-Hall, 1978), and Training for Effective Parenting (Dinkmeyer & McKay, 1976).

Self-Awareness

A third domain in which parent education goals have been formulated might be described as improving self-awareness. Goals in this domain could include becoming aware of the manner in which our parents have influenced our own parenting styles and how our values predispose us to influence our children in directions which may not be in their best interest. Goals for parent education may go beyond values clarification to include bringing about changes in parent value systems. One can infer from the literature, for example, that it may be beneficial to change the beliefs and attitudes of authoritarian parents so that they are warmer and less punitive with their children.

An article by Fine and Jennings (1985) describes the application of a number of family therapy techniques to parent education programs, with the goals of helping parents toward greater self-awareness, emotional separation from their own parenting experiences, and more appropriate response to the needs of their family.

Problem Solving

The fourth domain which has frequently been addressed in parent-education groups is applied problem solving. The aim is to teach parents a basic problem-solving paradigm which is applicable to a broad spectrum of child development problems and which may generate interventions representing a variety of theoretical camps. The problem-solving components typically include identifying the problem, determining problem ownership, exploring options for interventions, anticipating probable outcomes of these actions, selecting and implementing a plan, and evaluating the effectiveness of the plan once implemented.

This phase of parenting programs still requires monitoring and feedback by the leader when parents report how they handled home situations. These are excellent occasions for the parent to receive encouragement and constructive feedback. In some instances the use of video or audio tapes allows for a clearer presentation by the parent of what occurred and permits helpful feedback by the leader and other group members.

Differentiating Goals and Content

Most parent education programs include each of these domains, but to varying degrees. Parent education programs for parents of infants often focus almost exclusively on sharing information about infant developmental milestones, stimulation, and health care, with little or no attention being devoted to skill building or developing increased self-awareness. Behavioral parent-training programs such as the Responsive Parenting Program (Clark-Hall, 1978) and The Family Living Series (Patterson & Forgatch, 1976) emphasize information sharing and skill building but devote little attention to improving self-awareness. Psychoanalytically oriented parent education typically emphasizes increased self-awareness of parents' own intrapsychic functioning (Reisinger, Ora, & Frangia, 1976).

While the content of parent education programs is potentially very broad, a survey of parent-training manuals (Bernal & North, 1978) revealed a tendency toward narrowness of focus. The content was often skill-building and application oriented. The theoretical and philosophical beliefs of the parent educator no doubt greatly influence the formulation of particular program goals.

Group Composition

Grouping parents on the basis of the child's age or problem has been viewed by some as a means of providing parents with a program that best addresses their immediate concerns. As an example, a parent education program for parents of preschoolers would presumably be quite different from one designed for parents of adolescents. The developmental tasks which must be accomplished by the children and appropriate parent-intervention techniques at these two levels are quite different. The socioeconomic status of the parents might also affect goal selection in that it may be advisable to emphasize skill-building goals rather than information sharing with parents from limited educational backgrounds.

While the above case for greater homogeneity in relation to specific problem areas or participant background may make common sense, there are counter positions. For example, parents with older children may have some valuable experiences to share with parents of preschoolers. A range of children's ages and parental concerns may help to more broadly educate parents in terms of the continuity of parenting through the years. Once again, the specific goals of the parenting program need to be considered in relation to group composition. It might be argued that the narrower the program focus and the greater the group homogeneity, the narrower and less generalizable will be the outcome.

Value Issues

It seems quite evident that parent education programs are not value free and are intertwined with our cultural heritage. The commercially available programs and most others seem based on white middle-class values. Their appropriateness for use with parents of various minority groups is open to question. First, one may question if techniques found to be effective with middle-class family systems are likely to work in lower-class or minority-group family systems which may differ considerably in values, structure, interaction, and distribution of power. Second, even where the effectiveness of given techniques can be shown to generalize to these families, one may question whether it is somehow a subversion of their particular cultural heritage. The new information may create divisiveness or conflict within a family or between the parents. A question that gets raised is whether programs should offer parents the skills to achieve their own goals within their family or whether the program is intended to produce a new or different way of understanding child–parent relationships.

In summary, any parenting program should be expected to explicitly identify its emphasis and means to achieve its goals. The appropriateness of the program for a particular population should be examined, and consideration needs to be given to the value issues inherent in any program. The more that parents are aware of program goals and values, the better they will be able to choose the extent to which they want to participate and the kind of applications that they are willing to introduce within their families.

The Effectiveness of Parent Education

The effectiveness of parent education programs is typically assessed in terms of the program's ability to achieve goals. Since each parenting program has a unique set of goals, comparison of outcome criteria becomes problematic. Some would argue that it does not make sense to evaluate a program in terms of goals to which it does not even subscribe. To do so would constitute a paradigm clash (Kuhn, 1962). Every program's outcome will likely reflect its unique pattern of emphasis.

Some observations on program effectiveness by writers in the field ought to be noted. Harmon and Brim (1980) state that "Our summation of the available evaluation research . . . rests on the premise that it is woefully inadequate—a reflection on the state of research and not necessarily on parent education itself" (p. 254). Fine (1980) added the following observations to this critical view of the field.

> The findings to date are mainly that parents like parent education programs, each type of parent education program has its devotees, and many parents report that they are being helped. More empirical evidence is needed to support or refute these impressions, to discriminate among the input variables in parent education programs in relation to outcomes, and to study more holistically the effects of parent participation on family structure. Such research will inevitably lead the practitioner to develop and implement more effective parent education programs. (p. 23)

An evaluation of major parent education programs by Dembo, Sweitzer, and Lauritzen (1985) supports these earlier conclusions. They conclude that changes in parent attitude and child behavior do occur but that quality and type of research varied widely. The authors believe that there were not enough well-designed studies from which one could conclude general effectiveness or the extent to which one program may be more effective with a given population.

Some Generalizations

Given the different programs' emphases, some generalizations can be tendered regarding the likelihood of certain outcomes. Thus, if we ask which programs are most effective in producing immediate behavioral changes in children, several reviews (Berkowitz & Graziano, 1972; Forehand & Atkeson, 1977; Johnson & Katz, 1973; O'Dell, 1974) indicate that the answer if almost certainly behavioral parent-training programs. The impact of behavior programs on parent attitudes and feelings, however, has been studied considerably less. If we ask which types of programs are more effective in changing parent attitudes, feeling, and interactive communication, the answer is probably Dreikurs or communications-focused programs such as Parent Effectiveness Training (Gordon, 1970). The Dreikursian and communications approaches have often reported producing changes in parent attitudes, feelings, and communications, but have often failed to obtain or in some cases even assess changes in the behavior of children (Berrett, 1975; Carkuff & Bierman, 1970; Freeman, 1975; Hetrick, 1979; McDonough, 1976; Mitchell & McManis, 1977; Moore & Dean-Zubritsky, 1979; Rinn & Markle, 1977).

Interactional Considerations

It seems that one basis of the lack of clarity of findings is the interaction taking place between program type and variables such as the age of the children involved, and the parents' socioeconomic background, values, or preexisting style of child rearing. The prospective parent educator who is faced with the decision of selecting or designing a parent education program needs to carefully consider the desired outcomes and potential interactions between program type and target population.

The question of a more general evaluation of parent education programs is complicated but provocative. As stated, the data are mainly the results of researchers examining outcomes along predetermined lines consistent with the professed intention of the program. Behavioral programs, for example, look for change in behavior while communications programs look for changes in the pattern of communications. What is missed in such theme-bound investigations is a "spread of effects" phenomenon. Many good and possibly some undesirable happenings in areas of parent and family life may not be being studied.

Researchers seem to prefer to examine unitary outcomes rather than broader family pattern changes. Yet, if a parent establishes a new pattern of communication or limit setting, the behavior of others in the family will necessarily change, leading to additional changes.

In summary, there is a growing empirical literature from which we can conclude the general usefulness of parenting programs. The literature does discriminate the relative effectiveness of certain program types for certain kinds of child problems. The broader questions of the impact of a specific parenting program on overall family functioning and the consideration of undesirable results have not been adequately researched.

Parent Education versus Psychotherapy

This issue was discussed by Fine (1980) and is a continuing professional concern. The theoretical orientation of practitioners has a major influence upon the manner in which they respond to this question. Those with behavioral beliefs may be inclined to see little or no difference between parent education and psychotherapy. Both would be defined in terms of bringing about changes in a parent's observable behaviors. Parents would be taught to utilize behavioral principles in their interaction with children. Behavioral practitioners might well prefer the use of the term "parent training" over the terms "psychotherapy" or "parent education."

For those who assume a more psychodynamic view of behavior, the distinction between parent education and therapy is more readily apparent and important. Psychotherapy would typically be seen as a process whereby changes are made in aspects of the client's personality structure. The client's intrapsychic life is a focal point of the change process even though attention may be devoted to surface behaviors. Problematic interpersonal situations would be interpreted as reflecting intrapsychic conflicts.

Parent education would be seen from this viewpoint as being concerned mainly with the imparting of information and skills which are supportive of good parenting. In contrast, changes brought about through parent education would presumably be more superficial and have a less pervasive impact on the client's overall functioning than would be expected from changes occurring in psychotherapy.

Other differentiations between parent education and therapy have been offered. Brim (1965) developed what he described as a "working distinction" between these two activities:

> Educational techniques are those directed to the conscious (and near-conscious) aspects of the individual personality and exposure to educational programs ideally should arouse only conscious beliefs and conscious mo-

tives. In contrast, therapeutic techniques are directed to unconscious motives, expectations, and attitudes, and the instrumental goal of therapy is to make the individual ready to profit from subsequent educational experiences. (p. 21)

Fine (1980) has drawn a number of differences between psychotherapy and parent education:

1. Provision of psychotherapy is limited (by statute in most states) to those holding mental health training credentials, while parent education is engaged in by persons of more diverse backgrounds, including teachers, nurses, and ministers, as well as mental health practitioners.
2. Psychotherapy is characterized by the sharing of "private" information.
3. The psychotherapist is generally more willing to become involved in a parent's personal problems than is a parent educator.
4. Psychotherapy may continue indefinitely, while parent education typically is a time-limited experience.
5. There is usually less confrontation in parent education than is psychotherapy. For example, in therapy, client resistance may be dealt with head-on, while in parent education, parent resistance may be ignored or worked around.
6. Psychotherapy is used to tackle more serious and pervasive problems than is parent education.

The Differences in Actual Practice

Although such distinctions can be made, the separation between parent education and therapy tends to dissolve in actual practice. When a group of people come together repeatedly, sharing their personal experiences and concerns, the process soon takes on a certain "air" of group therapy even when the ostensible goals are educational.

Sometimes in the course of a parent education program it becomes apparent to the leader that a particular parent has needs which can probably be better addressed through a formal therapeutic experience. The intensity of such a parent's problems may unfairly monopolize the group's time and generally undermine the quality of the experience. Such individuals are best counseled out of the group and into a more appropriate experience. There are also occasions when parents attempt to move the group's activities in the direction of psychotherapy. It is not uncommon for parents to make and explore interpretations of their own behavior or of others in the group. The group leader needs to be alert to such shifts and make a decision as to the appropriateness of continuing in the therapeutic direction.

Fine and Jennings (1985) also point out that the more experiential and process-oriented the parent education program, the greater the temptation for the group to shift from an education to a therapy format. There seems to be a clear responsibility for the leader to establish some demarcation between the two areas and, in a professionally responsible and ethical fashion, to maintain this important distinction.

In summary, the differentiation of education and therapy may be blurred but relates to important ethical considerations for the instructor and the well-being of the participants. While experientially oriented programs may tend to become more therapy-like, the posture and awareness of the leader may be more important. The distinction between therapy and education is important and needs to be maintained.

Group Leader Responsibilities

There are a number of fairly obvious responsibilities that must be assumed by parent educators. These include recruitment of parents, selection or design of program content, and scheduling meeting times and location. One of the key responsibilities for a leader is the protection of group members.

The Protection Function

The tendency for parent education groups to drift into a group psychotherapy experience was discussed earlier. This transition may be characterized by increased self-disclosure, confrontation, or challenges to the rationality of a group member's behavior. While such activities can play a meaningful role in group therapy, their appropriateness in parent education is questionable. The effective and appropriate utilization of such activities requires sensitivity, skill, and knowledge that we could expect to be ethically provided by a trained mental health professional in an appropriate setting.

The potential for therapist-induced deterioration is at its height in group therapy (Lambert, Bergin, & Collins, 1977). Group members who do not receive adequate support from the leader and who are subject to aggressive confrontation from the group leader or other members are at risk for deterioration. Clearly, the parent education group leader has a responsibility to protect the participants from aggressive confrontation and to make sure they are adequately supported. Some confrontation may be desirable, but it is crucial that it be provided only where there is a general atmosphere of support.

The group leader also has a responsibility to make sure that the participants are aware of the ground rules for discussion and interaction. If the parent education group is to assume qualities of a group therapy experience, this intention ought to be understood by all who decide to participate. Otherwise, there will be an absence of voluntary and informed consent for participation in the therapy.

Other forms of protection should also be provided to parents, including protection from being trained to use questionable or controversial child-rearing techniques. Parents should not be coerced by the leader or the group to change their behavior when they do not feel comfortable doing so. Parents should also be well enough trained to minimize the chances of harmful misapplication of parenting techniques which they learn. The group leader has a responsibility to head off such misapplications where they can be anticipated. As an example, one parent misapplied the very useful concept of "logical consequences" by keeping a child out of school for not completing a homework assignment.

It seems reasonable and ethical for the leader to emphasize that in the final analysis it is the participating parents who must judge the appropriateness of and assume the responsibility for particular applications with their own children.

In summary, leaders need to assume an important protection function. This relates to the earlier concerns with therapy versus education, but is broader in terms of the session-by-session activities and group intervention. The protective function also includes emphasizing the responsibility of the parents for what they accept and apply in their own families.

Leader Qualifications and Training

Parent education programs have a history of being led by virtually anyone who deems himself or herself appropriate and is motivated to do so. One conflict seems to be between those who argue that "parents can lead parents," and those who think that parent education is a professional endeavor requiring professional-level skills.

In the absence of good evaluative data, the answer to the question of which position is valid is "It all depends." Dreikurs and Soltz (1964) took the stance that parents could be trained to become group discussion leaders using Dreikurs's materials. A manual was prepared and parents were offered some basic training as group leaders (Soltz, 1967).

As an important adjunct to Parent Effectiveness Training (Gordon, 1970), an instructor training program was implemented. The qualifications for participation were "soft" and in effect permitted parents without a related professional background (psychology, social work, teaching, etc.) to present themselves in a leadership position. Systematic Training for Effective Parenting (STEP) (Dinkmeyer & McKay, 1976) seems to have taken what some would consider the extreme position that persons without formal training can assume the leadership role.

In referring back to the question of parent-training effectiveness, one can readily see that instructor characteristics become important to consider and vary greatly. The kinds of training and competencies that are needed are likely to vary with the conception of the leader function. In some instances, the leader is a discussion leader attempting to facilitate group participation, for example, in relation to a book the participants read. In other instances, the leader is attempting to impart some basic information regarding child development, normal versus problem child behavior, and effective parenting skills. In yet another setting, the instructor is an information disseminator, discussion leader, and trainer in specific skills that the parents are expected to apply and then report back to the group. Each of these three possibilities would seem to demand progressively more knowledge and skill on the part of the instructor, and accordingly increases the need for professional-level training by the instructor.

Gamson and associates (this volume) present a detailed and extended training program clearly based on the belief that being a parent educator is a professional responsibility requiring extensive training.

In general, there seems to be a discernible movement toward formalized training. More courses on parenting are being offered at the college level, and the interest in family therapy has precipitated the growth of many academic programs at the graduate level concerned with family life (Kerckhoff, Ulmschneider, & Adams, 1976). Newer parenting programs, such as Active Parenting (Popkin, 1983), include sophisticated training components and present parent education as a professional endeavor.

The earlier section concerning group leader responsibilities presents some of the danger points in the group process. It takes a person with skill in group dynamics, a range of knowledge and skills regarding child development and behavior, and a keen ethical awareness to offer the participants appropriate guidance and protection.

In summary, an argument can be made for the importance of specific training and knowledge requirements for parent educators. While instructor-training programs exist, there are also a number of commercial parenting programs that downplay the importance of leader qualifications.

With the increased legitimizing of the field of parent education, the trend is clearly toward more extensive professional training.

The Future

There is growing recognition in our society that assuming the role of parent is one of the most challenging tasks that can be undertaken. The dependence of young children on their parents for providing physical and emotional nurturance and guidance is obvious, and yet the vast majority of parents have had no formal training in child rearing and are left to use their own upbringing or the approaches of friends as models. Fortunately, "doing what comes naturally" does work in many instances. But in other cases, poor parenting practices simply get perpetuated. The acquisition of knowledge about how to raise children to be well-adjusted adults is not something that a wise society would leave to chance. We have begun to establish a body of knowledge that can guide us in teaching parents how to effectively promote their children's healthy development.

The field of parenting is becoming broader as society becomes more concerned with the overall quality of family life, including the relationships of mature persons to their aged parents. This burgeoning field continues to be in need of research to produce a sound empirical basis for programs.

"Professional" parent educators concerned with disseminating information and skills need to remain cognizant of the many professional issues that exist. The future is a positive one in many respects because of the growing attention to the area, the development and dissemination of progressively more sophisticated programs, and the increasing involvement of professional persons from diversified backgrounds.

References

Baldwin, A. L., Kalhorn, J., & Breese, F. H. (1945). Patterns of parent behavior. *Psychological Monograph, 58* (3).

Baldwin, A.L., Kalhorn, J., & Breese, F. H. (1949). The appraisal of parent behavior. *Psychological Monograph, 63,* (4).

Baumrind, D. (1967). Child care practices anteceding three patterns of preschool behavior. *Genetic Psychology Monograph, 75,* 43–88.

Baumrind, D. (1971). Current patterns of parental authority. *Developmental Psychology Monograph, 4,* (4, Pt. 2).

Baumrind, D. (1972). Socialization and instrumental competence in young children. In W. W. Hartup (Ed.), *The young child: Reviews of research* (Vol. 2). Washington, DC: National Association for the Education of Young Children.

Becker, W. C. (1964). Consequences of different kinds of parental discipline. In M. L. Hoffman & L. W. Hoffman (Eds.), *Review of child development research*. New York: Russell Sage Foundation.

Berkowitz, D. P., & Graziano, A. M. (1972). Training parents as behavior therapists: A review. *Behaviour Research and Therapy, 10,* 297–317.

Bernal, M., & North, J. (1978). A survey of parent training manuals. *Journal of Applied Behavior Analysis, 11,* 533–544.

Berrett, R. D. (1975). Adlerian mother study groups: An evaluation. *Journal of Individual Psychology, 30*(2), 179–182.

Brim, O. G. (1965). *Education for child rearing*. New York: Russell Sage Foundation.

Brown, C. C. (1976, November) It changed my life. *Psychology Today*.

Carkuff, R. R., & Bierman, R. (1970). Training as a preferred mode of treatment of parents of emotionally disturbed children. *Journal of Counseling Psychology, 17*(2), 157–161.

Clarke-Stewart, K. (1981). Parent education in the 1970's. *Educational Evaluation and Policy Analysis, 3,* 47–58.

Clark-Hall, M. (1978). *Responsive parenting manual*. Lawrence, KS: H & H Enterprises.

Croake, J. W., & Glover, K. E. (1977). A history and evaluation of parent education. *Family Coordinator, 26*(2), 151–158.

Davis, E. A., & McGinnis, E. (1939). *Parent education: A survey of the Minnesota program*. Westport, CT: Greenwood Press.

Dembo, M., Sweitzer, M., & Lauritzen, P. (1985). An evaluation of group parent education programs: Behavioral, PET, and Adlerian programs. *Review of Educational Research, 55,* 155–200.

Dinkmeyer, D., & McKay, G. (1976). *Systematic training for effective parenting*. Circle Pines, MN: American Guidance Service.

Dreikurs, R., & Soltz, V. (1964). *Children: The challenge*. New York: Meredith Press.

Fine, M. J. (Ed.), (1980). *Handbook on parent education*. New York: Academic Press.

Fine, M. J. (in press). Intervening with abusive parents of handicapped children. *Techniques*.

Fine, M., & Brownstein, C. (1983). Parent education: Problems, promises, and implications for school social workers. *Social Work in Education, 6,* 44–55.

Fine, M. J., & Jennings. (1985). What parent education can learn from family therapy. *Social Work in Education, 8,* 14–31.

Forehand, R., & Atkeson, B. M. (1977). Generality of treatment effects with parents as therapists: A review of assessment and implementation procedures. *Behavior Therapy, 8,* 575–593.

Freeman, C. W. (1975). Adlerian mother study groups: Effects on attitudes and behavior. *Journal of Individual Psychology, 31*(1), 37–50.

Gordon, T. (1970). *Parent effectiveness training*. New York: Wyden.

Greer, K. (1986, October). Today's parents: How well are they doing? *Better Homes and Gardens,* pp. 36–46.

Harmon, D., & Brim, O. (1980). *Learning to be parents*. Beverly Hills, CA: Sage.

Hattendorf, K. W., Ojemann, R. H., Shaus, H. S., Jack, L. M., Nystrom, G. H., & Remer, L. L. (1932). *Researches in parent education* (Vol. 1). Iowa City, IA: University of Iowa Press.

Hetrick, E. W. (1979). Training parents of learning disabled children in facilitative communication skills. *Journal of Learning Disabilities, 12,* 275–277.

Johnson, C. A., & Katz, R. C. (1973). Using parents as change agents for their children: A review. *Journal of Child Psychology and Psychiatry, 14,* 181–200.

Kagan, J., & Moss, H. A. (1962). *Birth to maturity*. New York: Wiley.

Kerckhoff, F., Ulmschneider, A., & Adams, C. (1976). College and University programs in parent education. *Family Coordinator, 25,* 131–133.

Kuhn, T. S. (1962). *The structure of scientific revolutions.* Chicago: University of Chicago Press.

Lambert, M. J., Bergin, A. E., & Collins, J. L. (1977). In A. S. Gurman & A. M. Razin (Eds.), *Effective psychotherapy: A handbook of research.* Oxford, England: Pergamon Press.

Lewis, J., Beavers, W., Gossett, J., & Phillips, V. (1976). *No single thread: Psychological health in family systems.* New York: Bruner/Mazel.

McClelland, D. C., Constantian, C. A., Regalado, D., & Stone, C. (1978, June). Making it to maturity. *Psychology Today,* pp. 41–53.

McDonough, J. J. (1976). Approaches to Adlerian family education research. *Journal of Individual Psychology, 32*(2), 224–231.

Mitchell, J., & McManis, D. L. (1977). Effects of P.E.T. on authoritarian attitudes toward child rearing in parents and non-parents. *Psychological Reports, 41,* 215–218.

Moore, M. H., & Dean-Zubritsky, C. (1979). Adlerian parent study groups: An assessment of attitude and behavior change. *Journal of Individual Psychology, 35*(2), 225–234.

O'Dell, S. (1974). Training parents in behavior modification: A review. *Psychological Bulleting, 81,* 418–433.

Ojemann, R. H., Roberts, M. P., Phillips, D. P., Fillmore, E. A., Pollack, J., & Hanson, R. C. (1932). *Researches in parent education* (Vol. 2). Iowa City, IA: University of Iowa Press.

Olson, D., McCubbin, H., Barnes, H., Larsen, A., Muxen, M., & Wilson, M. (1983). *Families: What makes them work?* New York: Sage.

Patterson, G. R., & Forgatch, M. S. (1976). *Family living series* (Ps. 1 and 2). Champaign, IL: Research Press.

Popkin, M. (1983). *Active parenting handbook.* Atlanta, GA: Active Parenting.

Reisinger, J. J., Ora, J. P., & Frangia, G. W. (1976). Parents as change agents for their children: A review. *Journal of Community Psychology, 1,* 103–123.

Rinn, R. C., & Markle, A. (1977). Parent effectiveness training: A review. *Psychological Reports, 41,* 95–109.

Schaefer, E. S. (1961). Converging conceptual models for maternal and for child behavior. In J. C. Glidewell (Ed.), *Parental attitudes and child behavior.* Springfield, IL: Charles C. Thomas.

Sears, R., Maccoby, E., & Levin, H. (1957). *Patterns of child rearing.* New York: Harper & Row.

Soltz, V. (1967). *Study group leader's manual for children: The challenge.* Chicago: Alfred Adler Institute of Chicago.

2

National Family Policy: Renegotiating the Government–Family Contract

Marvin S. Kaplan
Helga E. Kaplan

Introduction

Although there is no written constitution outlining the fundamental rules of the relationship between family and government as there is between the states and the national government, the analogy to our system of federalism is instructive. In both cases there is a mutual respect for the integrity and viability of the partners. Government has recognized the nuclear family as the "most favored condition" for its citizens and families have "agreed" to raise their children as loyal supporters of a democratic system based on individualism. There is also acceptance in principle of the doctrine of separation of powers, albeit considerable disagreement about where the lines of responsibility should be drawn: For example, the nation has long accepted government's role as keeper of its vital statistics (census and life cycle records), but there is more difficulty with government involved in such functions as education, abortion, and child care.

Moreover, just as the balance of power has shifted from the states to more centralized control, so too government in general (all of our legislatures, courts, executive agencies), as well as the national government in particular, has claimed increasing authority over family affairs. These shifts in power have regularly been accompanied by "states' rights" arguments on the one hand and "family rights" propositions on the other.

Possibly the most far-reaching proposal for a change in the "contract" between government and the family is the call for a national family policy. The reasons this subject has surfaced at this particular time in our history are open to speculation. Perhaps it relates to how America now sees

The Second Handbook on Parent Education

itself. Rich, mighty, somewhat disillusioned with the outcome of technology and the pursuit of materialism, we seem preoccupied with and able to afford the time and resources to seek quality in life—be it in health care, development of the arts, or clean air, water, and roadsides. In personal life, "quality" has come to be associated with fragile psychological factors such as emotional support and close, intimate relationships, specifically as centered in the family. If government is expected to develop a national policy on ecology to maintain our natural resources, why not a family policy to strengthen our interpersonal environment?

Another answer to Why now? relates more directly to the current revolution in social demographics (changing women's roles in work, divorce, single parents, etc.) which generates pressure for political accommodation. The loss of faith in experts has contributed to a renewed preference for the family as the major social problem-solver, with the resources of government carefully marshalled to support family effort.

The idea that the United States ought to have a national family policy entered American political awareness in 1965 with the publication of a paper by Senator Daniel Moynihan. In it the senator noted that even such an apparently family-centered program as AFDC provided help only after a family had disintegrated. By contrast, most other industralized nations have coordinated family-support policies and view our program of intervention after collapse as "insanity" (Moynihan, 1965).

The policy gap seems even more glaring when we consider that families are affected by far more than government's recent interest in such intimate decisions as treatment of severely handicapped newborn infants, abortion, and family violence. For example, highway construction and mortgage and tax policies influence where and how we live; labor laws and school rules limit control of our children; Social Security and Medicare provisions alter the responsibilities we assume for our parents—not to mention the economic impact the IRS has on every American family's standard of living. In most government programs, however, the family has been the dependent variable rather than the main target of governmental action. The problem this can create is illustrated by governmental attacks on inflation which can cause economic and psychological distress to the many families who lose jobs and homes and have to leave their communities to create new lives elsewhere. Federal actions are dominated by overall economic policies, not the specific needs of families (Shorr, 1979).

Despite the logic of having a national policy which lends coherence and direction to the impact of government actions on families, despite the examples of other nations, and despite our own recent indigeneous proposals, governmental coordination in this field will be difficult to achieve. National concensus will be difficult to achieve because we hold conflicting beliefs about whether, when, and how much government should be involved in family affairs and indeed whether or not family affairs should be a major determinant of governmental policy. Furthermore, we have a long history of reacting to social problems only when they become severe and initiate political pressure that can no longer be ignored (Pardeck, 1984). Finally, the incredible diversity of this society virtually guarantees a wide spectrum of often irreconcilable beliefs about how a family should be defined. Concomitantly, we disagree about the particular kind of family (or even families) what warrant social and governmental encouragement and support.

Professionals in the field of family and child care (among them parent educators, school officials, and welfare agency personnel) bring different concerns to the family policy debate. Their interests are not so much in setting limits for government (indeed they often are governmental employees) or in designating "worthy" families, as they are in altering social living units as they find them, most typically in ways they believe will improve the lives of children. Acting in accord with prevailing scientific beliefs and the ideology of individualism, professionals implement programs either without being aware of or failing to make explicit the underlying assumptions that these programs (e.g., behavioral, Parent Effectiveness Training) make about what constitutes an ideal family. (That such ideals do exist is evident in the programmatic goals which professionals set for their clients, e.g., client-centered therapy which encourages egalitarian rather than hierarchical relationships.)

In this chapter we propose to contribute to an understanding of the national family policy issue by (1) reviewing the history of government–family relations; (2) discussing family policy in its ideological and social context; (3) surveying several major family policy proposals; (4) focusing on the special implications of this controversy for professionals in the field of family and child care.

Government–Family Relations

Even the most cursory review of American history leaves no doubt that government in its broadest sense (i.e., federal, state, and local levels; executive, legislative, and judicial branches) has always influenced and maintained some kind of control over both family structure and function (Mencher, 1967). While we are most concerned with governmental preoccupation and intervention in the ongoing daily activities of family life (i.e., functions) in this chapter, it is important to acknowledge the long-standing role of government vis-à-vis family structure (e.g., which relationships are permissible and how they are legitimized and dissolved). Thus, for the Puritans in the northern colonies, marriage and divorce laws were primarily a state and secular rather than a religious responsibility. Further to the south, seventeenth- and eighteenth-century legislation prohibited interracial marriages and miscegenation.

Similarly, legislatures and courts have passed judgment on the use of contraceptives, the nature of married couples' private sexual practices, abortion, divorce, homosexuality, child custody, and child abuse. While some of these actions have fallen by the legal wayside, the federal government has increased its involvement in other areas, for example, the Supreme Court's decision permitting abortion under specified conditions (*Roe v. Wade*, 1973) and its willingness to review fathers' child-custody rights. The primacy of government over other institutions in matters of family structure is vividly demonstrated by the United States Supreme Court's denial to Mormons of the right to practice religiously sanctioned polygamy in *Canon v. U.S.* (1885) (Levitan & Belous, 1981). Contracts can typically be broken at the agreement of the participating parties, but this not so with the marriage contract—government plays a part.

Child care and rearing problems have been the most frequent and direct cause of governmental intervention in how families carry out their functional responsibilities. Compulsory education, child welfare, and day care are three examples of government's willingness to act and if necessary to override the family in areas previously reserved to the authority of the family. It is interesting to compare the social and historical circumstances which precipitate governmental action, the groups pressuring for action and those affected by proposed policies, as well as to explore the use of family rights arguments.

Family and Compulsory Education

Requiring basic education for all children was probably the earliest family function assumed by the state. The common school, locally run and financed, was promoted in the first half of the nineteenth century by educational reformers such as Horace Mann (Butts, 1978). This was a period of unusual social change as the first major wave of nineteenth-century immigrants reached an only recently established nation. The immigrant families did not regard the common school as an unmitigated blessing, given their need for their children's wages and their desire to maintain their own ethnic values and life styles. Opponents charged that compulsory school attendance was an unwarranted interference with parental authority and argued that parents rather than the state should be held responsible for the education of their children (Greenblatt, 1977).

However, the Pennsylvania Board of Charities concluded, "It is precisely those children whose parents and guardians are unable or indisposed to provide them with education for whom the state is most interested to provide and secure it" (Kirp & Yudof, 1974, p. 5). Education was deemed too important to be left to parental discretion. Consequently, "enlightened" and nativist forces became strange bedfellows in the movement to educate and Americanize the poor and the new immigrants by compulsory education. First enacted in Massachusetts in 1852, compulsory school attendance was the law in 28 states shortly after the Civil War and by the beginning of the twentieth century, it was well on the way to universal acceptance (Kirp & Yudof, 1974). Universal, compulsory schooling was a very advanced notion. "It constituted in the service of a unified society, a radical intrusion of the state into the previously private domain of the family. No other country had done anything like it" (Hobbs, 1978, p. 757).

In the 1920s the argument shifted from the issue of whether children had to attend school to the question of where they attended (public vs. private schools). Once again the historical circumstances surrounding the debate involved a major immigration movement—the 1880–1929 influx from southern and eastern Europe. The issue reached the United States Supreme Court in the case of *Pierce v. Society of Sisters* (1925). The challenged act had been promoted in Oregon by the Ku Klux Klan and the Masons to "Americanize" the immigrant students. One Klansman noted, "Somehow the mongrel hordes must be Americanized; failing that deportation is the only remedy" (cited in Kirp & Yudof, 1974, p. 5). The Supreme Court reached a compromise: States could mandate compulsory education but must respect parental choice of public or private schools.

Throughout our history, balancing state and family prerogatives in education has continued at both the state and federal levels with gains on each side. The federal government won in its efforts to educate the poor and black at ever-earlier ages (e.g., prekindergarten in Operation Head Start); Amish families successfully argued (*Yoder v. Wisconsin,* 1972) that religious beliefs can supercede state educational requirements (e.g., Amish children were not required to stay in school until the age of 16); secular parents have been minimially successful in gaining the right to provide formal education at home for their children (Kirp & Yudof, 1974).

The Family and Child Welfare

Paralleling the debate on the parameters of parental and governmental control of education are the deliberations on child welfare. Government actions to protect children can be traced to the colonial period, when it was the poor who were the primary beneficiaries or victims. Following the tradition of English poor law, public authorities provided for orphans and paupers' children by placing these children in selected homes, poorhouses, and indentured service. This out-of-home care extended into the nineteenth century with cyclical waves of reform advocating first expansion of poorhouses (houses including destitute adults, children, the insane, and retarded individuals) and then elimination of poorhouses in favor of state- and locally funded homes for children or subsidies to voluntary agencies responsible for child care (Greenblatt, 1977). Juvenile delinquents, who made up the bulk of contacts between state and youth, were also removed from family units and placed at various times in poorhouses, asylums, and reform schools (McGowan, 1983).

Twentieth century government–family relations are characterized by at least a rhetorical shift from "rescue and removal" (in effect often condemning and rejecting the family) to in-home assistance and by a more prominint role for the federal government. For example, the 1909 White House Conference on Children recommended that aid should be given as necessary to maintain suitable homes for

> children of parents of working character, suffering from temporary misfortune, and children of reasonably efficient and deserving mothers who are without the support of the normal breadwinners, [who] should as a rule be kept with their parents, such aid being given as may be necessary to maintain suitable homes for the rearing of the children. (cited in McGowan, 1983, p. 64)

The first congressional recognition of federal responsibility for the welfare of all children was represented by the establishment of the Children's Bureau in 1912. Thus the federal government affirmed public responsibility for the well-being of all children, not only the poor, neglected, disturbed, and delinquent. Again, this action was not without its critics. McGowan (1983) cites a "Senator from Kansas" who viewed the legislation to establish the Bureau as an assertion that "the American people do not know how to take care of themselves; and that the state must force its official nose into the private homes of people" (p. 61).

By 1923 the number of children receiving aid in their own homes began to approximate the number in institutions and exceeded those placed in foster homes (McGowan, 1983). Within a decade, virtually all the states had introduced mothers' pension/aid laws, and the expressed goal of child welfare services was to keep children in their homes. However, the amount of money available was "never sufficient . . . and mothers, often after a terrific struggle, ultimately . . . gave up their children" (Bell, 1965, p. 15). Others, such as the elderly, ill, and deviant continued to be viewed as separate individuals requiring professional care, special housing, and/or institutional placement.

During the Great Depression, the federal government alone was capable of responding to the monumental crisis affecting families. The president and Congress departed from tradition and specifically adopted the goal of strengthening family life. Thus, the Social Security Act of 1935 for the first time provided recognition that family problems stemmed from economic conditions rather than moral weaknesses. Aid to Dependent Children (ADC) made it easier to assist children at home through their caretakers. Out-of-home care did not disappear, however, and ADC and foster care legislation provided for children unable to benefit from family-oriented measures (e.g., southern black children whose caretakers were ineligible for welfare assistance).

The Family and Day Care

The Great Depression nurtured yet another precedent for federal involvement in family functions—preschool day care programs. (In contrast to nineteenth century examples of public education and child welfare, day care has historically been limited to private charitable institutions.) This new governmental venture, however, was not initiated to meet the needs of working mothers, but rather to create jobs for the unemployed. The WPA preschool programs were expected to serve families on relief. As it turned out, they attracted families from all socioeconomic levels, and by 1937, 40,000 preschoolers were attending 1,500 WPA nursery schools across the country (Greenblatt, 1977).

Another crisis, World War II, built on this depression era precedent; it led to interpreting the Community Facilities (Lanham) Act (1941) so as to allow federal funds to be used to support child day care for mothers engaged in war production (Greenblatt, 1977). This child-care aid cut across class lines and involved over 3,000 centers with expenditures of $130,000,000 over a 2 and one-half-year period. When the war ended in 1945, all such assistance came to an end and women who agitated for continuation of the programs were called "communists" (Greenblatt, 1977). In the 1970s, legislation supporting child day care specifically including middle-class children was vetoed by President Nixon, in part he said because it would contribute to neglect of parental responsibilities (McCathern, 1981).

The societal belief that mothers should not work was altered for the affirmed poor (AFDC mothers) in the early 1960s when welfare costs and an unbalanced national budget became major concerns. The resulting political pressures for the first time made financial aid contingent on mothers leaving their children (day care was provided) and accepting work training or employement (Greenblatt, 1977).

The Idea of a Family Policy

Compulsory education, child welfare, and day care do not exhaust the examples of government's historical involvement in the functions of the family, especially as these relate to children. Traditionally family obligations for the economic, physical, and emotional support of the young have also been regulated by legislation regarding child labor, health care, and child abuse. These laws, however, were initiated to redress disturbing abuses in the work and health conditions of individual citizens, not to enhance the quality of family life. Sometimes operational at the state and sometimes at the federal level, these laws clearly do not reflect the conscious aim of strengthening American family life to some predetermined standard (as, for example, antipollution laws further the nation's goal of clean air and water by specifying a predefined level of purity).

Despite the tentative moves towards family support associated with the depression and World War II, the federal role was not one of strengthening families:

> The traditional ways social services have been carried out are to substitute for the family more than to support it, to focus on the individual more than the family, and to emphasize a professional–client relationship more than mutual support and the utilization of informal support networks and the family's own capacities. (Grotberg, 1981, p. 9)

Even today, government help is more readily available for individual family members placed out of the home than those cared for in it. James Carr, executive director of the 1981 White House Conference on Families, notes that this is especially so in the case of older or handicapped individuals where "our laws and regulations (have) a tremendous bias for institutionalization" (Caldwell, 1980, p. 4). Child development researcher Bettye Caldwell adds, "Almost no one in this country would say that institutionalization is our philosophy . . . if you asked. But then you look at the laws and it's there" (Caldwell, 1980, p. 4).

The above history of governement–family relations takes on a significant, and for our purposes, critical, turn with the emergence of a conscious national family policy movement. Indicative of steps in this direction were Senator Moynihan's 1965 statement cited at the beginning of this chapter and the Senate hearings on American families (*American Families: Trends and Pressures* (1974) held by the Congressional Subcommittee on Children and Youth chaired by Senator Walter Mondale in 1973. Mondale observed that federal actions taken in realms seemingly separate from the family (e.g., economic actions) must be considered in terms of their direct consequences for the family (Haberkorn, 1976).

Presidents Kennedy, Johnson, and Nixon had addressed government's role in strengthening poor families, but President Carter in 1976 was the first to address the family cause generally, without limiting it to any ethnic or economic group (Steiner, 1981).

Around the same time, commissions appointed by the National Academy of Sciences (Advisory Committee on Child Development) and the Carnegie Council on Children, expected to issue reports on children's needs, instead issued reports calling for a comprehensive national family policy (*Toward a National Policy,* 1976; Keniston & Carnegie Council on Children, 1977).

The impetus to keep families intact reached a new level of legislative concern with the Adoption Assistance and Child Welfare Act (1980). Under this act, federal funds are provided to help families stay together or, if separated, to be brought back together again. Professionals responsible for implementing the act are required to indicate measures taken to encourage family unification and to avoid placement of children outside of the home. The power of parents is increased by giving them an active role in the review of childcare decisions (Allen & Knitzer, 1983). Also in 1980, President Carter created the Federal Office of Families and in addition, to provide a major national forum for the review and discussion of the needs of families, initiated the 1980 White House Conference on Families. (In 1984 President Reagan merged the Office of Families with the Runaway and Homeless Youth Programs. The merged agency is known as the Family and Youth Services Bureau.)

The tasks of the White House Conference were barely completed when the election of Ronald Reagan resulted in a shift away from plans for either a comprehensive family policy or a national welfare system. While the 1980 Republican national platform broke new ground by inserting a family plank, it called for private and local initiatives rather than a national and comprehensive effort. The platform recognized that childcare for working mothers was inadequate but it recommended community-based solutions to this problem. National attention, instead, was directed to inflation, the designated chief destroyer of the family. The Republican platform accepted welfare philosophy favoring noninstitutionalized childcare and agreed that policies should be formulated with the (traditional) family in mind but specified that this did not signal an intent to "shape a national family order" (*Congressional Quarterly Almanac,* 1980).

Those who opposed Reagan's policies were dismayed at the increasing influence of the antiabortion and protraditional-family forces as well as signs of governmental incursions into the patient–physician relationship in the care of newborn severely handicapped children. Liberal supporters of a national family policy recognized that such a policy might become synonymous with the views of the Moral Majority and conservative advocates for the traditional family. In addition, policy analysts questioned the utility of such a policy given the difficulty in defining its boundaries and the lack of consensus on the definition of *family* (Cherlin, 1984). Consequently, the notion of a national and comprehensive policy was seen by many as unrealistic, and references began to appear to national family polic*ies*, or even famil*ies* polic*ies*.

Ideological Positions and Social Realities

Up to this point we have reviewed the historical background of the debate over a national family policy. However, to appreciate why this issue is so emotional, controversial, and resistant to concensus, it is also necessary to consider the complex set of ideological convictions and social realities that influence views of the family.

The Ideal American Family

Historically there have been three models of the American family, each viewed in their time as being the morally correct form (Degler, 1980; Hareven, 1977, 1982; Seward, 1978). The first model, characteristic of the colonial and early national period, existed in a predominantly rural society. Marriage was viewed as primarily an ecnomic necessity rather than a relationship initiated by romantic affection (affection was deemed a desirable but not essential outcome of the marital bond). Both husband and wife worked, although at gender-related tasks, typically in close proximity and at a shared exterprise (be it farm, mill, or shop). Children were treated as though they were little adults. In essence, the family was a microcosm of the outer world, public and private domains were not sharply differentiated, and neither privacy nor individual autonomy was particularly respected or valued.

By the 1830s, the second "ideal" family type had emerged: the Victorian family, now known as the traditional family. In a newly industrializing society, marriage retained its importance as an economic relationship, but increased importance was attached to romantic mate selection. The workplace was geographically and psychologically removed from the dwelling place, and the home became a private sanctuary apart from the external "jungle" environment of cutthroat competition. The father's role was that of sole breadwinner who assured the survival of his dependent and vulnerable children sometimes by working at more than one job. Expanding bourgeois wealth made it possible to withdraw wives from the marketplace and to install them instead as full-time household managers and as status symbols of male economic success. During the nineteenth century only 3% of married women worked out of the home, despite job opportunities, labor-saving devices, readily available transportation, and declining birth rates (Hareven, 1982). The wife was regarded by herself and society as the moral and cultural superior of her husband, albeit his legal and social inferior. Accompanying the wife's domesticity, children were now believed to be significantly different from adults. They were highly valued and seen a requiring special affection and protection (Degler, 1980).

The sharply differentiated gender roles and functions associated with this ideal family were believed to be God-given, natural, and the fortunate consequence of innate male and female biological characteristics. Men were regarded as naturally suited to a competitive marketplace role given their innate aggressiveness, orientation to societal and moral issues, and ability to join other men in defending their families. By contrast, women were naturally nurturant, patient, caring, responsive to children's needs, and less concerned with outerworld problems than happenings within their own family unit.

Most of the history of government–family relations outlined in the previous section coincides with the hegemony of the traditional family both as social reality and dominant cultural ideology. This accounts for government's rhetorical respect for the sanctity and privacy of the family and the basic premise that public assistance is only warranted if families admit to failure. Public funds were primarily for minor children in peril and then only if the male breadwinner was not on hand to meet his moral obligations. Indeed, providing aid with an adult male present was viewed as promoting irresponsibility. Not until 1985 was a bill proposed in the U.S. Senate requiring states to provide AFCD benefits to poor two-parent families whose principal wage earner was unemployed (*Update,* 1985).

With the exception of the crisis of World War II, which temporarily disrupted the normalcy of traditional family life, variations from the Victorian (traditional) ideal were viewed as deviant and immoral. Thus, lower-class families in which both husband and wife were employed were condemned, as were upper class families whose women were "too worldly" and whose children were cared for by nannies and boarding schools (Greenblatt, 1977, p. 81). Beginning in the 1960s, however, major social changes such as working women and single-parent families began to erode the demographic base underlying the traditional family. It should be noted that prior to 1960 the conventional family was virtually the only form imaginable (Scanzoni, 1982). By the early 1980s, support for such traditional values as the domestic wife and a hierarchical husband–wife relationship had dwindled to a substantial minority (Hartford Connecticut, 1981). Furthermore, the socioeconomic profile of the typical traditional family had significantly shifted. The educated middle class was decreasingly traditional in behavior and accordingly was condemned by some as a "decadent cultural elite" who, even if they verbally supported traditional values, actually practiced serial marriage. According to Berger and Berger (1983), the chief supporters of the traditional family today are the new immigrants, "ethnics," and religious fundamentalists, perhaps aided by more prosperous conservatives represented by President Ronald Reagan. The 1980 Republican National Convention platform advocated strengthening the traditional family structure, the first time in history that a national political party has openly and explicitly favored government support of a single type of family (Parkhurst & Houseknecht, 1983).

The implications of such a traditional value system on the family policy debate are substantial: Traditional values present a sharply delineated definition of "family" and easy identification of families meriting welfare. While typically in favor of maximizing family privacy and opportunities for family decision making, traditional family advocates support intervention if it seems likely to enhance traditional values such as antiabortion, prayer in schools, or male dominance (Reiss, 1981).

The third family model is variously called the nontraditional, contemporary, or progressive family. It also defines the home as private and separate from the "rat race" of the work world. However, this family is less an economic arrangement than its predecessors and instead serves as a mental "R & R" center and especially a source of emotional support to members. Gender roles are blurred and no longer sanctioned by God or biology, wives and mothers pursue careers, and it is socially appropriate for husbands to take an active part in running the household and the care of the children. Success of the relationship is typically defined in terms of the equality of the partners and the emotional satisfaction each partner derives (Cherlin, 1983).

Scanzoni (1982, pp. 287–290) provides a comparative analysis of the "moral norms" of what he calls the "progressive" and "conservative" family models:

Progressive	Conservative
1. All work and intimacy matters should be negotiable.	1. Certain work, household and intimate patterns are not negotiable.

2. The ultimate goal of decision making should be equality, justice, and absence of exploitation.

3. Each partner should cultivate skills to function effectively in both household and marketplace.

4. The primary objective of child socialization is active involvement of the child in decisions in age–appropriate ways.

2. The prime goal of household interaction is order and predictability.

3. Gender ultimately shapes the sphere in which each person is expected to function most effectively.

4. The chief task of socialization is content transmission (of culture) rather than creative problem solving.

The progressive family is not dependent upon mate exchange of services (they can be purchased or are provided by government); services exchanged need not be gender determined; and the relationship is not based on economic necessity, since it is expected that both partners will be employed; and it is not hierarchical. Instead, the steadfastness of the relationship is predicated on the provision of companionship and especially on the often–fragile condition of mutual support. (The authors attended a marriage ceremony the couple modified from "as long as we shall live" to "as long as we shall love.")

The Demographic Changes

The dramatic shift in goals and relationships represented by the progressive ideal parallels the social and demographic changes mentioned earlier. Probably the most revolutionary social event of recent generations involves the change in labor force participation by married women. In the relatively short time between 1950 and 1984, the number of married women employed outside the home more than doubled (24 % to 53%), thereby transforming a minority trend into a majority social pattern: The working married woman has become the norm. Even more astonishing is the significantly altered work pattern of married women with children under the age of 6. By 1984 over half of all women with children in this category were working (only 12% had been so employed a generation earlier) (*Statistical Abstract,* 1984).

Second only to the dramatic shift in the number of women working is the parallel change in patterns of marriage. Census statistics indicate just how significant these changes are:

LATE MARRIAGE. Between 1970 and 1983, the percentage of never-married males and females increased at every age level from 18 to 39 years. Those who did marry did so approximately 2 years later than in the preceding period (*Cenus Bureau*, 1983). Despite this postponement of marriage, 95% of Americans can still expect to marry at some point in their lives, and marriage remains an integral part of the lives of almost all adults (Kahn & Kammerman, 1982).

DIVORCE RATE. Divorce rate per 1,000 of the population climbed from a low of 0.9 in 1910 to a historic high of 5.3 in 1981. However, since 1981 there has been a leveling off and a slight decrease in divorce rates (1983, 5.0; 1984 and 1985, 4.9) (National Center for Health Statistics, 1985).

SINGLE-PARENT HOUSEHOLDS. Between 1970 and 1983, single-parent households increased by 107%. (As a percentage of all families, this represents an increase from 11 to 22%.) Most of this increase involved households headed by single women. Thus, by 1982, 19% of all families were single-parent families as compared to 7.4% in 1960. If we focus on the children living in single-parent households in a given year (1983), the following data emerge: 42% lived with a divorced parent, 26% with a separated parent, 24% with a never-married parent, and 8% with a widowed parent (*Census Bureau*, 1983).

The Causes of Family Change

As might be expected, there are widely different interpretations of the cause and the impact on society of these reported events. In the absence of agreement as to why these changes are occurring and whether they are good or bad for families, the development of a general policy concensus is extremely difficult. The magnitude of the dispute is suggested by the following interpretations.

Guttentag and Secord (1983) link the increasing number of women in the labor market to changing male/female ratios in the population. They present data indicating that from 1790 to World War II there were more men than women in the United States and that the reverse has been true since World War II. They conclude that having fewer marriageable-age males invariably has "profound effects . . . on patterns of marriage and divorce, childrearing conditions and practices, family stability, and certain structural aspects of society itself" (p. 9). While having more marriageable-age females than males is a new phenomenon for our country, in other countries such ratios, "typically are associated with increased numbers of unmarried singles, rising divorce rates, increased illegitimacy, transient marital relationships, active feminism, and substantial attempts by women to establish themselves as separate and independent persons'' (p. 21).

The dominant societal value of individualism in its psychological guise of "self-actualization" is also held responsible for encouraging individuals to seek changes in their "assigned" roles (e.g., gender roles, marital status, jobs) so that they can feel more consistent with their perceived "real self" (Yankelovich, 1981). While Lasch (1977) views self-actualization as a form of destructive narcissism, Yankelovich (1981) find it "well within the American tradition of individual self improvement" (p. 69). Certainly emotional satisfaction and opportunities for personal growth (self-actualization) in the marital relationship have become significant factors weighed in decisions to divorce (Cherlin, 1983).

Legal decisions of the 1970s and 1980s which emphasize individual as contrasted to family rights have also contributed to change. For example, courts and legislatures have reduced the penalties of illegitimacy, supported no-fault divorce, and permitted unrestricted availability of contraceptives and legalized abortion, thus placing the focus upon the individual rather than the traditional family in defining rights and prerogatives (Rega, 1979–1980). A very different explanation for women working and increased divorce is proposed by M. G. Robertson, founder and president of the Christian Broadcasting Network. He charges that the economic burden resulting from deficit spending forced women to enter the work force for family economic survival. The consequences include tired mothers, neglected children, conflicts with husbands and, ultimately, divorce (cited in Cherlin, 1983).

Social movements such as feminism have been credited with or blamed for the altered social statistics. Thus, the Women's Movement, or more specifically, the liberal, equal rights branch of feminism, subscribes to out-of-home career employment, negotiated material decisions based on a relationship between equals, equality before the law, and freedom for women to control their bodies in such matters as contraception and abortion.

The feminist movement, according to Scanzoni (1982), represents the reemergence of individualism within the family—a repetition of the nineteenth century clash between feminists and the politically powerful conservative evangelicals who controlled state legislatures and ensured exclusive legal recognition of the traditional family. In this context, the increase in divorce is interpreted by Scanzoni and others (see, e.g., Stone, 1977) as individualism gaining ground against evangelical anti-individualist family values which made divorce unacceptable. From a minister's perspective (Dobson, 1980), feminist values and "confusion in sex role identity'' are not the result of random social evolution. They are, instead, the products of ''a virtual conspiracy by the liberal media and humanistic scientists to discredit the traditional biblical role of manliness and to attain revolution within the family'' (p. 155).

Finally, some would argue that the current social statistics are not all that they seem. Cherlin (1983) contends that the trend toward women becoming more independent of men and working outside the home and increasing divorce is not new but rather represents a continuing pattern dating from at least the 1820s. Hareven (1982) contends that rising divorce rates do not indicate family breakdown but rather reflect new solutions to old problems previously managed by separation, desertion, ''living like strangers,'' or continuous conflict. Stone (1977) suggests that in comparison with the 1750s, ''the current rate of divorce is little more than a functional substitute for marriage broken by death'' (p. 56).

It is difficult if not impossible to separate the explanations of current social statistics from the value judgments and strong emotional responses associated with the interpretations of those facts and figures. Thus, as is apparent, some view the trends with considerable approval, envisaging a newly emergent and more adaptive family unit (Rapoport, Rapoport, & Strelitz, 1977), while others fear imminent family disintegration leading to the collapse of Western civilization (Berger & Berger, 1983). In the camp of those who see moral decay, Lasch (1977) views self-centeredness, selfishness, and divorce as the inevitable concomitants of the ideology of self-actualization. As early as 1958, sociologist and family expert C. Zimmerman claimed the social statistics signaled a transformation of marriage from a sacred to a secular institution and the critical loss of time for family life. He predicted lack of parental control of children, a decline in the spirit of self-sacrifice, and an eroding familism associated with women's decisions to raise smaller families (cited in Dempsey, 1981).

More optimistically, Folson (also in 1958) predicted a reorganized and strengthened family better adjusted to a democratic society. He applauded the declining double standard in sex, voluntary choice of mates, the reduction in household drudgery, and the increasing equality of women in families and before the law (cited in Dempsey, 1981). Similarly, Monroney (1976) concludes from his studies that the contemporary family is strong, viable, and in Bane's (1976) words, ''here to stay.'' Despite the numbers of working wives and mothers and the population's geographical mobility, Monroney found that families continue to assume major responsibility not only for handicapped children but also for elderly parents. Citing data that the majority of Americans approve of egalitarian marital relationships, some commentators (Rapoport et al., 1977, Scanzoni, 1982) condemn the legal institutionalization of traditional male dominance which prevents mates from making creative adjustments to the current conditions of life. Families are in trouble, according to Rapoport et al. (1977), not because they are changing but rather because they "have inherited conceptions of family life that are inadequate to cope with the requirements of modern living" (p. 364).

Individualism and American Society

We cannot leave this discussion of the ideologies and social realities associated with the American family as an institution without discussing the overall philosophical values of American society. While many belief systems coexist in a society as diverse as ours, individualism has long been central to American ideology and continues to have a significant impact on both our behavior and our institutions. The rights that Thomas Jefferson hailed as inalienable and those safeguarded by the Bill of Rights accrue to individuals, not families. Early in the nineteenth century Tocqueville reported the pervasiveness of individualism in America, and Arieli (1964), in a monograph on American society, concludes that by the end of the Civil War this philosophical outlook was permanently linked to the uniqueness of the American national character.

Consider the following postulates: society is an aggregate of individuals rather than a collection of families or groups; individuals can rise above their family origins and difficulties if they put forth the will and work, while society simply needs to provide equal opportunity and access to the mechanisms of social mobility (e.g., education); self-development and personal achievement are more praiseworthy than self-sacrifice and perpetuation of group traditions (ethnic exclusivity); merit and competition should determine the distribution of society's rewards rather than family connections and group affiliations. (By appointing his brother attorney general, President Kennedy in effect violated both the "proven merit" and the antinepotism rules. He escaped severe criticism by the effective use of humor: "Where can a young man get experience nowadays?") The above assertions of individualism are in some respects incompatible with the beliefs Americans have held about the family. Consistent with individualism, recent studies confirm that American families have always believed that they should "launch" their children into independent adult orbits, that is, children should establish nuclear families of their own rather than maintain extended families (Hareven, 1982). In their dealings with the outside world, children are encouraged to "make it on their own" and granted social approval for seeking occupational and social positions that differ from those of their parents. American families have accepted traditional social services, which have primarily focused on the needs of individuals (Grotberg, 1981). Nontraditional contemporary families have expanded the commitment to individualism by advocating separate career goals for female family members (the new individualism) and by defining the family's primary role as a support system for members in their separate life pursuits (Parkhurst & Houseknecht, 1983).

On the other hand, and at considerable odds with the assumptions and goals of individualism, traditional as well as contemporary American families confer acceptance based on membership rather than on performance. Cooperation takes precedence over competition, and it is generally assumed that family members will give according to their abilities and receive according to their needs. The supportive environment of the family differs significantly from individualism's credo: from each according to ability, to each according to achievements. The traditional family deviates further from individualism than does the contemporary progressive family in that there is an expectation that wives and mothers will place the overall needs of the family ahead of their personal aspirations. In addition, it is expected that husband–wife relationships will be hierarchical rather than equal. To the extent that family values are at odds with individualism, there will be tension between the family and government and disagreement about the nature of a national family policy.

Family Policy Proposals

This section examines some specific proposals made for inclusion in a national family policy. What they share is commitment to an explicit, conscious, and responsible approach by government to families. They differ in almost every other respect (e.g., a single comprehensive policy vs. multiple fragmented policies; active vs. restricted governmental powers vis-à-vis families; a separate family government ministry vs. a special presidential advisor). This diversity is hardly surprising given, first, the newness of the idea of a national policy designed to strengthen all families (as novel to the 1970s and 1980s as Roosevelt's idea in the 1930s that the federal government was responsible for solving the Great Depression), and second, the range of special interest groups with stakes in strengthening one or another type of family (i.e., the traditionalists, including the Moral Majority, new immigrants, and the "ethnics" with the support of political and ideological conservatives; the progressives, including feminists, civil rights advocates, and many professionals in the family service fields).

This chapter began with a reference to Senator Moynihan's early advocacy of a national family policy. His 1965 proposal was modest and limited to securing a statement of intent that "it is the policy of . . . government to promote the stability and well being of the American family" and that "the social program of the federal government be formulated and administered with this in mind" and a directive for gathering relevant family data:

> That the President, or some person designated by him . . . will report to the Congress on the condition of the American family in all its facets—not *the* American family, for there is no such thing, but rather the great range of American families in terms of region, national origin and economic status. (Moynihan, 1965, p. 281)

Specific implementing measures were left to the outcome of national debate and ultimately to the actions of legislatures and administrators. After 20 years this proposal remains an untried viable family-policy option.

Eight years after Moynihan's proposal, Margaret Mead and Edward Zigler, first developer of the U.S. Office of Child Development presented to the Senate Subcommittee on Children and Youth the concept of a Family Impact Statement (like those prepared for legislation potentially affecting the environment) (*American Families,* 1974). It was proposed that prior to passage of a particular piece of legislation Congress would require a report of its potential effects on family life. A seminar to study this proposal was organized at Catholic University (Hubbell, 1981), and the participants, 24 academicians and policy makers, concluded that in the environmental field at least, such impact statements had "resulted in a large bureaucracy, cumbersome procedures . . . indigestible reports, lengthy lawsuits and considerable delays" (Ooms, 1984, p. 173). Formal family impact analysis for every piece of legislation was deemed inappropriate" for a subject as value laden and difficult to measure as family impact" (Ooms, 1984, p. 173). Instead, the seminar group recommended the establishment of independent commissions, reportedly operating effectively in Great Britain and Australia. They viewed such commissions as having more influence and visibility than cabinet or government agencies and recommended that each year such commissions prepare a small number of analyses of government policies. Advisory commissions in our country could operate at local, state, and national levels and have substantial educational impact.

In their review of family policy in 14 countries, Kammerman and Kahn (1978) provide an interesting analysis of where in the government a family policy unit should be located. They conclude that European family ministries have been unsuccessful largely because of their overlapping concerns with other major governmental units. Kammerman and Kahn believe that adding an agency which seeks to have a monopoly on all family-related matters is not likely to be successful. If such an agency were unable to assume a harmonizing role on behalf of policies affecting all families, it would be reduced to setting narrow goals and working on limited projects funded by restricted budgets. Kammerman and Kahn (1978) propose instead that a family-oriented advisor be placed in government in order to coordinate the activities of departments before action is taken (p. 490). A good analogy is that of the National Security Advisor who seeks to balance the views of such agencies as the Departments of Defense and State just prior to presentation to the president for decision. Zigler and Muenchow (1984) on the other hand believe that "a strong and effective federal agency is needed to provide a focal point for developing and implementing social policy for children and families" (p. 418).

Regardless of where in government the advocates of family policy are located, they will confront many controversies inherent in the idea of a national family policy (e.g., the kinds of families benefiting from such policies and the degree of government involvement). While liberals and conservatives differ sharply as to the kinds of families government should support, they agree that government should be an active partner in strengthening families. The opposing view in this case is represented by Berger and Berger (1983), who argue for a national policy which will guarantee protection for the family, specifically the traditional family which they regard as both ideal and essential, from government. Their proposal stresses the following:

1. Recognition of the primacy of the family. The family and no other conceivable structure is the basic institution of society; there are no alternatives or substitutes. Basic needs are best taken care of within the family and where allowances are granted, they should be provided to care for family members at home.

2. Restoration of the private. Legislate only for public behavior. Living with practices that may offend is the price of democracy. Private matters (e.g., sex) should not be part of public policy.

3. Respect for pluralism. Non-middle-class standards need to be acknowledged and ethnic differences tolerated.

4. Autonomy and empowerment. Reduce state intervention into the family (e.g., welfare). Empower the family by letting them choose needed services. The family has surrendered too much to a monopolistic and coercive educational system. Provide vouchers and support autonomy.

5. Restoration of parental rights. Trust parents to make decisions for their children even though they are not experts.

6. Maintenance of community. Community ethnic, racial, church, and voluntary associations give meaning to private life. Such organizations should be utilized before recourse to professional help.

Caplow (1977) takes this limited government position even further, stating that not only does the government lack the necessary moral basis for prescribing for the family, but that previous attempts to prescribe have been disastrous: "On the whole the government's expenditure of many billions of dollars for the improvement of family life has done more harm than good—mysteriously frustrated by something in the social machinery. . . . AFDC continues to function as a family smashing device. . . . Government is . . . incapable of improving [the family]" (pp. 7–10).

Barbaro (1979, p. 457) agrees with Caplow that a national family policy risks violation of civil rights. Such a policy "is unmanageable, potentially dangerous and promises more than it can deliver. Even if there were agreement on goals . . . society has not developed the tools of social engineering and the political skills to influence this complex human relationship."

In contrast to these statements that the main priority is to control government interference in the family, Kammerman and Kahn (1983) believe that the proper concern of family policy is assured government support to all families. Indeed, they believe that unless there is a broad basic program underwriting the fundamental requirements of typical families, no welfare policy can be effective for families with special needs. They believe that vouchers and other attempts to guarantee freedom from governmental and professional control are inadequate to meet family needs. They add that families cannot be strong as long as the national government ignores the differences between wages and minimal economic requirements, fails to provide a universal health-care system, overlooks the need to compensate families for lost economic resources due to childbearing and child rearing, and fails to provide time off for the essential psychological bonding of parents with newborn children. Thus, their family policy favors a guaranteed baseline of adequate food, clothing, income, medical care, education, housing, and employment. It encourages such special programs as paid and substantial employment leave after childbirth and professional human service assistance to support families struggling with life-cycle crises (loss of a mate, severe illness, job loss, etc.). Kammerman and Kahn (1983) accept a wide variety of family types, structures, roles, and relationships.

Although there are other major differences, Kammerman and Kahn (1983) join Cherlin (1984) in their primary concern for families that include children, and they and Berger and Berger (1983) agree with Hareven (1982) that family policy must utilize and strengthen informal support networks of kin and neighborhood without bureaucratizing these groups. Kammerman and Kahn (1983) include in their definition of family policy both governmental and nongovernmental policies which "seek to affect primary relationships and structure" (p. 153).

Perhaps the most pragmatic proposals for a national family policy are those suggested by interest groups who deliberately avoid highly politicized issues (e.g., abortion) and focus instead on problems where consensus across ideological groups is possible (e.g., assuring child support by absent fathers). The drawback of this approach is its fragmented gains, its advantage that at least some families will benefit and be strengthened.

Professionals and National Family Policy

> Everywhere as people push against the professionalized institutional structures we've inherited from the past, they try to think of alternatives but increasingly turn to the family. (Featherstone, 1979, p. 35)

In the political and ideological tug-of-war over a national family policy, the role of the expert deserves special attention. As a society we have increasingly relied on the professions as the resource to explain and prescribe in virtually all areas and stages of our lives. Significant advice and sometimes control of our physical and mental well-being, learning, and critical life choices have been transferred to scientists, technologies, and special institutional settings (from obstetrician to gerontologist; from preschool teacher to career planning center). Since professionals (from theoreticians to service providers) have influenced government–family relationships in the past, it may be assumed that they will play an important role in the debate on a formal family policy as well.

The work of both theorists and researchers has been used by advocates of various family models to bolster their points of view. For example, psychoanalysis in both its orthodox and modified Ericksonian forms has been used to substantiate the sex-determined social roles characterizing the traditional family. Individuals unhappy with traditionally prescribed family role requirements may be diagnosed as having a "pathology" and requiring "mental health" treatment. Similarly, the work of Talcott Parsons assumes biologically based gender roles and is seen as confirming the traditional assignment of males to "instrumental" and females to "expressive" behaviors. (These behaviors are seen as sex-linked traits.) Instrumental behaviors enable fathers to bring external and universal values to their children, while expressive traits result in mothers nurturing their children and negotiating differences within the family (Rapoport et al., 1977).

Another dimension of the problem between professionals and the family is the tension caused by the ideology of individualism: Committed to helping individuals rather than families, psychoanalysts are an archetypal example of a wide range of professionals who are reluctant to talk with family members because the family members are not "the patient," and talking with the family members may negatively affect treatment (Appleton, 1974). Sampson (1977); a psychologist, writes that "the value basis of the discipline [psychology] thwarts effective problem solving on anything other than a purely individual level" (p. 783). Similarly, Schneiderman (1979) says that parent educators reveal their grounding in individualism by focusing on the "defects" or lack of knowledge of individual family members rather than emphasizing the social forces and political events which are at least partly causal of family difficulty.

The value society has put on new knowledge and the authority of specialists (as against the knowledge of its senior citizens) has exacted too high a price according to Berger and Berger (1983), Lasch (1977), and others. Indeed, they argue that professional helpers have become the problem (e.g., the authors are aware of a respected pediatrician who warns new mothers against "succumbing" to the advice of their parents regarding infant feeding schedules even though the scientific data is ambiguous!) Such unwisely used influence erodes the relationship between generations. Those without specialized credentials (i.e., the family) are reduced to very limited helper status. This is especially evident whenever a problem is "medicalized," thereby turning it into one that can be treated only by those with highly technical training (Monroney & Dokecki, 1984).

Experts typically treat individuals on professional turf rather than in the family home or on neutral ground. The rules governing care in professional settings are designed to meet bureaucratic and scientific standards rather than enhance family effectiveness. For example, by limiting visiting hours and preventing children from seeing sick relatives, family contact and support are reduced when they are often most needed. Courts incarcerate and treat delinquent individuals and ignore families and family conflict which may have precipitated the difficulty. In traditional medicine and psychiatry, the family is hardly regarded as an indispensable asset to the treatment process (Preister, 1984). The schools are yet another important institution which asserts professional and bureaucratic control and tends to keep families at arm's length, making them scarcely more welcome than they are at work.

The revolt against professional power includes legislation empowering parents over schools in the case of handicapped children, due process rights for mental patients, and patient rights to participate and review professional decision making (PL 94-142, the Rights of Handicapped

Children Act; PL 96-272, the Adoption Assistance and Child Welfare Act of 1980, etc.).

The fivefold increase in the number of professionals in the past 50 years has intensified the impact of a professionalized service society which downgrades the family. The backlash resulting from families' loss of control makes the family "a key symbol in an ongoing assault on institution and professions—a continuation of the romantic mutinies against modern professionalized society" (Featherstone, 1979, p. 33).

The implications for professionals are clear: They must create a more constructive balance with families. Berger and Berger (1983) see part of the solution as a movement away from the medical or pathology model which assigns individuals to experts and unnecessarily excludes family helpers. Families with supportive services can provide more personal and better help at lower cost (Monroney & Dokecki, 1984).

Professional Roles

Beyond being responsive to the usurpation of power, what roles can and should professionals take in the development of a national family policy? How can they promote coordinated government policies which will lead to stronger families?

Professional participation in the national debate on family policy is essential and allows for a wide range of activities. Certainly there is a need for the performance of traditional professional and scientific tasks including the collection of data and the monitoring of the current status of families and children. (Knitzer, 1984, reports that current national data are scarce on even such matters as the number of adolescents being seen for mental health services.) There are also the more technical tasks of developing effective instruments to determine family strengths and weaknesses. Reiss (1981) adds that although science cannot settle which ideology is best, "it can deal with such questions as genetic differences between the sexes, the meaning of terms like normality. . . . Social sciences offer a comprehensive perspective on the competing ideologies and an overview of the social scene that is not available elsewhere" (p. 282).

Zigler and Muenchow (1984) suggest that professionals testify as frequently as possible before federal Senate and House committees dealing with children and families (e.g., the Senate Children's Caucus, the House Select Committee on Children, Youth, and Family). They view government leaders as needing to be made aware of the importance of research on families as well as the ways in which current legislation affects or fails to affect families.

Data collected locally regarding unmet needs of children and families can also be communicated to state representatives and state government leaders who may be more accessible to some professionals than those at the federal level. Certainly professionals should become familar with the state legislative committees that are concerned with families and children, seek to report their findings, and indicate the need to coordinate government policy. In this regard, Zigler and Muenchow (1984) advise that in communication with legislators and government officials "We must learn how to listen and how to compromise, even in those instances where we are reasonably certain of the idea we wish to sell" (p. 420).

Another option for professionals is to emulate the Massachusetts example by encouraging governors to appoint family advisory committees. Such committees could hold hearings prior to the submission of state agency goals and budgets and could require agencies to explain the effects of their proposals on families. Although, as recommended by Calhoun (1980), such committees would have no line authority, they could draft recommendations to the governor, offer their perspectives, hold press conferences, and generally keep the concern about families visible to both the public and governmental leaders. The task of obtaining the appointment of a state family advisory committee may become the common goal of professional organizations within each state.

Specific "how to do it" suggestions are provided by Edelman (1978), who spells out 12 guidelines for children and family advocates, among them the careful setting of goals and the development of powerful political networks. Another means of involvement is proposed by Darling and Bulbolz (1980). They present a curricular model useful in increasing student awareness of public policy issues. The goals of their curriculum are to increase familiarity with, understanding of, and the ability to analyze public policy formation and to stimulate student involvement in public policy issues affecting the family.

Summary and Conclusions

To review the background of the national family policy debate: State and community have always regulated and influenced the family. More specifically, the state since colonial days has regulated family structure and the federal government has gradually overcome a philosophical reluctance to intervene in family functioning, especially when children are deemed at peril. Twentieth century crises precipitated increased national attention to family problems along with a new commitment in principle, if not in practice, to in-home service (support for families) rather than out-of-home placements for individuals.

Beginning in the mid-1960s, the idea of a national family policy which would go beyond the welfare needs of the poor and address a new national priority for strengthening all families became a public political issue. Since then, disagreement about definition, jurisdiction, means and ends, as well as ideology has prevented agreement on the direction such a policy (or policies) should take. Nevertheless, national conferences, presidential endorsements, executive agencies, court decisions, congressional committees, political party platforms, family advocate lobbies, and professional writing and research have kept the debate very much alive. This is probably so because while it is difficult to gain agreement on particulars, the idea of a policy to strengthen families is "irresistible" in the abstract (Steiner, 1981). Conservatives and liberals alike have favored a family policy, especially when they felt confident their version would be enacted.

The content of the family policy proposals that have emerged is directly related to ideological positions about the family and reflects different beliefs about the cause of changing social and demographic data. For example, acceptance of different historical models of the ideal family influences definitions and judgments about what a family is and should be and which families merit inclusion or exclusion from special family support programs. Americans are often suspicious of strong central government and government planning, while those who subscribe to traditional family values in most cases tend to proscribe, rather than prescribe, how government should intervene in family decision making. Goode (1977) comments that

> This is surely the first period in [history] in which people have suggested that the government should improve respectable classes. That is we have come to believe that not only the lower classes but also the middle and upper classes exhibit failure in their family behavior and that, as a government, we should do something about it. (p. 15)

He goes on to say, "We can do many things to weaken or undermine the family, but we have little knowledge about how to strengthen it" (p. 17).

Those generally against government intervention to help the family often make two exceptions: They favor laws against abortion and they also favor government action to protect the lives (as against parental judgments) of severely impaired newborn infants.

Any comprehensive family policy inevitably must take into account our strong national affinity for individualism which predisposes academics, legislators, and social activists to think in terms of individuals and not family units. It must also reconcile conflicts between individualism and core family values (e.g., competition and autonomy vs. cooperation and community). As important as these ideological positions are, they are matched in significance by the realities of changing attitudes toward activities of women, high divorce rates, increasing numbers of single parents, and so forth.

In response to this complex set of attitudes and social data, proposals for family policy have ranged from calls for legislative "impact statements" to research on the current status of families, to special advisors, commissions, and so on. The role of professionals and existing institutions vis-à-vis the national policy debate is viewed with wariness. There is widespread concern about the usurpation by professionals and institutions of control that can be discharged by families alone, or in concert with a more limited professional role. On the other hand, professionals are widely regarded as essential providers of research, supportive services, and lobbying and teaching skills.

To this point we have deliberately avoided explicit endorsement of the specific form any family policy or policies should take, choosing instead to provide an overview of the subject, to raise relevant questions and outline several available options. If anything, our own reading has made us more open to the viability of a range of differing approaches than we were when we began this study. As the closing paragraph draws near, however, we feel we would be remiss if we failed to present at least some tentative conclusions and recommendations. And so we propose the following:

1. *Defining the parameters of a national family policy.* We argue simultaneously for a wide and narrow approach. It is wide in the potential impact of governmental actions on all areas of family life. As Walter Mondale wrote in his introduction to Zigler, Kagan, and Klugman's text in 1983, "When government touches family life—as it does every day—we should make sure it supports and maintains rather than undermines and weakens American families" (p. XIII). The examples he cites range from the negative impact of taxes on marriage to housing policies which discriminate against families with young children. Beyond this alerting function, family policy can and should be comprehensive in its commitment to strengthening all families and children. This means recognition that the family (and we deliberately leave it loosely defined) is the basic unit of society (and to date the most effective social form known) and that as such it deserves government and societal help as it strives to support society's members throughout their life span.

There is, however, a countervailing pressure to keep the focus of family policy within restricted bounds. While policy should support the family in general, care must be taken that the problem of clashing definitions of *family* and *policy* according to one or another theoretical or political philosophy do not result in total stalemate or destructive divisiveness (e.g., the abortion issue and homosexual "families" are cases in point). Any aspect of family policy is hard enough to enact, given government's historical predilection to make family needs subservient to public policy considerations as they affect individuals, corporations, and other institutions. We are sympathetic to Steiner's view that "Unless family policy is broken into component parts, it is only an abstract theme that neither blesses nor damns, neither rewards nor punishes. Only the components of family policy are susceptible to legislative action or administrative order" (1981, p. 199).

2. *Setting priorities for family policy objectives.* Assuming a partial, piecemeal approach, the primary imperative for family interest groups (of which there are some 200) is using their particular understandings of family needs to set priorities for governmental action, with the expectation that compromise will establish mutually acceptable goals. For example, while we rank single-parent families with children as top priority for any family policy, we concede that this priority might have to be reconciled with other acceptable, but lower-on-the-wishlist, priorities such as primary care for children in low-income traditional two-parent families. Consensus in this case might hinge on the question of child assistance, since historically there has been general agreement that this population is the most worthy of support and the data indicate that children are the most impoverished and disabled group in our society (Children's Defense Fund, 1985).

3. *Providing a locus for implementing family policy.* Family policy must inevitably interact with government, and therefore families must be strongly represented at the national level. The issues are quite analogous to the stakes in national security and the natural environment. Furthermore, the federal government is the only source with funds sufficient to carry out a wide-scale effort in this regard. This is not to deny initiative in this area to the states but to argue for nationally visible commitment and responsibility.

As to where in the national hierarchy such responsibility should rest, we would argue against cabinet or agency-level designation, preferring instead an executive branch presidential advisor supplemented by commissions analogous to those described in this chapter. This by no means implies that Congress can be overlooked. To the contrary, close attention and liaison need to be effected both with important long-standing committees such as the House Ways and Means Committee and with special committees such as the House Select Committee on Children, Youth, and Families.

4. *Developing a strategy for action.* The major remaining step in implementing family policy goals is formulating an effective strategy to insure their enactment. This requires first and formost the gathering and disseminating of reliable data. As Steiner (1981) notes, "The minimum conditon for success in developing public policies as remedies for family dysfunction are reliable data about dysfunction." (p. 207). Beyond this, appropriate strategy requires effective lobbying. Kagan, Klugman, and Zigler (1983) cite as an example of successful strategy the coalition of some 30 organizations who reviewed and modified the 1980 Federal Interagency Day Care Requirements, which the Secretary of Health and Human Services subsequently approved. (The measure's failure in Congress underscores the need for more effective education at this level.) At the state level, lobbies have been active and successful, especially in California and Texas (Kagan et al., 1983).

It is in these two areas—providing information and lobbying—that professionals in the field of family affairs have a special role. It is they who can lend the benefits of their specialized knowledge and experience to promote constructive movement in the area of family policy. Finally, it is professionals with their research and data-based perspective who can keep the ultimate family policy goal of strengthening all families from disappearing in the press of the narrower, albeit important, goal of securing welfare for the impoverished.

References

Adoption Assistance and Child Welfare Act, 42 U.S.C. §670 (1980).

Allen, M., & Knitzer,J. (1983). Child welfare: Examining the policy framework. In B. G. McGowan & W. Meezan (Eds.), *Child welfare. Current dilemmas. Future directions* (pp. 93–142). Itasca, IL: Peacock.

American Families: Trends and pressures. (1974). Hearings before the Subcommittee on Children and Youth of the Committee on Labor and Public Welfare, U.S. Senate 93rd Congress, First Session, September 24–26, 1973. Washington, DC: U.S. Government Printing Office.

Appleton, W. S. (1974). Mistreatment of patients' families by psychiatrists. *American Journal of Psychiatry, 131,* 650–657.

Arieli, Y. (1964). *Individualism and nationalism in American ideology.* Cambridge, MA: Harvard University Press.

Bane, M. J. (1976). *Here to stay: American families in the twentieth century.* New York: Basic Books.

Barbaro, F. (1979). The case against family policy. *Social Work, 24*(6), 455–457.

Bell, W. (1965). *Aid to dependent children.* New York: Columbia University Press.

Berger, B., & Berger, P. L. (1983). *The war over the family: Capturing the middle ground.* Garden City, NY: Anchor Press/Doubleday.

Butts, R. F. (1978). *Public education in the United States: From revolution to reform.* New York: Holt, Rinehart & Winston.

Caldwell, B. (1980). White House conference on families: An interview with John Carr, executive director, White House conference. *Educational Horizons, 59,* 4–9.

Calhoun, J. A. (1980, March–April). Developing a family perspective. *Children Today,* pp. 3–8.

Cannon v. United States, 116 U.S. 55 (1885).

Caplow, T. (1977). The loco parent: Federal policy and family life. In B. A. Chadwick (Ed.), *Government impact on family life* (pp. 1–12). Provo, UT: Brigham Young University Press.

Census Bureau Current Population Reports. Marital Status and Living Arrangements. (1983, March). Washington, DC: Department of Commerce, Bureau of Census.

Cherlin, A. (1983). Family policy: The conservative challenge and the professional response. *Journal of Family Issues, 4*(3), 427–438.

Cherlin, A. (1984). Family policy and family professionals. *Journal of Family Issues, 5*(2), 155–159.

Children's Defense Fund, (1985). *Black and white children in America.* Washington, DC: Author.

Community Facilities (Lanham) Act, U.S.C. 260, 55 Stat. 361 (1941).

Congressional Quarterly Almanac. (1980). 76th Congress, 2nd Session, Vol. 34, pp. 58–71. Washington, DC.

Darling, C. A., & Bulbolz, M. M. (1980). Public policy and the family: An integrative course. *Journal of Home Economics, 27*(1), 20–23.

Degler, C. N. (1980). *At odds women and family in America from the revolution to the present.* New York: Oxford University Press.

Dempsey, J. J. (1981). *The family and public policy: The issues of the '80s.* Baltimore: Paul H. Brookes.

Dobson, J. C. (1980). *Straight talk to men and their wives.* Waco, TX: World Books.

Edelman, M. W. (1978, March). Today's promises—tomorrow's Americans: Putting children first on the national agenda. *Young Children, 33,* 4–9.

Featherstone, J. (1979). Family matters. *Harvard Educational Review, 49*(1), 20–52.

Goode, W. (1977). State intervention and the family: Problems of policy. In B. Chadwick (Ed.), *Government impact on family life* (pp. 13–19). Provo, UT: Brigham Young University Press.

Greenblatt, T. (1977). *Responsibility for child care.* San Francisco, CA: Jossey-Bass.

Grotberg, E. H. (1981). The federal role in family policies. In H. C. Wallach (Ed.), *Approaches to child and family policy. AAAS selected symposium* (pp. 9–24). Boulder, CO: Westview Press.

Guttentag, M., & Secord, P. F. (1983). *Too many women? The sex ratio question.* Beverly Hills, CA: Sage.

Haberkorn, F. E. (1976, January). An interview with W. F. Mondale. *Young Child,* pp. 98–105.

Hareven, T. K. (1977). The family and gender roles in historical perspective. In I. A. Carter & A. F. Scott (Eds.), *Women and men: Changing roles and relationships and perceptions* (pp. 93–118). New York: Praeger.

Hareven, T. K. (1982). American family in transition: Historical perspective on change. In F. Walsh (Ed.), *Normal family processes* (chap. 18). New York: Guilford Press.

Hartford Connecticut Mutual Life Insurance Company. (1981). *The Connecticut Mutual Life report on American values in the 1980's: The impact of belief.* Hartford, Ct: Author.

Hobbs, N. (1978). Family school and communities: An ecosystem for children. *Teacher College Record, 79*(4), 756–766.

Hubbell, R. (1981). Family impact seminar: A new approach to policy analysis. In H. C. Wallach (Ed.), *Approaches to family policy. AAAS selected symposium* (pp. 35–46). Boulder, CO: Westview Press.

Kagan, S., Klugman, E., & Zigler, E. (1983). Shaping child and family policies: Criteria and strategies for a new decade. In E. Zigler, S. Kagan, & E. Klugman (Eds.), *Children, families, and government: Perspectives on American policy* (pp. 415–440). Cambridge, MA: Harvard University Press.

Kahn, A. J., & Kammerman, S. B. (1982). *Helping America's families.* Philadelphia: Temple University Press.

Kammerman, S. B., & Kahn, A. J. (Eds.). (1978). *Family policy, government and families in 14 countries.* New York: Columbia University Press.

Kammerman, S. B., & Kahn, A. J. (1983). Child welfare of families with children: A child and family policy agenda. In B. G. McGowan & W. Meezan (Eds.), *Child welfare. Current dilemmas. Future directions* (pp. 143–168). Itaska, IL: Peacock.

Keniston, K., & Carnegie Council on Children. (1977). *All our children: The American family under pressure.* New York: Harcourt Brace Jovanovich.

Kirp, D. L., & Yudof, M. G. (1974). *Educational policy and the law.* Berkeley, CA: McCutchan Press.

Knitzer, J. (1984). Mental health services to children and adolescents. A national view of public policies. *American Psychologist, 39*(8), 905–911.

Lasch, A. (1977). *Haven in a heartless world.* New York: Basic Books.

Levitan. S., & Belous, R. S. (1981). *What's happening to the American family?* Baltimore: Johns Hopkins University Press.

McCathern, R. R. (1981). The demise of federal child care legislation: Lessons for the 80's from the failures of the 70's. In H. C. Wallach (Ed.), *Approaches to child and family policy* (pp. 101–143). Boulder, CO: Westview Press.

McGowan, B. G. (1983). Historical evolution of child welfare services. In B. G. McGowan & W. Meezan (Eds.), *Child welfare. Current dilemmas. Future directions* (pp. 45–90). Itaska, IL: Peacock.

Mencher, S. (1967). Social authority and the family. *Journal of Marriage and Family, 29,* 164–192.

Monroney, R. M. (1976). *The family and the state: Consideratons for social policy.* London: Longman.

Monroney, R. M., & Dokecki, P. R. (1984). The family and the professions. *Journal of Family Issues, 5*(2), 224–238.

Moynihan, D. D. (1965, September). A family policy for the nation. *America,* pp. 280–283.

National Center for Health Statistics. (1985, July). Births, marriages, divorces, and deaths for April 1985. *Monthly Vital Statistics Report, 34*(4). Washington, DC: U.S. Department of Health and Human Services.

Ooms, T. (1984). The necessity of a family policy. *Journal of Family Issues, 5*(2), 160–181.

Pardeck, J. T. (1984). Development of a family policy through social crises. *Family Therapy, 9*(2), 97–104.

Parkhurst, J. G., & Houseknecht, S. K. (1983). The family, politics and religion in the '80's. *Journal of Family Issues, 4*(1), 5–34.

Pierce v. Society of Sisters, 268 U.S. 510 (1925).

Preister, S. (1984, September). *American Family. The National Newsletter on Family Policy and Programs. 7*(9). Washington, DC: Youth Policy Institute, St. Johns Hall, Cardinal Station.

Rapoport, R., Rapoport, R. N., & Strelitz, A. (1977). *Fathers, mothers, and society. Toward new alliances.* New York: Basic Books.

Rega, P. J. (1979–1980). The supreme court's view of marriage and the family: Tradition or transition. *Journal of Family Law, 18,* 301–330.

Reiss, I. L. (1981). Some observations on ideology and sexuality in America. *Journal of Marriage and the Family, 43,* 271–283.

Roe v. Wade, 410 U.S. 113 (1973).

Sampson, E. E. (1977). Psychology and the American ideal. *Journal of Personality and Social Psychology, 35,* 767–782.

Scanzoni, J. (1982). Considering family policy: Status quo or force for change. *Journal of Family Issues, 3*(3), 227–300.

Schneiderman, L. (1979). Against the family. *Social Work, 24*(6), 386–389.

Seward, R. R. (1978). *The American family: A demographic history* (Vol. 70). Beverly Hills, CA: Sage.

Shorr, A. (1979). Views of family policy. *Journal of Marital and Family Therapy, 41*(3), 465–467.

Statistical Abstract of the United States (104th ed). (1984). Washington, DC: U.S. Department of Commerce, Bureau of the Census.

Steiner, G. (1981). *The futility of family policy.* Washington, DC: Brookings Institution.

Stone, L. (1977). *The family: Sex and marriage in England 1500–1800.* New York: Harper Press.

Toward a National Policy for Children and Families. (1976). Washington, DC: National Academy of Sciences, Advisory Committee on Child Development.

Update, (1985, November). *Mental Health Law Project, 4*(5). Washington, DC.

White House Conference on Families. (1980). *Listening to America's families: Action for the 80's. The report to the president, congress and families of the nation.* Washington, DC: U.S. Government Printing Office.

Yankelovich, D. (1981). *New rules, searching for self-fulfillment in a world turned upside down.* New York: Random House.

Yoder v. Wisconsin, 406 U.S. 205 (1972).

Zigler, E., & Muenchow, S. (1984). How to influence social policy affecting children and families. *American Psychologist, 39*(4), 415–420.

Zigler, E., Kagan, S., & Klugman, E. (Eds.). (1983). *Children, families, and government: Perspectives on American social policy.* Cambridge, MA: Harvard University Press.

3

The Healthy Family: Is It Possible?

Nick Stinnett
John DeFrain

Introduction

Research on strong families, involving more than 3,000 families and more than 30 separate investigations, has been carried out by the authors of this chapter for more than a decade. An undertaking of this scope is not, of course, the work of only one or two individuals. More than 30 masters and doctoral students have worked on the various projects. The most comprehensive and readable report of this effort appears in *Secrets of Strong Families*, a popular book written for a wide audience (Stinnett & DeFrain, 1986). As a result of our research, we believe that healthy families are possible, but that considerable commitment and effort are required.

Research Background

Our studies of strong families began in the early 1970s in Oklahoma. The first author, based at Oklahoma State University, asked family life and home economics specialists in the Cooperative Extension Service to recommend a few families in each county of the state which they felt exhibited healthy family behaviors. The Extension Service was a likely organization to ask for help because the personnel had professional training in family study, their jobs were concerned with improving the quality of family life, and as Extension Specialists they had a great deal of contact with a wide range of families—rural and urban, rich and poor, black, white, Spanish-American, American Indian.

The recommended families were then contacted. (This particular study, by the way, focused on two-parent families with at least one child at home; a later study looked at young single-parent families.) If the parents reported very high marriage satisfaction and very high satisfaction with the parent–child relationship, the family was included in the study. The 130 families who met the criteria came from farms and ranches, small towns, medium-sized cities, and large urban areas.

Interview and questionnaire data were gathered and separate studies of various aspects of family life were done: communication patterns (Ball, 1976), vital/total marriage relationships (Ammons & Stinnett, 1980), personality characteristics and commitment (Leland, 1977; Stevenson et al., 1983), religious orientation (Matthews, 1977), ways of spending time together (Wright, 1975), patterns of dealing with conflict (McCumber, 1977), relationship patterns (Stinnett & Sauer, 1977; Wall, 1977), and power structure (Tomlinson, 1977).

When Stinnett moved to the University of Nebraska-Lincoln in 1977, the work was expanded nationwide. Each study was conducted in a different manner than the one before. The researchers felt diverse methods would shed more light on a very intricate and difficult research topic. In one study, for example, newspaper stories were placed in about 50 papers around the country:

STRONG FAMILIES NEEDED FOR NATIONAL RESEARCH

Lincoln, Nebraska—Researchers at the University of Nebraska are seeking volunteers for a nationwide study of strong families.

"If you live in a strong family, we'd like you to contact us by mail," Dr. Nick Stinnett, Chairman of the Department of Human Development and the Family, noted. "We know a lot these days about what makes families fail, but we really need to know a lot more about what makes families succeed. Your help is urgently requested."

The news story was tiny and usually buried far back in the newspaper. The researchers were shocked and overjoyed when more than 850 parents volunteered for the study. Many wrote to say they were delighted someone was finally doing something on happy families. In this particular study, the volunteers filled out 17 pages of questionnaire materials which peered deeply into their family relationships (Stinnett, Sanders, & DeFrain, 1981).

Many more studies followed. When the researchers placed stories in newspapers around the country asking for strong single-parent families (Elmen, 1983; Fricke, 1982), more than 1,100 letters poured in.

The list of studies is too long to recount here, but a sample of the work should be instructive: strengths of black families (King, 1980); leisure in high-strength, middle-strength, and low-strength families (Lynn, 1983);

religiosity and purpose in life (Rampey, 1983); the strengths and stresses of executive families (Stinnett, Smith, Tucker, and Schell, 1985); family strengths and personal well-being (Stinnett, Lynn, Kimmons, Fuenning, & DeFrain, 1984); strengths of remarried families (Knaub, Hanna, & Stinnett, 1984); family strengths concepts and marriage enrichment programs (Gutz, 1980; Johnson, 1984); an analysis of the characteristics of strong families and the effectiveness of marriage and family life education (Luetchens, 1981); and parent–child relationships in strong families (Strand, 1979).

Graduate students from foreign countries and U.S. graduate students with an interest in other cultures convinced us the work should be expanded into other corners of the globe. One study focused on Latin American family strengths. Families from 12 countries participated in that survey (Casas, Stinnett, DeFrain, Williams, & Lee, 1984). German, Swiss, and Austrian family strengths were studied in another project (Stoll, 1984).

One student tried for several months to figure out a way to learn more about the strengths of families in the Soviet Union, but finally had to settle for a look at families who had recently immigrated from Russia to the United States (Porter, 1981).

Another student traveled with her family to Johannesburg, South Africa, on missionary assignment. Her research focused on the strengths of South African black families in Soweto, a very poor, strife-torn black ghetto outside of Johannesburg. Intensive interviews with a small number of families there yielded fascinating results (V. P. Weber, 1984).

Yet another population was studied by Brigman, Schons, and Stinnett (1986), who collected data on the characteristics of strong families in Iraq. While other studies are underway and more anticipated, we are at a point in our research where we can discuss some common characteristics of strong, healthy families.

The Six Major Qualities of Strong Families

The behavioral scientist's job is to try to make sense of an often chaotic world—to try to simplify human experience and report research results in a manner in which people can comprehend and use the findings. Margaret Mead once said that the family is the most difficult institution in the world to study and explain. It is a very closed institution, and the diversity of family types in the United States and around the world is astounding.

John Spiegel, a psychiatrist, and a group of associates set out to define the "normal American family" a few years ago. The task seemed simple enough, for they would do this by straightforwardly describing the normal American family's day-to-day behavior. Spiegel and his colleagues found the task almost impossible:

> Instead of finding a clear-cut definition of the family easy to achieve, we discovered that families exhibited the most astonishing variance in their structure and function. . . . Not only were various and differing functions assigned to the family in different social milieus, but even those functions which were apparently universal, such as the socialization of children, the satisfaction of sexual needs, or the biological and material maintenance of the members of the family, were carried out in such various ways and with such interesting implications, that it proved impossible to obtain meaningful patterns without reference to the surrounding social system. (Spiegel, 1971, p. 144)

In proposing six major qualities of strong families, we are acutely aware of the extreme complexity and diversity of family life in this country. The handful of cross-cultural studies reinforced our belief that it is very difficult to understand American families and that the researcher compounds the challenges by looking at families in other lands.

Yet, after looking at the results of 30 different studies with 3,000 families in every state of the United States and several foreign countries, we are willing to present some useful hypotheses here. We believe that six major qualities or themes appear in the life of millions of strong families in this country and in other countries, especially among the Western industrial societies and the more technologically oriented nations of the globe:

1. Commitment
2. Appreciation
3. Communication
4. Time together
5. Spiritual wellness
6. The ability to cope with stress and crisis

Each family is unique and functions somewhat differently from other families. When asked to describe the qualities that make for success, individual families tend to use different words. Thus, there are dangers in overgeneralizing when speaking about the qualities of strong families. Not all six qualities are apparent in every family, and the emphasis in one family of necessity is different from the emphasis in another family.

Given the above disclaimers, we believe the six listed qualities do come through very often (Stinnett, 1983, 1985). Other researchers, as we discuss later in this chapter, have come to surprisingly similar conclusions. Although they may not have made a list of six qualities or used the same terminology, the essence of healthy families as described by other researchers appears to be very similar to our findings.

Commitment

On occasion people ask us to single out the most important quality of strong families. This is difficult to do, and in some ways impossible, because all of the qualities are interrelated, making it hard to separate one from the other. But we do have a great deal of evidence that commitment is very important to the strong families—it is the invisible tie that binds them together and perhaps the foundation for the other five qualities.

The strong families generally are committed to the family above all else. (Many say that their commitment is to God and that family commitment is a logical extension of this higher commitment.) They tend to view the family as the foundation of society, and certainly as the foundation of individual well-being for themselves.

Many people these days pay lip service to the notion of the family. Strong family members put action behind their words. They make a determined effort to invest their time and energy in family activities, and keep their jobs, volunteer work, and housework under control.

In the words of the strong family members, it is clear the family comes first: "My wife and kids are the most important part of my life," one father told us. Another said quite eloquently, "What we have as a family is a treasure."

Commitment does not mean the family members stifle each other, however. "We give each other the freedom and encouragement to pursue individual goals," a husband explained. "Yet either of us would cut out activities or goals that threaten our existence as a couple." He continued, "She has a wonderful job that she loves, but she wouldn't transfer to another city if I couldn't go happily, and vice versa."

Commitment includes sexual fidelity. Though some of the individuals we surveyed admitted to having engaged in an extramarital affair at some time earlier in the marriage, none felt that in the long run the affair did anything extraordinarily positive for the marriage relationship. "Being faithful to each other sexually is just a part of being honest with each other," a young woman told us.

An older man explained that he and his wife promised 40 years ago in their wedding vows to be faithful to each other. They have taken the vows seriously. Though they could go looking elsewhere for sex, they both commented, "What good is a broken promise?"

Some couples saw an extramarital affair as a cry for help in a failing marriage and used the affair to build a stronger relationship. "I suppose we could have divorced after her affair, but I saw that she was looking for warmth, for intimacy in life, and I was too busy at work to provide it for her. But her relationship with Jim shocked me into realizing that I was a pretty poor husband at that time and today I'm a pretty good one!"

Appreciation

When we report the six qualities of strong families that come up repeatedly in our research, people sometimes say, "Well, that one sure is just plain common sense."

It is always interesting to us, however, that one particular quality that seems commonsensical to one person may be very surprising to another. For example, it seems reasonable to us that people who love and care about each other would express a good deal of appreciation to other family members. But many people do not think of this quality at all when they try to guess what the six qualities of strong families might be. In fact, when Nick Stinnett surveyed a long list of marriage and family life textbooks in the early 1970s, he found to his surprise that very few authors had much to say about appreciation when they talked about what might make for a successful relationship.

Some people do not think it is important to tell their loved ones how thankful they are for having them in the family: "She puts dinner on the table every evening, but it never occurred to me to thank her for it. Why should I, really? She doesn't thank me for going to work every day."

But it takes a great deal of hard work and drive to do all the things in life that we are "supposed" to do, and that tiny expression of appreciation for each other not only builds the self-esteem of the one being appreciated, it also builds a bond of caring between both "appreciatee" and "appreciator."

"I make a point of giving a sincere compliment to every person in my family every day," one middle-aged mother told us. Another wife added, "He makes me feel good about me and about us as a couple. Very few days go by without him saying something like 'You look really nice today' or 'The house is so clean and neat; it's a real pleasure to be home' or 'Great dinner' or 'I'd rather stay home with you; let's skip that party.'"

Some of the strong families use a technique that we believe would be valuable to everyone. If you have to make a constructive criticism of another family member, make sure that you follow the 10-to-1 rule: Criticize, but criticize with kindness, and make sure that you express appreciation for something positive the person does at least 10 times for each negative thing you say.

By keeping a high ratio of positives to negatives, we estimate 10-to-1 or more, people can insure a healthy family atmosphere. The good feelings tend to flow back and forth among members. If Mom feels good about herself, she is more likely to make kind comments to Sister. And when Sister feels good, she's not as likely to give Brother trouble. The positive energy charges everyone in a strong family, and the accomplishments of the individuals are great.

People in dysfunctional, unhealthy families tend to focus on the negative and often try to gain energy by feeding off the self-esteem of other family members. What usually happens is that the good in each person is quickly depleted and only destructive feelings are left.

Another important area of appreciation in families is the sexual area. In strong families, positive sexual relationships are not narrowly time-defined such as beginning at 10:30 P.M. on Saturday night. Rather, it begins Monday morning when Dad takes out the garbage, and continues on Tuesday when Mom compliments the children on their art work, and on Wednesday when Mom asks Dad out for lunch. In other words, the good feelings that energize the family members make a warm and comfortable sexual relationship more likely for the parents. Also, positive sexual experiences are a natural continuation of the ongoing positive and supportive family relationships.

"The times when sex was best have been times when my wife and I felt especially close and in tune with each other," one middle-aged husband told us, "when we've solved a problem or when we're working on a project together." A wife said, "I learned a long time ago that I can't gripe about my husband's sloppy ways, insinuate he doesn't bring home enough money, or drool over Burt Reynolds on TV, and still expect him to be very thrilled about me either."

Communication

A researcher, interested in the amount of time that the average husband and wife spend in conversation each week, wired portable microphones to a number of couples. Each time they spoke, their voices were recorded. The microphone may have made some a bit self-conscious, but we suspect that after a short while people forgot the tiny apparatus was even there and that the data are probably valid. One startling finding was that the average couple spent only 17 of the 10,080 minutes there are in a week in conversation (McGinnis, 1979).

The feedback we received from the strong families we have studied indicates that considerably more than 17 minutes a week is spent in conversation. They talk about important things, and are often very task-oriented in their communication: what-needs-to-be-done and how-are-we-going-to-get-it-done types of conversations. Strong family members also spend a lot of time talking about small things. They just enjoy talking with each other on issues from the trivial to the sublime.

This fact is often ignored by therapists who have a problem-solving orientation. The strong families we have studied teach us that communication is important not only to solve problems, but also as recognition that the people in the family simply enjoy each other's company. Otherwise, if family members talk only about how to solve problems, the relationship is not much different from the relationship with one's plumber or dentist. It may accomplish narrow tasks, but it is not a warm, exciting, or growing relationship.

The more involved family members become in outside activities, the less time there is for quiet, calm, "fun" communication. Some parents are so scheduled, so task-oriented, that they try to treat family like just another job. "Now I'm going to sit down with my teenaged daughter and really communicate with her for three minutes!" the parent seems to believe. "And then I'll take the car to be greased, and then I'll meet with the boss."

Members of strong family have differences, of course. To live is to experience conflict with other people. Troubled families tend to err in one of two ways: They either fight too much or they do not argue at all. But members of strong families have positive ways of resolving the inevitable differences, and they tend not to go to either of the two extremes.

Constant hostilities and violence in a family do not support the development of healthy relationships. At the other extreme, though, are families who are so afraid of conflict that they do not bring up differences at all. These families are prime candidates for marriage burnout. Afraid to talk about genuine differences, the couples over a long period of time lose any feeling, negative or positive, for each other (Lingren et al., 1982).

In the strong families we find a modest amount of bickering. When something comes up the family members try to solve the problem very quickly by speaking very directly, very honestly, and trying not to blame or pour out hostility. Hostilities occur on occasion, of course, because strong family members are genuinely human. But the hostilities generally do not get to an extreme level.

In an unhealthy family erring on the side of silence, the members "gunnysack" their feelings. They hide the complaints, believing that to complain or express a tinge of anger is somehow wrong. Pressure builds and builds in these families, and in some cases can explode into tremendous angry outbursts or even violence. After several episodes like this, the members teach themselves to avoid differences at all cost, for fear of a blowup. They walk out the door, or they go off and drink, or find a friend or therapist who will listen to their complaints. But they do not communicate with each other in a way that solves the problem in the long run, and marriage and family relationships are likely to become even more problematic and dissatisfying.

Here are a few important points we have learned from our research on communication patterns of strong families:

1. The individuals have good perspective on life and human beings. They realize that good things take time and that having positive communication patterns in a family requires a great deal of time.

2. The strong family members know how to listen. They avoid sermonizing. They are intelligent enough to know that getting along well with others often means placing a hold on expressing their opinions long enough to hear what other family members are really saying.

3. They check things out with each other by asking questions: "How do you feel today?" "What's on your mind?" "It's been pretty tough, I guess, huh?"

4. They avoid trying to read each other's minds. Loved ones who really know each other realize that they often do not know what the other person is thinking or believes. Rather than trying to speak for each other, they believe it is important for the loved one to speak for himself or herself. And rather than assume something is going on in the other's head, they check it out first. This avoids the problems that follow when persons incorrectly assume what others are thinking or feeling and then act on those erroneous impressions.

5. Strong family members get inside the other person's world. They do this by listening, and when empathy is built in this way it makes family relations a lot easier. When people disagree on an issue, it usually is not because one is right and the other wrong. Rather, it is because they hold different perceptions, and when we can understand the other person's views we can respond more empathically and less combatively.

6. They create a caring communion. It seems to be a natural inclination for many people to hide their fears and frustrations from each other. A number of men are especially adept at this, because they have been told from childhood not to show hurt or reveal their emotions, especially tender ones. By creating a caring communion in the

family, each member receives the permission to express fears, failings, and triumphs. We accept each other for our insecurities and support each other in our efforts to succeed.

7. They avoid criticism, evaluating, psychoanalysis, and acting superior, all barriers to positive communication. These behaviors produce a defensiveness and competitiveness in families and counteract the development of strong and positive family relationships.

8. Strong families keep it honest. Communication patterns are characterized by honesty and openness. Honesty is more than not lying; it is the absence of manipulation.

9. They avoid brutal honesty. Some people use honesty as an excuse to be destructively critical and injure the loved one. There is a fine line between honesty and mental cruelty, and even a young child can learn the difference.

10. Strong family members tend to air their differences when they are still warm, rather than sit on the difference and add tension in the household for a long time before the trouble comes out. They are also smart enough to wait at least until angry feelings have dissipated enough to have a rational discussion. Attempting a discussion when one or several family members are extremely upset can lead to dissatisfactory outcomes.

11. In a strong family one problem at a time is handled. By gunnysacking problems, we usually find that everything finally is dumped out in one big, unmanageable pile. By handling issues one at a time, we have a much greater chance of resolving them and keeping problems in perspective. When problems build up and are then brought up, the extent of resentment and magnitude of problems make a reasonable resolution considerably harder to achieve.

12. They are specific and define terms, breaking problems down into logical components. "For a long time I kept telling my wife she was spending too much money," one husband told us. "Finally, I realized that wasn't quite true. I simply was upset about how much money she spent on the kids' clothes. On groceries and other items, she was doing terrific." By being more specific, the problem became much more manageable and the couple could find a reasonable compromise.

13. Members of strong families tend to become allies, attacking the problem rather than each other. "There is a genuine difference of opinion between us," the reasoning should go. "How can we work together to find a solution to this difference of opinion, since we are both honorable and good people?"

14. They "ban the bomb." Some dysfunctional families use what we

call "A bombs." These are the most destructive, hurtful things that a person can bring up in an argument. We all know what really hurts our loved ones. Maybe they feel bad about their weight, an extramarital affair long past, or their inability to get into law school. The list of sore spots is endless. Using an "A Bomb" in a family argument is unfair and only encourages the injured party to also fight dirty.

15. Perhaps most important, strong families look at differences in a very creative way. A disagreement can easily end up in a brawl and does so in many, many families. Strong families use active problem-solving techniques and look at a disagreement as an opportunity for growth and enrichment. Communication is used not only to smooth out differences, but more importantly, to sustain mental health and nurture intimacy.

Communication is the lifeblood of strong relationships.

Time Together

A survey of 1,500 schoolchildren included this enticing question: "What do you think makes a happy family?" The children, with a tremendous amount of wisdom, did not list money, cars, fancy homes, or television sets. Their most frequent response was that a family is happy because they do things together (Jacobsen, 1969).

This seems simple enough, but how many times have you heard the over-used saying: "I don't have a lot of time with my family, but I try to make it quality time." The strong families correct this trite rationalization and make it ring true: "We have quality time, and in great quantity!"

One of the exercises we do with families is to ask them to go on a "journey of happy memories." They think back to their childhood and pinpoint the experiences with their families that were the most memorable, the most dear to them. The adults come up with things like this:

> I remember stories Mom and Dad told me when they tucked me in to bed.

> Going with Dad to work on the farm. I felt so important. So superior, cause my little brother wasn't big enough to go.

> Having the whole family together at Christmas was special. All the grandpas and grandmas and aunts and uncles, and thousands of kids. They made us kids eat in the kitchen together. I thought it was so neat then, and it must have been pandemonium.

> Singing altogether, yes. Singing. We had an old piano, and I learned to play, and we would all sing corny old songs.

Vacation. We would go 50 miles to the lake and rent a cabin, and Dad would swim with us and dunk me.

My dad and I would cook together on Sunday. Lunch. It was great. We were all too busy during the week to take much time, but Sundays Dad and I would make something special like hamburgers or bean sandwiches.

The common denominator in all these happy memories of childhood, of course, is that the family members were enjoying each other's company. Most often, the people in the strong families we study tell us about activities together that do not cost a lot of money. So the point here is not the cost of such activities, but the quality of the time spent in the activities.

While we have stressed time together, it is also important that individuals have time alone and time outside the family so that the bonds do not become chains. David Olson at the University of Minnesota-St. Paul stresses that there is a middle ground on this issue (Olson et al., 1983). Too little family time signifies a disengaged type of family in which the group lacks cohesion and support for each other. Too much family time leads to psychological enmeshment. The individuals are not free to explore the world independently and grow.

Without the opportunity for persons to grow as individuals, the family cannot grow as a unit. The family's strength depends on the strength of each member.

Popular activities of family members include: meals together; house and yard chores; outdoor recreation, including camping, playing catch and yard games, canoeing, hiking, picnicking, stargazing, league sports, bicycling, walking, and swimming; church, synagogue, or other religious activities; and special events including holidays, vacations, birthdays.

It is important to recognize that these activities are relatively common-place and within the financial reach of the vast majority of creative people. The key, of course, is commitment to spending time together.

A New Mexico wife and mother we know has "temporarily retired" from teaching to nurture her own four children. At the end of every "typical" day she is hard pressed to report even a small sample of all the different activites she shared with her very active youngsters. The kids flow in and out of her sight, bringing things they have found in their explorations of the world to share with her. And they bring sore knees and arguments to settle. The day is a veritable roller coaster for her, but she manages to be good natured about it most of the time. Her philosophy is summed up in a poem by an anonymous author decorating a hallway wall:

Cleaning and scrubbing
Can wait 'til tomorrow
For babies grow up,
We've learned to our sorrow—
So quiet down, cobwebs,
Dust, go to sleep—
I'm rocking my baby,
And babies don't keep.

Strong marriages which are a vital aspect of strong families do not automatically happen. To maintain a strong marriage, many of the people in our studies recommended that parents make a tremendous effort to avoid committing more energy and love to child rearing than they do to their spouses. We have seen many couples who do a wonderful job in caring for the children but end up in divorce anyway. The marriage somehow got lost in the shuffle.

Kathy Simon, a family researcher in Omaha, recently asked 700 fathers nationwide what was the greatest gift they could give their children. The most common reply: "a happy marriage." The fathers were arguing that a stable marital relationship is not only a good model for the children's future but insures security in the here and now (Simon, 1986). And a happy marriage takes time.

Spiritual Wellness

This is possibly the most controversial finding in our research, and yet it is undeniable that for many strong families religion—or spiritual wellness, or feelings of optimism or hope, or an ethical value system, or whatever you wish to call it—are important themes in their lives.

One dictionary defines spiritual as "non material; of or pertaining to the spirit or soul" (E. B. Williams, 1979). Many people regard the soul as the immortal part of a human being; for others, the soul is the part of human nature where feelings, ideas, and morals are centered.

Spiritual wellness for many of the strong families we have surveyed is the unifying force, the caring center within each individual that promotes sharing, love, and compassion for other people. It is a force helping us to transcend the self and tap into something greater.

Many of the strong family members in our studies manifest their spiritual nature through membership in religious organizations— churches, synagogues, temples. Other manifest their spiritual nature in adherence to deeply felt values and involvement in causes they deem worthy.

However they express their spiritual or ethical nature, these beliefs have tremendous benefits for their families. These people tell us their beliefs give them purpose or meaning in life. Some tell us, "My purpose is to serve God." Others say, "I am here to make the world a little bit better than before I came." Whatever they say, this purpose helps them transcend the everyday frustrations and pettiness that human existence so often is burdened with.

Their beliefs give them a positive, confident outlook on life. "If God is in control, all is well in my world." one father told us. Another sat at the edge of the Grand Canyon of the Colorado and was awestruck by its immensity and his own insignificance: "I gain perspective by going out into nature and 'talking with God,' " the young man explained. "On the edge of the Grand Canyon my problems don't seem so big. And I feel like I'm a part of something so much greater, so much more important than my little, insignificant life."

The spiritual values, the sense of reverence for life and living we develop through our days, firmly ground us. We develop guidelines for living that often grow and change as we grow. Listen to some of the strong family members:

> We remind ourselves that all living creatures are wonderful and marvelous. That certainly includes humans. So even when they do dumb things, they still are worthwhile. I love my husband and my son even when I don't like what they're doing. That kind of philosophy helps me to be more patient and forgiving.

> The belief that we are not alone helps us to deal with conflict and anger. We believe we have divine guidance to show us the best way when we disagree.

> The old, old rule of treating other people as you'd like to be treated just can't be beat as a succinct guide for good relationships.

> Most of the religions I'm familiar with value behaviors that are helpful in creating good family relationships. By that I mean that things like responsibility and concern for others, empathy, love, forgiveness, honesty, controlling anger, gentleness, and patience are all taught as virtues.

Religious or spiritual communities often provide tremendous support for their members. The community helps people in time of illness, death, birth, natural disaster, and accident. And during good times, contact with others whose values you respect can be a great source of encouragement and a model for conduct. Also, groups of couples meeting occasionally for dinner and discussion reaffirms the value of marriage and intimacy in a time when many marriages are threatened.

The ways the strong families expressed their spiritual or transcendent values were as numerous as the radii emanating from the center of a circle—in reality there are an infinite variety of ways to express our spiritual nature. The common denominator in all of these beliefs seemed to be the need to search out the greater good in a difficult world, to identify with it, and to gain strength from it.

In working with families we have found that it is a disservice to them to ignore their values. Rather, by trying to understand the values they hold dear, we as professionals can help the families to tap the potential for healing and growth inherent in many spiritual and religious communities. We are not interested in debating the details of one particular theology or another. Instead, we seek to use the power of the adherents of a particular faith or belief system for the good of the troubled family.

Coping with Stress and Crisis

Finally, strong family members in our research are enormously creative and adaptable. They experience stress in their life on a daily basis, just as anyone else does, and major crises can rock the foundations of their families, (W.C. Weber, 1981). However, they respond as survivors. They have developed ways of coping with the trials and tribulations of life, and the family is for many the most important source of strength.

Here are some of the things the families do:

1. They pull together. No individual is completely responsible for the situation. Each person, down to the youngest child, can do things to ease the burden for all.

2. They get help. Members of strong families are often seen at counseling centers or talking with a priest or rabbi or dropping by a social agency for ideas. Many of them do not know how to fix the transmission of a car, so they take it to a specialist. Likewise, they also recognize the fact that they often do not know how to "fix" a marriage problem, a dispute with in-laws, or a teenager who is depressed. In short, they are smart enough to know not only what they do know, but also what they do not know.

3. They use their spiritual resources. Through prayer, a walk in the woods, a talk with a pastor or religious educator, or finding the courage to reach out to the people in their church or neighborhood they gain help in solving a problem which is much bigger than they are.

4. They have open lines of communication. Because the problem is not

the sole property of any one individual, the family members share the problem and feelings with each other without fear of negative reaction from the members. It is okay to hurt in a strong family; it is okay to feel upset and overwhelmed. But it is not okay to "bite the bullet" when many other people are aching to be of help.

5. Strong families go with the flow of life. One old proverb reminds us about the mighty oak so tall and firm that it breaks in a strong wind, while the spindly looking reeds bend to the ground but do not snap. In a crisis, the old ways to approach life, the old rules of the game, may simply not work any more. The strong family is creative enough to think of new ways to adapt to new and stressful situations.

6. They are not afraid to laugh; they are not afraid to cry. Sometimes life is so crazy or so terrible that we have only two choices: to laugh or to cry. Either approach can be very helpful. Recent physiological studies indicate that laughter and tears may help rid our bodies of the buildup of chemicals we generated in preparing to fight off stress. Many people know the value of "a good cry." And a healthy, black sense of humor sometimes keeps a person from going crazy. Dr. Jon Wuerffel, a chaplain at the U.S. Air Force Academy in Colorado Springs, recently completed a pioneering study of family strengths and their relationship to family humor. He is convinced that humor is an essential element of family health, and his data demonstrate his contention (Wuerffel, 1986).

7. Strong families take one step at a time. They realize that solving any great problem in life is not done overnight. It may take many months, even years. And sometimes the problem cannot really be solved—we must simply adapt to it. The key, in any event, is hanging on until help arrives and some type of resolution is reached.

8. Another common coping technique strong families employ is attending to problems at the time something can be done about them, and they "zone out" the problem when nothing can be done. The key is figuring out when something can be done, and when nothing can be done. This is certainly not easy, but by working together and brainstorming possibilities, strong family members become extremely adept.

9. Strong families are aware of tremendous trifles. People can get hysterical over little things, perhaps because they feel bombarded by petty irritations and overreact. This usually is a time to shut the office door or forget about the leaky kitchen faucet and go out for a walk or some relaxation. By simply changing scenery members of strong families can turn off the torrent of trivia that threatens mental stability. If you are holding a loved one's hand and walking in the park, it is hard for the leaky faucet to get you down. After relaxation and refreshment there will be time to worry about tiny things.

One father would shut his office door on particularly stressful days and remind himself as he walked out that "no matter what happens in this mess, the level of the Mississippi River probably won't raise or lower one inch." In a great, cosmic sense, the little things that were disturbing him did not mean a thing. This realization helped him go home to his wife and children with a clearer head.

10. Physical activity is an important part of the lives of many strong families. The fatigue produced by some form of strenuous activity is certainly one of the world's safest tranquilizers.

11. Strong families help their members minimize fragmentation. Husbands and wives remind each other on occasion what is important in life and what is not important. Since the family is important, it is easier to cut out the trivia that overload us. One of the first things family therapists do to help troubled couples is look at their appointment books and help them cut big chunks out of the schedule. "Is this meeting more important than your marriage?" counselors often ask. "Is this club more important than reading stories to your daughter?" Loved ones need time to gaze into each other's eyes, if their love is to last. Strong families have told us this many times.

12. "The secret to not being overwhelmed," one woman told us, "is to be able to see the daily challenges and frustrations as contributing to something larger. Keep the big picture in mind. See those PTA meetings as improving the school; see your volunteer hours as easing someone's misery; see the work of caring for your family as creating healthy, productive people who will make the world a better place."

Other Research on Healthy Families

Our research is certainly not the only research on strong families, or healthy families, or successful families. A number of other prominent researchers have looked at this important question, and it is interesting to us how similar the findings of our colleagues are to our own findings, even though they may have employed somewhat different research procedures. This, we believe, lends credibility to all the studies.

To discuss all of the studies is beyond the scope of this chapter. But for the serious student of family strengths or healthy families, we recommend reading the work of the following researchers and theoreticians: Herbert Otto, the pioneer in family strengths research (1962a, 1962b, 1971a, 1971b, 1971c, 1976); Otto and Griffiths (1965); Kantor and Lehr (1975); Epstein, Bishop, and Levin (1978); Olson et al. (1983); Olson, Russell, and Sprenkle (1980a, 1980b); Olson, Sprenkle, and Russell (1979); Reiss (1981); and Beavers and Voellers (1983).

Also, we recommend the Family Strengths Book Series.[1] Currently there are seven volumes of articles focusing on building family strengths. Each Annual volume has 30 to 40 articles by counselors, authors, family-life educators, theoreticians, and researchers (Rowe et al., 1984; Stinnett, Chesser, & DeFrain, 1979; Stinnett, Chesser, DeFrain, & Knaub, 1980; Stinnett, DeFrain, King, Knaub, & Rowe, 1981; Stinnett et al., 1982; Stinnett, Knorr, DeFrain, & Rowe, 1981; Van Zandt et al., 1986; R. Williams et al., 1985).

The University of Nebraska sponsors the National Symposium on Building Family Strengths each May in Lincoln. For a decade hundreds of people from 30 to 40 states interested in improving the quality of family life have come to the symposium to share ideas.[2] An Eastern Symposium on Building Family Strengths is sponsored by Pennsylvania State University.[3] A Southern Regional Conference on Family Strengths is sponsored by Arkansas State University in Jonesboro, and an International Conference on Family Strengths has been established by Pepperdine University in Los Angeles, California.

Using These Ideas in Parent Education

It is very clear to us that the family strengths research can be very helpful in parent education programs. The 3,000 strong families we have studied serve as tremendous models. Our book, *Secrets of Strong Families* (Stinnett & DeFrain, 1986), is written specifically for mothers and fathers and is quite useful in parent education classes and programming. A 6-week series can easily be planned around the six family strengths; activities and discussion topics are included in each chapter.

As parent educators, our goal is often to help parents solve problems. "What do I do about bedwetting?" "When he hits his sister I'd like to break his neck. How should I respond?" The questions parents pose are enormously challenging. The answers are not always easy, and both parent and facilitator run the risk of getting bogged down in the endless

[1] Available from the Center for Family Strengths, University of Nebraska, Lincoln, NE 68583.

[2] Contact the Nebraska Center for Continuing Education, University of Nebraska-Lincoln, for information.

[3] Contact the Pennsylvania State University Cooperative Extension Service for information.

details of parenthood when we need to sit back and think more philosophically sometimes: What is the process of parenthood all about? Where are we going? What is my purpose in life? My title is "parent." What does that mean? Those are important questions and concerns experienced by parents.

The six qualities of strong families give us something to reflect upon and offer a foundation from which to build. The enterprise of parenthood is perhaps the most challenging task we face as human beings. The information and knowledge gained from the many studies of strong families offers concrete direction for parents and professionals alike. As stated earlier, healthy families are possible but require considerable and ongoing commitment and effort. The results in terms of human happiness and the healthy emotional development of children are well worth the effort.

References

Ammons, P., & Stinnett, N. (1980). The vital marriage: A closer look. *Family Relations, 19,* 37–42.

Ball, O. L. (1976). *Communication patterns in strong families.* Unpublished master's thesis, Oklahoma State University, Stillwater.

Beavers, W., & Voellers, M. N. (1983). Family models: Comparing and contrasting the Olsen circumplex model with the Beavers system model. *Family Process, 21,* 250–260.

Brigman, K., Schons, J., & Stinnett, N. (1986). Strengths of families in a society under stress: A study of strong families in Iraq. *Family Perspective, 20,* 61–73.

Casas, C., Stinnett, N., DeFrain, J., Williams, R., & Lee, P. (1984). Latin American family strengths. *Family Perspective, 18,* 11–17.

Elmen, J. (1983). *Sole custody and joint custody: A nationwide assessment of divorced parents and children.* Unpublished master's thesis, University of Nebraska, Lincoln.

Epstein, N. B., Bishop, D. S., & Levin, S. (1978). The McMaster model of family functioning. *Journal of Marriage and Family Counseling, 40,* 19–31.

Fricke, J. M. (1982). *Coping as divorced fathers and mothers: A nationwide study of sole, joint, and split custody.* Unpublished master's thesis, University of Nebraska, Lincoln.

Gutz, G. K. T. (1980). *Couples' enrichment: Program development, implementation, and evaluation.* Unpublished master's thesis, University of Nebraska, Lincoln.

Jacobsen, M. L. (1969). *How to keep your family together and still have fun.* Grand Rapids, MI: Zondervan.

Johnson, S. (1984). *The effects of marriage enrichment on marital adaptability, cohesion, and family strengths.* Unpublished doctoral dissertation, University of Nebraska, Lincoln.

Kantor, D., & Lehr, W. (1975). *Inside the family.* San Francisco: Jossey-Bass.

King, J. (1980). *The strengths of Black families.* Unpublished doctoral dissertation, University of Nebraska, Lincoln.

Knaub, P., Hanna, S., & Stinnett, N. (1984). Strengths of remarried families. *Journal of Divorce, 7*(Fall), 41–55.

Leland, C. (1977). *The relationship of family strengths to personality characteristics and commitment.* Unpublished master's thesis, Oklahoma State University, Stillwater.

Lingren, H., Stinnett, N., VanZandt, S., & Rowe, G. (1982). Strengths and skills throughout the life cycle. In N. Stinnett, J. DeFrain, K. King, H. Lingren, S. VanZandt, & R. Williams (Eds.), *Family strengths* (Vol. 4) (pp. 385–406). Lincoln: University of Nebraska.

Luetchens, M. (1981). *An analysis of some characteristics of strong families and the effectiveness of marriage and family life education.* Unpublished doctoral dissertation, University of Nebraska, Lincoln.

Lynn, D. W. (1983). *Leisure activities in high strength, middle strength, and low strength families.* Unpublished doctoral dissertation, University of Nebraska, Lincoln.

Matthews, W. D. (1977). *Family strengths, commitment and religious orientation.* Unpublished master's thesis, Oklahoma State University, Stillwater.

McCumber, A. K. (1977). *Patterns of dealing with conflict in strong families.* Unpublished doctoral dissertation, Oklahoma State University, Stillwater.

McGinnis, A. L. (1979). *The friendship factor.* Minneapolis: Augsburg.

Olson, D. H., McCubbin, H., Barnes, H., Larsen, A., Muxen, M., & Wilson, M. (1983). *Families: What makes them work.* Beverly Hills, CA: Sage.

Olson, D. H., Russell, C. S., & Sprenkle, D. (1980a). Circumplex model of marital and family systems II: Empirical studies and clinical intervention. In J. Vincent (Ed.), *Advances in family intervention, assessment and theory* (pp. 128–176). Greenwich, CT: JAI.

Olson, D. H., Russell, C. S., & Sprenkle, D. (1980b). Marital and family therapy: A decade review. *Journal of Marriage and the Family, 42,* 973–993.

Olson, D. H., Sprenkle, D. H., & Russell, C. (1979). Circumplex model of marital and family systems I: Cohesion and adaptability dimensions, family types, and clinical applications. *Family Process, 18,* 3–28.

Otto, H. A. (1962a). The personal and family resource development programs: A preliminary report. *International Journal of Social Psychiatry, 8,* 185–195.

Otto, H. A. (1962b). The personal and family strength research projects: Some implications for the therapist. *Mental Hygiene, 48,* 439–450.

Otto, H. A. (1971a). *The family cluster: A multi-base alternative.* Los Angeles: Holistic Press.

Otto, H. A. (1971b). *Group methods to actualize human potential: A handbook.* Los Angeles: Holistic Press.

Otto, H. A. (1971c). The human potentialities movement: An overview. *Journal of Creative Behavior, 5,* 258–265.

Otto, H. A. (1976). *Marriage and family enrichment: New perspectives and programs.* Nashville, TN: Abingdon.

Otto, H. A., & Griffiths, A. C. (1965). Personality strength concepts in the helping professions. *Psychiatric Quarterly, 39,* 632–645.

Porter, R. W. (1981). *Strengths of Russian emigrant families.* Unpublished master's thesis, University of Nebraska, Lincoln.

Rampey, T. S. (1983). *Religiosity, purpose in life, and other factors related to family success: A national study.* Unpublished doctoral dissertation, University of Nebraska, Lincoln.

Reiss, D. (1981). *The family's construction of reality.* Cambridge, MA: Harvard University Press.

Rowe, G., DeFrain, J., Lingren, H., MacDonald, R., Stinnett, N., VanZandt, S., & Williams, R. (Eds.), (1984). *Family strengths: Vol. 5. Continuity and diversity.* Newton, MA: Education Development Center.

Simon, K. (1986). *Recycled fathers: Fathering at midlife.* Unpublished master's thesis, University of Nebraska, Lincoln.

Spiegel, J. (1971). *Transactions: The interplay between individual, family and society.* New York: Science House.

Stevenson, P., Lee, P., Stinnett, N., & DeFrain, J. (1983). Family commitment and marital need satisfaction. *Family Perspective, 16,* 157–164.

Stinnett, N. (1983). Strong families: A portrait. In D. Mace (Ed.), *Prevention in family service: Approaches to family wellness.* Beverly Hills, CA: Sage.

Stinnett, N. (1985). Research on strong families. In G. A. Rekers (Eds.), *National leadership forum on strong families.* Ventura, CA: Regal Books.

Stinnett, N., Chesser, B., & DeFrain, J. (Eds.). (1979). *Building family strengths: Vol. 1. Blueprints for action.* Lincoln: University of Nebraska Press.

Stinnett, N., Chesser, B., DeFrain, J., & Knaub, P. (Eds.). (1980). *Family strengths: Vol. 2. Positive models for family life.* Lincoln: University of Nebraska Press.

Stinnett, N., & DeFrain, J. (1986). *Secrets of strong families.* Boston: Little, Brown.

Stinnett, N., DeFrain, J., King, K., Knaub, P., & Rowe, G. (Eds.). (1981). *Family strengths: Vol. 3. Roots of well-being.* Lincoln: University of Nebraska Press.

Stinnett, N., DeFrain, J., King, K., Lingren, H., Rowe, G., VanZandt, S., & Williams, R. (Eds.). (1982). *Family strengths: Vol. 4. Positive support systems.* Lincoln: University of Nebraska Press.

Stinnett, N., Knorr, B., DeFrain, J., & Rowe, G. (1981). How strong families cope with crisis. *Family Perspective, 15,* 159–166.

Stinnett, N., Lynn, D., Kimmons, L., Fuenning, S., & DeFrain, J. (1984). Family strengths and personal wellness. *Wellness Perspectives, 1,* 25–31.

Stinnett, N., Sanders, G., & DeFrain, J. (1981). Strong families: A national study. In N. Stinnett, J. DeFrain, K. King, P. Knaub, & G. Rowe (Eds.), *Family strengths: Vol. 3. Roots of well-being* (pp. 33–41). Lincoln: University of Nebraska Press.

Stinnett, N., & Sauer, K. H. (1977). Relationship characteristics of strong families. *Family Perspective, 11,* 3–11.

Stinnett, N., Smith, R., Tucker, D., & Schell, D. (1985). Executive families: Strengths, stresses, and loneliness. *Wellness Perspectives, 1,* 25–31.

Stinnett, N., Walters, J., & Kaye, E. (1984). *Relationships in marriage and the family.* (2nd ed.). New York: Macmillan.

Stoll, B. (1984). *Family strengths in Austria, Germany, and Switzerland.* Unpublished master's thesis, University of Nebraska, Lincoln.

Strand, K. (1979). *Parent–child relationships among strong families.* Unpublished master's thesis, University of Nebraska, Lincoln.

Tomlinson, D. L. (1977). *Power structure of strong families.* Unpublished master's thesis, Oklahoma State University, Stillwater.

VanZandt, S. (Ed.). (1986). *Family strengths.* Lincoln: University of Nebraska, Center for Family Strengths.

Wall, J. A. K. (1977). *Characteristics of strong families.* Unpublished master's thesis, Oklahoma State University, Stillwater.

Weber, V. P. (1984). *The strengths of Black families in Soweto, Johannesburg, South Africa.* Unpublished master's thesis, University of Nebraska, Lincoln.

Weber, W. C. (1981). *Families cope with stress: A study of family strengths in families where a spouse has end-stage renal disease.* Unpublished doctoral dissertation, University of Nebraska, Lincoln.

Williams, E. B. (Ed.). (1979). *The Scribner–Bantam English dictionary.* New York: Bantam Books.

Williams, R., Lingren, H., Rowe, G., VanZandt, S., Lee, P., & Stinnett, N. (Eds.). (1985).

Family strengths: Vol. 6. Enhancement of interaction. Lincoln: University of Nebraska, Center for Family Strengths.

Wright, R. M. (1975). *The manner in which strong families participate in activities which comprise a large segment of potential family interaction time.* Unpublished master's thesis, Oklahoma State University, Stillwater.

Wuerffel, J. (1986). *The relationship between family strengths and humor.* Unpublished doctoral dissertation, University of Nebraska, Lincoln.

II

Delivery Systems of Parenting Education

4

Active Parenting: A Video-Based Program

Michael H. Popkin

Introduction

A group of parents look expectantly at the TV screen as the leader turns on the video cassette player (VCR). On the screen 5-year-old Danny is playing a game. Danny's mother comes in reminding him to pick up his toys. The parents in the group gulp as Danny says, "No, I don't have to." The group leader observes the parents' looks and nods of familiarity as they watch the ensuing power struggle develop. Back on the screen Mother sends Danny off to bed with a spank, then drops to her knees in parental frustration.

The leader turns off the VCR and asks, "How many of you have ever felt like this mother?" As every head nods in agreement, the leader moves the group into a discussion of parent–child dynamics. Analyzing this vignette, the parents reflect on how Mother was provoked into a power struggle, and how her autocratic parenting tactics actually worsened the problem. Later, the leader will return to the VCR to show the group how Mother could have better handled Danny's challenge.

These video dramatizations are 2 of 45 that form the core of *Active Parenting: A Video-Based Program* (Popkin, 1983a, 1983b). As the title implies, the innovative feature of *Active Parenting* is not the course content, but rather the process by which it is taught: the video-based delivery system.

The Need for a New Delivery System

The 1960s and 1970s saw rapid changes in American society, many of which directly or indirectly affected the American family. One of the results of such changes was the need on the part of parents for new information and skills from which to prepare their children for life in this new society. A response to this need was made by a cross section of helping professionals and volunteers in many diverse settings. Counselors, social workers, psychologists, nurses, teachers, ministers, and others took up the call to "parent education" in such diverse settings as schools, churches, mental health centers, YMCAs, synagogues, hospitals, and even hotels.

Though parent education was not a new phenomenon (prior to World War II, the Austrian psychiatrist, Alfred Adler, 1920, had set up over 30 family education centers in Vienna), during the 1970s it became a full-fledged movement. Programs such as Parent Effectivenss Training (P.E.T.) (Gordon, 1970) and Systematic Training for Effective Parenting (S.T.E.P.) (Dinkmeyer & McKay, 1976) flourished. Books such as *Children: The Challenge* (Dreikurs & Soltz, 1964) and *Between Parent and Child* (Ginott, 1965) became best sellers.

Where once such books stood alone on bookstore shelves, today there are literally hundreds of parent education titles in print. Where once P.E.T. and S.T.E.P. dominated the field like Hertz and Avis, today dozens of programs are offered to group leaders for consideration.

So what is the problem? We have acted as if the problem were one of content. What should we teach parents? Should we teach S.T.E.P. or P.E.T. or Tough Love or How to Talk So Kids Will Listen (Faber & Mazlich, 1980), or should we write our own? We have offered parents and leaders a plethora of choices regarding content. Ironically, even these choices are a little thin if not completely bogus. With parenting education so "hot" in the publishing business, every house has sought its authors. The rationale seemed to be that even if authors had nothing new to say, perhaps they could say it in a different way.

The truth may be that the content is all in, and has been all in for some time. In fact, ever since Thomas Gordon developed the communication skills for the P.E.T. program (Gordon, 1970), we have had the perfect complement for Dreikurs's discipline and guidance techniques (Dreikers, 1964). Together, they form the basis of most of the real content taught in parent education groups today. The only real content choices still being debated are along democratic–autocratic lines. Even there, the issue is usually one of degree and not absolute. Furthermore, almost everyone seems to promote the basic skills of communication, encouragement, and consequences.

What then is the problem? With 55 million parents in the United States alone, the question that must be answered is how to train so many parents. This shift from content (the "what" of parent education) to process (the "how") is vitally important, but not altogether new. For example, the S.T.E.P. program made such a shift in 1976 and rapidly replaced P.E.T. as the most-widespread parenting education program. S.T.E.P. offered very little that was new in content (it simply merged the Adler–Dreikurs concepts with those of Gordon); however, it offered a very new process for teaching these skills. As the first audiocassette-based package for teaching parenting education, it afforded leaders the unique opportunity to model the skills taught using actors on audio-cassette.

At this point it is pertinent to inject a concept from the marketing field. The term *lag time* refers to the amount of time that occurs between the invention of a new product or technique and it's introduction into the marketplace. The lag time in electronics, for example, is 18 months, and is considered very short. The lag time in education, on the other hand, has been estimated at about 50 years.

Until S.T.E.P., most parenting education was based on reading and lecturing—educational delivery systems that have been around since the invention of the printing press. S.T.E.P. took the "how" of parenting education out of the Middle Ages and placed it firmly in the 1940s, specifically, 1948, the date that the Wire Recording Corporation of America introduced the reel-to-reel tape recorder, a device that could have been used to accomplish the same purpose as audiocassettes in the S.T.E.P. program.

This point is not made to belittle the very real contribution made by S.T.E.P. Rather, it is meant to emphasize the tremendous resistance inherent in educational innovation. That educational lag time is an accepted part of our reality is highlighted by the fact that the same parents who watched television in their homes thought nothing about listening to audiocassette dramatizations during their S.T.E.P. group. However, as major a contribution as S.T.E.P. made to parenting education, it has still not enabled parent educators to meet the expanding need that exists. How are we to educate all parents for preparing children who will thrive in a complex modern democratic world?

What You See Is What You Get—Twice as Fast

There are sayings in our language such as "What you see is what you get," "A picture is worth a thousand words," and "Seeing is believing" that underscore an important fact: Most people are visual learners. When a person explains, "I'm from Missouri; show me," he or she may be expressing a view popular in the other 49 states as well. In fact, an often-cited set of statistics among human resource development people in business and industry indicates that we only retain 10% of what we read, 20% of what we hear, 30% of what we read and hear, but 50% of what we see. Though nobody seems to have a source for these statistics, there are ample examples of major corporations saving millions of dollars in training costs by applying this knowledge and using some form of video in their training programs.

Now 30 years old, videotape is being used in virtually every major corporation in the country (Bretz, 1976). By 1978 there were 70 television studios with AT&T alone (Thomas, 1978) and most *Fortune* 100 companies were spending over a million dollars a year in video production and playback equipment. The federal government had over 500 video systems, and over $25 million a year was being spent on religious programming. Clearly video use was booming. Why? Again, because we "get" more of what we see. We are a very visual species. Consider the fact that in the United States there are more television sets than toilets!

From Video to Video-Based Training

As a training tool, video by itself will not do the job. Even accepting the 50% retention rate as accurate, that still leaves another 50% that is not retained. In technical, skill-oriented training, that is an unacceptable figure.

This, by the way, is why a film series is not an effective method of teaching parenting skills. Even if 50% of the information is retained, there is not enough learning to lead to the application of new skills. Parents return home inspired, but a week later are parenting much as before.

In order to maximize the visual communication power of video, companies began integrating it into a comprehensive training programs. Writing in the *Training and Development Journal*, Willard Thomas (1980), a leader in this area, put it this way: "The decision to 'shoot the works' has recently been made by a number of organizations. The concept they adopted is called 'the videobased training package.' It combines all the theory, techniques and media into a combined method to train people rapidly, efficiently and economically."

For example, when the U.S. Bureau of the Census needed to train 6,000 temporary workers to process data on 85 million forms in just 3 months, they developed a video-based training program to do the job. Since the mid 1970s, dozens of corporations, such as Phillips Petroleum, Mobil Oil, Dresser-Atlas, Perkin-Elmer-ETEC, Texas Instruments, and Miller

Brewing have also utilized video-based delivery systems in their training programs.

Why the bandwagon effect? For the same reason that usually motivates business: It's efficient. For example, an item in a 1975 issue of the *Training and Development Journal* reported an early experience with video-based training: "Elwell-Parker Electric Co. has found a way to put new impact into the training of customer maintenance and operations personnel, and at the same time has decreased the amount of time it takes." Nine years later, Thomas and Thomas (1984) concluded that "The most efficient medium for presenting massive amounts of information and examples is videotape. Some media purists may argue for slide-audio, film or even videodisc, but they have yet to produce a two-week course that replaced four weeks of traditional instruction."

That video-based training has been found to be twice as efficient as other methods should come as no surprise to anyone familiar with the research on behavior modeling. Bandura (1977) has demonstrated quite clearly the power of modeling—learning by watching others—for the development of skills. In fact, parent educators are quick to point out in their groups that much of a person's own parenting style is developed in childhood by watching his or her parents actively parenting.

Modeling, of course, can be in vivo but it can also be vicarious through oral story, radio, film, TV, or video. Since most parents in today's parenting education groups grew up on TV, the real parent educators of the 1950s may well have been the script writers for "Leave It to Beaver," "Donna Reed," "Father Knows Best," and other family television shows. At least one study found that "children who frequently watched family shows appear to believe that families in real life show support and concern for each other" (Buerkel-Rothfus, Greenberg, Atkin, & Neuendorf, 1982).

All of which reminds me of a story . . .

A scientist had invented the most sophisticated mainframe computer in existence. In fact, it was so complex that he began thinking about the potential of a computer to think like a human. So, he typed in this question: "Will a computer ever be able to think like a human?" The computer's discs spun a few seconds and out came this answer: "That reminds me of a story . . . "

This story illustrates very simply the essence of human thinking. We think and learn in pictures and stories. What's more, we associate these stories to our own experience (other stories) through pictures in our mind's eye.

Great teachers have always known that a story or parable could create

Table 4.1 Comparison of Delivery Systems

System	Effective?	Reason
Computers	No	Efficient, but expensive; too individualized—group support missing
Films	No	Passive medium; reduces interaction
Audiocassette-based training	No	Limited appeal; fine for narration, but dialogue often sounds like old radio; visual component missed
Filmstrips	No	Hard to hold audience attention; lack movement/not real life
Live seminars	No	Costly; too much emphasis placed on leader; long preparation time required
Video-based training	Yes	Excellent results found in business; encourages group interaction; engaging medium; maximizes leader's strengths; better retention of material in less time; cost effective

a picture in a person's mind that was much more permanent than abstract words. These pictures were very powerful learning tools for helping people live their lives more effectively.

However, unless one is a master storyteller, the oral medium will not create a vivid picture. Furthermore, speech is a very slow way to communicate information. The eyes, with thousands of rods and cones, can receive information much more rapidly than the ears. Now, with the advent of video, it is not only possible for anyone to be a master storyteller, but also to stop the pictures at any point to analyze, discuss, role play, or otherwise process the information. With a litle imagination, communication and training possibilities become extraordinary.

It is no wonder that when we evaluated various delivery systems in designing Active Parenting that video-based training was rated very favorably. Table 4.1 offers an overview of our analysis.

Components of the Active Parenting Program

The Active Parenting video-based training package brings together the following elements to create a synergistic learning experience. That is, the sum of the components in a video-based package is inevitably more powerful than one would imagine:

The Leader's Guide

Anyone who attempts to replace a leader with a film is missing the boat. Films and videos do not train; they simply enable a leader to train more effectively. The key to an Active Parenting group is still the leader, and therefore the *Active Parenting Leader's Guide* (Popkin et al., 1983) is an essential element of the training package. Because the content can be more efficiently presented by the video and the *Active Parenting Handbook* (Popkin, 1983b), the leader's role is to provide structure, organization, and feedback. This means that an effective leader may be either an expert in the content area or a beginner—the essential qualification is only that the leader be an effective facilitator.

The *Leader's Guide* is divided into six sections, one for each group session, with an additional section about leader preparation. Each section includes a session organizer that breaks down the session into topic areas, group exercises, and video scenes (see Figure 4.1). This aids the leader in organizing the session and reviewing it before future sessions.

The *Active Parenting Leader's Guide* contains questions (and answers) for processing the video, instructions for all group activities, brief explanations to be made by the leader, and home activity assignments. It is sufficiently detailed that a beginning leader can follow it in a step-by-step manner and lead a successful group. However, it is emphasized that the *Active Parenting Leader's Guide* is just that, a guide. Leaders are encouraged to personalize their groups by selecting some of the exercises presented and omitting others, and otherwise "doctoring" the program as their experience and expertise allow.

Video Content Carrier

The video carries a full visual presentation and demonstration of the content. It usually provides a negative example of how an autocratic or permissive parenting technique fails to handle a situation, and always models the alternative democratic skill. In two scenes, colorful paintings are used to complement brief narrated teaching stories. However, most of the 45 scenes depict three families, played by professional actors, engaged in a variety of typical family situations. Most scenes are under 2 minutes in length with the longest being 6 mintues. The total video content is 95 minutes, which, spread out over 6 sessions, is about 16 minutes per 2-hour session. These 7 to 8 brief vignettes allow each of the 2-hour sessions to stay fully interactive. It is noteworthy to remember that most people do not absorb more than 6 minutes of video at a time (another reason that films alone do not train).

DEVELOPING RESPONSIBILITY

	TOPIC	EXERCISE	VIDEO	
I.	SHOW AND TELL			
II.	INTRODUCTION TO RESPONSIBILITY			
III.	AVOIDING RESPONSIBILITY	*Can Do/Can't Do*		
IV.	RESPONSIBILITY AND PROBLEM HANDLING	★ *Video Practice: Who Owns the Problem*	#1	Whose Problem *Is* This, Anyway?
			#2	Who Owns the Problem?
V.	"I" MESSAGES		#3	"I" Messages
VI.	CONSEQUENCES		#4	"The Butterfly's Wings"
			#5	Natural Consequences
			#6	Logical Consequences/ Punishment
		★ *Video Practice: Logical Consequences*	#7	Video Practice: Logical Consequences
VII.	SUMMARY			
VIII.	OVERVIEW			
IX.	FAMILY ENRICHMENT ACTIVITY	*Remember When . . .*	#8	Mutual Respect
X.	HOME ACTIVITIES			

★ *Highly recommended.*

59

Figure 4.1. Sample divider and session organizer from the Active Parenting Leader's Guide.

Although the content of Active Parenting is generic, the three families include a single-parent family and a minority family. This was done to facilitate the audience's ability to identify with the characters. Likewise, a wide range of ages (5 to 15) was selected for the children.

The video is narrated by Dave Moore, a professional newscaster with expert commentary presented by Dr. Linda Albert, a parent education author, and this author. These narratives and dialogues, though brief, serve to provide additional information and analysis to the group.

Parents' Handbook

The *Active Parenting Handbook* (Popkin, 1983b) is the other major content carrier for the program, and in fact contains all of the information covered in Active Parenting. As the text for the course, it provides the parents with their first exposure to the information and skills they will be learning. By reading each of the six sessions at home, precious group time can be maximally used to demonstrate, discuss, practice, and otherwise integrate the material into usable form.

To encourage this important preview reading, the *Active Parenting Handbook* was designed to be what computer people would call "user friendly." Streamlined to just 89 pages of information, examples, charts, and photographs, the two-color format with wide margins invites entry. Two special review features are also included. About 100 key points were extracted from the text and reprinted in red in the margins. In addition, 70 photographs taken during the video production appear in the text. When parents review the text in the future, these pictures will hopefully remind them of the video scenes presented in the group and the discussion that followed.

Parents' Action Guide

An important factor in facilitating retention in any video-based training program is the active participation of the learner. Active Parenting is itself a very active program. The *Active Parenting Action Guide* (Popkin, 1983a) provides self-monitored review questions to accompany the *Active Parenting Handbook* content, forms for the video practice activities done in the group, guide sheets for completing the home activities, and group activity sheets. Having all of these items in one 64-page guide saves the leader much preparation time and increases the participation of the parents.

Job Performance Aid

This is a summary of the steps involved in a given task or other information that the learner can take back "on the job." In the case of Active Parenting, the Job Performance Aid is a 17" × 22" poster describing goals of children's behavior and misbehavior, how to analyze the child's purpose, and most importantly, actions the parent can take to solve problems. It is designed in chart form with attractive illustrations and can be taped to the back of a door for easy reference.

Video Practice Activities

Task simulation is an important part of video-based training, because it allows realistic practice. A true video simulation, such as is used by the Miami Police Department to enable officers to practice shooting at criminals on a giant screen, would be ideal. It would also cost over a million dollars . . . per location! The next best simulation would be an interactive system utilizing a computer wired to a video. The cost of that is about $5,000 per location. A video-based simulation offers a good cost-effective alternative.

Using brief (5–6 sec each) "stimulus vignettes," parents in Active Parenting groups are asked to respond to what the child or parent on the video has just said or done. The response is usually written in the *Active Parenting Action Guide,* (Popkin, 1983a), then shared verbally, and often role played. After this simulated practice, the parent will try the skill at home with his or her children, then return to the group the following week for feedback.

Posttest

Most video-based training packages also include a pretest; however, these programs are used in employment situations where the learner has little choice about attending. Because of the sensitive nature of parenting education, and because of the negative mindset of many people about testing, no pretest is used in Active Parenting. In fact, the posttest is optional for most groups, an exception being Active Parenting's 35 fieldtest groups of 274 parents. Results of these posttests is reported later in this chapter.

The omisson of a pretest or control group limits the interpretation of these fieldtest data. However, such research is currently underway in at least two universities and should aid in developing a better understanding of how this video-based program affects parenting skills and children's behavior.

The Active Parenting Learning System

It is more than just the use of video that make video-based training so much more effective than traditional delivery systems. It is video integrated into a total training package that includes at least eight separate steps. Each major topic or skill is experienced by the parent at least eight times (Fig 4.2). The repetition and interaction through various communication modes is particularly effective.

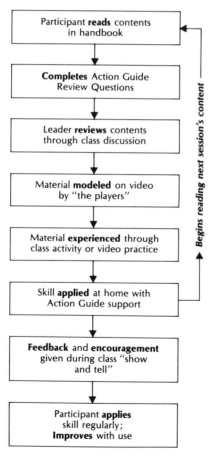

Figure 4.2. The Active Parenting learning system.

The Content of Active Parenting

The purpose of this chapter is to describe the unique delivery system of video-based training as it is being applied to parent education through the Active Parenting program. Therefore, rather than a detailed exploration of the program's content, a simple outline of the six sessions is offered as an orientation:

1. The Active Parent
   a. Why "active" parenting
   b. The concept of equality
   c. Styles of parenting
   d. What kind of child do we want to raise?
   e. Family enrichment activities
2. Understanding Your Child
   a. Self-esteem
   b. The four goals of children's behavior
   c. Dreikurs's four mistaken goals of misbehavior
   d. Parenting and anger
3. Instilling Courage
   a. How parents (too often) discourage their own children
   b. Methods of encouragement
4. Developing Responsibility
   a. Freedom and the limits to freedom
   b. The problem-handling model for parents
   c. Who owns the problem
   d. "I" messages
   e. Natural and logical consequences
   f. Mutual respect
5. Winning Cooperation
   a. Communication: The road to cooperation
   b. Avoiding communication blocks
   c. Active communication
   d. Expressing love
6. The Democratic Family in Action
   a. The family council meeting
   b. How to handle problems in a group
   c. Emphasizing the family unit

The Video in Video-Based Training

Although beginning leaders use Active Parenting as a structured program following the *Active Parenting Leader's Guide* (Popkin, Garcia, & Woodward, 1983) closely, the multiple uses of each video vignette is really limited only by imagination. The following examples highlight some of the ways in which the video scenes are being effectively used.

TO HELP DEVELOP GROUP COHESIVENESS. One of the strengths of parent education is the sense of mutual support and group problem solving that is often fostered among participants. Almost any of the family action scenes can be used to help generate an awareness of common experience that helps build cohesiveness among group members. For example, consider the dialogue from the following scene:

FATHER: Allison! It's time to brush your teeth.
ALLISON: Oh, do I have to? I just did it this morning.
FATHER: Yes, you know you're supposed to do it before bedtime.
ALLISON: Will you come and tell me a story while I do it?
FATHER: Sure, baby. I'd love to.
ALLISON: And you won't leave early like you did last time?
FATHER: Allison, you just brush your teeth and don't worry about the story.
ALLISON: You promise you'll stay till I'm done?
FATHER: Yes, I promise.
ALLISON: And then you'll come and tuck me in.
FATHER: Brush your teeth, Allison, and I'll be right in.
ALLISON: O.K. After you tuck me in, will you sing to me for awhile, too?

As the voice of Allison's older brother, Dexter, mimics "Will you sing to me, too?" in the background the camera freezes on Dad's expression of frustration and bewilderment. The humor of the scene is reflected in the spontaneous laughter of the group. As they share this response, the leader can deepen their awareness by asking, "How many of you have ever felt like Dad does here?" The realization that all parents share many common experiences not only brings the group closer together, but offers encouragement to each parent individually.

TO TEACH THROUGH METAPHOR AND STORY. The two brief parables presented in Active Parenting offer a simple yet profound method of driving home key points in a memorable way. Illustrated with color graphics, they also offer a visual treat and change from the live action. For example, to introduce the important concept of "consequences," the following tale, "The Butterfly's Wings," is used. Imagine the mystical sound of a sitar playing in the background as watercolor images fade in and out to complement the narrator's skillful voice.

A Master once sent his student into a wood in order that he might observe a cocoon. The young man watched as the butterfly's wings began to break their house of silken fibers. He watched and waited and watched and grew impatient. Unable to simply observe any longer, he reached in and helped the butterfly out of the cocoon. The tender butterfly flew a few feet then spiraled to the earth and died. The student, his eyes wet with tears, hurried back to the Master and asked what had happened. The Master explained, "When you reached in and opened the cocoon, you deprived the butterfly of the chance to strengthen its wings in the struggle."

TO ANALYZE PARENT–CHILD DYNAMICS. One of the central themes of any form of education is the importance of learning from the experience of others. Because of our ability to communicate, we do not have to make all the mistakes ourselves. Throughout Active Parenting, scenes portraying typical parent–child conflicts are used by the group leader to help parents understand how parents and children influence each other. By analyzing these conflicts, parents can learn how to avoid common pitfalls and look for alternative actions. The following scene depicts the power struggle between Mother and 5-year-old Dan used to open this chapter.

MOTHER: It's time to clean up. Put your toys away.
DAN: No, I don't have to.
MOTHER: Put your toys away.
DAN: You can't make me. I don't have to.
MOTHER: Yes, you do—they're your toys. Now put them away.
DAN: You can't make me!
MOTHER: (Grabbing Dan's arm and jerking him) Don't you talk to me like that, young man. Now pick them up! I'll be back in 5 minutes and if this room isn't clean, you'll get a spanking!
(Mother leaves, then returns to find toys still out.)
MOTHER: I thought I told you to pick these toys up! (Grabs Dan and spanks him a couple of times.) Now go to your room and stay there!
DAN: I hate you. I hate you. (Runs to his room)
(Mother bends to pick up toys. Picks up first few rapidly, then slows as she picks up a well-used stuffed animal. She is looking at it dejectedly as scene fades.)

There are several levels of analysis that leaders might apply to this scene depending on the experience of the group. A simple analysis might begin by asking questions such as, "How did Mother feel during this confrontation?" "Did she win or lose the battle?" "What mistakes did she make?" A more thorough analysis would look at Dan's behavior in terms of Dreikurs and Cassel's (1964) four goals of misbehavior. Finally, most Active Parenting groups utilize a form from the *Active Parenting Action Guide* to fully understand what we call "the parent–child cycle." Based on an integration of Dreikurs and Cassel's four goals and the rational emotive theory of Albert Ellis (1962), this video practice activity illustrated in Fig. 4.3, has proven exceptionally effective in Active Parenting groups.

FOUR GOALS RECOGNITION

SCENE #2 (Dan and his toys)

CHILD'S BASIC GOAL:

CHILD'S MISTAKEN APPROACH

BEGIN HERE

PARENT'S ACTIVATING EVENT
(Child's Misbehavior)

CHILD'S RESPONSE
TO CORRECTION:

D becomes A

D

C

B

A

PARENT'S
THOUGHTS/BELIEFS

A

B

C

D

CHILD'S FEELING

PARENT'S FEELING

CHILD'S
THOUGHTS/BELIEFS

PARENT'S BEHAVIOR
(To Correct Misbehavior)

CHILD'S ACTIVATING EVENT
(Parent's Correction)

A becomes D

PARENT'S STYLE

MISTAKES PARENT MADE:

MISTAKEN BELIEFS: _____

MISTAKEN ACTIONS: _____

DEMOCRATIC ALTERNATIVES:

BELIEFS: _____

ACTIONS: _____

13

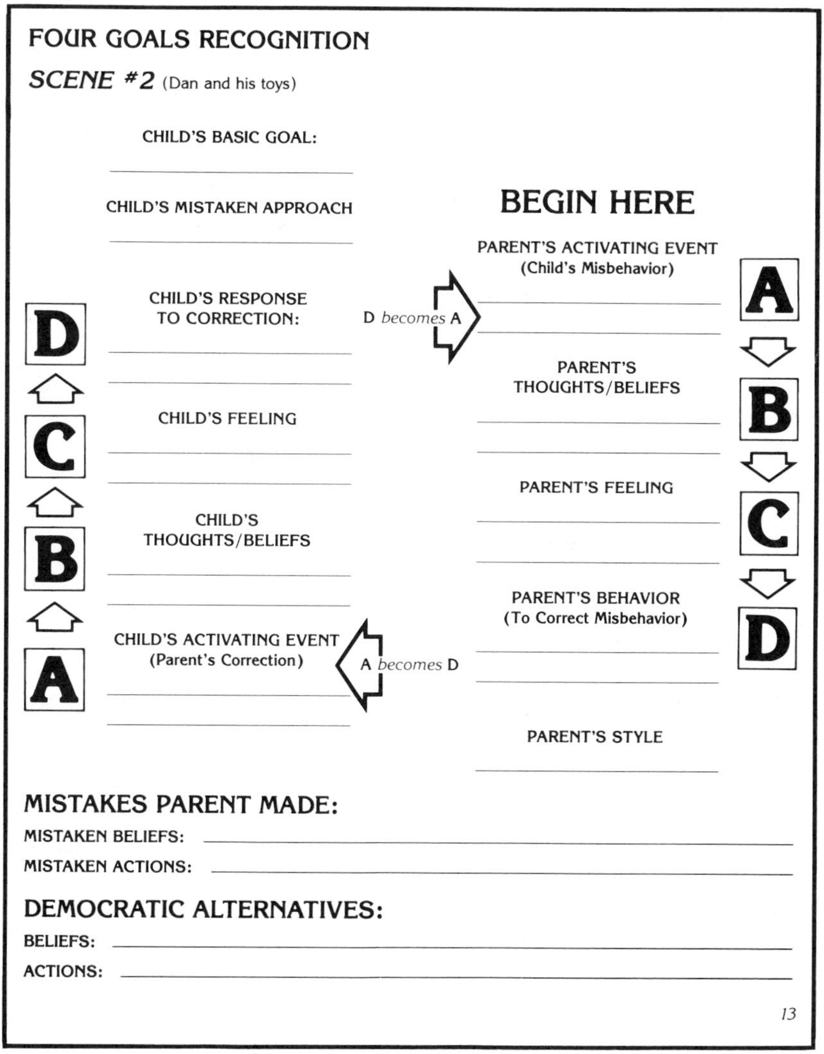

Figure 4.3. Video-based practice activity.

TO MODEL EFFECTIVE PARENTING SKILLS. The leading feature of video-based training is its ability to visually model the skill to be learned. By first showing a conflict situation poorly handled through autocratic or permissive techniques, the participant's interest is already piqued. A "democratic alternative" can then be modeled with maximum impact. For example, the Active Parenting narrator asks the group, "In the power struggle with Danny, what alternatives does Mom have?" The scene following this question shows Mother using a blend of logical consequences and other democratic methods to bring about a better result. Keep in mind as you read that the important differences in voice tone, facial expression, and body language are lost in the written script.

MOTHER: It's time to pick up your toys, Danny. Would you like to pick them up yourself or would you like me to help you.

DAN: I don't have to.

MOTHER: Now come on, Dan. We made a deal. Either you put away your toys or I'll put them away and you can have them again tomorrow.

DAN: (Looking around and weighing the choices) Oh . . . all right. I'll pick them up.

(Mother leaves the room. Dan picks up a couple of toys, then begins playing another video game. Mother returns.)

MOTHER: Have you finished putting them away?

DAN: Uh oh.

MOTHER: Oh, I see you are having trouble putting away your toys. I'll tell you what; I'll put them away for the day, and you can try again tomorrow.

DAN: (Protesting) But . . . I . . . put away some . . .

MOTHER: (Interrupting) That's okay, honey. You can try again tomorrow.

DAN: (Dejectedly going out of the room) Tomorrow's long!

TO HELP THE PARENT GENERALIZE SKILLS. Once a democratic alternative is shown, the leader can still use the video to help parents generalize the skills presented to other situations. One technique is to play a game of "what if" with the group. For example, following the previous scene, the leader might ask, "What if Dan had a temper tantrum when Mother began putting the toys away? How could she still stay out of the power struggle?" Of course, the essential generalization is for parents to learn to apply the skills taught in the *Handbook* and modeled on video to their own families.

This is one reason why the group leader plays such an important role in

Active Parenting: The leader helps the group come up with their own examples for each principle or skill taught. This is done either in written exercise, group discussion, or both.

TO TEACH PARENTS HOW TO EMPATHIZE. Remembering how the world looks through a child's eyes is a big advantage when parenting. Whether this involves "listening for feelings" (Session 5) or becoming aware of our own discouraging comments (Session 3), the video vignettes can be a tremendous help.

For example, in the following video practice, parents are asked to imagine they are the child in the scene. Using a page in the *Action Guide,* they record what they might be thinking and feeling and how they might behave in the future. Later, as they share their observations with each other, the parents become more aware that how a comment is intended is not always how it is perceived by the child.

> FATHER: Lisa, honey. What are we going to do about that Biology grade?
>
> LISA: (Lisa is age 15). Raise it, I guess.
>
> FATHER: I sure hope so. It's a shame to ruin a good report card with a C. And now that I look at it, I think you're smarter than a B in Geometry.
>
> LISA: But I got A's in English, Government, Music, and even Spanish . . . and you know how hard Spanish is for me.
>
> FATHER: I know it is, honey. Mom and I just expect a lot from you. We wouldn't expect the best if you couldn't do it. But you're bright and we just want you to use that brain of yours to the fullest. D'you see?
>
> LISA: (Fighting back tears) Uh uh.
>
> FATHER: And you want to get into a good college like your cousin Vickie, don't you?
>
> LISA: I guess so.
>
> FATHER: That's my girl. Now you better hit those books . . . give that bright brain of yours a workout . . . so you can get all A's next time.

TO INCREASE GROUP ATTENDANCE. The action-packed video vignettes add a dimension of entertainment to what is essentially an educational experience. The humor and drama of the scenes heightens motivation to sign up for an Active Parenting group to begin with, and to continue for the full six sessions.

TO PROVIDE SIMULATED PRACTICE. This exceptional feature of video-based training was described earlier. By encouraging participants to respond to brief stimulus vignettes on the video, leaders can make the transition to home applicaton much easier for their group.

TO MOVE PARENTS TO ACTION. A philosophical theme that democracy is a positive way of life, that it has a positive place in families, and that it need not undermine the parents' rightful leadership role in the family is woven throughout the video. Accompanying this theme are the ideas that families are "the backbone of civilization" and that effective parenting is active parenting. The video strongly promotes action and leadership by parents who learn to show respect and responsibility for the children they lead.

Field Test Report

Results from 35 field-test groups conducted between January and March of 1984 showed strong support for the Active Parenting video-based approach. A brief report of this research is presented below.

SUBJECTS

Subjects were 274 parents self-selected for Active Parenting groups offered in either a school (45%), church (42%), health care facility (4%), or other community location (9%). The average age of participants was 40.7 years with 202 females (74%) and 72 males (26%). 67% had at least a college degree; 92% were white; the median family income was approximately $35,000 a year with 13% between $10,000 and $20,000 and 44% over $40,000. There were 12% single parents and 1% grandparents. Of the married parents (87%), 51% attended the group with their spouse. The ages of the subject's children were 0–5 years (33%); 6–11 years (39%); 11–14 years (18%); 15–17 years (10%).

METHOD

Field-test locations were self-selected by leaders who chose to sign up for an opportunity to try *Active Parenting: A Video-based Program* (Popkin & Woodward, 1983) free of charge for a trial course. Leaders were shipped the program as usual with no special instructions and were not required to take any special training. They promoted their groups as they chose, charging their usual fee for a parent education group (usually $10–$50). All groups were held for the complete six sessions and each parent had an *Active Parenting Handbook* and an *Active Parenting Action Guide*.

Leaders were given course evaluations for their participants that included two behavior checklists. One checklist was used by parents to rate themselves on parenting behaviors before and after their Active Parenting group. The other was used to rate their children's behavior before and after Active Parenting. All evaluations were completed at the end of the sixth session and mailed by the leader back to Active Parenting, Inc. The evaluations were made anonymously.

RESULTS

Of the 274 parents, 97% reported positive changes in their own parenting following 6 weeks of Active Parenting. Using the four-point rating system (4, more than once a day; 3, once a day, 2; every 2–3 days; 1, never), parents moved an average of 0.68 points in the desired direction, an improvement of approximately 27%. The ten item scores are shown in Table 4.2.

Results of the behavior checklist, "About Your Child," indicated that 84% of the parents reported an improvement in their children's behavior by the end of the sixth Active Parenting session. Using the same 4-point scale, the average improvement was 0.49 or 20%. The item averages are shown in Table 4.3.

In addition to the behavior checklists, 97% of the parents indicated that they would be recommending Active Parenting to their friends. All 35 group leaders (100%) reported that they intended to recommend Active Parenting to other group leaders.

Table 4.2 Responses to Items in "About You as a Parent"

Behavior	Desired change	Average improvement	% improvement
Yelling	Less	0.94	38
Logical consequences	More	1.02	41
Punishment	Less	0.65	26
Family conferences	More	0.29	12
I messages	More	1.22	49
Touching	More	0.18	7
Discouragement	Less	0.89	36
Encouragement	More	0.67	27
Power struggles	Less	0.90	36
Reward	Less	0.31	12
Average	—	0.68	27
Possible improvement	—	1.50	60

Table 4.3 Responses to Items in "About Your Child"

Behavior	Desired change	Average improvement	% improvement
Acts rebelliously	Less	0.68	27
Accepts responsibility	More	0.68	27
Yells	Less	0.57	23
Exhibits self-confidence	More	0.40	16
Gives up easily	Less	0.39	16
Cooperates	More	0.45	18
Demands undue attention	Less	0.55	22
Responds to requests	More	0.56	22
Has temper tantrums	Less	0.39	16
Expresses affection	More	0.28	10
Average	—	0.49	20
Possible improvement	—	1.50	60

DISCUSSION

The results indicate that positive changes in both parent and child behaviors occur following Active Parenting groups. As expected, the largest changes occurred in the parent skill areas such as using *I* messages and logical consequences. The slightly lower level of change in child behaviors may be due to the timing of the survey. At the end of the six sessions, these new skills have only been used a few weeks. A follow-up survey would help determine how much parents continued to use their new skills, and how much subsequent improvement or backsliding was made by their children.

An applied program such as Active Parenting often moves ahead of its research. These field test data are a beginning to the research that will follow. Currently, there are two doctoral dissertations in progress, with many other studies needed to examine the efficacy of this video-based approach to parent education. As indicated earlier, control groups and pretest data are needed, as well as longitudinal studies. In the meantime, Active Parenting groups are forming in communities throughout North America at an ever-increasing rate.

Summary

This chapter has focused on the application of an advanced learning technology, video-based training, to the important area of parenting education. A brief history of various delivery systems utilized in parenting education outlined the field's progression from book-oriented study groups to audio-cassette-based programs and finally, the video-based medium. Special emphasis was placed on the development of training packages in business and industry during the 1970s, and the rapid move of video-based training to become the standard among training and development specialists in the 1980s.

Active Parenting: A Video-Based Program was introduced as the synthesis between this video-based learning technology and the content of widely accepted parenting concepts. The components of a video-based package as exemplified by Active Parenting were described: The *Leader's Guide,* video content carrier, parents' *Handbook,* parents' *Action Guide,* job performance aid, video-practice activities, and posttest. It was suggested that multimodal components combine synergistically to create a unique and powerful learning experience.

Several of the Active Parenting video scenes were transcribed in order to demonstrate the wide range of applications of brief video vignettes. Examples included the use of metaphor, analysis of parent–child dynamics, effective modeling of parenting skills, teaching empathy, and developing group cohesiveness. Finally, results of the Active Parenting field test were presented, underscoring positive changes in both parenting skills and child behavior. The appeal of this effective new approach to parenting education is highlighted by the fact that 97% of the parents in the field test indicated a desire to recommend Active Parenting to other parents. With over 4,000 programs now in use, it appears that video-based parenting education is an accepted innovation in parenting education.

References

Adler, A. (1920). *The practice and theory of individual psychology.* New York: Harcourt, Brace.

Ansbacher, H. L., & Ansbacher, R. (1964). *The individual psychology of Alfred Adler.* New York: Harper Torchbooks.

Bandura, A. (1977). *Social learning theory.* Englewood Cliffs, NJ: Prentice-Hall.

Brentz,R. (1976). In-school television and the new technology. *Educational Technology, 16,* 50–53.

Buerkel-Rothfuss, N., Greenberg, B., Atkin, C., & Neuendorf, K. (1982). Learning about the family from television. *Journal of Communication, 34,* 191–201.

Dinkmeyer, D., & McKay, G. (1976). *Systematic training for effective parenting.* Circle Pines, MN: American Guidance Services.

Dreikurs, R. (1950). *Fundamentals of Adlerian psychology.* Chicago: Alfred Adler Institute.

Dreikurs, R., & Cassel, P. (1964). *Discipline without tears.* New York: Hawthorn Books.

Dreikurs, R., & Soltz, V. (1964). *Children: The challenge.* Des Moines, IA: Meredith Press.

Ellis, A. (1962). *Reason and emotion in psychotherapy.* New York: Lyle Stuart.

Faber, A., & Mazlich, E. (1980). *How to talk so kids will listen.* New York: Avon.

Ginott, H. (1965). *Between parent and child.* New York: Macmillan.

Gordon, T. (1970). *Parent effectiveness training.* New York: Peter H. Wyden.

Greenburg, B. S., Edison, N., Korzenny, F., Fernandez-Collado, C., & Atkin, C. K. (1980). Antisocial and prosocial behaviors on television. In B. S. Greenberg et al. (Eds.), *Life on television.* Norwood, NJ: Ablex.

Moore, J. (1982). Institutional television and technological change: New approaches and opportunities. *Educational Technology, 26–28.*

Popkin, M. (1983a). *Active Parenting Action Guide.* Atlanta, GA: Active Parenting.

Popkin, M. (1983b). *Active Parenting Handbook.* Atlanta, GA: Active Parenting.

Popkin, M., Garcia, E., & Woodward, H. (1983). *Active Parenting Leader's Guide.* Atlanta, GA: Active Parenting.

Popkin, M., & Woodward, H. (1983). *Active Parenting Videotapes.* Atlanta, GA: Active Parenting.

Prince, S. (1981). Education by video with the human touch. *Business Screen, 42,* 16–46.

Reavis, H., Rice, J., & Hamel, K. (1986). Home teaching packages for parents. *Audiovisual Instruction, 21,* 45–46.

Staff. (1975). Video tape helps train consumer personnel. *Training and Development Journal, 29,* 13–15.

Thomas, W. (1978). Video: The promise is real, the payoff depends on you. *Training and Development Journal, 32,* 3–5.

Thomas, W. (1980). Shoots the works with videobased training. *Training and Development Journal, 34,* 83–87.

Thomas, W., & Thomas, C. (1984). Update and analysis of video-based training. *Training and Development Journal, 38,* 28–31.

5

Parents as First Teachers

Sue Vartuli
Mildred Winter

Introduction

Researchers and educators have searched for years to find ways to give children a good start in life. The focus of these efforts has been on children at the preschool age (Head Start and day care centers) and in grades K through 3 (The Follow-Through Program). Homestart, the Verbal Interaction Project, (Levenstein, 1970), the Parent–Child Development Centers and the Child and Family Resource Programs all shifted the trend from educating children in centers to working with parents in the home in order to begin intervention at earlier ages. The major reasons for this shift were that (1) by 3 years of age deficits were often clearly present and remedial intervention comes too late, and (2) working with the family, focusing on the first years of life, appears to be a genuinely effective approach.

Burton White developed a model for educating parents as the child's first and most important teachers. In this model, prospective parents begin a course of study in their child's third trimester of gestation to help them prepare for the baby's arrival. The program focuses on first-time parents because research from the Harvard Preschool Project found that first-time parents were far more eager for educational support.

The parents as teachers model is based on 13 years of research (1965–1978) on early development conducted by the Harvard University Preschool Project. Using techniques similar to those of Arnold Gesell, White and his associates observed children in their homes. In addition to employing Gesell's natural-history approach, however, White investigated the effects of planned intevention as well. The major goal of the project was "to determine how experiences during the first years of life

influence the development of all major abilities of any preschool child"
(White, 1981a, p. 212).

Building the Model

White hoped to identify through "induction" the most salient environmental factors that influence development and subsequently to examine
these factors in experimental tests. Child-rearing pattern was one of the
first factors identified. An assessment scale was developed to measure the
responses of the caregiver to overtures by the child and behaviors
initiated by the caregiver toward the child. Eight categories were developed to measure the quality and latency of the adult's responses, adult
language usage, and quality of the child's needs satisfaction.

The longitudinal study and previously established information on early
growth and development convinced the researchers that children generally manage to reach the age of 8 months with their potential for education
for the most part intact. Four areas of development critical to later
educational success appear to be at risk between 8 and 36 months:
(1) language, (2) curiosity development, (3) social skills and attachment,
and (4) sensory–motor intelligence. In White's experimental training
program, parents were made more aware of the course of development in
these four areas, helped to emulate the child-rearing practices of successful parents, and helped to avoid child-rearing practices of apparently
unsuccessful parents (White, Kaban, Attanucci, & Shapiro, 1978).

Looking for other environmental factors influencing development,
White was led to extensive observation of the abilities or competencies of
well-developed 3- to 6-year-old children. The research attempted to use
scientific methods to generate reliable information on good education for
infants and toddlers by observing families who appeared to be unusually
successful. This natural history approach deliberately sought to be as
atheoretical as possible given the conviction that theories are limited in
their likely utility by the amount of existing relevant empirical data
(White, 1978).

White's model was field-tested as part of a comprehensive educational
support system for parents known as the Brookline Early Education
Project (BEEP). This 5-year test of the feasibility of a public school
system assuming a formal role in guiding the educational development of
children from birth exhibited the following major features:

> 1. Strengthening each family's capacity to rear young children through
> provision of parent education, professional consultation, and support and
> materials when needed.

2. Identification of educationally relevant handicaps as early as possible through a systematic medical and psychological diagnostic program administered continuously from before the child is born on through the preschool years.

3. Treatment of identified handicaps such a sensory deficits, language acquisition and other learning difficulties, mental retardation beginning at birth.

4. A high likelihood of continuity with elementary educational experiences by virtue of the fact that the school system is the initiator and director of this experimental venture. (White, 1972, p. 611)

Parents were induced to participate by promises that their child would not go through the program with an undetected, untreated educational handicap. Families participating in the BEEP seemed to value the experience very highly (White, 1981a).

Education for Parenthood

Through the Harvard Preschool Project's research, White and his associates have attempted to bridge basic research and applied research, focusing on current social problems. One of White's desires is to see education for parenthood become the cornerstone of society's educational efforts. He believes that the American educational system must create a partnership between the family and school and that educators should have a responsibility to help prepare and assist the family to give the child a solid educational foundation. White (1980, pp. 341–342) suggests that

1. "Long before the child is born, we should teach each and every prospective parent all the known and accepted fundamentals about educational development in the first years of life" (p. 341).

2. In order to reduce parents' trauma immediately preceding and following the baby's birth, they need to be informed that their experiences are not unique but quite common.

3. For the first 6 years of a child's life, especially the first three, continuing low-pressure, strictly voluntary training for parents should be made available.

4. We must provide referral services for special needs.

5. We must provide remedial assistance as soon as possible.

Other educators support White's view that there should be education for parenthood. T. H. Bell, former U.S. Secretary of Education, has been an unusually strong supporter of the concept of public schools reaching out to new parents (Bell, 1974). At a 1976 meeting of UNESCO in Paris, 20 countries also supported education in the first 6 years of life as it relates to lifelong learning. All of the countries saw the need to help parents become educators of their own children and to employ well-qualified personnel to work with children and parents. The nations agreed that

1. The first three years of life are of critical importance in the development of language, approaches to problem-solving and social behavior and emotional growth.
2. Basic motivation to learn is inherent in children but it is nourished as a result of the influence of adult within the environment. Thus children learn to learn or learn not to learn as a result of how adults handle their development during the first three years of life.
3. The period after 7 months appears to be of critical importance for the development of language, curiosity, social behavior, and the beginnings of intelligence and emotional growth.
4. Language plays an important role in concept development and social behavior. It begins to develop rapidly about the age of 7 or 8 months and especially during the two years or so that follow. Most of the basic language acquisitions—grammar, syntax, basic vocabulary, etc.—are already present by the end of the third year.
5. The parents, particularly the mother or the person most in contact with the child, influence the acquisition of language by the way in which explanations are made to the child and the way in which verbal behavior is reinforced, rewarded, punished, or ignored.
6. Deep curiosity is invariably present in all but seriously damaged children at the age of 8 months, but unless this curiosity is encouraged and rewarded, it can easily be somewhat retarded by the age of two years, or even sharply reduced.
7. Social development is particularly noticeable at the age of 8 months, and by the age of two years it is being used to acquire attention, utilize adults as a resource, and seek the support of others.
8. The roots of intelligence as described by Piaget are nourished by the environment and in favorable environments intelligence is well developed by the age of four years (cf. Benjamin Bloom). (White, Kaban, Attanucci, & Shapiro, 1978, pp. 199–200)

Educational Focus

Educational intervention programs can influence the child's development and parental attitudes and child-rearing practices. As White is quick to point out, however, educational programs have limited utility and are no substitute for multifaceted social service programs. The family's basic needs have to be met as a precondition of successful educational intervention. A comprehensive referral system is needed so educators can refer parents to appropriate specialists. Housing, employment, and counseling are needs other professionals can and should address. The basic survival needs must be met before parents can focus on educational assistance (White, 1980).

To get more people interested in providing better education in the first 3 years of life and to provide services to professionals working in the field, White and Meyerhoff established the Center for Parent Education in 1978. This center offers services including workshops, a bimonthly newsletter, consulting, and conference activities. By integrating the models of the Harvard Preschool Project and the Brookline Early Education Project, White and associates were able to combine the educational focus with supplemental features of a neighborhood center into a parent education model. The model reflects translation of hypotheses about effective child-rearing practices into a workable program for average families. Two programs evolving from White's model, the BEEP and the New Parents as Teachers Project (Missouri), have demonstrated workable parent education programs for average families.

Model Goals and Services

The goal of the Parent Education Model designed by White and his associates is to strengthen the capacity of families to be their children's first educational delivery system. Intervention should begin during the third trimester of pregnancy and focus on educating the child's parents, thus altering the child's home environment during the first 3 years of life.

Two major premises of the model are (1) that the informal education that families provide for their children makes more of an impact on the child's total educational development than the formal educational system, and (2) that 2 years of age is already too late to begin to look at a child's educational development (White, 1975). Based on these premises, the model provided parents with information on parenting and child development.

The model was developed with suggestions to help parents achieve the very best results and have the most pleasure in rearing their children. When parents use the ideas in this program, they should be able to avoid needless anxiety and stress and benefit family life. Services to families include home visits, group meetings, periodic medical and educational screening of the child, and provision of a resource center which includes a toy-lending, book, and film library.

Program Components

Information describing the program components is from White's (1981b) *Outline for a Parent Education Program.*

PERSONNEL

To serve a population of 60 families, the staff should consist of two full-time educators, a half-time secretary, and a psychological tester. (It is important to note that in the Missouri program each parent educator served more than 30 families and did not use a psychological tester.) It is recommended that the parent educators be women and mothers in order to facilitate their reception into homes of participating families and to strengthen their credibility. It is widely believed that motherhood provides an education in family management and child development that cannot be duplicated.

The director of the program should devote 20% of her time to home visits, 30% to planning and implementing group meetings, and the rest to administrative duties. A bachelor's or master's degree in education, nursing, social work, or a related field as well as specialized training in parent education is required for the position of program director. Administrative experience and community involvement and experience working with young children are also important.

The home visitor or parent educator is responsible for making home visits, screening infants, making referrals, and running the resource center. The qualifications of the parent educator are a bachelor's or master's degree in early childhood education or a related field and some experience in working with young children.

PHYSICAL PLAN

The Parent Education Program ideally requires five rooms to be used as offices and/or service areas. The educational staff and secretary's offices need to be separate from the resource library, playroom, and quiet room for testing and/or napping.

RECRUITMENT AND COMMUNITY RELATIONS

Recruitment of parents and public relations efforts are interrelated. Staff must advertise the program focusing on the target population. Methods of announcing the program include (1) dissemination of flyers in elementary schools, doctors' offices, health clinics, family service agencies, hospitals, prenatal classes, and other locations; (2) referrals by obstetricians and pediatricians; (3) posters in shopping centers; (4) public service announcements on the radio and television; and (5) articles in local newspapers. Staff members can also use community or state birth records to locate new parents and write them directly.

At the time of recruitment, parent educators should explain the benefits and requirements of the program. Recruitment efforts normally take less time once the program has been established and word of mouth becomes the major source of advertising.

The community's network of human service agencies plays an important role in referring new parents to the parent education program, as well as providing specialized assistance for families. Contacts should be made with churches, welfare agencies, social service agencies, nursery schools, day care centers, doctors, elementary schools, special education and diagnostic services, and local universities.

Educational Components

PERSONAL VISITS

Personal visits, either at the home or center, are a key component of the parent education program. Each visit takes approximately one hour and is scheduled, ideally, when the infant is awake. This provides opportunities for the parent educator to observe parent–child interactions and make comments on observed behavior. Observing the parent and the child enables the parent educator to personalize the educational guidance given to the family. Although one staff member may have prime responsibility for visits to particular families, it is advisable that the family be visited periodically by the other staff member. This scheduling prevents the development of a dependency relationship and promotes more objective guidance to the family.

The frequency and content of the visits varies over the 3-year period. Visits are initially made monthly to build rapport and because the child's development is so rapid during the first 18 months. As the pace of development slows, the frequency of the visits decreases.

During the first visits, parents should be introduced to the program goals and recommended child-rearing practices. During the 8-to-18 month period, four foundations of educational development are the core of the curriculum for all visits: curiosity, social development, language, and intellectual development.

Parents are encouraged to view themselves as (1) designers, creating a safe environment to stimulate their child's curiosity, allowing for exploration and practice of developing skills; (2) consultants, available to the child and responding promptly and enthusiastically (when appropriate) using appropriate language; and (3) controllers, setting firm and consistent limits.

Parents are encouraged to view themselves as the child's educational managers during the 19-to-36 month period. Practical child-rearing practices such as safety-proofing and toilet training, and decisions such as selecting nursery schools are discussed.

Parent educators keep confidential records of each visit, including content of the visit, parental issues, general comments, and plans for the next home visit. These reports serve as background material for staff discussions on each family and help parent educators keep track of both the child's and family's progress.

GROUP MEETINGS

Parents learn more about their child's development when they attend group meetings. The meetings give parents the opportunity to share common concerns about their children's behavior. Parents are assigned to groups of approximately 20 other parents who have children in the same age range. Some of the meetings are held in the evenings or on weekends so the greatest number of parents can attend.

The teacher/director of the parent program has the responsibility to plan, run, and keep records on the meetings. Parents meet more frequently during the period from pregnancy to 18 months. Meetings are scheduled monthly during the first 18 months and then reduced to one every 6 months for the remaining period.

Resource people from the community can be invited to address topics of interest. Parents can recommend topics for group meetings, but throughout the 3-year period every meeting has the same basic format: an informal lecture on their children's current growth and development patterns and educational and management implications followed by a film (if appropriate) and a discussion.

A group-meeting record form is completed that includes attendance, content covered, issues raised by the parents, and a general evaluation of the session. Also, parents' written evaluatons of each session are helpful for planning future meetings.

SCREENING

Screening is an important component of the program. Tests of hearing, vision, and development of abilities such as language and social skills are administered as early in life as feasible to assure that the child will not enter school with an undetected educational disability.

Since parents are the primary advocates for their child's educational development, they are fully informed of the results of all screening exams. Parents and staff meet to discuss the results and identify problems needing attention for possible referral or special services. The child's development is always monitored so staff and parents feel confident regarding the child's well-being.

RESOURCE CENTER

Families enrolled in the program have access to a resource center containing a toy, book, and film library. The center is open at scheduled times during the day and evening. The reading material in the center is available on loan for families, and the films are used during the group meetings. The secretary or parent educator monitors the library during the scheduled hours to check out books for parents.

The toy library is a collection of recommended toys for each age level. The toys are not allowed to circulate. The resource center can also serve as an informal meeting place for parents. Records are kept on the general utilization of the resource center and an account is made of the books in circulation.

The playroom for drop-in care is included in the resource center. The playroom is used for the children to play while their parents attend group meetings or use the library. During designated prescheduled hours, parents can leave their children at the playroom for a brief respite. Volunteers from the community can help the parent educator staff the playroom so the adult–child ratio is one adult for every two children. The babysitting service can provide the mental and physical support parents need to keep their interactions with their children positive and healthy.

EVALUATION OF THE PROGRAM

All aspects of the parent education program are evaluated. Evaluations of the children's development and family participation are made after every group meeting and personal visit. This information is useful to the parent educators as they plan for future interactions.

Utilization of the program's resources are recorded and suggestions from parents are encouraged to improve services. Periodically, staff need to assess their role as parent educators and/or administrators. This information can be used to improve the services offered to parents.

To assess whether the program goals are being met, a simple pre/post measure of parents' knowledge about child development and attitudes toward child rearing can be developed. Informal parental feedback about the usefulness of the information can also be used to measure whether program goals are achieved.

Missouri Adoption of White's Model

History

Initial impetus for the New Parents as Teachers (NPAT) program came from the 1981 Conference for Decision Makers on Early Education and Parent Education—Direction for the Eighties. Research supporting parent education and early intervention was presented to state legislators and decision makers. Dr. Burton White and Dr. David Weikart were the primary speakers for the conference.

The Missouri Department of Elementary and Secondary Education (DESE) has been committed to early childhood education since 1972. Leadership from former Commissioner of Education, Arthur Mallory, and support from (former) Governor Christopher S. Bond and the Missouri State Board of Education made implementation of the parent education program a reality.

Implementation

The NPAT project was started during the 1981–82 school year in four Missouri school districts representing urban, suburban, and rural communities. Under the direction of Mildred Winter, state director of early childhood education, and with consultation from Dr. White and his associates, the four sites offered parent education services to more than 300 families in Missouri.

The model programs were funded by the Missouri Department of Elementary and Secondary Education, the four participating school districts, and the Danforth Foundation of St. Louis. The goal of the project was to demonstrate that through a partnership between home and school beginning at the onset of learning, the child can get the best possible start in life. Only first-time parents were recruited for the project for two reasons: (1) the Harvard Preschool Project research found that first-time parents are the most eager for this type of educational support, and (2) the effects of the program can be monitored more clearly with new parents than with parents who have previous child-rearing experience.

Parents participating in this program represented a broad range of socioeconomic and educational levels, including single parents and families where both parents worked. Community advisory groups helped in recruitment efforts to seek out eligible families in order to mitigate the effects of self-selection. The information and advice shared with families was not designed to produce "superbabies" but to help parents feel more comfortable with their roles as parents.

> Unlike the many "infant stimulation" or "superbaby" programs that have sprung up in recent years, the Missouri program focused on a comfortable, constructive style of parenting designed to make the early educational process enjoyable as well as effective rather than intensive and highly structured. In our opinion, such high-pressure programs tend to dampen the children's intrinsic interest in learning and take much of the fun out of the typical daily interactions between parents and children. (Meyerhoff & White, 1986, p. 43)

The NPAT project offered parents participating in the 3-year program the following services:

1. Information and guidance before the baby is born to help first-time parents prepare themselves psychologically.
2. Information about things to look for and expect in a growing child, and guidance in fostering language, cognitive, social, and motor skill development.
3. Periodic checkups of the child's educational and sensory (hearing and vision) development to detect possible problems or handicaps. If serious problems are discovered, help is sought from other agencies or professionals.
4. A parent resource center, located in a school building, which provides a meeting place for parents and staff, and facilities for child care during parent meetings.
5. Monthly hour-long private visits in the home or at the center to individualize the education program for each family.
6. Monthly group meetings with other new parents to share experiences and discuss topics of interest. (Winter, 1985, p. 23)

The basic purpose of the program was to provide information and assistance to parents to make their job, as parent, less stressful, more pleasurable, and to help them to be better prepared to be their child's first teacher. Much of this information pertained to the seven phases of child development from birth to 3 years found in White's (1975) *The First Three Years of Life*. The specific goals of the program were

1. To establish a practical, community-based system for providing helpful information and services to first-time parents.
2. To identify conditions which might interfere with normal development during the child's preschool years and with later academic success in school.
3. To help families provide a home environment that aids the child's physical, intellectual, and social development.
4. To show feasibility of parents' and educators' working together on a part-time basis to help each child develop as fully as possible during the crucial period from birth to age 3.
5. To show that the program was an economical way of preventing learning problems and enhancing children's development.
6. To provide information which communities could use in determining the desirability of such programs. (Brochure: *Facts about New Parents as Teachers*)

Each of the four sites had an advisory committee made up of representatives from the community to build a broad base of community awareness, involvement, and support. The state supervisory committee provided guidance to the programs.

Evaluation

At the end of the 3-year project, outcomes were measured by outside evaluators, Research Training and Associates of Overland Park, Kansas. Six hypotheses and five research questions were addressed.

The hypotheses were

1. Children of participating parents will demonstrate better intellectual and language development as compared to a comparison group or to the normed group of nationally representative children;
2. Children of participating parents will demonstrate more positive social development as compared to a comparison group of children;
3. Children of participating parents will demonstrate fewer undetected incidences of handicapping conditions, particularly in hearing, as compared to a comparison group of children;
4. Participating parents will demonstrate increased knowledge of child development and child-rearing practices;
5. Participating parents will demonstrate positive feelings about the program's usefulness; and
6. Participating parents will demonstrate positive attitudes toward the school district.

The questions were

1. To what extent did early detections of potentially handicapping conditions by NPAT staff reduce the size of the "at-risk" population at age three?
2. Are traditional measures of "at-risk" family characteristics (e.g., single-parent households, parents' age and education, receipt of public assistance, quality of alternate care, etc.) related to a child's ability at age three?
3. Is parent knowledge of child development related to the child's ability at age 3?
4. Is the extent to which parents participate in project activities related to the child's performance at age three?
5. Do parents with certain background and family characteristics tend to be "better" NPAT participants? (Pfannenstiel & Seltzer, 1985, p. II-2)

The research report confirmed that the NPAT project significantly enhanced the child's intellectual, language, and social abilities at age 3:

Children of parents participating in the New Parents As Teacher Project (NPAT) consistently scored significantly higher (at least .001) on all measures of intelligence, achievement, auditory comprehension, verbal ability and language ability than did comparison children. NPAT children scored seven scores higher than did comparison children on the intelligence (mental processing) scale of the Kaufman Assessment Battery for Children (KABC). (Pfannenstiel & Seltzer, 1985, p. III-1)

The Kaufman Assessment Battery Scales is a standardized test for gauging the learning progress of young children. The children in the parent education program placed more than 10 scores higher on measures assessing general information and school-related success. On the Zimmerman Preschool Language Scales the 3 year olds participating in the NPAT program tested more than six scores higher than their peers in the control group on language development.

Parents participating in the parent education program were more likely to have their child's hearing professionally tested by age 3. The NPAT parents were significantly more knowledgeable than the comparison group about discipline and child development in the first 3 years of life. Parents attending more meetings were more knowledgeable in certain areas of child development. The greater the parental participation in home visits, the more likely children were to demonstrate positive aspects of social development.

Benefits of the program even extended to the sponsoring school districts where participating parents were more likely to regard their school districts as responsive to their child's needs. Almost all of the participants reported a high degree of satisfaction with each of the program's services and considered home visits as the most helpful project service (Pfannenstiel & Seltzer, 1985, pp. III-15–III-16).

Further State Efforts

Since the pilot project had such positive results, Parents as Teachers programs are now being implemented in school districts across Missouri under the Early Childhood Development Act of 1984. Parent education for all parents of children under the age of 3 has been authorized for state funding by this bill. Screening for children 1 and 2 years of age has also been included in the funding.

School districts are now providing a concentrated program of parent education for parents of children, birth to 3 years of age. The Missouri Department of Elementary and Secondary Education, under the guidance of Mildred Winter, offers training, preservice, and inservice sessions for parent educators, project staff, and school administrators. Inservice training is provided on an ongoing basis. Each school district submitted an implementation plan for the parent education program to the state Department of Education for approval. Efforts are carefully being monitored.

Statewide Training Opportunities

PARENT EDUCATOR TRAINING

All parent educators are required to participate in a week-long institute for initial training conducted by professional staff involved in the original NPAT program. The institutes can be taken for 2 hours' university graduate or undergraduate credit. In response to requests from other states the institutes are now open to a limited number of applicants from outside Missouri.

In order to be approved as a parent educator by the Missouri Department of Elementary and Secondary Education, students (1) attend 30 hours of classroom instruction, (2) read White's *The First Three Years of Life* and other selected readings, (3) demonstrate their understanding of the information presented by making at least a C on daily tests, and (4) submit an acceptable implementation plan of the Parents as Teachers program for their local school district.

Students learn how to implement the Parents as Teachers program in their local district during the institute. Content of the institute includes topics such as working with families, private visits with families, and phases of development and learning from birth to age 3. Parent educators learn how to screen young children and how to market the program within their district and community.

After the initial institute, parent educators attend a series of 1- and 2-day follow-up regional training sessions. All sessions are open to administrators. The follow-up regional training sessions include such workshop topics as: (1) the research base supporting the Parents as Teachers program, (2) a critique of video-taped home visits involving more than one child under age 3, and (3) lesson plans and topics for group meetings appropriate for each phase of development.

TELEPHONE CONSULTATION

In addition to the planned institutes, administrators and parent educators can call in their questions during regularly scheduled hours at each of the original New Parents as Teachers sites. This offers the opportunity for parent educators to have their questions answered in a timely fashion.

TRAINING PERSONNEL

Statewide training is conducted primarily by four parent educators who implemented the pilot New Parents as Teachers program and the state Department of Elementary and Secondary Education's early childhood consultant. Specialists are brought in as needed.

Program Implementation under Senate Bill 658

As of January 1986, the Parents as Teachers program was implemented under state funding in 536 of the 543 eligible school districts. This funding provides for services to 10% (17,000+) of the families with children under age of 3 in Missouri. The Missouri General Assembly doubled the funding for 1986–87. The program served 20% of the families with children under 3 in Missouri, and local school districts were reimbursed by the state for providing this service. State funding was provided to serve 30% (53,000) of the families in all 543 school districts during 1987–1988. A 5% increase in enrollment is projected for each succeeding year.

Second-Wave Research

Forty-two school districts meeting selected criteria were invited to participate in a second wave of PAT model programs to collect further data on program outcomes and to study a broader sample of programs. The criteria used included (1) diversity as to location, district size, and type of community, (2) high degree of philosophical and financial commitment to the program by the school district, and (3) strong administrative support and supervision.

Involvement in the program includes (1) provision of monthly private visits (which continue until the child reaches age 3) to a designated number of families entering the program during the 1986–87 school year with children under 8 months of age; (2) provision of required group meetings and screening of children at required intervals with prescribed instruments and procedures; (3) administration of the pre- and post-program parent questionnaire used in the original research study; (4) measurement of certain parental risk conditions which were found in the original research study to correlate with children's achievement; (5) tracing the children once they enter school; (6) provision of released staff time and travel expenses to parent educators receiving training.

At each of the second-wave sites extra staff training and consultation is provided. An on-site needs assessment is conducted at each site to individualize training needs. Observation and critique of the home visits and group meetings conducted by the parent educators is part of the monitoring for quality and consistency of services. The collection of these data will give further credibility to existing evidence of the program's success.

Ingredients for Success

When starting a new program like the Parents as Teachers program, one needs to be aware of certain factors which in part determine the success of the outcome. Among these factors are the following:

1. Grassroots support. The Parents as Teachers program in Missouri has been fortunate to have support from both the public and private community. The Commissioner of Education appointed a committee composed of influential people across the state to help promote public awareness of this program. The members of the Commissioner of Education's Comitteee on Parents as Teachers have been the program's strongest advocates. They have helped to raise money and donated expertise and time to provide leadership for the program. The fact that the Parents as Teachers program has been so successful has been partly due to this public–private partnership.

2. Dissemintion and quality monitoring. The Missouri Department of Elementary and Secondary Education acknowledges that expanding the parent education services from 4 to 546 school districts with less than a year of planning has been a challenge and has not been an ideal situation. But given the scarcity of opportunity and money for efforts of this sort, it was decided to accept the challenge and implement the program with specific quality-control measures. Thus, the department has linked up with the state university system to offer training and regional support. Grant monies, such as a grant from the Green Foundation of Mexico, Missouri, enables trainers of parent educators to visit individual school districts to provide on-site training and critique home visits. In addition, all school districts involved in the second-wave research project receive extra training, monitoring, and consultation. Efforts for monitoring quality starts with the initial training institutes where all parent educators must meet designated requirements. On going in-service hours and written documentation of the services each parent educator provides assists the Department of Elementary and Secondary Education in keeping track of the quantity and quality of services provided to parents.

3. Sponsorship. Every public school district in Missouri can receive state funding for providing services to parents included in the Parents as

Teachers program. School districts are located in every community in the state and are generally associated with enhancing learning of people within the community. Schools were selected as dissemination sites because, unlike many public agencies, they are not perceived by the public as connected with family problems. Generally, there are positive feelings toward public schools, and parents feel comfortable meeting at and going to them.

4. Qualifications of parent educators. Ideally every school district would like to be able to hire parent educators who have degrees in early childhood education or child development. Since the need for parent educators for every school district is great, it is impossible to require such high educational standards. Most school districts require 60 college hours and prefer that the parent educators be a parent. The lower educational requirements have enabled many people who live in specific ethnic neighborhoods to apply for the job. This has enabled parent educators to relate better to and recruit parents. The only negative aspect of lower educational requirements is that the parent educators need more extensive training and information on parenting skills and normal child growth and development. Regional workshops and institutes have provided all parent educators with information and resources.

5. Limited applicability. The Parents as Teachers program has benefited many parents and their children. This parent education model is only one example of how parenting skills can be enhanced. Every parent education program has its limitations and Parents as Teachers is no exception. The Parents as Teachers program cannot solve every social problem. Children with severe handicapping conditions or parents with overwhelming personal problems need services in addition to those provided by the program. Since Parents as Teachers is an educational program, it cannot provide for every parental need.

For the majority of parents, however, the Parents as Teachers program works. Thus, Meyerhoff and White (1986) conclude their evaluation of the program as follows: "The results of the evaluation seem applicable to the approximately 85 percent of the population without such special problems. We had success with families in which both parents had doctoral degrees and with families in which both parents had failed to finish high school" (Meyerhoff & White, 1986, p. 45).

When parent educators become aware of needs that are beyond the scope of the program, they can refer the parent to the proper resources. All parent educators are expected to be knowledgeable about available resources. The Parents as Teachers program conveys to parents in every community that parenting and being a parent is important. There are particular skills and knowledge which can enhance parent–child interactions. Conveying the value of parenting and being a parent is one of the greatest benefits this program can offer.

Summary

Burton White's dream of educating parents about the first 3 years of life is at least a reality in the state of Missouri. Other states are considering starting a similar program and the Parents as Teachers programs could spread across the nation. The plan to empower parents using local school districts' resources is feasible. White's research demonstrates that the first 3 years of life are critical to the child's well being, and parents are the best advocates for their own children.

The Parents as Teachers program provides parents with the needed support and information to be more effective in their role as parents. Parents gain confidence in their abilities and feel success in their role as a parent. Children benefit from more positive parent interactions and from the support systems structured into the parent education services. When screening indicates delays in development, appropriate guidance is provided to parents, with referral to outside resources as needed. The program seems to benefit everyone who participates. A second research study has been initiated to further document the program's effectiveness.

References

Bell, T. H. (1974, July). *The family, the young child, and the school*. Paper presented at the 10th Annual Conference of South Carolina School Officials, Myrtle Beach, SC.

Facts about "New Parents as Teachers." (N.D.) Brochure, Early Education Program, Ferguson-Florissant School District, Florissant, MO.

Levenstein, P. (1970, April). Cognitive growth in preschoolers through verbal interaction with mothers. *American Journal of Orthopsychiatry, 40*, 426–432.

Meyerhoff, M. & White, B. (1986, September). Making the grade as parents. *Psychology Today, 20*, 38–45.

Parents as Teachers: A program planning and implementation guide (rev. ed.). (1986). (Available from Missouri Department of Elementary and Secondary Education, Box 480, Jefferson City, MO 65102)

Pfannenstiel, J. C., & Seltzer, D. (1985). *Evaluation report: New Parents as Teachers project*. (Available from Missouri Department of Elementary and Secondaty Education, Box 480, Jefferson City, MO 65102)

White, B. L. (1972, June). When should schooling begin? *Phi Delta Kappan, 53*, 610–614.

White, B. L. (1975). *The first three years of life*. Englewood Cliffs, NJ: Prentice-Hall.

White, B. L. (1978, May). Love is not enough. *UNESCO Courier*, 22–24.

White, B. L. (1980). Primary prevention: Beginning at the beginning. *Personnel and Guidance Journal, 58,* 338–343.

White, B. L. (1981a). Education for parenthood 1981. *Journal of Education, 163,* 205–218.

White, B. L. (1981b). *Outline for a parent education program.* Unpublished manuscript. Handout at Parents As Teachers Institute, St. Louis, MO.

White, B. L., Kaban, B. T., Attanucci, J., & Shapiro, B. B. (1978). *Experience and environment: Major influences on the development of the young child* (Vol. 2). Englewood Cliffs, NJ: Prentice-Hall.

Winter, M. M. (1985, May). Parents as first teachers. *Principal, 64,* 22–24.

6

School-Based Parent Involvement Programs

Roger Kroth

Introduction

Parent involvement in the treatment and education of exceptional children has a long history. It was not surprising when this type of interaction was written into law in the Education for All Handicapped Children Act, PL 94-142, in 1974. In addition, the Family Educational Rights and Privacy Act in 1975 defined a number of rights to privacy for both parents and their children. By the 1980s most special education programs had made provisions for systematic parent contact.

Most school districts have policies which encourage and define parent involvement. Some districts rely heavily on parent advisory groups; some Title programs require such activities. Other districts have made provisions for periodic parent–teacher conferences, and most districts encourage parent-teacher organizations such as PTA or PTO.

Just how effective these attempts to promote interaction between the significant adults in a child's life have been remains in question. Some educators have suggested that the federal legislation has caused more problems than it has solved. Some parents have felt that the doors have not been opened as wide as they should be and that educators have used the law to hide behind (Kroth, 1985).

New Mexico was the lone holdout of the states in accepting the funding provided by PL 94-142. Although New Mexico has capitulated and begun full participation in the federally funded program, parent involvement has long been a vital part of the educational procedures in the state. Albuquerque has had, and still maintains, a parent involvement center. A variety of parent programs have been in operation in the surrounding rural areas during the time that New Mexico was not receiving monies through

PL 94-142. These programs were frequently funded by the Developmental Disabilities Planning Council and sometimes by local school districts. A number of parent and professional organizations joined forces in a lawsuit against state officials in 1975 to force provision of services for children that were required by federal guidelines. The parent–professional connection in New Mexico is compatible with the values and practices of the people of the state.

The Mirror Model of Parent Involvement which is the framework for most of the programs described in this chapter (Kroth, 1985; Kroth & Otteni, 1983) is explained so the reader has a road map for understanding the decisions that were made in the programs outlined. The Parent Center in Albuquerque, which grew out of federal funding and continues to exist many years after those monies were depleted, was based on this model and used the assumptions and activities as a blueprint for action in a large school system (school-based) program. A program for parents in rural New Mexico is also outlined.

The Mirror Model of Parental Involvement was conceived as a means to define the parameters of a comprehensive parent-involvement program in a public school setting. It is based on the philosophy that parents are capable of managing much of their own behavior and that they are willing and able to take responsibility for much of their child's growth and development. Nicholas Hobbs said it well: "Parents have to be recognized as the special educators, the true experts on their children; and professional people—teachers, pediatricians, psychologists, and others—have to learn to be consultants to parents" (Hobbs, 1978). The helping professions seem to have a tendency to own many of the problems of their clients or patients, rather than to take the time to help the clients learn to be their own case managers.

For instance, in the rural areas of New Mexico and even in the urban areas, there are many different pueblos with their own languages, and many different cultures with their own customs and beliefs. New Mexico is truly a multicultured state. In one elementary school in Albuquerque, five different interpreters are employed to help in parent–teacher–child interaction.

Assumptions

A number of assumptions were made when the Mirror Model was conceptualized (Kroth & Otteni, 1983). The assumptions that one makes about the conditions that affect parent involvement influence the activities in which one engages as programs are designed. One is certainly entitled to formulate his or her own assumptions, but the following five considerations were recognized as influencing parent involvement in parent activities and in the delivery of service in a large school system (child population of over 75,000) and in a sparsely populated state which has at least one county of less than 2,000 people. While they appear obvious, these assumptions are the reality that one must work within.

Money

Finances always force program personnel into choices. It would be nice to produce videotapes for small groups or be able to provide parents with takehome computers, but few school districts can consider the possibility.

Therapeutic parent groups or counseling usually involves only a few parents and becomes a very expensive component. In-depth services for small numbers are often the first to go in times of a money crunch. It therefore becomes necessary in developing services to place this component in perspective. Often program personnel decide that these are cases that need to be referred to other community agencies. It is a matter of spending money in areas one feels will yield the biggest payoff.

There will never be enough money to do what one may want to do or know how to do. For instance, in those cases where we could pay for motels, travel, food, and materials, it was possible to have representative populations from different pueblos or tribes for 2 or 3 days at a time. If we had had enough money to pay parents for time away from the job, we could have had even more participation.

To illustrate the point more clearly, imagine if one told the professionals who complain that they are not able to get parent participation that every parent attending a meeting could have $1,000 and that the meeting would be held at Disneyland with all expenses paid. Most professionals could have a nice-sized meeting.

The question remains one of establishing priorities. There will never be that kind of money for parent involvement.

Time

Even if money were not an issue, time probably would be. There is seldom enough time to do what one knows how to do. Teacher time to prepare for interaction with parents and to actually call or interview parents is limited. The amount of time that parents have to attend meetings is limited.

Setting aside time for parent–child interaction for most families means rearranging priorities. While most professionals feel this should be done, for a variety of reasons it is not always practical for parents of handicapped children. The same problem arises when one suggests that teachers or educators spend more time working with parents.

Does one merely respond to crises, which could take all of one's time, or does one take an active stance and initiate certain training programs? Time is a commodity that must be considered, and there is never enough of it.

Personnel

The assumption is made by the writer that there are not, nor probably ever will be, enough trained personnel to facilitate the interaction between parents and teachers or to train parents in strategies to work more effectively with their children. There still are many colleges and universities which do not offer any courses in parent conferencing or parent counseling (Kroth, Otteni, & Parks, 1982).

The lack of training affects the type of services that can be offered in a community. If there are limited numbers of trained personnel, one has to ask how the maximum benefit can be derived from these individuals. Guerney (1969) proposes that professionals multiply their impact by teaching their skills to others, such as parents or other professionals. In rural areas where there will never be enough trained personnel to provide programs for all who need them, the question arises as to whether one should try to provide case-management services to everyone or try to train some parents to provide their own case management services. Some have suggested that the County Agent or County Nurse network be used to provide support to parents. In New Mexico we took the position that whenever possible the parents should be taught to be their own case managers to the extent that they are able, because professionals are not always around when they might be needed.

Heterogeneity of Parents

Most professionals recognize that parents of exceptional children are not a homogeneous group. Still, this assumption is continually being violated by almost everything that is designed for parents. Teachers who are excellent at individualizing programs for children seldom individualize for parents.

It is not uncommon to attend a parent meeting and have someone say, "The parents who should be here for this information are not here tonight." As Bridge (1976) noted, in addition to the variables of ethnicity, religion, education, and income, a wide variety of attitudes, values, and child-rearing practices must be taken into account. It is difficult for some people to recognize that not all people have the same priorities. Some parents are having a struggle to survive. A mother once said, "I have eight children, my husband's shot at me twice, I'm on welfare, and I'm having a hard time keeping clean clothes on my kids and food on the table. I just can't come to your meetings. 'Sides I don't have transportation."

Glenn and Warner (1982) discuss the transitions that have taken place in families from the 1930s to the present. They point out the change in family structure over time. Figure 6.1 highlights some of the changes that might affect the interaction between parents and school personnel. In addition to the factors listed, consider that the percentage of births to unwed mothers has more than quadrupled.

Professionals often act as if structures were the same as they were years ago. The "Ozzie and Harriet" type family where the father went off to work in the morning, the mother stayed home, and there were two children, a dog named Spot, and a cat named Mitten, represents only about 7–10% of the families today (Nadelson & Nadelson, 1980). In large cities like Albuquerque, it is not uncommon to find 70% of the children having both parents working or the only parent working in a single-parent family. Only about one-third of the children who are labeled behaviorally disordered are living with their birth parents (Casey, 1983), and about 50% are living in a single-parent family. In the 1980s, over half of the children may be living in a single-parent family by age 15 (Black, 1979; Hamner & Turner, 1985; Wallerstein & Kelly, 1979; Wattenberg & Reinhardt, 1979).

These factors will affect the decisions about attending meetings at school. Most conferences and parent–staff meetings are scheduled during the work day when it is almost impossible for parents to attend. In trying times, some parents are afraid to ask for time off for fear they will lose their jobs.

Educators often have to decide who is to be invited to meetings because of the alternative family constellations that exist. The move away from the extended family has made it difficult for parents to leave the child and siblings with relatives while they attend meetings.

The educational level of parents is often not adequate to understand information sent from school. Some can read and some cannot, and yet the materials that are sent home seem to assume that all parents can read at high school level. Some of the pamphlets sent home to explain the services available to parents and children, for example, diagnosticians or occupational therapy, are at the college-graduate level. One wonders about issues such as informed consent if the parents cannot read the

	then — 50 years — now

	then	— 50 years —	now
family composition	Many members Extended Intact (Ozzie and Harriet)		Few Members Nuclear Reconstituted, Alternative styles
family interaction	Work, play games, talk together (2-3 hours a day) Intergenerational		Little family work Parallel TV viewing (average, 7 hours a day) 15-20 minutes interaction a day
family work	Mainly fathers Family businesses		Both parents (70% of the time)
neighborhoods	Much interaction Ethnic Rural/small town		Anonymity Integrated Urban
education	Less than ½ finished HS Few went past HS		Most finished HS Many go to post HS
orphanages	Some		Very rare
child abuse	? ? ? ? ? ?		Currently a problem
divorce	Rare		Common (over ½ of children will live in single parent family by age 15)

Figure 6.1.   Families (style and structure).

materials. The author has examined materials prepared by state agencies
for parents and often found them lacking in readability and clarity.

Some parents are wealthy and some are poor. Some have large families
and some have only one child. Some families have both parents working
and some have no parents working. In some families there is only one
parent and some children have to adjust to a large number of parents over
time. In fact, some families have a large number of adults living in a single

dwelling. Some children are raised by grandparents. It was not uncommon when we were doing training with some of the Native American groups to have aunts and grandparents in attendance.

Unfortunately, people who provide training and service to Native American groups often do not consider the cultural differences that exist between the various tribes and pueblos. This may be true even when the trainers are Native Americans themselves. For instance, it is not uncommon to find that certain pueblos or tribes do not have words for some of the handicapping conditions that are funded under PL 19-142 or the developmental disabilities programs. Some of the "reasons" for the handicapping condition may be "explained" by cultural beliefs rather than medical factors, and thus may be viewed differently from group to group. Not too long ago children born with certain visible handicaps were left to die in certain tribes. It is not too difficult to understand why parents of these children may not want to attend parent meetings when the traditions are not far removed historically. Treating parents as if they were homogenous groups is vastly unfair. They should be provided with individualized parent programs, just as children should be provided with individualized educational programs (IEPs).

The heterogeneity of parents is a complex factor that will confuse and compound problems of communication between school and home. Recognizing it and attempting to provide for it was an underlying assumption in the development of the Mirror Model.

Recent work by Jennifer Olson at the University of Idaho, Ann Turnbull and her staff at the University of Kansas, and Damon Lamb in Marshaltown, Iowa has begun to shed light on the Family System Analysis as a strategy for considering the whole family in treatment programs for the handicapped children. While most of this work has been done with families of young children, it has application for school-age children and their families. It is a major consideration that should influence the work of professionals who work in the area of exceptional children.

Needs and Strengths

A fifth basic assumption in the development of comprehensive parent-involvement programs was that all parents had needs, and all parents had strengths. Failure to recognize the strength factor in parents leads one to the automatic assumption that parents are not capable.

By law, there are some basic facts that all parents must be provided with in order to make decisions about interventions for their children (Dominguez, 1982). In many instances, professionals believe they have communicated clearly with parents but the parents do not recognize that they have been provided with the information, thus creating a communication gap (Korsch & Negrete, 1972).

In summary, certain assumptions about working conditions and parent populations underlie the Mirror Model of Parental Involvement:

1. There will never be enough money to do the things school personnel know need to be done.
2. Time will always be lacking for both parents and professionals in accomplishing desired goals.
3. There probably will never be enough training programs to satisfy parents or staff.
4. Parents of exceptional children are not a homogeneous group and should not be treated as one.
5. All parents of exceptional children have strengths to be used, and all have needs to be met.

The Mirror Model of Parental Involvement

The Mirror Model of Parental Involvement (Fig. 6.2) was developed based on the assumptions presented above and years of experience in teaching and working with teachers and parents in the public schools and special interest groups. It is an attempt to provide a model for comprehensive parent programs and to serve as a guide in planning. The top half of the model addresses needs and the bottom half reflects the strengths that parents have. The various levels reflect the recognition that parents are not homogeneous and therefore will need to be treated differently. The left-hand side of the model indicates needs and strengths and the right-hand side of the model indicates how these might be accommodated with some suggested activities.

All parents do not have the same needs, therefore the model has different levels. It is assumed that all parents need some things but not all parents need *all* things. The various levels are discussed in some detail to show how they influence the activities that one might find in a school system. They also have relevance for training activities. For instance, the thrust of the Parent Involvement Center activity has been on Level 1 and 2 activities, those in the four center levels of the chart, because those are the things that impact the greater number of parents and teachers. This is not to downgrade Level 3 and 4 activities but rather to put them in perspective because of limited resources in any organization. The Mirror

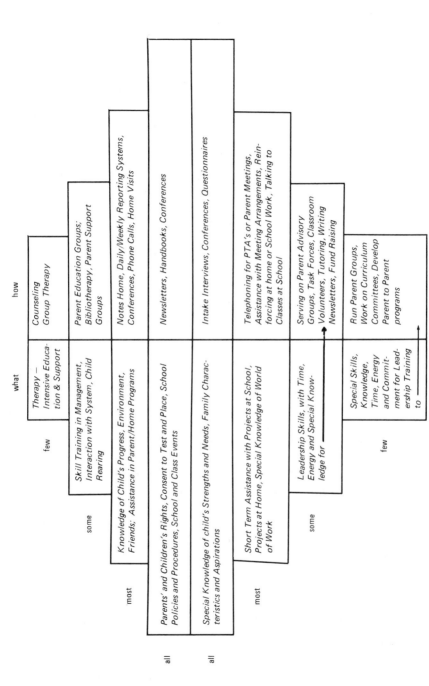

Figure 6.2. Mirror model of parental involvement.

Model is intended to serve as a guide for decision making in the development of delivery systems of parent involvement in school systems.

Needs

LEVEL 4

One of the most expensive services that can be offered by a school district to families is therapy. It is time consuming, provides for only a few families at a time, and usually requires professionals with a certain type of expertise. Since only a few parents need this level of service, the role of the school personnel is often that of referral to other community agencies. The percentage of parents needing this service is unknown. It probably is no more than 5% of the total population of parents, but for a large district this can be a substantial number.

Although the number of parents requiring this level of service is not directly related to the severity of handicap, some professionals feel that parents of severely emotionally disturbed children may need more counseling or group therapy than other parents. This might be related to Bell's bidirectional theory (Bell, 1968; Bell & Harper, 1977), which suggests that not only do adults influence child behavior, but children influence adult behavior. Therefore, disturbed children probably can produce disturbed parents. School personnel must have the ability to recognize the need for help and refer parents to appropriate community service.

Another service that is needed by only a few parents is relocation. Knowledgeable parents realize that not all communities offer the same levels of program for their children. At the same time, the adult population is mobile, approximately 16% of households moving each year. Helping parents check out services and prepare for the move from one community to another is a service that can be provided to those few parents who need it. Often a couple of phone calls to program directors can clear up problems before the family moves.

Some services at this level can be handled by preparing community directories, guides for community services, and other handouts for parents. Guiding them to the right service may be the most important function at this level. In this way, disproportionate amounts of monies probably need not be allocated for this level of service.

LEVEL 3

Parent group work is quite popular in the literature (Cooper & Edge, 1978; Guerney, 1969; Kroth & Scholl, 1978; Rutherford & Edgar, 1979; Wagonseller, Burnett, Salzberg, & Burnett, 1977; Wagonseller & Mc-

Dowell, 1982). Procedures for designing, implementing, and evaluating parent groups are discussed and recommended by many authors. There are also many parent programs in kit form. Only some parents will take advantage of these offerings. Perhaps 20% of the parents will attend skill training or support groups over time. For instance, the teacher with a class of 10 children might expect two or three parents to be willing to devote three or four sessions in a parent group.

Most of the groups are designed for groups of 10 or less. Since a teacher or leader is expected to attend on a regular basis to facilitate the group, this becomes an expensive program. Fortunately, many communities have support groups available and these are publicized in the newspapers or the yellow pages of the phone book.

For teachers or educators who want to implement parent groups, the commercial materials are often well written with leader's guides, workbooks, posters, and various supplementary materials. Most of the "canned" programs need to be modified for the target populations.

It is desirable to analyze the parent population for the needs that should be met by the program. At the Parent Involvement Center in Albuquerque, New Mexico, many parent group programs have been designed over the past 6 or 7 years. They have been designed to teach parents

1. To test their own children
2. To write their own IEPs
3. To make nutritional snacks
4. To make the transition between levels of education, for example, preschool and elementary
5. To be active participants in conferences
6. Their rights
7. To be their own case managers
8. A variety of skills and information.

Parent programs grow out of observed and expressed needs. One can carry out a needs–strength assessment or one can become attuned to the needs expressed by parents in everyday contacts. Trained staff usually enjoy conducting parent groups. It might be a more profitable use of their time to teach others (parents and teachers) to design and run these groups, since only some of the parents will be involved.

LEVEL 2

Most parents of exceptional children want to know more about the causes of their children's problems, how their children are doing in the treatment programs, and what they can do to help. They usually want this information from the primary source, that is, the teacher, the doctor, the diagnostician, and they want it in understandable terms (Dembinski & Mauser, 1977, 1978).

Since these needs seem to affect about 80% of the parent population, it is important to spend time on how to receive information from parents and how to convey meaningful data to parents. Dembinski and Mauser (1977, 1978) and a series of studies by Korsch (Korsch & Negrete, 1972) have addressed the communication gaps that seem to exist between professionals and parents.

The improvement of communication between the teacher and parent is the primary goal. To this end, teacher-training programs at the University of New Mexico and the Parent Involvement Center pay attention to such things as handbooks, handouts, conferencing tips and skills, daily report card systems, and other materials that facilitate the understanding between parents and teachers. Computer readability programs have reduced the labor of analyzing materials to the point that it is almost inexcusable to send materials home that are beyond the reading and comprehension level of the parents. Some examples of tip sheets and information sheets can be found in *Communicating with Parents of Exceptional Children* (Kroth, 1985).

Another way to consider conveying information to larger aduiences is through topical conferences. A variety of general interest presentations have been sponsored by the Albuquerque Public School (APS) through the Parent Involvement Center. Topics that seem to be of widespread interest are discipline, divorce, sex education, drugs and alcohol, adolescence, and stress management. There are some good materials available to help in the preparation of discipline workshop topics (Canter & Canter, 1982; Smith, 1984).

A number of authors have been concerned with the interaction that is meant to occur at Levels 1 and 2 (Coletta, 1977; Kroth, 1985; Kroth & Simpson, 1977; Lillie & Place, 1982; Seligman, 1979; Simpson, 1982). Parents regard the teachers as their primary source of information and support. The more skilled the teacher is in this role, the more satisfaction will be derived by parents, and the better the programming will be for children.

LEVEL 1

By state and federal law, all parents are to be apprised of their rights and the rights of their children. School district personnel must therefore put time and resources into activities and materials that explain these rights. Unfortunately, many school district administrators feel apprehensive about conveying this information. Even school districts that are doing a good job in this regard should be aware that their message does not always get across. Dominguez (1982) found that even though school district records showed that parents had signed the various permission slips and forms required by law, they reported that they were unaware of what they had done. Williams (1983) also found that when diagnosticians spent a great deal of time explaining test scores and interpretations, parents often were not able to recall the information.

Many school districts prepare handbooks and supplementary materials for parents. Even when this is done, the materials are often not checked for reading levels. A sampling of such materials was found to be at the 10th- and 11th-grade reading level, and explanatory materials on supplementary services was at the college level. Translating the materials into the parents' primary language (often Spanish) usually misses the mark. The language is often textbook Spanish and the parents may use a combination of Spanish and English.

Since Level 1 is an area that affects all parents, resources should be put into developing materials and strategies for meeting the needs of that level. Some commercial materials may help, with modifications made for any particular population.

Strengths

LEVEL 1

All parents know some things about their children or family structure that professionals need to know. Skilled professionals are able to elicit this information with good interviewing skills or observational techniques.

It is entirely possible that parents of exceptional children may be working with a large number of professionals. In a series of weekend camps for families of visually impaired children sponsored by the Texas Commission for the Blind, it was found that some of the parents were being seen by as many as 20 different professionals because of the multiplicity of handicapping conditions. This can be overwhelming, because all professionals feel that their programs need to be carried out. Even well-meaning professionals with exemplary programs may produce negative effects on families because the demands of the programs exceed the strengths of the parents to participate (Doernberg, 1978).

LEVEL 2

Most parents have the strength, time, and energy to do more than just provide the professionals with information. They may be able to set up a program at home that reinforces what the teacher is doing in the classroom, for example, reward growth recorded on the child's daily or weekly report card system.

These parents might be willing to call other parents as part of a telephone tree, address envelopes, make cookies, or carry out a number of other one-shot activities. Sensitive teachers can take advantage of parents' willingness to help but allow them the opportunity to "take a breather" once in a while. Unfortunately, parents who volunteer their services often get overworked. They can get "burned out" just like teachers, and they do not even get the summer off.

LEVEL 3

Remembering the heterogeneity of the parent population, one realizes that some parents will have the knowledge, training, and skill to provide training for other parents and teachers in training. Some participants in our program have benefited many parents and professionals with their teaching and leadership positions in organizations. This does not mean that they do not have needs of their own, but they have special talents plus the insights of being parents.

Some parents have the time, strength, and energy to provide assistance in the classroom. They may be able to teach children or provide help to teachers. Some may serve on advisory boards or participate in parent panels.

Sometimes parents are asked to participate in roles for which they have not been prepared. This can be unfortunate. If parents are asked to serve in the role of aide in the classroom, the expectations should be made clear. If parents are asked to serve on committees or boards, the roles should be clear and training should be offered if it is needed.

This area of parent involvement is often neglected. Parents can be a rich source of assistance for the welfare of children and a help to professionals and other parents. Not using a parent who has writing skills and the time to help with newsletters and handbooks is a disservice to the parent and to the professional.

LEVEL 4

Parents have long been recognized as the major sources of strength for other parents. A number of parent support groups have been formed. For instance, in Albuquerque there is a group called Parents Reaching Out (PRO), made up of parents who provide support for each other, produce a newsletter, keep an eye on legislation, provide speakers for interested groups, and are generally available for the unique services that parents need from time to time. A number of communities have the Pilot Parent program, a support group of parents of handicapped children who assist each other through the grief cycle.

In Grand Junction, Colorado, the Effective Parenting Project has sponsored "The Roundhouse" for the past 5 years. Parents have provided leadership for workshops and training programs to help parents work through the mourning process for the Roundhouse conference and parent-to-parent projects around the state. This program, which has been jointly sponsored by the Colorado State Department of Education, local school districts, and funding projects, has had a tremendous impact on parents in Colorado and other parts of the country.

A Parent Support Network has been formed in New Mexico to train parents and professionals to develop support services in their own communities. The strategy of combining parents and professionals from the same community for training was deliberate. Often parents attend meetings and garner many good ideas, but when they return home they have no place to meet, no access to equipment or phones. Professionals may be able to provide these resources.

Large communities have support groups available. These often have a minimum amount of professional assistance. School personnel may help parents locate these groups. The number of parents who are not aware of organizations such as the Association for Children with Learning Disabilities, the Association for Retarded Citizens, or the Association for Gifted and Talented Students is often surprising. Support groups such as Recovery, Parents Anonymous, and Tough Love are active in many communities.

Using the Mirror Model as a framework and attending to the assumptions outlined, some programs that "work" are outlined below. The Parent Center is primarily an urban program, while the rural program focuses on teaching parents case management skills.

The Parent Center

The Parent Center is located in Inez Elementary School in the APS. It was originally funded as a demonstration program by the Office of Special Education and as such provided services to APS professionals and parents. Although primary attention is by necessity focused on APS, parents and professionals from all the other 49 states and from some foreign countries have visited and been trained by Center staff. Materials developed by staff at the Center are being used by university trainers and staff development personnel in most of the states.

From the beginning, the Center has been staffed by University of New Mexico personnel and APS professionals. When funding from the federal government stopped, APS picked up the project financially and continued to support the services being offered, and the administration shifted to APS with consultation from the University of New Mexico.

Services of the Center

In order to perpetuate the philosophy of a partnership between home and school, services of the center may be categorized as follows:

1. Services to schools
   a. Assisting school staffs in planning and implementing parent involvement in the classroom or building
   b. Conducting inservice training on the awareness, knowledge, and skills related to home–school communications
   c. Providing consultation and support services to school personnel as they work with parents
   d. Offering on-site graduate coursework in parent involvement through the University of New Mexico
2. Services to parents
   a. Helping parents locate community resources
   b. Conducting parent workshops, seminars, and support groups
   c. Offering relocation service to parents of exceptional children who are moving to another locale
3. Materials development
   a. Collecting and compiling information that facilitates better understanding and improved practices between school and home
   b. Acquiring and designing materials for use in parent and teacher workshops and seminars
   c. Providing information related to home–school needs through distribution of newsletters, handbooks, and other source materials
   d. Maintaining a parent and professional use library that houses current books, articles, and other resource materials on issues and skills in parent involvement

Since the Parent Center began operation in 1978, most of the over 100 schools in the school district that serves over 75,000 students, including approximately 11,000 exceptional children have had inservice sessions conducted by center staff. Many of the sessions have concentrated on the parent–teacher conference; however, there have been sessions on stress management, understanding the families of handicapped children, preparing for mainstreaming students, and helping regular education staff members prepare for the introduction of special education programs into their buildings.

There has been a conscious effort on the part of the Parent Center staff not to "own" the parents of any particular school. In this respect, staff members try to enhance the local school personnel by providing materials and consultative services rather than intervening directly. The thrust of the Center personnel, then, has been to train, support, and assist in the maintenance of the direct relationship between teachers and parents in the education of each child.

There have been additional efforts to reach the "hard-to-reach" parents. In order to accomplish this, a series of workshops on how to negotiate the system, how to help the child build good study habits, techniques of discipline, and other topics of interest have been developed. These workshops have been presented on-site in local industries such as Digital Equipment Corporation, Public Service of New Mexico, and Sandia Laboratories during lunch periods. Employees have been encouraged to bring a brown bag lunch and to interact with the Parent Center staff.

In addition, staff members have appeared on local television and radio interview programs to provide "conference tips" to parents, and the local cable television station has permitted Center personnel to provide other informational programs. The staff has also used public service announcements, free radio and television service available to public agencies, as a way of providing tips to parents. These have been presented in the Zuni, Navajo, Spanish, and English languages.

Another technique that has been used to reach parents is a Saturday mini-conference. It is put together much like any professional conference with a welcome address by the superintendent or a designee, a keynote address, and then a series of breakout sessions. Each parent is permitted to attend two sessions. In order to facilitate the activity, parents are informed by their neighborhood school and asked to call the Parent Center to register for the conference. This gives the staff an opportunity to make sure some sessions are not overloaded and that the rooms are large enough, or to cancel sessions that do not seem to be of interest to participants.

Over 600 parents attended the first year of the conference; almost 1,000 parents preregistered the second year (1985); the third year was snowed out and had to be rescheduled. Parents were asked to evaluate their experience and each session. There seemed to be overwhelming support for the conference evidenced by positive evaluations by parents and the increase in attendance.

Rural and Sparsely Populated Areas

Eliciting parental involvement in rural, sparsely populated areas is difficult at best, and it is particularly difficult when one is dealing with a variety of cultures, such as Native Americans, Hispanic, and Anglo, in the same settings. The Mirror Model of Parental Involvement provided a structure for planning activities and services. The same basic assumptions that were made previously seemed to hold regardless of the population.

Case Management Strategies

A basic underlying respect for parents was the basis for developing a program where they could be expected to take charge of their own future. Working under this philosophy allows the parents to make cultural adjustments wherever they need to, and it does provide them with some of the knowledge and skills they may need to deal with the professionals they encounter. It could be hypothesized that all parents need some help but some parents could provide most of their own management services.

The first order of business was to develop a survey form which would include many of the problem areas or needs expressed by parents over time. Parents were asked to respond to the survey prior to any training and their responses were used to guide the workshop leaders. The most frequently mentioned areas and those that seemed to be of greatest concern to the parent centered around knowledge of IEPs, rights, and community services, and providing support to other parents.

Some of the training strategies and some of the information contained in the assumptions came about through the experience of Roberta Krehbiel and Kroth (1983) during a train-the-trainers workshop for Navajos in Gallup, NM, and Pat Putnam and Kroth in training parents in the Southern Pueblo Agency area in New Mexico. Much of the rest was developed by Kroth and Robert and Jeanelle Pasternak (Kroth, Pasternak, & Livingston-Pasternak, 1985; Pasternak, Livingston-Pasternak, & Kroth, 1984a, 1984b).

Case Management Training

Training was generally carried out using a group strategy. The following is a brief description of the materials used.

RECORD KEEPING.   One of the first things for us to keep in mind when becoming a case manager was to record the information available for one's own use or for use by another helper. A record-keeping book was developed for helping parents keep track of the information that they collected. The cover was designed by R. C. Gorman, a noted Indian artist. It was felt that the parents would keep the book for the cover if for no other reason.

Different sections were designed and pockets were provided for parents to insert records such as IEPs, reports from specialists, or just nice notes. There was a place for pictures and journal entries, and places to record telephone contacts and special helpers. As part of the workshop, parents were asked to bring any materials they had about their children. They were shown how to file the materials.

CASE MANAGEMENT GUIDE. Special care was used to prepare the guide at a sixth- or seventh-grade reading level. There are readability programs available for most computers, so we felt it was inexcusable to use materials for parents that were beyond the reading level of an "Ann Landers" newspaper column. The most difficult part of that activity was writing special education technical terms in readable language.

One short section of the guide told of the feelings that many parents experience when they find they have an exceptional child. This section was accompanied by a video tape of parents and their children, with the parents discussing what they had gone through.

A short explanation of what a developmental disability is was presented, and a list of places to contact for more information was included. This was important because many services which may be available to parents depend on the child being eligible as an exceptional child.

A section listing questions that parents should ask included a number of single sheets for different professionals and programs the parents might encounter. There was a list of questions for the audiologist, the physical therapist, or the occupational therapist, and questions the parent may want to ask about the individual plan. There was a check list for the IEP. There were also suggestions of what the parent might want to look for in a program. Each of the sections on "questions to ask" ended with "May I have a copy of your report for my files?"

A section on getting along with the program staff and hints for parent–teacher conferences helped with a critical part of the parent–professional interaction. An "information for my babysitter section" was provided, although babysitting is not as often an issue in Native American populations.

Most parents need to consider the total family. Siblings may be neglected because professionals tend to focus on the handicapped child. A pueblo mother recently related how her "normal" daughter asked why they never played together any more. This was on a trip to Albuquerque where the mother took the handicapped child regularly for therapy. As their own case manager, parents need to continually assess how they are using their resources. For instance, as was mentioned earlier, it was found that the parents were being seen by an average of 12 professionals and some by as many as 20 different people, all asking a little bit of their time.

Pamphlets on how to apply for SSI money were made available as well as immunization record cards. In addition, many organizations, such as the Red Cross and the American Heart Association, have pamphlets on first aid and CPR that were incorporated as handouts.

The materials that were used were written at an easy reading level. A number of materials were written on wallet-sized cards, such as Tips for Conferences or immunization records. One card listed important telephone numbers to call for help, numbers that were "where the buck stops," such as the Protection and Advocacy number.

To make a CEC filmstrip on "Procedural Safeguards" more meaningful, Mel Keeto, a Navajo professional, did a "voice over" in Navajo.

Continually, the trainers had to remember not to "own the parent's problems" and to provide the participants with strategies to use to get at their own answers. Parents are not a homogeneous group, but they are the major educators of their own children, and the job of professionals is to help them solve their own problems.

"Train the Trainers" Model

Parent conferencing coursework has been offered at the University of New Mexico through the 1970s and into the 1980s. The coursework was developed in recognition of the vital role that parents and teachers— working together—have in the education of the children. The content of the class centered around basic communication skills, such as the interview or conference, how to make and implement daily report card systems, and how to design handbooks. Since the target population was the classroom teacher, little time was spent on how to form and conduct group meetings.

Most special education teachers know how to formulate an individualized education plan. Writing long-term goals and short-term objectives has lost its mystery. They can manage a learning environment and the behavior of their children. They are expert in the various aspects of direct child instruction and techniques for measuring growth or lack of growth. The part of their training program is often missing is expertise in communicating this information to parents and techniques for eliciting the assistance of the parents in the education of the children (Kroth et al., 1982).

Parents have traditionally had high regard for their children's teachers, usually considering the teacher as the next most significant adult in the child's life. According to a literature review by Seligman (1979), parents view teachers in a positive light, for the most part:

> Although parents have made complaints about and widely hold negative attitudes toward professionals in general, teachers tend to be spared. . . . On the whole, parents tend to value their child's teacher as one who is generally knowledgeable, a specialist in working with children and a source of encouragement and support. (pp. 31–32)

Since teachers are held in such high regard, it is unfortunate that parent–teacher interaction techniques are not a typical part of the teacher training curriculum.

Developing the "Course in a Box"

Because of the rural nature of New Mexico and other southwestern states, there was a need to design a transportable course to provide instructors with some training and skills in working with other teachers. The concept of a multiplying effect dictated that training those who were in a position to train teachers might be efficacious. Therefore, the target group became college staff and staff development personnel, although teachers, counselors, and parents were not excluded.

The "box" contained a training manual, with directions on delivery of lectures (audio tapes were included), transparencies, and handouts. Instructional materials were identified, and a variety of activities to provide the participants with learning experiences were outlined. There was enough material, with timelines for presentations, to provide an instructor with a 2-credit-hour course.

For the purpose of designing a delivery system, six individuals were selected as a working advisory committee. These were people who (1) had demonstrated leadership and experience in university training programs of parent education, (2) had publications in the area of parent involvement, and (3) could serve as members of a network core of trainers. The following professionals served as advisors and trainers for the Institute's "Strategies for Effective Parent–Teacher Interaction" module: Dr. Ray Dembinski, Northern Illinois State University; Dr. Denzil Edge, University of Louisville; Dr. Kay Hartwell, Arizona State University; Dr. Jennifer Olson, University of Idaho; Dr. Richard Simpson, University of Kansas; and Dr. Bill Wagonseller, University of Nevada at Las Vegas.

This committee has provided assistance in the development of materials and recruitment of participants throughout the project.

Effects of the Program

It is difficult to determine the far-reaching effects of the program because of the intentional attempt to multiply. For instance, a prime example of the multiplying effects is Project Enrich in Kentucky. Staff from the State Department of Special Education have trained hundreds of trainers; they estimate that over 5,000 teachers and parents will have benefited from training in a 4-year period. The training is still going on in Kentucky.

Lita Aldridge, from Gallaudet College, was one of the early trainees. In her role as outreach director for the Special School of the Future, she has conducted training sessions throughout the United States and Canada. One of the early summer sessions conducted at Gallaudet College received a special award. Some of the materials have been translated into Spanish and have been used in Gallaudet's outreach efforts in Central and South America.

Course Content

The course content in many ways follows *Communicating with Parents of Exceptional Children,* (Kroth, 1975, 1985). The major topics are the following:

1. Values system. Teachers need to understand their own value system and to realize the heterogeneity of the value systems of the parents they work with. There are a variety of activities that help with this knowledge.

2. Family dynamics. Most teachers and professionals need to become more aware of what having a handicapped child in the family is like and the effects on all of the members of the family. There is some literature and some video tapes that help. The use of parent panels is also explored.

3. Communication techniques. Since not all parents can attend school functions or work as closely s school personnel might hope for, a variety of other forms of communication are presented. Parents appreciate receiving notes, phone calls, handbooks, daily or weekly report cards, and other forms of information.

4. Informational needs of parents. Teachers are taught how to write public service announcements and develop informational handbooks on such items as summer programs, community resources, field trips for parents and their children, and books to read.

5. Conferencing skills. These include listening skills as well as techniques for presenting growth information to parents. Since all teachers must hold conferences, considerable emphasis is placed on these skills.

6. Legal information. The whole issue of informed consent and parents' rights still seems a little cloudy to most educators. Program changes are made without informing parents. IEPs are written before parents come to meetings, and parents are merely asked to sign. Due-process procedures are not explained and sometimes not followed. Higher levels of informed involvement are encouraged.

Over the years there seems to be an increased interest in parent involvement and effective parent–teacher interaction. To perpetuate the original mission of the Institute and the trainers, the "course in a box" was put on a pay-as-you-go basis when federal funds ceased. Participants are charged a fee for materials and training. All in all, the programs that have been described have often been started on federal money, but have continued after the original grants were stopped. In many ways that has been the strongest evaluation statement.

Summary and Conclusions

Working with parents and professionals who work with parents is rewarding and exciting. The program described above is primarily a school-based program located in a large school district with tentacles reaching out into the state and dealing with many diverse cultures.

The advantage of working in the school environment is that one quickly has to be reality based. One has almost immediate feedback as to whether programs and services are viable. As one trainer said, "Parents vote with their feet. They walk out or don't come back."

Any parent–professional involvement program is based on some assumptions about one's target population and the resources of the deliverers of service. The assumptions of the Parent Center and the Mirror Model of Parent Involvement are obvious and straightforward and are discussed early in this chapter.

The Mirror Model is a framework for designing programs. It is useful in helping monitor one's activities to make sure that the most people are being served most of the time. For instance, it was useful to realize 13–20% of the adult population is functionally illiterate. The reading level and format of materials have to be capable of communicating to all parents, which is required by law.

Another strategy was to help parents become their own case managers.

This required the deliverers of service to remember that many parents can take care of most of their needs if they are taught a strategy. Some parents only need a little information while others need a great deal of support, but they all do not need to be taught the same things.

Frequently, trainers need to go to the "market place." As a result, arrangements were made to provide some training from time to time for parents during brown bag sessions at their places of employment.

Working in Parent Involvement in a large school district is like having a big laboratory for a scientist. There are so many opportunities to try new and different programs. Since the task is overwhelming in the first place, this gives the creator a chance to create different ways to get the job done. As one special educator used to say, "Try another way!"

References

Bell, R. Q. (1968). A reinterpretation of the direction of effects in studies of socialization. *Psychological Review, 75*, 81–95.

Bell, R. Q., & Harper, L. V. (1977). *Child effects on adults*. Hillsdale, NJ: Erlbaum.

Black, K. N. (1979, January). What about the child from a one-parent home? *Teacher*, pp. 24–28.

Bridge, R. G. (1976). Parent participation in school innovation. *Teachers College Record, 77*, 366–384.

Canter, L., & Canter, M. (1982). *Assertive discipline for parents*. Santa Monica, CA: Harper & Row.

Casey, R. (1983). *The relationship between school performance during residential treatment and post-discharge school adjustment of emotionally disturbed children*. Unpublished doctoral dissertation, University of New Mexico, Albuquerque.

Coletta, A. (1977). *Working together: A guide to parent involvement*. Atlanta, GA: Humanities Unlimited.

Cooper, J. O., & Edge, D. (1978). *Parenting strategies and educational methods*. Columbus, OH: Charles E. Merrill.

Dembinski, R. J., & Mauser, A. J. (1977). What parents of the learning disabled really want from professionals. *Journal of Learning Disabilities, 10*(9), 49–56.

Dembinski, R. J., & Mauser, A. J. (1978). Parents of the gifted: Perceptions of psychologists and teachers. *Journal for Education of the Gifted, 1*(2), 5–14.

Doernberg, N. (1978). Some negative effects on family integration of health and educational services for young handicapped children. *Rehabilitation Literature, 39*(4), 107–110.

Dominquez, J. C. (1982). *The effects of training on special education teachers' perceptions, knowledge, and interactions with parents*. Unpublished doctoral dissertation, University of New Mexico, Albuquerque.

Glenn, H. S., & Warner, J. W. (1982). *Developing capable young people*. Hurst, TX: Humansphere.

Guerney, B. G. (1969). *Psychotherapeutic agents: New roles for non-professional, parents, and teachers*. New York: Holt, Rinehart & Winston.

Hamner, T., & Turner, P. (1985). *Parenting in contemporary society*. Englewood Cliffs, NJ: Prentice-Hall.

Hobbs, N. (1978). Classification options: A conversation with Nicholas Hobbs on exceptional child education. *Exceptional Children, 44,* 494–497.

Korsch, B. M., & Negrete, V. F. (1972). Doctor–patient communication. *Scientific American, 227,* 66–74.

Kroth, R. (1985). *Communicating with parents of exceptional chidren* (2nd ed.) Denver: Love.

Kroth, R. L., & Krehbiel, R. (1983). *Parent–teacher interaction.* Washington, DC: American Association of Colleges for Teacher Education.

Kroth, R., & Otteni, H. (1983). Parent education programs that work: A model. *Focus on Exceptional Children, 15*(8), 1–16.

Kroth, R., Otteni, H., & Parks, P. (1982). Parent involvement: A challenge for teacher training institutions. *Building an alliance for children,* pp. 181–205.

Kroth, R., Pasternak, R., & Livingston-Pasternak, J. (1985). *Teaching parents of handicapped children to be their own case managers: A model for rural areas.* Unpublished manuscript.

Kroth, R., & Scholl, G. T. (1978). *Getting schools involved with parents.* Reston, VA: Council for Exceptional Children.

Kroth, R., & Simpson, R. L. (1977). *Parent conferences as a teaching strategy.* Denver: Love.

Lille, D., & Place, P. (1982). *Partners: A guide to working with schools for parents of children with special instructional needs.* Glenview, IL: Scott, Foresman.

Pasternak, R., Livingston-Pasternak, J., & Kroth, R. (1984a). *A parents guide to case management.* Taos, NM: ENSENAR.

Pasternak, R., Livingston-Pasternak, J., & Kroth, R. (1984b). *Growing up: The first five years.* Taos, NM: ENSENAR.

Rutherford, R. B., & Edgar, E. (1979). *Teachers and parents: A guide to interaction and cooperation.* Boston: Allyn & Bacon.

Seligman, M. (1979). *Strategies for helping parents of exceptional children.* New York: Free Press.

Simpson, R. L. (1982). *Conferencing parents of exceptional children.* Rockville, MD: Aspen Systems.

Smith, D. D. (1984). *Effective discipline: A positive approach to discipline for educators in all settings.* Austin, TX: Pro-ed.

Wagonseller, B., Burnett, M., Salzberg, B., & Burnett, J. (1977). *The art of parenting.* Champaign, IL: Research Press.

Wagonseller, F., & McDowell, R. (1982). *Teaching involved parenting.* Champaign, IL: Research Press.

Wallerstein, J. S., & Kelly, J. B. (1979). Children and divorce: A review. *Social Work, 24,* 468–475.

Wattenberg, E., & Reinhardt, H. (1979). Female-headed families: Trends and implications. *Social Work, 24,* 460–466.

Williams, B. (1983). *Diagnostician–parent communication.* Unpublished doctoral dissertation, University of New Mexico, Albuquerque.

7

Parent Participation in Individualized Educational Program (IEP) Conferences: A Case for Individualization

Richard L. Simpson
Craig R. Fiedler

Introduction

Public Law 94-142, the Education for All Handicapped Children Act, guarantees not only the right to a free and appropriate education for all children with disabilities, it also ensures the continuous involvement of parents in educational planning, decision making, and implementation. This clearly stated policy of support for parent involvement represents a radical departure from past attitudes and practices. Historically, parents have often been blamed for their children's educational problems and isolated from professional decision making concerning the development and welfare of their disabled children (Donnellan & Mirenda, 1984; Karnes & Lee, 1980). In contrast, current policies and practices of allowing and encouraging parent involvement in educational matters which affect their children are mandated and ensure a certain level of involvement for all parents. It is ironic that even though our parent involvement policies have changed drastically, the individual needs and concerns of parents and families are still largely neglected or misunderstood. This chapter focuses on ways to individualize parent (or family) involvement in the education of children with disabilities. In particular, we address policies and practices for involving parents in individualized Education Program (IEP) conferences, as such meetings represent the most typical interactions between parents and school personnel. The chapter provides a rationale and implementation guidelines for an individualized approach to parent IEP conference involvement. Specifically, we discuss (1) the historical development of parent IEP involvement; (2) the legal bases (as stated in P.L. 94-142) for parent involvement; (3) the need (rationale) for individualizing parent IEP involvement; (4) requirements

The Second Handbook on Parent Education

for an individualized parent involvement approach; and (5) procedures and suggestions for individualizing parent IEP involvement before, during, and after the IEP conference.

A Brief History of Parent Involvement

Gaining a historical perspective on parent involvement in IEP conferences requires an understanding of the forces that have affected both parent–child and home–school relationships. Major among these are societal factors and governmental policy as enacted through federal legislation.

In the early years of our country's history, the economy was basically agrarian and families lived together, worked together, played together, and learned together. Family influences on the children were many, whereas outside influences were few. The Industrial Revolution, however, changed family life dramatically. The amount of interaction between parents and their children decreased and families no longer were the focal point of information dissemination to the children. Instead, the influences on children by outside forces, particularly the public schools (Lombana, 1983), increased dramatically. Since 1950, further sociologic, economic, and educational changes have impacted both parents and the public schools, resulting in major changes of their relationships. Some of the major societal forces behind these changes include technological advances, changes in values, increase in the number of working mothers and single parents, family mobility, and busing (Lombana, 1983; Simpson, 1982).

Concurrent with the aforementioned general societal changes which affected parents of both disabled and nondisabled children, the prevailing practice of caring for disabled children underwent significant changes. During the first half of this century the predominant practice was to institutionalize severely (and often not-so-severely) handicapped children. As Turnbull and Winton (1984, p. 378) remark,

Institutionalization as a form of treatment was recommended to promote positive outcomes for the family (e.g., "a mongoloid child is seen as having a destructive impact upon the family") as well as positive outcomes for the child (e.g., "the child is presumably much better off and happier in an institution"). Furthermore, the role of parents was clearly to adhere to the recommendation of the physician rather than to participate in the decision-making process.

Through the advocacy of parent organizations such as the National Association for Retarded Citizens (NARC, now known as the Association for Retarded Citizens/USA), governmental policy began to recognize the participatory rights of parents in educational decision making. Thus, NARC published an Educational Bill of Rights for the Retarded Child as a policy statement in 1954 (Boggs, 1978). As an indication of parental concern for this active involvement as decision makers, the following statement was contained in the NARC Bill of Rights: "And [the child's] parents have the right to determine for themselves, on the basis of competent advice, the course of care, training, and treatment, among those open to them which they believe best for their family; and to have their decisions respected by others" (NARC, 1954, cited in Boggs, 1978, p. 60).

In their analysis of governmental parent-involvement policy, Turnbull and Winton (1984) identify two prevalent perspectives. The first arose out of what has been referred to as the *cultural deficit model,* according to which parents were viewed as deficient in essential child-rearing knowledge and skills. Consequently, they were considered to be in need of remediation and their role was that of learner. A second, politically focused, perspective viewed parents of lower economic status as lacking in opportunities for decision making and political advocacy.

Consistent with this view, parents were to be empowered with a heightened sensitivity to the political process and the role of assertive advocacy in affecting governmental policies. Furthermore, the role of parents as decision makers was legitimized by granting them equal status as decision-making participants. The first federal legislation which implemented a policy of parent involvement was P. L. 89-794, which instituted Headstart programs (Wiegerink, Hocutt, Posante-Lorne, & Bristol, 1980). This law required parents to participate not only as learners and teachers, but also as decision makers. Another example of governmental policy in the area of parent involvement can be found in P.L. 90-538, which authorized the Handicapped Children's Early Education Program (HCEEP). Federal regulations specified the following modes for parent involvement:

1. parent assistance in the planning, development, operation, and evaluation of a project;
2. parent training as a project component;
3. parent participation in educational and therapeutic components of the project; and
4. opportunity for parents to advise and assist in information dissemination concerning the project. (Turnbull & Winton, 1984)

P.L. 94-142 Parent Involvement Provisions

Although precedents for parent involvement had been established in earlier federal legislation, the most significant event shaping current parent roles was the enactment of P.L. 94-142, The Education for All Handicapped Children Act, in 1975. With this law, parents were given participatory rights with regard to their children's education—rights which the public schools never before had to recognize or allow. Some of these include parents' right to be a part of the process of evaluating their child; challenge the accuracy of their child's evaluation, program, or placement; give or withhold consent to initial evaluation or placement; have access to school records; participate in public hearings on the state special education plan; and plan their child's educational program (i.e., participate in writing the IEP). According to Turnbull, Turnbull, and Wheat (1982), Congress provides for parent participation under P.L. 94-142 for two reasons: (1) parent participation was seen to be helpful to disabled children, their parents, and the schools; and (2) parent participation was made an enforceable right based on the belief that parents should not be relegated to assuming that their children were being properly evaluated. That is, parents were viewed as the most natural advocates to ensure that the schools would comply with all legal requirements and provide a free and appropriate education to all disabled children. Based on an investigation of the act's legislative history, Turnbull et al. (1982) identified the following three assumptions which underlay its passage: (1) parents should make decisions about their children's education, (2) parent participation would ensure that schools satisfy their legal obligations to children, and (3) parents can and would be their children's teachers.

As an ideal goal these assumptions are commendable; as a requirement or realistic expectation for all parents, however, they are seriously flawed. A brief review of studies on parents' roles in IEP conferences confirms that parent-stated preferences and actions differ significantly from the policy of P.L. 94-142, which envisions an active, as opposed to a passive, parent role. For example, even though parent attendance at IEP meetings is fairly high (Goldstein, Strickland, Turnbull, & Curry, 1980; Marver & David, 1978; National Committee for Citizens in Education, 1979), parent participation in actual decision making is limited. Undoubtedly, some of this parental passivity in educational planning and decision making is the result of a lack of knowledge (Goldstein et al., 1980), parental discomfort in such school interactions (Dembinski & Mauser, 1977), confusion about the parental role in the educational decision-making process (Hoff, Fenton, Yoshida, & Kaufman, 1978), and general noninvolvement in educational meetings (Mitchell, 1976). In addition, many parents prefer to receive and confirm information at IEP meetings as opposed to assuming an assertive role (Turnbull & Turnbull, 1982). Such a parental need to take a break from full-time educational responsibility for their child has been confirmed in a study by Winton and Turnbull (1981). For example, one upper-middle-class mother, who previously had been actively involved in an early intervention program, stated:

> A lot of times I get tired of having a role—God. I don't want to solve that—I'm paying you to take him for three hours and, lady, make it work! Maybe that's a nasty attitude toward teachers but I kind of feel that way sometimes. It's not worth it to me if I have to figure it out—I might as well have him with me at those times. (p. 15)

In a review of research on parents' participation in IEP conferences, Turnbull (1983) concluded, "It is clear that the current level of parent participation in IEP conferences can more accurately be described as passive rather than active" (p. 111). Yet, in many of the cited studies, parents reported a high level of satisfaction with their IEP involvement. The results of a growing body of research should cause us to question the underlying assumptions of P.L. 94-142 parent-involvement policies as applied to all parents. Thus, Turnbull and Turnbull (1982) have advocated that "Rather than mandating that all parents be equal participants with the school personnel to make decisions jointly, public policy should tolerate a range of parent involvement choices and options, matched to the needs and interests of the parents" (p. 120).

While P.L. 94-142 has effectively promoted an individualized perspective toward all children with disabilities, ironically it has not applied the same emphasis on individualization to parents. According to MacMillan and Turnbull (1983), parents should be entitled to a comfortable level of participation in their child's education. Therefore, decisions about the degree of parent involvement in IEP conferences should be made on the basis of individual preferences rather than generalized expectations.

Rationale for Individualizing Parent Involvement

Our rationale for individualizing parent (family) involvement in IEP conferences is based on our three major assumptions:

1. All parents (families) are unique in terms of their interest in and ability to be involved in their child's educational program. Families are heterogeneous groups with varying degrees of energy, time, resources, knowledge, skills, and other commitments.

2. Educational policies and practices should tolerate and encourage a range of parent involvement options matched to the needs and interests of each family.

3. More involvement by parents in IEP conference-related activities is not necessarily better involvement.

The first assumption is based on family systems theory, that is, all parts of the family are interrelated and events affecting one member of the family affect all others (Carter & McGoldrich, 1980; Hoffman, 1980). Turnbull, Summers, and Brotherson (1983) applied a family-systems approach to families with disabled children. Their conceptual framework for understanding and working with families is shown in Fig. 7.1. Their model consists of three components—family structure, family functions, and family life cycle—that shape family interaction, the central core of the system. We briefly outline each component with an emphasis on the need for involving parents on an individualized basis in their child's education, including IEP conference participation.

Family Structure

The diverse family compositional structures must be recognized when developing an individualize approach to parent involvement. For example, families vary according to membership characteristics, cultural style, and ideological style.

Family membership characteristics are determined by the family's size, individual member characteristics, and level of extrafamilial support. Primarily, family membership characteristics determine the needs and resources of a given family unit. For example, the needs of a single-parent family of five children are likely to be different from those of a two-parent family with only one child. Furthermore, extrafamilial support, such as relatives or close family friends, can have a significant impact on the availability and desire of parents to participate in their handicapped child's education. A family with substantial extrafamilial support to meet the burdens of daily care needs which a disabled child presents is likely to be in a better position (emotionally and physically) to actively participate in educational activities.

Families are also influenced by cultural and ideological factors, which greatly shape their values and perspectives on their disabled child's current and future needs. Parents react differently to the stress of coping with a disabled child. Some may become immersed in their child's educational program. Other parents, for equally valid reasons, may need to distance themselves from their child's school program. Both ap-

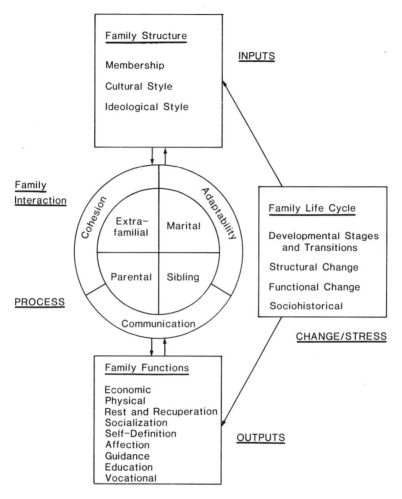

Figure 7.1. Family systems conceptual framework.

proaches can be effective coping strategies and should be treated with equal respect.

It is also important to consider a family's socioeconomic status when determining the educational involvement needs and support of particular parents. For instance, a financially struggling family may not be able to afford to become actively involved in their child's education. Instead, they may be working two jobs or taking on as much overtime as possible. In all likelihood, they will not be able to function as active educational decision makers or as teachers for their child. Rather, they are likely to be preoccupied with the priority of meeting the financial needs of maintaining their household.

Family Interaction

Family interaction, another component of the family systems framework presented here, involves the constant interplay among individual family members. The traditional nuclear family consists of four distinct subsystems: (1) marital (husband/wife), (2) parental (child/parent), (3) sibling (child/child), and (4) extrafamilial (interactions of entire family or individual members with others, including neighbors, friends, work associates, and professionals). Events affecting any of the four subsystems inevitably are felt by all family members. The parent involvement provisions in P.L. 94-142 maintain an exclusive focus on the disabled child witout considering potential effects on other family members. For example, in discussing the assumption that parents can and will be their child's teachers (at home), Turnbull et al. (1983) note:

> Consider the example of a mother who has agreed to work on a home training program in the area of feeding with her severely retarded child. Allowing her child to feed himself triples the time involved in each meal. While the mother is working with the child on feeding, her dinner conversation with her husband and other children is substantially limited. After the other family members finish dinner, the father cleans the kitchen and the siblings proceed to their homework all feeling that some of their needs have been overlooked. Meanwhile, the mother is feeling isolated from the rest of her family and frustrated over all the tasks to which she must attend before midnight. (p. 5)

The interaction of the four family subsystems is based on cohesion, adaptability, and communication (Olson, Russell, & Sprenkle, 1980). *Cohesion* refers to the force by which family members are held together. If a family is to function on a healthy level (i.e., adequately meet the needs of all family members), its subsystems should avoid enmeshment or disengagement in regard to the disabled family member. An enmeshed family situation is characterized by overconcern and overinvolvement by the parents, for example, in their disabled child's education. Such overinvolvement typically comes at the expense of the other family subsystems (e.g., siblings feel neglected by their parents). On the other hand, families must also avoid becoming disengaged. Disengaged families maintain rigid boundaries between subsystems, resulting in poor communication and, frequently, little family unity or loyalty. Another determinant of family subsystem interaction refers to the family's ability to conform to new or changed circumstances. If parent-involvement practices were truly individualized, school personnel would recognize that some parents are more effective at planning changes in educational programming than others. Consequently, a continuum of parent-involvement options should be available.

The last major component of the family interactional system is communication. Fully functioning families must be able to communicate openly by sending clear messages, listening with genuine interest, and providing constructive feedback. As discussed later in this chapter, educators should model appropriate communication skills in their interactions with parents. Effective communication is a prerequisite to ensuring a family's preferred level of educational involvement and should be accurately modeled and understood by school personnel.

Family Functioning

The tasks a family performs are referred to as *functions,* or outputs, of the family system. A family serves the collective and individual needs of its members by carrying out the following nine functions: economic, physical, rest and recuperation, socialization, self definition, affection, guidance, education, and vocation. Without specifically addressing each of these functions, it is important to note that education is but one of the functions which a family must concern itself with in order to remain a viable entity. Overemphasis or overinvolvement in one family function seriously erodes the family's capacity to effectively address needs in the other areas. Parents' lack of active involvement in educational programs as advocates or teachers of their child does not imply that they are not involved with their children in meeting needs in other functional areas (MacMillan & Turnbull, 1983). Therefore, a realistic parent educational-involvement policy would recognize that some parents may have to delegate full educational responsibility to the schools to allow themselves additional time to respond to their disabled child's needs in other functional areas or to their own needs, as well as those of other family members.

Family Life Cycle

The final component of the family systems framework, family life cycle, is described by Goldenberg and Goldenberg (1980) as "successive patterns within the continuity of family living over the years of its existence—with members aging and passing through a succession of family roles" (p. 14). There are two fundamental reasons that school personnel must be aware of the life-cycle events that impact families of disabled children (Benson & Turnbull, 1985). First, life-cycle events clarify the changing nature of the family's needs and characteristics over time. For instance, a recently divorced parent would probably have substantially less time and energy to be actively involved in the child's education than when the family was functioning as a two-parent household. Second, a knowledge of family life-cycle events heightens educators' sensitivity to the sources of stress that impact the family. Again, parents experiencing stressful times will undoubtedly expend their personal resources in the area(s) that cause them the most stress. Consequently, their educational involvement may assume a lower priority, at least temporarily.

Families usually experience four types of change throughout their life cycle: (1) developmental stages and transitions, (2) structural change, (3) functional change, and (4) sociohistorical change (Turnbull, Summers, & Brotherson, 1986).

Developmental changes refer to major life events that impact families as their members age, including such stages as couple, childbearing, school age, adolescence, postparental family, and aging. A movement from one stage to another leads to transition periods, which are frequently accompanied by considerable stress. With stress comes changing needs and capabilities for parental involvement in certain areas of family functioning. As mentioned, this may lead to reduced or increased parent involvement in educational matters. In this connection, it is important that educators do not consider a reduced level of parent involvement to be indicative of parental disregard for their child's education. Indeed, such a parental response may be a logical way of handling transitional periods in their family's life cycle.

Structural changes in the family include institutionalization or deinstitutionalization of a member, death, divorce, birth, or unemployment. Stress is again comonly associated with such changes.

Functional change occurs when a family changes the way it fulfills its functions. Families with disabled children (especially severely disabled) often must make functional changes which so-called normal families typically do not need to consider. For example, severely disabled children are usually not capable of caring for themselves and contributing to the household in the same manner as nondisabled children, who assume increasingly more responsibility as they grow older. When one family member is unable to help fulfill the needs of the family, more responsibility is placed on the remaining family members. Therefore, parents of disabled children tend to have more functional responsibilities at home and are often less capable of assuming active educational responsibilities.

Sociohistorical change was defined by Benson and Turnbull (1985) as "effected by cultural and political trends, the state of the economy, and formative events such as natural disasters and participation in activist movements'' (p. 147). In this respect, educators must be aware that certain educational trends (e.g., mainstreaming, learning in natural environments) may not be met with the same degree of enthusiasm by different parents due to dissimilar value orientations or parental concern or fear of the unknown. Parent involvement in educational decision making would be greatly facilitated if school personnel recognized and respected the impact of certain sociohistorical changes on parents and families.

Levels of Potential Parent Involvement

If a range of parent-involvement options is to become a reality, such involvement must be available at several levels. The following seven potential parent-involvement levels (Turnbull et al., 1983) are offered as examples of the direction in which educational policies and practices must proceed to achieve this goal. As illustrated in Fig. 7.2, the suggested levels of potential parent involvement are not hierarchical, that is, active involvement is not necessarily better for a particular parent. Instead, the needs, interests, dynamics, and abilities of parents and the entire family must be matched to the most appropriate level of involvement. The seven

Figure 7.2. Levels of potential parent involvement in IEP conference-related activities.

levels of potential parent involvement will be used as a framework for assisting families in selecting preferred levels of involvement.

1. Attendance and approval of teacher priorities. Parents attend IEP meetings, receive feedback about their child, and receive and approve proposed IEP goals.

2. Sharing information. Parents provide information to the educational staff regarding, for example, their child's current level of functioning within the family, effective and ineffective teaching strategies, preferred and nonpreferred activities.

3. Suggesting goals. Parents suggest specific skills or goals that they would like to see incorporated into the educational program.

4. Negotiating goals. When differences of opinion arise, parents and educational staff negotiate to agreement on IEP goals and implementation strategies.

5. Collaboratively analyzing and monitoring implementation. After reaching agreement on the IEP, parents help monitor day-to-day performance to assure achievement of goals, help include new goals when performance criteria are met, and reexamine goals that are not being met for respecification of goals or procedures.

6. Joint programming. Parents select specific IEP goals that they will implement in the home and/or in community settings, simultaneously and in cooperation with the school's implementation of the goal.

7. Independent programming. Parents undertake training in the home or in the community of educational goals that are not being trained at school.

The various levels of parent educational involvement are further illustrated in the following vignettes describing parent–school IEP-related interactions.

LEVEL 1: ATTENDANCE AND APPROVAL OF TEACHER PRIORITIES. Mr. and Mrs. Smith both work full-time to make ends meet for their family of seven children. The youngest child, Marie, has Down's Syndrome and attends a special education class at a local junior high school. Marie's teacher corresponds daily with the Smiths via a spiral notebook. Similarly, Mr. and Mrs. Smith write messages to the teacher in the notebook. Recently, the Smiths were asked to attend a school meeting to discuss Marie's educational program. They were unable to attend but sent a letter outlining their concerns for educational goals and objectives for the upcoming school year.

LEVEL 2: SHARING INFORMATION. John's special education teacher requests a home visit to meet with his mother. John and his family are new to the school district and little information is available on John's past educational performance and family history. During the home visit, John's teacher asks his mother many questions. John's mother cheerfully talks about his previous schools and teachers, his problems and frustrations in school, his out-of-school activities, and his medical history.

LEVEL 3: SUGGESTING GOALS. Mr. and Mrs. Jones were dissatisfied with their son's special education program last year. They felt that there was too much emphasis on purely academic tasks, and that what their son needed was prevocational and vocational training since he would be graduating from high school in 3 years. This year, Mr. and Mrs. Jones have vowed to avert a disaster similar to that of the previous year. In preparation for the initial meeting with their son's new teacher, Mr. and Mrs. Jones have talked to their son and together made a list of five skills that they would like the school to address.

LEVEL 4: NEGOTIATING GOALS. Mrs. Quinn has asked a friend to come with her to a meeting concerning her daughter's educational program. Mrs. Quinn wants some support at this meeting since she knows the school will have five or six people there, and she is afraid of being intimidated and getting upset and confused. At the meeting, Mrs. Quinn requests that speech therapy be provided for her daughter. The school psychologist informs Mrs. Quinn that it was the evaluation team's consensus that such services were not necessary and, furthermore, the school's speech pathologist already had an overwhelming caseload. Mrs. Quinn, with the assistance of her friend, remains firm in maintaining the importance of this service. At the very least, Mrs. Quinn argues, a speech pathologist ought to be able to develop some programming and provide consultation to the classroom teacher. After much discussion, the school psychologist agrees to provide speech therapy services once a week with consultation to the classroom teacher.

LEVEL 5: COLLABORATIVELY ANALYZING AND MONITORING IMPLEMENTATION. William Duffy is 13 years old and has moderate-to-severe mental retardation. Since his enrollment in the public schools 8 years ago,

William has attended a self-contained classroom for trainable mentally retarded children. William's parents have always tried to work closely with his teachers to insure his continued development. Mr. and Mrs. Duffy know exactly what educational goals and objectives are being pursued with William. Many of the educational objectives involve self-care skills (e.g., dressing, eating, laundry, grooming) which William works on at home. Mr. and Mrs. Duffy have devised an evaluation sheet on which they write anecdotal accounts and other pertinent information summarizing William's performance on educational objectives carried out in the home.

LEVEL 6: JOINT PROGRAMMING. At the last educational planning meeting to develop Jane Welch's school program, both her parents and participating school personnel agreed upon a number of specific objectives for the current school year. Jane is 15 years old and enrolled in a high school SMH program. Mr. and Mrs. Welch are most concerned about Jane's tantruming (when she does not get her way) and her bed-wetting. Jane's teacher employs behavioral techniques in meeting these two educational objectives while Jane is at school. However, Jane exhibits these two behaviors quite often at home. In an effort to improve Jane's functioning in both environments—school and home—Jane's parents have requested assistance from the school so that they may carry out behavioral programming for Jane at home.

LEVEL 7: INDEPENDENT PROGRAMMING. Jill Davis is 18 years old and lives with her parents and three siblings. Jill attends a public school program for students with severe mental retardation (a TMR program). Jill's parents are actively trying to prepare Jill for the day when she will no longer attend public school (when she turns 21 years old) and might be employed at a sheltered workshop and reside in a group home or supervised apartment living arrangement. As part of their efforts, Mr. and Mrs. Davis and their other children take Jill out into the community as often as possible. Currently, the Davis family is teaching Jill how to ride the local bus and how to plan, shop, and prepare some basic meals.

More Parent Involvement Is Not Necessarily Better Involvement

Through a truly individualized approach to parent involvement in their child's education, school personnel should be able to recognize and respect the unique needs of every parent and, consequently, establish a variety of appropriate training and involvement activities. Parents should be able to receive information and assistance to help them move from one level of involvement to another as dictated by changes in time and energy for educational participation as a result of various life cycles. It is a false and destructive dichotomy for educators to imply that "good" parents are actively involved (*actively* as defined by school personnel's expectations for parents) in their child's education and that "less than active" involvement is indicative of "bad" parents. Expecting families to exhibit greater involvement than they are able may have detrimental effects on both the child and the parents. Therefore, careful consideration of possible benefits and detriments to both parents and children must be a part of identifying the most appropriate level of parent educational involvement.

Establishing an Appropriate Level of Parent Involvement

In any attempt at determining the appropriate level of parent involvement, two major factors must be considered: (1) parent and family needs and (2) parents' preferred level of involvement. While no precise assessment formula exists, general decision-making guidelines may be applied.

Parental and family needs will, at least in part, be assessed by means of the family-system model discussed previously. In particular, family structure, parent and family functions, parent and family interactions, and family cycles will yield an understanding of involvement potential.

Assessment of *family structure* is faciliated by consideration of (1) family makeup; (2) family characteristics, including ages and sex of members, socioeconomic and educational background, religious affiliation, and ethnicity; (3) nature and severity of the exceptional child's disability; and (4) available resources for responding to the disability, including economic, family, and community.

Assessment of parent and *family functions* focuses on the handicapped child's disability relative to family members' performance of role functions. Needed information in this domain may be derived from considering the impact of the handicapped child's disability on the performance of duties within and outside the home and restrictions associated with the disability, including financial, recreational, custodial, and personal.

Parent and family interactions relative to the exceptional family member may be assessed by studying the emotional climate of the family, including level of family communication, support, and involvement; decision-making processes within the family; and level of understanding and degree of support of exceptional family member.

Finally, the *family cycle* analysis revolves around the role of the exceptional child as a family member and expectations for his or her future. Specifically, the degree to which family members respond to the exceptional child in an age-appropriate manner and family members' expectations for the exceptional child may be considered.

Via this family systems analysis, educators will gain an understanding of parents needs and concerns related to raising an exceptional child. Although interpretations of these data are vulnerable to the values and perceptions of individual educators, they will serve as a basis for better understanding parent's involvement potential.

Even more important than professionals' analysis of parents' needs is a consideration of parents' desired involvement level. Too often parents have reported encountering little flexibility in the degree to which they are expected to be involved in their exceptional child's education (Kroth, 1985). Educators must communicate to parents that a variety of participating levels is acceptable. Such an emphasis on direct communication should not be interpreted to mean that parents must specify, at an initial conference, to what degree they will be involved in their child's education, including participation in IEP meetings. Rather, the intent is for educators not to rigidly establish the same participation expectations for all parents at all times, but to tolerate a variety of participation levels. Additionally, educators may observe parents' level of participation as a basis for discussing with them whether or not their behavior reflects the desired degree of involvement. In instances where parents express a desire to change their involvement level and where change is considered appropriate based upon other information (e.g., family systems assessment), strategies for adjusting participation levels may be presented. Thus, combined, results of family systems assessment and establishment of parents' preferred level of involvement will enhance appropriate individualization of parent participation in school-related activities.

Conditions for Cooperative and Individualized Parent Involvement

Educators' Attitudes and Training

Educators, parents, and legal authorities continue to struggle to define and clarify the meaning and parameters of the Education for All Handicapped Children Act. However, in spite of the difficulty involved in interpreting this enactment, it was soon recognized that parent–educator cooperation is something that extends beyond legislation and that interpersonal, not legislative, conditions are the basis of cooperative involvement. In particular, four interpersonal factors appear fundamental to establishing cooperative and productive parent–educator relationships: (1) willingness to listen, (2) recognition of trust as a basic element of cooperation, (3) knowledge and acceptance of individual values, and (4) willingness to accommodate a partnership relationship. These conditions apply to all participation levels. That is, regardless of the degree of involvement, parents will respond to the interpersonal conditions established by educators.

WILLINGNESS TO LISTEN

Listening to parents is the most fundamental way in which educators can communicate interest and willingness to accept parents as educational partners. Yet it remains a relatively undeveloped skill as illustrated in the following description of an IEP conference by the mother of a recently diagnosed learning-disabled child. The meeting was attended by 11 persons, all of whom were professional educators except the parent. The mother reported that while she was introduced as "Larry's mother," other participants were introduced neither by name nor title. She also noted that she was the only person in the room without an information folder. According to Larry's mother, the other participants were absorbed throughout the session with the contents of their folders such that they provided little eye contact or personal attention. Further, she reported feeling like a nonentity because her name was only mentioned in a third-person context, for example, "according to the mother . . . ," "Mrs. Tyler indicated to me that . . . ," On one occasion the other IEP participants discussed what Mrs. Tyler had meant by a statement to a school psychologist without ever seeking clarification directly from her. According to this parent, the meeting could have been held without her; in fact, for all practical purposes, it was.

Although it might be argued that the unfortunate circumstances of the above encounter are atypical, there is every indication that parents attending group educational conferences, including IEP meetings, are provided less than optimal listening environments. Thus, such settings fail to communicate to parents that their input is not only accepted, but needed, regardless of verbal messages to the contrary.

Increasingly, the power of listening is being recognized. Japanese businessmen, known for efficiency and quality products, suggest that a salient correlate of such outcomes is an atmosphere of allowing their workers to be heard and involved. Peters and Waterman, in *In Search of Excellence* (1982), also observed that the most successful businesses are those that listen to and work closely with their consumers. Although schools and educational programs differ from profit-oriented businesses, the importance of listening applies equally to both situations: Only with an acceptable listening atmosphere will parents be optimally functional and cooperative members of a conference team.

RECOGNITION OF TRUST AS A BASIC ELEMENT OF COOPERATION

Any sustained and productive relationship is based on the confidence that another person will behave in an honest and dependable manner. Advertisers commonly invoke their customers' trust via such terminology as *honest, trustworthy, dependable,* and *loyal.* Similarly, educators must invite the trust of the parents with whom they are involved in a more subtle fashion.

Rapport and trust are particularly needed during the initial stages of parent–professional involvement (when IEP conferences are first held), when parents are apt to feel most vulnerable and the responses of educators are most likely to be misinterpreted. Being informed that their offspring has an educationally significant learning or behavior problem will create self-doubts and questions in most parents. While such responses are accepted as natural and potentially therapeutic, they must not be exacerbated by doubts about educators' trustworthiness. Simpson (1982) identified the following seven requirements for developing parent–professional trust: willingness to be involved in the educational process, acceptance that both parents and educators have a commitment to children, willingness to serve as a child advocate, positive outlook, willingness on the part of parents and professionals to reinforce and confront one another, sensitivity to individual needs and emotions, and desire to trust. While demanding deliberate efforts on the part of both parents and educators, these conditions help create an atmosphere in which parents are able to play an appropriate role in planning and implementing their children's education.

KNOWLEDGE AND ACCEPTANCE OF INDIVIDUAL VALUES

Increasingly, experts agree that personal values determine many of our decisions and much of our behavior. Accordingly, a person's beliefs, opinions, and subjective biases are often the basis for behavior. Consistent with this perception, Kroth and Simpson (1977) observed that "The importance of assessing your own values is that ultimately you tend to act on those values you cherish the most" (p. 8). One mother of a severely retarded child reported feeling uncomfortable during an IEP conference when she realized that her son's program would contain no academic goals. She later indicated that although she recognized that her son's priority needs did not lie in traditional academic areas, her personal beliefs and values made her wish to see her son involved in reading and math activities.

By dictating students' goals and objectives and hence the way in which their time in school will be spent, the IEP is replete with potential value issues. Ideally, educators should be able to recommend and construe IEP goals based on assessment data and other professional information. However, educators must recognize that without such data the basis for their recommendations, just as with parents, will be personal values. Accordingly, educators must not presume that their values are more acceptable than those of parents. Rather, when attempting to make value-based decisions, professionals should anticipate differences of opinion. Such differences should not be perceived as problematic; however, they do require that parents as well as educators recognize their own values and accept that others will often have different goals and beliefs.

WILLINGNESS TO ACCOMMODATE A PARTNERSHIP RELATIONSHIP

A willingness to listen to parents, develop a trusting relationship, and accept differing values are contingent upon educators' willingness to allow parents to gain individualized participatory status. Hence, educators must actively promote and accept parents as participants in the educational process. Although parents and educators have long spoken of the need to cooperate and communicate, until recently professional educators determined students' curricula, programs, and procedures independent of parents. The IEP process clearly allows the participation of parents as decision makers. In spite of this mandate, however, parental cooperative involvement will occur only if educators accept parents' rights and privilege to be involved in their child's education. Such participation will vary across parents and time, yet parents must be assured of their role in their child's education.

Administrative Arrangements

Administrative structures and policies also determine parental involvement. Thus, insuring that parents' rights to meaningful involvement and participation in their child's education is properly communicated requires encouragement for parental participation at various levels, administrative arrangements conducive to such involvement, and willingness to share information and procedures.

ENCOURAGEMENT FOR PARENTAL PARTICIPATION

Administrators' capacity to facilitate change and establish standards is well documented. Hence, principals, directors of special education, coordinators, and other administrative personnel often determine the extent to which parents are provided an opportunity for various levels of participation in their child's education. If administrators encourage staff to involve parents in activities and meetings, including IEP sessions, and set standards for such participation beyond minimal compliance, parents will be more apt to respond. One school principal behaved in ways which conveyed to parents in her district an authentic desire to include them in educational processes. Upon learning that a student had been tentatively assigned to a special education program in her school, the principal phoned the child's family. During this initial contact, which was coordinated with diagnostic and special education personnel, she personally welcomed the parents to the program and invited them to observe the class to which their child had been assigned. Further, the principal indicated that she would be available to them when the need arose. At this time she also told parents that they would be receiving by mail information about the Education for all Handicapped Children Act. This information packet, which had been developed by school personnel, outlined parental and school rights and responsibilities in an easily understandable manner. As a part of this overview parents received information about IEP conferences and their roles in these meetings. Finally, the principal modeled parent participation responses for her staff and directed them in making similar responses. These activities clearly established a pattern whereby both parents and staff recognized that parents were to be accepted as educational participants.

ADMINISTRATIVE ARRANGEMENTS CONDUCIVE TO PARENT INVOLVEMENT

Administrators must not only instruct and model parent involvement, they must utilize their power to establish conditions that are supportive of such involvement. First and foremost, administrators must ensure that the appropriate individuals attend conferences, particularly IEP sessions, and that these meetings are scheduled at convenient times (parents must be informed that meetings can be arranged to accommodate their schedules). Additionally, administrators should require all personnel who will be providing direct educational services to attend the IEP meeting so that IEP annual goals and short-term objectives will be based on the broadest possible range of input. Administrators should also secure suitable physical facilities for meetings and make sure that an agenda and established protocol are followed and that all necessary materials and procedures are available. Finally, in addition to setting the appropriate interpersonal tone, administrators must be knowledgeable of local, state, and federal program standards and requirements, including:

1. The district or program's educational philosophy for exceptional students.

2. Community and parental information-dissemination activities related to exceptional education.

3. Special education service alternatives for students in private and parochial programs.

4. Referral, screening, identification, and evaluation programs and procedures utilized by the district or program.

5. Parental notification and permission procedures required by local, state, and federal mandates.

6. IEP program requirements and procedures, including meeting participants, document content, and related procedures.

7. Least restrictive environment requirements and documentation procedures.

8. Procedural due process considerations, including student and parental rights, parental notification and permission procedures, and due process hearing procedures and requirements.

9. Confidentiality requirements and procedures, including parental and student access to records and parental rights regarding the amendment of such documents.

10. District graduation requirements for exceptional students.

11. The nature and appropriateness of physical facilities for exceptional students.

12. District or program inservice training procedures and alternatives.

13. Procedures and results of program evaluations.

WILLINGNESS TO SHARE INFORMATION AND PROCEDURES

An atmosphere where parents recognize that they have access to documents about their own child as well as information about district and program changes represents another administrative vehicle for advancing parent rapport and participation. In communities where parents have the opportunity to read newspaper accounts of school events, listen to radio and TV coverage of policies and procedures, and receive other school-related information, parents seem not only to be knowledgeable, but also supportive of district activities.

The most successful special education programs routinely disseminate information to parents about the procedures used in the programs in which their children are enrolled. For example, parents receive pamphlets and other materials describing assessment and diagnostic procedures, the program to which their child is being assigned (schedules, program philosophy, remediation strategies, management programs, related ser-

vices offered), student evaluation procedures, and problem-solving resources available to the student and family. Such documents not only
provide parents with valuable information, they also communicate the
willingness of school personnel to accommodate parents in the educational process.

Preparing Parents to Be IEP Conference Participants

The Education for All Handicapped Children Act has given parents the
opportunity to become meaningfully involved in their child's education.
Prominent among these involvement opportunities is participation in the
IEP process whereby parents may suggest and react to annual goals,
short-term objectives, specialized procedures, the extent of their child's
involvement with nonhandicapped students, and other important areas
related to their child's education. Parents must not only be allowed to
participate in these conferences to an extent commensurate with their
needs and abilities, they should also be afforded support and structure for
the desired participation level. Hence, after an acceptable level has been
chosen, parents should receive information and guidance about how to
function at that level. Not all parents will avail themselves of such
training; yet, it must be available.

Table 7.1 suggests the type of information and guidance to be offered
within each of seven involvement levels: attendance, sharing information,
suggesting goals, negotiating goals, monitoring implementation, joint
programming and independent programming. Considerations for each
level of involvement are provided for three phrases: prior to the IEP
conference, during the conference, and after the IEP meeting.

The considerations listed in Table 7.1 within the various participation
levels and phases are not intended to be comprehensive, and implementation of these considerations may take many forms. For example, reading
materials can be provided for various independent activities, parents and
parent groups may also provide information and arrange for workshops,
and finally, professional educators can be expected to assume some
training responsibility. For more advanced training, formal workshops
and classes are required.

Summary

Parent participation in educational conferences, including IEP meetings, must be individualized and based on a number of family-system
considerations. Further, if parents are to assume a meaningful role in their

Table 7.1 Considerations for Parent IEP Involvement, by Level of Involvement and Phase of Participation

Pre IEP conference[a]	During IEP conference	Post IEP conference
	Attendance and Approval	
	Maintain a positive attitude during the conference.	Be willing to attend future meetings and to offer support and approval.
Plan for the meeting: (1) determine the site of the conference, (2) plan to arrive on time, (3) identify a baby sitter to avoid having to bring young children to the meeting, (4) determine how much time has been allotted for the conference, (5) attempt to identify who will attend the meeting.	Maintain a businesslike demeanor: (1) dress in a businesslike manner, (2) bring writing materials, (3) avoid isolation via the seating arrangement, (4) listen carefully, (5) introduce yourself and request that others at the meeting do the same, including specifying their role.	
Consider bringing a friend or relative to the meeting if you are uncomfortable attending alone.	Be willing to accept responsibility for problems which are outside school. Similarly, do not expect school personnel to solve your personal or family problems. However, you may seek referrals from school personnel for such services.	
Develop a positive attitude regarding the meeting as opposed to assuming an adversarial position.		
Familiarize yourself with legal and legislative special education mandates. In particular, review handbooks and pamphlets relating to PL 94-142.		

(continued)

Table 7.1 *Continued*

Pre IEP conference[a]	During IEP conference	Post IEP conference
	Sharing Information	
Maintain and organize developmental, school, and clinical records on your children and review these records (including previous IEPs).	Bring writing materials, background information, and other information which you may wish to share at the conference.	Obtain and file a copy of the IEP and any other information needed for future reference.
Develop a list of information and other data you wish to share at IEP conferences. Write this information down because you may not remember it at conference time.		Provide conference information to family members, including the child about whom the meeting was held (if appropriate).
	Suggesting Goals	
Identify with family members (including the child about whom the conference will be held) prioritized goals for the child.	Assertively maintain a participatory status during the conference. Ask for clarification about items and concepts which you fail to understand and which are not explained; solicit input and feedback from individuals who might not otherwise share information; make suggestions you consider important; request a copy of the completed IEP; and request additional meeting time if the allotted schedule is insufficient for completing the IEP.	Prepare notes about the meeting. These notes should reflect happenings during the conference and should be filed with the student's IEP.
	Present to IEP participants parent and family goals for the child.	Contact the appropriate personnel if clarification or additional information is required.
		Reinforce educators for their work, for example, through letters and phone calls.

Negotiating Goals

Positively and assertively work with educators. Present and advocate priority goals. However, avoid arguing over minor details or attempting to dominate the meeting.

Consider enrolling in assertiveness training and problem-solving workshops.

Monitoring Implementation

Establish the manner in which goals and objectives will be monitored and how this information will be communicated to educators.

Consider enrolling in workshops on child and program assessment and evaluation.

Maintain an ongoing record of IEP progress and skill development.

Engaging in Joint Programming

Establish the manner in which goals and objectives will be jointly monitored and how this information will be communicated.

Familiarize yourself with teaching strategies and behavior management techniques.

Engaging in Independent Programming

Establish the conditions under which goals and objectives will be independently pursued by parents and the manner in which this information will be communicated.

Develop proficiency in independently carrying out teaching strategies and behavior management procedures.

---

[a] Activities at each level of involvement are cumulative (e.g., activities at the second level include those of the first level).

exceptional child's education, educators must demonstrate cooperative attitudes and behaviors along with providing appropriate parent training for various participation levels.

References

Benson, H., & Turnbull, A. P. (1985). Approaching families from an individualized perspective. In R. H. Horner, L. M. Voeltz, & H. D. Fredericks (Eds.), *Education of learners with severe handicaps: Exemplary service strategies* (pp. 127–160). Baltimore: Paul H. Brookes.

Boggs, E. M. (1978). Who is putting whose head in the sand or in the clouds as the case may be? In A. P. Turnbull & H. R. Turnbull (Eds.), *Parents speak out* (pp. 50–68). Columbus, OH: Charles E. Merrill.

Carter, E., & McGoldrich, M. (1980). The family life cycle and family therapy: An overview. In E. Carter & M. McGoldrich (Eds.), *The family life cycle: A framework for family therapy* (pp. 3–19). New York: Gardner Press.

Dembinski, R. J., & Mauser, A. J. (1977). What parents of the learning disabled really went from professionals. *Journal of Learning Disabilities, 10,* 578–584.

Donnelian, A. M., & Mirenda, P. L. (1984). Issues related to professional involvement with families of individuals with autism and other severe handicaps. *Journal of the Association for Persons with Severe Handicaps, 9* (1), 16–24.

Goldenberg, I., & Goldenberg, H. (1980). *Family therapy: An overview*. Belmont, CA: Brooks/Cole.

Goldstein, S., Strickland, B., Turnbull, A. P., & Curry, L. (1980). An observational analysis of the IEP conference. *Exceptional Children, 46*(4), 278–286.

Hoff, M. K., Fenton, K. S., Yoshida, R., & Kaufman, M. J. (1978). Notice and consent: The school's responsibility to inform parents. *Journal of School Psychology, 16,* 265–273.

Hoffman, L. (1980). The family life cycle and discontinuous change. In E. Carter & M. McGoldrich (Eds.), *The family life cycle: A framework for family therapy* (pp. 53–68). New York: Gardner Press.

Karnes, M. B., & Lee, R. C. (1980). Involving parents in the education of their handicapped children: An essential component of an exemplary program. In M. J. Fine (Ed.), *Handbook on parent education* (pp. 201–225). New York: Academic Press.

Kroth, R. L. (1985). *Communicating with parents of exceptional children*. Denver: Love.

Kroth, R. L., & Simpson, R. L. (1977). *Parent conferences as a teaching strategy*. Denver: Love.

Lombana, J. H. (1983). *Home–school partnerships: Guidelines and strategies for educators*. New York: Grune & Stratton.

MacMillan, D. L., & Turnbull, A. P. (1983). Parent involvement with special education: Respecting individual preferences. *Education and Training of the Mentally Retarded, 18*(1), 4–9.

Marver, J. D., & David, J. L. (1978). *The implementation of individualized education program requirements of P.L. 94-142*. Trends Park, CA: SRI International.

Mitchell, S. (1976). *Parental perceptions of their experiences with due process in special education: A preliminary report*. Paper presented at the annual meeting of the American Educational Research Association, San Francisco. (ERIC Document Reproduction Service, No. ED 130–482).

National Association for Retarded Children. (1954). *The educator's viewpoint*. New York: NARC.

National Committee for Citizens in Education. (1979). Unpublished manuscript serving as basis for Congressional testimony.

Olson, D. H., Russell, C. S., & Sprenkle, D. H. (1980). Marital and family therapy: A decade review. *Journal of Marriage and the Family, 42*(4), 973–993.

Peters, T. J., & Waterman, R. H. (1982). *In search of excellence*. New York: Harper & Row.

Simpson, R. L. (1982). *Conferencing parents of exceptional children*. Rockville, MD: Aspen Press.

Turnbull, A. P. (1983). Parental participation in the IEP process. In J. A. Mulick & S. M. Pueschel (Eds.), *Parent–professional partnerships in developmental disability services* (pp. 107–122). Cambridge, MA: Ware Press.

Turnbull, A. P., Summers, J. A., & Brotherson, M. J. (1984). *Working with families with disabled members: A family systems perspective*. Lawrence, KS: University of Kansas, Research and Training Center on Independent Living.

Turnbull, A. P., Summers, J. A., & Brotherson, M. J. (1986). Family life cycle: Theoretical and empirical implications and future directions for families with mentally retarded members. In J. J. Gallagher & P. Vietze (Eds.), *Future research directions: Families with handicapped children* (pp. 45–65). Baltimore: University Park Press.

Turnbull, H. R., & Turnbull, A. P. (1982). Parent involvement in the education of handicapped children: A critique. *Mental Retardation, 20*(3), 115–122.

Turnbull, H. R., Turnbull, A. P., & Wheat, M. (1982). Assumptions about parental participation: A legislative history. *Exceptional Education Quarterly, 3*(2), 1–8.

Turnbull, A. P., & Winton, P. J. (1984). Parent involvement policy and practice: Current research and implications for families of young severely handicapped children. In J. Blacher (Ed.), *Severely handicapped young children and their families: Research in review* (pp. 377–397). New York: Academic Press.

Wiegerink, R., Hocutt, A., Posante-Lorne, R., & Bristol, M. (1980). Parent involvement in early education programs for handicapped children. In J. J. Gallagher (Ed.), *New directions for exceptional children: Ecology of exceptional children* (pp. 67–85). San Francisco: Jossey-Bass.

Winton, P., & Turnbull, A. P. (1981). Parent involvement as viewed by parents of preschool handicapped children. *Topics in Early Childhood Special Education, 1*(3), 11–19.

8

Teenage Pregnancy and Parenthood Education

Marlene A. Merrill

Introduction

Because of increasing numbers of unwed adolescent parents, the crisis of unscheduled parenthood has become a grim reality of the 1980s. The overall pregnancy rate for all sexually active adolescents, aged 15 to 19, has increased to 33% (Conger & Peterson, 1984). Scott, Field, and Robertson (1981) report the proportion of births to mothers 15 to 19 years old rose from 17% in 1966 to 19% in 1975. Teenagers are responsible for 46% of all out-of-wedlock births (Alan Guttmacher Institute, 1981). Today half of all black children are born to unmarried and typically teenage mothers (Anderson, 1984). Among whites the teenage birth rate is also high. The teenage birthrate in the United States is among the highest of the developed countries and is higher than many developing countries (Alan Guttmacher Institute, 1981). These teen parents face the normal struggles of growing up compounded by the demands of being a parent.

This chapter includes a discussion of the characteristics of adolescent mothers and the consequences of their early parenthood, an overview of several school-based programs providing parenting programs and services for teenage mothers, an examination of the available research, and recommendations for parenthood education for teenage mothers.

Teenage Mothers: Characteristics and Consequences

Adolescence is transition period from child to adult. It is a time when a multitude of developmental changes take place. While there is considerable individual variation in the maturation process, adolescents all have

The Second Handbook on Parent Education   173

concerns about sexuality, dependence–independence, acceptance by peers, competence, values, and identity (Conger & Peterson, 1984). These changes take place within the framework of life-cycle stages. "Unscheduled parenthood" (Russell, 1980) presents severe difficulties in three areas: developmental conflicts, discontinuity with traditional life-cycle stages, and parental perceptions of adolescent behavior problems.

Implicit in the notion of developmental tasks is the idea that earlier tasks must be completed before later tasks may be successfully accomplished. The teenager must confront the issues of identity formation, establishment of intimacy with age mates, and completion of vocational and educational objectives (Erikson, 1950). Along with these typical adolescent developmental tasks, the teenage mother must also reconcile jumping ahead in her life-cycle development (Carter & McGoldrick, 1980). The teen is "off-time" regarding leaving home and establishing a family. Early parenthood disrupts the developmental schedule in terms of personal development, family development, school completion, and economic self-sufficiency (Russell, 1980).

Fraiberg (1982) describes the interlocking developmental conflicts of adolescence and motherhood. The unplanned pregnancy of the teenager brings with it unexpected conflicts between the teenage mother's dependency upon her parents and her own desire to become independent, her conception of her mothering role, and her own strong needs for nurturance. It is understandable how the baby itself can then get caught up in the teenager's fantasy about motherhood. Fraiberg says when the adolescent becomes a parent, self-love and self-centered goals come in conflict with the needs of the baby and the requirements of parenthood.

Unscheduled parenthood in the family sociology literature is seen from three perspectives: (1) as a transition to parenthood, (2) as accelerated role transition, and (3) as a crisis of family accession (Russell, 1980). Unscheduled parenthood represents a discontinuity in the cycling of the family life cycle (Feldman & Feldman, 1975). It presents a "crisis" for the teenage mother. This crisis can be an opportunity for family growth if the teenager can reenter the educational system and if the teen and her family can develop an adaptive relationship (Osofsky & Osofsky, 1983; Russell, 1980).

Teenage pregnancy can impose lasting hardships, including the likelihood that teenage mothers and their offspring will live in poverty. Teenage mothers are half as likely to finish high school and they are likely to earn half as much money as those teenagers who postpone childbearing (Furstenberg, 1976; Hardy, King, Shipp, & Welcher, 1981; Wallis, 1985). Klein (1975) describes the consequences as a "syndrome of failure" because 90% of the girls in his study dropped out of school and failed to return, infant mortality ranged from 21.9 to 43.5 per 1000 births, the girls failed to develop self-confidence and a sense of personal identity, and these teenage parents failed to develop adequate mothering skills.

Programs For Teen Mothers

Programs for teenage mothers tend to focus on providing prenatal information and providing information on child development and child-rearing techniques. A number of programs have been established in hospitals, schools, or social service institutions. Parent education programs for teens vary widely, as each seeks to adapt its program to meet local needs and use resources that are available. Several surveys have compiled a broad overview of services being offered teenage mothers (Goldstein, Zalar, & Grady, 1973; McCarthy & Radish, 1983; Wallace, Gold, Goldstein, & Oglesby, 1973; Washington, 1975). Many of these programs targeted their services to low-income, inner city teenagers. McCarthy and Radish (1983) list programs in Kalamazoo, Michigan; Yale/New Haven, Connecticut; St. Paul, Minnesota; San Francisco, California; and Fort Worth, Texas, among others, that provide educational and other services to adolescent mothers. In 1976 there were 1,132 programs referenced as providing some services to teenage mothers, according to the National Alliance Concerned with School-Age Parents (NACSAP). However, only 54 of these programs (4.8%) had comprehensive services (Jekel & Klerman, 1983).

As a minimum, a comprehensive program needs to provide education on a classroom basis, early and consistent prenatal care, postpartum health services, and counseling services (Howard, 1972; Klerman, 1975). It is important that the program addresses four major areas: medical, education, social, and psychological (St. Pierre & St. Pierre, 1980). Helpful additional areas include a vocational component, an infant day care component, and a young fathers component. The numbers and kinds of components are limited only by the planner's conceptualization of need and the constraints placed on the program, such as availability of staff and funding sources (Howard, 1972).

A variety of educational programs for teenage mothers are in operation. Programs may include clinic or hospital components and such educational services as special classes, adult educational classes, homebound education, alternative settings, or remaining in the home school. The programs reviewed in this chapter give the reader an understanding of the organization, curriculum, and services provided. Program strengths frequently include flexibility in length of school day, individualization of teaching techniques, smaller class sizes, flexibility in the curriculum, a school lunch program, and vocational and social counseling. Weaknesses typically cited include the lack of extracurricular activities, limited staff and curriculum, duplication of educational services with regular high schools, and transportation difficulties (Washington, 1975).

Several programs which characterize somewhat different approaches to involving teenage mothers are briefly described. The Topeka program is described in greater detail than the others because of the involvement of the author in that program.

Baltimore: A Hospital Program

A multidisciplinary, comprehensive program at Johns Hopkins Hospital in Baltimore, emphasizes early and periodic screening of medical, psychosocial, and educational needs, followed by diagnosis and treatment if necessary. Prevention is through health-related education. Referrals are made through the Baltimore City Maternal–Infant Care Center, and girls are registered at Johns Hopkins by the 14th week of their pregnancy. The teenage mothers make an average of 11 prenatal visits and are followed postpartum through well-baby visits. A strength of this program is that the teenage mothers deal with the same staff of people in the prenatal and postnatal phases of the program, which promotes development of trust in these helpers. Hardy et al. (1981) state that the program provides pregnancy care for 51% of teenage mothers 15 and younger and just over 30% of the care for those aged 16 and 17 in Baltimore. The educational component is not a direct part of the Johns Hopkins program. The pregnant teens attend a special city school, the Edgar Allen Poe School Program for Teenage Mothers. The school is under the direction of an appointed principal who interviews prospective staff members and coordinates the social services (Washington, 1975). According to the McCarthy and Radish (1983) survey, 85% of the participants in the Johns Hopkins program graduate from high school or remain in school.

Philadelphia: An Urban Alternative School

The Philadelphia Program for School-Age Parents (Magid, Gross, & Shuman, 1979) is designed to improve child-rearing skills and to teach child development. In Philadelphia, a pregnant teenager can elect to remain in her present school or to attend an alternative school. Funds for the creation of this program in 1972 originally came from Title IV-A of the Social Security Act. Teenage mothers who enter the program can remain to finish out the school year. The goals of the program are to provide social services such as family life information, information about community resources, and counseling in order to improve health care of the adolescent mothers and infants, to encourage completion of high school, and to improve parenting skills.

The parent education component consists of monthly discussion and the curriculum includes child development, child-rearing practices, and anticipatory guidance. Approximately 15 girls participate. An interesting technique is the interviewing of a "recent graduate" of the program by two developmental psychologists. The other girls sit around the mother–baby pair and listen as the mother talks with the psychologists about her child-rearing experiences and the competencies of her infant. The group is able to observe a real-life infant interacting with age-appropriate play materials. In a survey of 159 girls ages 13 to 20, 55% said they would like to have these sessions more often, and 26% said they would like to have this as a regular course in school (Magid et al., 1979).

Georgia: Teacher/Project Coordinator Model

During 1977 the state of Georgia began development of a program which could provide a school setting for teenage mothers to complete their education. The Vocational Act of 1976, Section 150, Consumer and Homemaker Education provided financial assistance for program development. State grants allowed school districts to hire a teacher, pay travel expenses, and purchase educational materials. This home economics teacher also functions as project coordinator, conducts two classes a day at the local high school, and is available one period a day to talk with students individually. The teaching in these classes aims to provide the teenage mother with parenting and nutrition skills. The teacher/project coordinator also makes home visits, chairs the advisory committee, and assists in curriculum development (Register & King, 1978).

Urbana, Illinois: Regular High School Program with Modifications

Urbana, Illinois has had a high school class for pregnant students for several years. It originally was taught by two community health nurses and coordinated by a counselor (Wilson, 1978). The program was changed and a social worker is now the coordinator. The program served 35 to 50 students a year. Students continue in their regular classes except for the addition of a 1-hour Home and Family Education class. The social worker interviews each student, discusses various options, and makes school schedule modifications. Both postpartum and prepartum students are encouraged to take the class. Teenage mothers are encouraged to stay in school as long as possible before starting the Homebound Program. After the birth of their child they return to school and their classes.

The Home and Family Education class is taught by a team which includes a social worker, school nurse, public health nurse, food service director, and a community resource coordinator. The social worker leads discussions relevant to parenting issues, interpersonal and family relationships, values clarification, communication skills, goal-setting skills, and assertiveness training. The school nurse teaches a child development unit. The others on the team teach units in their areas of expertise.

Due to changes in the numbers of pregnant teenagers, changes in high school graduation requirements, and funding changes, scheduling the Home and Family Education class became difficult. In recent years the program has served 20 to 30 pregnant teenagers each year. Students are taken out of PE class and placed in an independent study period to work on Home and Family Education materials. They work independently and at their own instructional pace. They meet with the school social worker weekly to discuss their progress. The Urbana school nurse estimates that 86 to 90% of these teenage mothers continue their high school studies upon completion of their pregnancy (C. Terstriep, personal communication, September 9, 1986).

Hartford: The Parent–Child Center

Weaver High School in Hartford, Connecticut is a large urban school whose student enrollment contains a large minority population. From 1978 to 1984, Weaver transferred about 150 students to the Hartford Teenage Parents Program, an alternative school for pregnant girls. In the late 1970s, in order to decrease the dropout rate for teen parents, the district started the Parent–Child Center. The Center offers a course titled "Parenting" as part of the home economics curriculum and includes infant day care as a laboratory component of the course. The center enrolls seven student parents and their babies, and continued attendance in school is the criterion, for remaining in the program. The director/teacher of the Center is a home economics teacher. The Center also employs one paraprofessional who directs student aides in providing care to the infants. Students form their own peer group and participate in a support group in which they listen to each other's problems, offer suggestions, exchange ideas, clothes, and resources. The parenting class enables the student to gain knowledge of human behavior, child care, communication, and the responsibilities of parenthood (Cobb, 1985).

The dropout rates from Weaver High School and the Parent–Child Center are similar. However, a comparison of Parent–Child Center students to other teenage parents indicates that a substantially higher percentage of Center students complete school. In 1981 the Alan Guttmacher Institute reported only 49.9% of students 17 years old and younger with children graduate from high school. The Parent–Child Center graduated 73% of its participants (Cobb, 1985).

Albuquerque: An Alternative School

New Futures School is a comprehensive program for adolescent parents located in Albuquerque, New Mexico. Begun by the Albuquerque YWCA, it is now an alternative school for the public school systems and it is also supported by a nonprofit community based organization. This program serves two populations: the first-time teenage mother in the Perinatal Program and school-age mothers or fathers in the Young Parents' Center. These programs serve 450 students a year. Required high school classes, special education classes, vocational classes, and classes in parenting and child development are offered for credit from accredited certified staff members. There is flexibility in scheduling; a student may take as few as two or as many as six classes. Classes are individually paced and strive to be success oriented. Nurse-health educators teach a daily class on perinatal health care, parenting, and family planning. A nutrition analysis is done for each new student. A breakfast and lunch program is available at the school. Family practice clinics, a weekly women, infants, and children clinic, a well-child clinic, and a weekly prenatal clinic are available at the school and are sponsored by the New Mexico School of Medicine and the Public Health Department (*New Futures School*, 1984).

Counseling and social service are a very important component of the New Futures program. Individual counseling is available when requested. Counselors are knowledgeable about community resources, vocational opportunities, and child-care facilities. A weekly counseling group is held for girls considering adoption as an alternative.

New Futures School has developed videotaped presentations and a guide entitled *Working With Childbearing Adolescents* (Barr & Monserrat, 1982). This guide presents a general strategy and methodology for working with pregnant adolescents and lesson plans for a student text titled *Teenage Pregnancy: A New Beginning* by Barr and Monserrat (1978).

The program at New Futures School has provided benefits for both its participants and the surrounding community. Teenage mothers who have participated in the New Futures program show repeat pregnancy rates that are less than one-third of the national rate. A study in 1981 found that

94% of former program participants had either completed high school or were still attending school (*New Futures School*, 1984).

Topeka: A School–Community Program

The Teen-Aid School in Topeka, Kansas is a comprehensive supportive program for teenage pregnant girls. It is a specialized program that helps the teenage mother continue her academic progress and encourages personal growth and learning of parenting skills. The program was begun in cooperation with the Crittenton Youth Home in the mid-1970s. It is now totally funded by the public schools and is located in the same building as the Alternative School. The Alternative School provides an educational option for those students who are unable to meet the demands of a regular high school structure and are in danger of dropping out of school. Teen-Aid assists 70 to 90 teenage mothers each year. The Alternative School serves slightly more than twice that number of students.

Any student enrolled in Topeka Public Schools who becomes pregnant and wishes to may attend Teen-Aid. Although most prenatal teenage mothers elect to attend Teen-Aid, some students continue to attend school in their assigned high school. The student's home–school counselor discusses the Teen-Aid program with the student and her parent(s). The counselor then contacts the Teen-Aid head teacher to arrange for the student and her parent(s) to visit the program. Enrollment and scheduling is completed after this interview. After the student's pregnancy is completed, the student normally returns to her home school at the end of the next grading period. Middle-school students or special education students return to their home schools 3 weeks after the delivery of the baby.

Since the Teen-Aid Program and the Alternative Education Program are located in the same facility, these programs share teaching staff. All of the required high school classes are offered and elective courses are limited to home economics, business, math, and human relations. Most of the Teen-Aid students prefer to be in classes with other pregnant girls, and the class scheduling typically allows this to occur. The curriculum at Teen-Aid also includes nutrition, prenatal care, parenting, practical living skills, and vocational skills. Class size is small with only 6 to 15 students per class period. Adaptive Physical Education is required for all students, which includes LaMaze Exercise and Labor and Delivery classes. Nurses provided by the Shawnee County Health department arrange hospital tours and meet with girls individually in the Maternal and Infant Program at the Health Department clinic.

Students at Teen-Aid are provided opportunity for consultation and counseling from community and school student-support services. Resources that are available to the Teen-Aid students include family guidance centers, a mother and infant pregnancy care clinic at the Shawnee County Health Department, Crittenton Home, a school counselor, a school social worker, and a school psychologist. The school social worker and school psychologist each spend a morning each week at Teen-Aid to be available for student or family counseling and teacher consultations.

Upon admission to the program, each teenage mother is interviewed by either the social worker or school psychologist in order to discuss health, family conditions and issues, pregnancy options, school history and long-range educational plans, resources needed to complete plans, and what they would like to learn at Teen Aid. This information is used by the team at Teen-Aid, which includes the head consulting teacher, counselor, social worker, and school psychologist, to develop an individualized plan which addresses any personal, social, emotional, or academic concerns, vocational or other casework needs. The school psychologist or social worker follow up with each student to determine if objectives are being met.

Students at Teen-Aid are urged to attend a weekly counseling discussion group. Although girls may enter or leave the group at various times, the group basically remains at a stable membership of 12 to 15 each week throughout the school year. Participation in the group is voluntary, but each student is urged during the initial interview to participate in at least one group session. Each group of teenage mothers has had different needs and therefore the focus of each year's group has been different. Topics for the group have included the following:

- Relationships with parents
- Others expectations for us
- Feelings about one's own body
- Thoughts and reactions to pregnancy
- Understanding and coping with moods
- Decision making about self and baby
- Family planning
- Parenting skills
- Discipline versus abuse
- Sexuality and relationships
- Teenage marriage

- Understanding the newborn's development
- Expectations about child development and the child's behavior
- Relationship with the father of the baby
- Independent living
- Solving conflicts
- Negotiating agreements
- Managing wants: finances
- Future plans: job? school?

Each week the group meets and informally discusses events occurring during the week that affected them, after which it considers a preselected topic. Worksheets, films, or small group activities are frequently used to stimulate conversation. Variety of topics and the manner of presentation keep the format of the group varied and interesting.

The group counseling discussions and sections of the home economics course on child development emphasize parenting education issues. The emphasis in parenting training is experienced-based as the girls bring to the group experiences from their own childhood rearing and their experience in parenting sibling, helping neighborhood children, or parenting their own child. In the group, analysis of child and caregiver behaviors takes place. A model of parenting training frequently utilized is the Adlerian concept of using one's own reaction to determine another person's behavioral goal. Dreikurs and Soltz (1964) state that behavior can be understood in terms of its purpose and can be described rather than talked about in explanatory terms. Because providing alternative parenting responses is encouraged, the group's discussion expands the teenage mother's parenting options and stresses decision-making skills. Instruction in concepts such as I-statements, natural and logical consequences, and encouragement rather than praise become part of the conversation of the group.

Our work with the group is based upon the following psychological principles. Positive relationships between parent and child are based on mutual respect. A positive attitude of discipline means discipline is administered with firmness and kindness. It is desirable to teach discipline by helping the child identify the social consequences of his or her behavior. Encouragement communicates love, respect, support, and a valuing of the child as a person who, like the parent, needs to feel a positive sense of self worth (Dinkmeyer & McKay, 1976). It is important to set realistic expectations for the child's behavior based upon a knowledge of child development. Finally, it is important to recognize and understand that children, while they love their parent, cannot be the vehicle by which the parent obtains affection, nurturance, and self satisfaction. Thus the goal for the Teen-Aid discussion group is to encourage an attitude of positive and responsible parenting, to teach knowledge and skills about parenting, and to teach problem-solving skills so that alternative choices can be explored and good decisions made.

As with the other programs providing services to teenage mothers, outcomes are difficult to assess. Evaluations completed by the participants appear to indicate increased confidence in the student's abilities to care for herself and to provide appropriate parenting for her child. Most of the participants of Teen-Aid either graduate from high school or complete the general equivalency diploma.

Research on Teenage Mothers

This chapter has identified the psychosocial consequences of teenage parenthood and reviewed several programs for teenage mothers. There has been fairly extensive research on important factors related to teenage parenting (Card & Wise, 1978; Furstenberg, 1976; Rogeness, Ritchey, Alex, Zuelzer, & Morris, 1981b). Teenagers who are also parents have more relationship problems with their own parents (Hawley, Shear, Stark, & Goodman, 1984). A popular song advises parents, "Papa, don't preach," because the teenager is not going to listen (Madonna, 1986). Teenage parents look to siblings or to their peer group for nurturance and support. Rogeness et al. (1981b) found significant isolation of some teenage mothers; these teens had less interest in work or school when compared to never-pregnant teenagers, which implies that they had "problems" which predated the pregnancy. This study indicated that neither the never-pregnant group nor the teenage parent group had acceptable skills in parenting. This would tend to place teenage parents in the high risk group for parenting problems (Altemeier et al., 1979; Egeland & Brunnguell, 1979).

Parents are charged with the well-being of their children, and teenage parents are faced with the double burden of growing up themselves and parenting their child. Numerous authors have pointed out the necessity of providing education for responsible parenthood (Fine, 1980; Goldman, 1984; Hardy et al., 1981; Mullis, Mullis, & Moore, 1984; Osofsky & Osofsky, 1983; Roosa, 1984; Russell, 1980; St. Pierre & St. Pierre, 1980). Parent counseling, both behavioral and insightful-reflective, has been found to produce successful therapeutic change with a variety of children's behaviors (Tavormina, 1974). Parent education programs have also helped parents to develop improved skill functioning and a sense of competence as they change their individual lifestyles (Chilman, 1968; Mullis et al., 1984; Mullis & Mullis, 1983; Pevsner, 1982; M. B. Smith, 1968; Stevens, 1978; Tavormina, 1974). Hawkins (1972) shows that parent training programs are capable of improving the quality of child-rearing practices and suggests that the school is the logical setting for such programs.

The research also suggests that there is a connection between child abuse and lack of parenting knowledge and skills (Lystad, 1975; Spinetta & Rigler, 1972). Studies indicating that the teenage mother is not very knowledgeable about parenting (Alan Guttmacher Institute, 1981; de Lissovoy, 1973) reinforce the stated need for parent training classes to teach child development and discipline and child management skills.

Outcomes of Parenting Programs

Although parent education for teenage mothers appears to be widely encouraged, there appears to have been little research to evaluate the effectiveness of teenage parenting programs (Klerman, 1981; Mullis et al., 1984). The literature on intervention programs for teenage mothers faces the difficulties of inadequate sampling due to unavailability of control groups, inappropriate selection of criteria to measure intervention effectiveness, and inadequate generalizability (McDonough, 1985). These problems are frequently faced by studies reporting intervention results in the human service field. Some studies imply that intervention can have a positive short-term effect on knowledge and interactional behavior of teenage mothers. A couple of these studies are worthy of our interest.

Badger (1981) reported on research conducted in mid-1973 for the Cincinnati Infant Stimulation/Mother Training project (IS/MT). The IS/MT model of weekly postnatal mother–infant classes was intended to reinforce the teenager's role as parent and as primary caretaker of the infant and to provide social supports for the mother. Analysis of infant testing using Uzziris-Hunt and Bayley scales showed that the infants of mothers who participated in the classes did better than those who were in the home-visit only group. Evaluation of the IS/MT project concluded that infants of adolescent socially disadvantaged mothers tend to lag in development very early in life if no intervention is received, young adolescent mothers are interested in learning good mothering techniques and will attend parenting classes after their babies are born, and the 15–16-year-old mother is more willing than the 18–19-year-old mother to participate in classes and take the time to learn parenting skills.

Attitudes of Teenage Mothers

Roosa (1984) evaluated the short-term impact of parenting programs upon the teenager's knowledge and attitudes about parenting and child development. Subjects for this study were recruited from three urban programs in Arizona, all of which stressed continuation of a high school education as well as the importance of parenting classes. Due to a high number of school dropouts, data from only a small sample, 31 out of 79 subjects, had usable pretest and posttest materials. The programs produced significant positive change on scores for knowledge of child development, but there was practically no change in maternal attitudes. Roosa suggests that these parenting programs need to put greater emphasis upon helping teenagers learn decision-making skills so that the teen can become more responsible in parenting behavior.

Influence of Social Supports

Unger and Wandersman (1985) used structured interviews to examine the influences of social support and support interventions on the adjustment of teenage mothes in two longitudinal studies in Columbia, South Carolina. The teenage mothers participated in educational support groups which included emotional support of the group as well as information about problem solving, child development, and parenting. At 1 month post-partum and again at 8 months the results show that greater perceived support was related to greater life satisfaction and better adjustment to their new parenting role for both urban and rural teenage mothers.

In addition, it appears that teenage mothers who participate in special education programs while they are pregnant and take advantage of post-partum infant care are most likely to continue their education (Badger & Burns, 1980; Klerman, 1981; Roosa & Vaughn, 1983). Rogeness, Ritchey, Alex, Zuelzer, and Missos (1981a) compared a group of teenage parents who attended a special school with a group that was not in a special school. This study found that participation in the special school resulted in more interest in education, less dependency upon others, and more realistic expectations about parenting. Roosa and Vaughn (1983) also found a strong relationship between enrollment in an alternative program and improved infant care and improved educational interest.

Very little research has been done to evaluate intervention programs for teenage mothers. Conclusions drawn from the existing research must be tentative due to weaknesses in this research. The difficulties include small sample size due to dropout of participants, difficulty maintaining adequate control groups, and selection of measurement criteria. Many intervention reports tend to be descriptive, advocatory, and lacking in a clearly defined theoretical focus (McDonough, 1985).

Recommendations for Teenage Parenting Programs

The present emphasis of teenage pregnancy and parenthood education programs is secondary prevention. The teenage mother does need society's help throughout the pregnancy and for several years afterward, particularily to ameliorate or minimize the consequences of the pregnancy. Therefore these programs have attempted to provide prenatal health care and have urged continuation of the teenage mother's education. Education is important if the teenage mother is to achieve her psychosocial and vocational potential and responsible parenting.

Education about reproductive anatomy, responsible sexuality, and birth control has been widely advocated by the government as well as by family and religious groups (Klerman, 1981). The federal government has also had limited involvement in encouraging family-life education. In 1972 the Office of Child Development was formed in collaboration with the Office of Education and the National Institute of Mental Health. The goal of this group has been to improve knowledge of child development and children's needs and to develop positive attitudes regarding parenting. The federal government provides some funds for family planning services and maternity and infant care projects, although the bulk of the funding typically comes from antipoverty programs, United Way, or state and city government.

Special programs for adolescent mothers need to examine the assumptions under which they operate. They need to address sociological concerns and help young people develop realistic plans for their lives. If teenagers have a hopeful sense of their future they may seek to avoid early pregnancy. Carrera (1985) in an address before the Kansas City Planned Parenthood Conference on Teenage Pregnancy reported that many teens, both males and females, see a future for themselves that holds little employment opportunity, lifelong poor economic status, inadequate opportunity for meaningful education, and family fragmentation. "Under such conditions it is no wonder that some young people, instead of becoming industrious and hopeful, become sexually intimate and fatalistic" (Carrera, 1985, p. 4). The goal of special program for pregnant teens needs to assist teenage mothers in the development of a positive sense of self-esteem, appropriate coping and decision-making skills, and information about sexuality and contraception so that additional pregnancy can be delayed until their education can be completed.

A second recommendation is the strengthening of the child development curriculum in parenting education classes. Although the typical female adolescent is biologically ready for motherhood, she is developmentally and psychologically ill-prepared for the role of teenage mother. The literature suggests that teenage mothers are less emotionally available to the infants, less able to provide cognitive stimulation, and have fewer verbal interactions with their offspring (Anastasiow, 1983; Lawrence, 1983; Phipps-Yonas, 1980). Because infancy is a critical period for the infant's development and because early parenthood is a critical transition for the teenage mother, it is important that educational interventions occur. For the teenage mother, a pregnancy-related special program may be her last opportunity to learn parenting skills and to modify her parenting attitudes.

Parenthood education can be defined as a systematic and conceptually organized program intended to provide knowledge, awareness, and skills about aspects of parenting (Fine, 1980). Additionally it enhances acquisition of the competencies necessary for proper physical, socioemotional, and intellectual care and development of the child (Kruger, 1975). A needs-based curriculum for parenthood education for teenage mothers provides a general education and vocational or career education as well as parenthood education. Health and social services resources must be available to support educational services (Goldman, 1984; Jekel & Klerman, 1983; Kruger, 1975; Sharpe, 1975, C. P. Smith, 1982).

Kruger (1975, p. 294) developed a list of topics for parenthood education that serves as a point of departure for curriculum development:

Biological Factors of Human Reproduction
Influences of Heredity and Environment
Pregnancy, Prenatal Development, and Childbirth
Prenatal and Postnatal Care for Mothers
   Influences of Maternal Nutrition
Infant Care
   Nutrition for Young children
   Health, Protection, and Safety of Children
   Meeting the Child's Need for Shelter, Clothing, and
      Medical Care
Child Growth and Development
   Personality and Social Development
      Separation Anxiety
      Approaches to Discipline
      Sibling Rivalry

Building Self-Esteem
Perceptual and Cognitive Development
  Speech and Language
  Number Concept
Physical Development
Sequential Aspects of Growth and Development
  The First Year
  Two and Three Year Olds
  Four and Five Year Olds
Individual Differences in Children
The Handicapped Child
  Prevention of Child Handicaps/Birth Defects
  Working with Handicapped Children
Creative Activities for Children
  Children's Play
    Developmental Toys
  Children's Art
  Music and Dance for Children
  Children's Literature/Television
  Children and the World of Work
Family Structure and Functions
  Influence of Family Environment on Child Behavior
Parental Roles and Responsibilities
  Male Equity
Human Sexuality and Responsible Sexual Behavior
Family Planning and Population Growth
Community Resources to Aid in Parenting
Child Care Arrangements
Skills Required for Effective Work with Children
  Observation
  Analysis of Behavior
  Communication
  Counseling
  Development of Value System
  Tutoring

At times the parenthood education curriculum appears to be synonymous with child development. However, child development provides a foundation upon which responsible and nurturant parenting rests. A comprehensive parenthood education curriculum develops from three topic areas: topics related to self-understanding and interpersonal relationships, topics related to child development, and topics related to family and environment (Bartz, 1980). Any list which makes suggestions for curriculum becomes a composite because it must be comprehensive, interdisciplinary, and competency-based.

A third recommended emphasis is that educational services for teenage mothers be a continuum of services that range from specialized classes which focus on the prepartum teen to classes that assist the teenage parent to reintegrate into the regular high school program. Several studies have suggested that short-term services during the crisis of the prenatal period have an immediate effect that declines rapidly after the services are ended (Cartoof, 1979). It has been argued the comprehensive service programs for pregnant and parenting adolescents need to continue providing services for 2 to 3 years in order to promote school completion and reduce subsequent pregnancies during adolescence (Jekel & Klerman, 1983). Carol Smith (1982) states the belief that the "least restrictive environment" for both the pregnant teenager and parenting teenager may be resource rooms in the regular high school to serve the health and social service needs of these teenagers. A parent–child center in a multipurpose space in the high school can provide classroom instruction and also lab space in which to practice the principles of parenthood education. Cobb (1985) describes a program that provides day care and parenthood education instruction which operates at Weaver High School in Hartford, Connecticut.

A fourth recommendation regards the quality of research. The literature reviewed shares the problems common to many other intervention studies on human services. Because of difficulties in the existing research, only tentative conclusions can be drawn.

A part of the difficulty with this type of research is that the variables are difficult to define and separate from other environmental factors. The constraints and incentives operating upon a person facing major life decisions are complex and dependent upon many other environmental factors. Research in adolescent parenting may have to eflect a "continuous adjustment" perspective (Caldwell, 1980). Behavior is a process of continuous adjustment to constantly changing conditons. Behavior is affected because persons modify their goals as a result of others' expectations, the consequences of earlier decisions, or the availability of resources. Caldwell (1980) suggests using a "continuous adjustment" perspective: treating research variables that are not independent in the long term as independent in order to include as variables major life decisions and events. Research then would more accurately portray the complexity of real-life events and how they impact people.

A final recommendation concerns teenage fathers. This chapter and much that has been written about adolescent parenthood has focused upon the needs and problems of teenage mothers. In the past, the male's role in pregnancy prevention, childbirth, and child care has been under-valued. Teenage father programs are being developed and teenage fathers have been found to be caring and desirous of involvement with their child (Rose, 1985).

Male adolescents are sexually active; various surveys suggest that 56 to 70% of males aged 13 to 17 engage in premarital sexual relations, but only 15 to 35% of these young men use contraception (Conger & Peterson, 1984; Phipps-Yonas, 1980). Although the teenage father may be stereotypically seen as insensitive and uninterested in his baby, recent studies suggest that differential factors separate teenage fathers from nonfathers. Teenage fathers are usually older, more likely to have been born out of wedlock, less trusting, and have a lower sense that they are in control of their lives (Williams-McCoy & Tyler, 1985). Having children may be perceived as assets by some of these young men (Phipps-Yonas, 1980).

Most reports of teenage fathers focus upon the teenage fathers' personality characteristics (Elster & Panzarine, 1980); Nakashima & Camp, 1984; Williams-McCoy & Tyler, 1985). Few reports focus on the results of their participation in intervention programs (McDonough, 1985). The teenage father has been overlooked frequently because the relationship with the teenage mother is unstable. The literature suggests that the teenage mother typically does not marry the teenage father and may or may not continue a close relationship with him (Jekel & Klerman, 1983; Phipps-Yonas, 1980). Williams-McCoy and Tyler (1985) suggest that teenage fathers do visit health service agencies and may be involved in an ongoing relationship with the child's mother and may be available to participate in child care. Sensitive casework is recommended to determine what role the teenage father will take. It is also important to consider the involvement of the teenage father in parenting education outreach and to encourage participation in pregnancy intervention programs.

Summary

Pregnant adolescents need special services. Pregnancy has been implicated as a major reason that many teenagers drop out of school before completing their education. The social and economic conditions in many households with teenage mothers are also ripe for child abuse. These teenage mothers become involved in the "failure syndrome" because they are ill-equiped to become either contributing members of society or adequate and responsible parents. Many communities are attempting to provide comprehensive educational programs which include parenthood education for these teenage parents. The various programs reviewed present both practical ideas for engaging these teenagers in discussion and counseling groups and curriculum ideas to assist educational completion of high school programs.It is important that programs be comprehensive and include general education, vocational education, medical services, social services, and parenthood education. Not only do the facts need to be taught, but as Roosa (1984) points out, positive parenting attitudes need to be conveyed and instilled in these teenage parents.

The reviewed research strengthens the need for building into educational programs social supports, placing emphasis upon teaching decision-making skills, and evaluating needs for reintegration into the regular high school. Recommendations for future teenage parenting programs include:

1. Emphasis upon continuing secondary prevention needs and expanding them to include both pregnancy prevention and parenthood education. In particular, the teaching of social–emotional coping skills and decision-making skills needs to be emphasized.

2. Inclusion of interventions that enhance acquisition of positive parenting attitudes and parenting skills. A needs-based curriculum provides for acquisition of parenting competencies necessary for the proper physical, social-emotional, intellectual, and developmental needs of the child.

3. A continuum of services. Services need to begin with specialized classes for the prenatal teen and continue with the postpartum teenage mother. A continuum of service will encourage maintenance of learned parenting skills, reinforcement of attitudinal changes, and completion of a high school education. In schools, child care facilities would be an asset in providing the "least restrictive environment" for teenage mothers.

4. Upgrading the quality of research. Careful definition of variables, including environmental factors and the constraints and incentives that operate upon a person's life, would allow research studies to more accurately describe real-life events. Conclusions drawn from such research would have greater applicability in assisting programs to make formative evaluations.

5. Considering teenage fathers, who have been a forgotten component of the teenage parenting situation. Teenage fathers may become an asset for the teenage mother if these young men can become participants in educational interventions. Involvement of teenage fathers in teenage pregnancy programs should be carefully evaluated. In programs where program objectives permit and constraints such as funding and staff are not hindrances, participation of teenage fathers needs to be encouraged.

Those of us concerned with the well-being of children entrusted to us for an education must become committed to providing timely and sufficient parenthood education to those teenagers who make the choice to become "unscheduled" parents, and we must also do all we can to prevent the occurrence of unscheduled parenthood.

References

Alan Guttmacher Institute. (1981). *Teenage pregnancy: The problem that hasn't gone away.* New York: Alan Guttmacher Institute.

Altemeier, W. A., Vietze, P. M., Sherrod, K. B., Sandler, H. M., Falsey, S., & O'Connor, S. (1979). Prediction of child maltreatment during pregnancy. *Journal of American Academy of Child Psychiatry, 18,* 205–218.

Anastasiow, N. J. (1983). Adolescent pregnancy and special education. *Exceptional Children, 49,* 396–401.

Anderson, K. (1984, May 14). A threat to the future: Coming to grips with the crumbling Black family. *Time,* p. 20.

Badger, E. (1981). Effects of parent education program on teenage mothers and their offspring. In K. Scott, T. Field, & E. Robertson (Eds), *Teenage parents and their offspring* (pp. 283–316). New York: Grune & Stratton.

Badger, E., & Burns, D. (1980). Impact of a parent education program on the personal development of teenage mothers. *Journal of Pediatric Psychology, 5,* 415–422.

Barr, L., & Monserrat, C. (1978). *Teenage pregnancy: A new beginning.* Albuquerque, NM: New Futures.

Barr, L., & Monserrat, C. (1982). *Working with childbearing adolescents.* Albuquerque, NM: New Futures.

Bartz, K. W. (1980). Parenting education for youth. In M. J. Fine (ed.), *Handbook on parent education* (pp. 271–290). New York: Academic Press.

Caldwell, S. (1980). Life course perspectives on adolescent parenthood research. *Journal of Social Issues, 36,* 130–145.

Card, J., & Wise, L. (1978). Teenage mothers and teenage fathers: The impact of early childbearing on parents' personal and professional lives. *Family Planning Perspective, 10,* 199–205.

Carrera, M. A. (1985, October). *We can make a difference.* Paper presented at the conference of Planned Parenthood, Kansas City, MO.

Carter, E. A., & McGoldrick, M. (Eds.). (1980). *The family life cycle.* New York: Gardner Press.

Cartoof, V. G. (1979). Postpartum services for adolescent mothers: Part 2. *Child Welfare, 58,* 673–680.

Chilman, C. S. (1968). Poor families and their patterns of child care: Some implications for service programs. In C. Chandler, R. S. Lourie, & A. D. Peters (Eds.), *Early child care: The new perspective.* New York: Atherton Press.

Cobb, P. C. (1985). How infants in high school keep their parents in school. *Illinois Teacher of Home Economics, 29,* 50–53.

Conger, J. J., & Peterson, A. D. (1984). *Adolescence and youth: Psychological development in a changeing world* (3rd Ed.) New York: Harper & Row.

de Lissovoy, V. (1973). Child care by adolescent parents. *Children Today, 2,* 20–25.

Dinkmeyer, D., & McKay, G. (1976). *Systematic training for effective parenting.* Circle Pines, MN: American Guidance Services.

Dreikurs, R., & Soltz, V. (1964). *Children: The challenge.* New York: Hawthorn Books.
Egeland, R., & Brunnguell, D. (1979). An at-risk approach to the study of child abuse: Some preliminary findings. *Journal of American Academy of Child Psychiatry, 18,* 219–235.
Elster, A. B., & Panzarine, S. (1980). Unwed teenage fathers. *Journal of Adolescent Health Care, 1,* 116–120.
Erikson, E. H. (1950). *Childhood and society.* New York: Norton.
Feldman, H., & Feldman, M. (1975). The family life cycle: Some suggestions for recycling. *Journal of Marriage and the Family, 37,* 277–284.
Fine, M. J. (1980). *Handbood on parent education.* New York: Academic Press.
Fraiberg, S. (1982). The adolescent mother and her infant. In S. C. Feinstein, J. G. Looney, A. Z. Schwartzberg, & A. D. Sorosky (Eds.), *Adolescent psychiatry: Developmental and clinical studies* (pp. 7–23). Chicago: University of Chicago Press.
Furstenberg, F. F., Jr. (1976). The social consequences of teenage pregnancy. *Family Planning Perspectives, 8,* 148–164.
Goldman, A. (1984). Today's parents: The alone generation. *Emotional First Aid, 1,* 31–33.
Goldstein, P. I., Zalar, M. K., & Grady, E. W. (1973). Vocational education: An unusual approach to adolescent pregnancy. *Journal of Reproductive Medicine, 10,* 77–79.
Hardy, J. B., King, T. M., Shipp, D. A., & Welcher, D. W. (1981). A comprehensive approach to adolescent pregnancy. In K. Scott, T. Field, & E. Robertson (Eds.), *Teenage parents and their offspring* (pp. 265–274). New York: Grune & Stratton.
Hawkins, R. P. (1972, November). It's time we taught the young how to be good parents (and don't you wish we'd started a long time ago?). *Psychology Today,* pp. 28–40.
Hawley, L. E., Shear, C. L., Stark, A. M., & Goodman, P. R. (1984). Resident and parental perceptions of adolescent problems and family communications in a low socioeconomic population. *Journal of Family Practice, 19,* 651–655.
Hooper, S. (1985, October 16). States setting initiatives to combat problem of teen pregnancies. *Education Week,* p. 6.
Howard, M. (1972). *Model components of comprehensive programs for pregnant school age girls.* Washington, DC: Consortium on Early Childbearing and Childrearing.
Jekel, J. F., & Klerman, L. V. (1983). Comprehensive service programs for pregnant and parenting adolescents. In E. R. McAnarney (Ed.), *Premature adolescent pregnancy and parenthood* (pp. 295–310). New York: Grune & Stratton.
Klein, L. (1975). Models of comprehensive service—regular school-based. *Journal of School Health, 45,* 271–273.
Klerman, L. V. (1975). Adolescent pregnancy: The need for new policies and new programs. *Journal of School Health, 45,* 263–267.
Klerman, L. V. (1981). Programs for pregnant adolescents and young parents: Their development and assessment. In K. Scott, T. Field, & E. Robertson (Eds.), *Teenage parents and their offspring* (pp. 227–248). New York: Grune & Stratton.
Kruger, W. S. (1975). Education for parenthood and school-age parents. *Journal of School Health, 45,* 292–295.
Lawrence, R. A. (1983). Early mothering by adolescents. In E. R. McAnarney (Ed.), *Premature adolescent pregnancy and parenthood* (pp. 207–218). New York: Grune & Stratton.
Lystad, M. H. (1975). Violence at home: A review of the literature. *American Journal of Orthopsychiatry, 45,* 328–345.
Madonna (Singer). (1986). Papa don't preach. Song on *True pure* (Record album 9-25442-4). New York: Sire Records.
Magid, D. T., Gross, B. D., & Shuman, B. J. (1979). Preparing pregnant teenagers for parenthood. *Family Coordinator, 28,* 359–362.

McCarthy, J., & Radish, E. (1983). Education and childbearing among teenagers. In E. R. McAnarney (Ed.), *Premature adolescent pregnancy and parenthood* (pp. 279–294). New York: Grune & Stratton.

McDonough, S. C. (1985). Intervention programs for adolescent mothers and their offspring. *Journal of Children in Contemporary Society, 17*, 67–78.

Mullis, A., & Mullis, R. (1983). Making parent education relevant. *Family Perspective, 17*, 167–173.

Mullis, A. K., Mullis, R. L., & Moore, J. J. (1984). Toward more effective parent education. *Journal of Child Care, 2*, 21–31.

Nakashima, I. I., & Camp, B. W. (1984). Fathers of infants born to adolescent mothers: A study of paternal characteristics. *American Journal of Diseases in the Child, 138*, 452–454.

New Futures School—An overview. (1984, October). Albuquerque, NM.

Osofsky, H. J., & Osofsky, J. D. (1983). Adolescent adaptation to pregnancy and parenthood. In E. R. McAnarney (Ed.), *Premature adolescent pregnancy and parenthood* (pp. 195–206). New York: Grune & Stratton.

Pevsner, R. (1982). Group parent training versus individual family therapy: An outcome study. *Journal of Therapy and Experiemental Psychiatry, 13*, 119–122.

Phipps-Yonas, S. (1980). Teenage pregnancy and motherhood. *American Journal of Orthopsychiatry, 50*, 403–431.

Register, A., & King, F. (1978). Helping teenage parents grow up. *Vocational Education, 53*, 27–29.

Rogeness, G. A., Ritchey, S., Alex, P. L., Zuelzer, M., & Morris, R. (1981a). Comparison of teen parents in a special school program with other corresponding students. *Education, 101*, 372–379.

Rogeness, G. A., Ritchey, S., Alex, P. L., Zuelzer, M., & Morris, R. (1981b). Family patterns and parenting attitudes in teenage parents. *Journal of Community Psychology, 9*, 239–245.

Roosa, M. W. (1984). Short-term effects of teenage parenting programs on knowledge and attitudes. *Adolescence, 19*, 73–76.

Roosa, M. W., & Vaughn, L. (1983). Teen mothers enrolled in an alternative parenting program. *Urban Education, 18*, 348–360.

Rose, E. (1985, October 15). Teen-age fathers caring, involved, study finds. *Education Week*, p. 6.

Rousseve, R. J. (1985, November). Unwed adolescents with babies: A grim american reality. *School Counselor, 33*, 85–87.

Russell, C. S. (1980). Unscheduled parenthood: Transition to "parent" for the teenager. *Journal of Social Issues, 36*, 45–63.

Scott, K. G., Field, T., & Robertson, E. G. (1981). *Teenage parents and their offspring.* New York: Grune & Stratton.

Sharpe, R. (1975). Counseling services for school-age pregnant girls. *Journal of School Health, 45*, 284–285.

Smith, C. P. (1982). A needs-based curriculum for teenage mothers. *Education, 102*, 254–257.

Smith, M. G. (1968). Competence and socialization. In J. A. Clausen (Ed.), *Socialization and society.* Boston: Brown and Company.

Spinetta, J. J., & Rigler, D. (1972). The child-abusing parent: A psychological review. *Psychological Bulletin, 77*, 296–304.

Stevens, J. H., Jr. (1978). Parent education programs: What determines effectiveness? *Young Children, 33*, 59–65.

St. Pierre, T., & St. Pierre, R. (1980). Adolescent pregnancy: Guidelines for a comprehensive school-based program. *Health Education, 11*, 12–13.

Tavormina, J. B. (1974). Basic models of parent counseling: A critical review. *Psychological Bulletin, 81*, 827–835.

Unger, D. G., & Wandersman, L.P. (1985). Social support and adolescent mothers: Action research contributions to theory and application. *Journal of Social Issues, 41*, 29–45.

Wallace, H. M., Gold, M. C., Goldstein, H., & Oglesby, A. C. (1973). A study of services and needs of teenage pregnant girls in the large cities of the United States. *American Journal of Public Health, 63*, 5–16.

Wallis, C. (1985, December 9). Children having children: Teen pregnancies are corroding America's social fabric. *Time*, pp. 78–90.

Washington, V. E. (1975). Models of comprehensive service—Special school-based. *Journal of School Health, 45*, 274–276.

Williams-McCoy, J. E., & Tyler, F. B. (1985). Selected psychological characteristics of Black unwed adolescent fathers. *Journal of Adolescent Health Care, 6*, 12–16.

Wilson, J. (1978). An innovative project to serve school-age parents. *Illinois Teacher of Home Economics, 21*, 210–211.

9

Parent Education and Involvement in Early Intervention Programs for Handicapped Children: A Different Perspective on Parent Needs and the Parent–Professional Relationship

Nancy L. Peterson
Carolyn S. Cooper

Introduction

Early childhood intervention for handicapped infants and preschoolers is a new field, rapidly gaining visibility, where services will expand dramatically throughout the nation. Why is this movement gaining momentum? Professionals have increasingly come to recognize the needs of children who are handicapped or whose development is not progressing normally before they reach school age. They are not only giving lip service to the notion that children's early years are a crucial time for acquiring basic developmental skills, but are now attempting to address the special needs of handicapped children during infancy and the preschool years. Professionals are recognizing that without additional training, some children are destined to fall so far behind by the time they enter kindergarten that a miraculous catch-up is unlikely and teachers are left only to wish, "If only someone had worked with these youngsters earlier." The once-common practice of keeping such children out of kindergarten for another year to wait for more maturation or for the child to overcome learning deficits is now viewed as an outmoded, unproductive approach. Special education, training, and active therapeutic intervention are now viewed as the appropriate action to take when children are delayed, lacking in appropriate skills, or handicapped in some way.

Federal leadership and funding is a second reason for the growth of early childhood–special education services. Early intervention services for handicapped children under school age is a major funding and service priority of the federal government and Department of Education. Programs such as Head Start, the Handicapped Children's Early Education Demonstration Programs (HCEEP) which have established exemplary model programs for early intervention, and State Planning Grants which have financially aided state agencies in planning and establishing statewide service systems for this population are a few examples of the federal support behind this growing movement. Many states have responded to these federal initiatives by establishing experimental demonstration intervention programs for handicapped children and by passing their own enabling legislation to assume programmatic and fiscal responsibility for services. Fifty states have legislative mandates requiring that early childhood–special education services be provided to all or some portion of the population of young children, birth thru age 5, who are handicapped or at risk for developmental disabilities. This significant national trend is shown in Table 9.1.

A final impetus for this movement was the passage of Public Law 99-457 in October 1986. This legislation amended and reauthorized certain provisions of P.L. 94-142, the monumental bill passed by Congress in 1975 known as the bill of rights for handicapped children and their parents. Congress took a significant step in this new law by extending the rights for a free, appropriate education to handicapped preschoolers, ages 3–5. States are mandated under P.L. 99-457 to establish early childhood intervention services for all 3–5 year olds with disabilities by the 1990–91 school year or lose certain federal funds. Financial incentives for states are also offered under the new law to create intervention services for babies and toddlers, birth through age 2, with handicapping or at-risk conditions. In describing the nature of those services, the law makes it clear that parent and family needs as well as those of the infant are to be addressed. Support to families and parent education and involvement is highlighted as an important component of effective early intervention.

These events not only give impetus to the growth of early intervention services across the United States but also set the stage for a new era in parent education and involvement as it applies to this unique population of individuals. The age of the target population and the role parents play in their lives, coupled with regulations in the new law outlining the scope of services for these children, plus the underlying philosophy about what early intervention entails, creates major implications for the roles professionals will play in this new arena. Early intervention programs embody a unique set of service priorities that focus not only upon the young child and his unique needs, but also upon the child's primary care environment and those persons therein who provide care and nurturance. This calls for

Table 9.1 State Mandated Services for Handicapped Children, Birth to Age 6[a,b]

Age range (years)					
0–5	2–5	3–5	4–5	5	6
Iowa	Virginia	Alaska	Minnesota	Alabama	Indiana
Maryland		Dist. of Columbia	Delaware[e]	Colorado	Vermont
Michigan		Hawaii	Oklahoma[f]	Florida	Arizona[k]
Nebraska		Illinois	Tennessee[g]	Georgia	Arkansas[l]
New Jersey		Massachusetts		Idaho	
South Dakota		Montana		Kansas	
Texas		New Hampshire		Kentucky	
North Dakota		Rhode Island		Maine	
Oregon		Wisconsin		Mississippi	
		California		Missouri	
		Connecticut[c]		New Mexico[h]	
		Louisiana[d]		New York	
		Washington		North Carolina	
		West Virginia		Ohio	
				Pennsylvania	
				Utah	
				Wyoming	
				Nevada[i]	
				South Carolina[j]	

[a]Updated version of summary published in the Seventh Annual Report to Congress on Implementation of the Education of the Handicapped Act (U.S. Department of Education, 1985).

[b] In footnotes following, A, autistic; AH, aurally handicapped; D, deaf; DB, deaf-blind; HI, hearing impaired; MH, mentally handicapped; PI, physically impaired; SH, severely handicapped; SMH, severely mentally handicapped; TMH, trainable mentally handicapped; VI, visually impaired; DD, developmentally disabled; all, all handicapping conditions.

[c] from 2.8 years, all.

[d] 3 years, all; from birth, children with serious handicapping conditions that, without intervention, will become progressively more difficult for successful intervention by school age.

[e] 4 years, all; from 3 years, TMH, SMH, PI; from birth, HI, VI, DB, A.

[f] 4 years, all; from birth VI, HI, SH.

[g] 4 years, all; from 3 years, D.

[h] 3 years, phase in DD by 1988.

[i] 5 years, all; from 3 years, MH; from birth, AH, VI.

[j] 5 years, all; from 4 years, VI, HI, D.

[k] 6 years, all; from 5 years, if LEA offers kindergarten.

[l] 6 years, all; from 6 years, if LEA offers kindergarten.

alternative service delivery approaches that are somewhat different from those traditionally used with school-aged students in regular and special education programs and their parents.

The premise of this chapter is that parent education and involvement and the parent–professional relationship within these evolving early intervention programs is a different "ballgame" than professionals have traditionally played in when working with parents of older, school-aged students. It calls for a different, new perspective about what constitutes "assistance" to parents. While wisdom can be gleaned from services for parents of older students in elementary and secondary schools, there is danger in assuming that traditional forms of parent education and involvement will be appropriate for parents of handicapped infants and preschoolers. Perhaps it is time for professionals to view parent education not as one single field where the application of professional expertise is similar to all clients, but as one where the application of parent education and involvement principles take on a unique character with each different subgroup. For example, parent education and involvement during a child's early years (birth to age 5 or 6) involves one set of needs, priorities, and methods of delivery that are different in many aspects from what is needed by parents when their youngster is in elementary or secondary school and spends the majority of his or her waking hours at school or in school-related activities. Likewise, parent education, involvement and consultation needs change again when their offspring are out of high school and are making transitions into the adult world and vocational independence.

This chapter describes the unique nature of parent education and involvement in early intervention programs. We describe why early intervention services demand a different perspective and set of skills and values from professionals and why professionals must assume a unique new view of their roles if they are to render constructive support to parents and families of young handicapped children. If professionals are to achieve the goals for which early intervention services are offered, what should the professional–parent relationship be in order to truly support parents in their caregiving, nurturing roles with a handicapped young family member? Our purpose is to describe some alternative approaches for rendering support to this unique group of parents during this stage of their own lives and their handicapped children's early life. Our intent is to help professionals recognize the need to build new skills for working with this particular clientele. We hope professionals will see more clearly how they can offer meaningful assistance to parents during the early years of a handicapped child's life.

Provisions under P.L. 99-457 Concerning Parent and Family Services and Involvement

The 1986 amendments to P.L. 94-142 establish clear authority and responsibility for state agencies to establish early intervention programs for 3–5 year olds and for infants from birth through age 2. That authority includes the establishment of service systems for parents and families as well as for the young handicapped child. This sets the stage for tremendous growth in services involving parents and professionals in collaborative relationships.

Parental roles and parent and family needs are addressed in several sections of the law. Title I, the section on handicapped infants and toddlers, sets forth a definition of "early intervention services" which includes seven criteria. Two of those criteria specifically relate to parent and family issues. One states that

> early intervention services include, but are not limited to: *family training, counseling,* and *home visits;* special instruction, speech pathology and audiology; occupational therapy, physical therapy; psychological services; *case management* services; medical services only for diagnostic or evaluation purposes; early identification, screening, and assessment services; and health services necessary to enable the infant or toddler to benefit from other early intervention services.

The law futher describes what case management services entail, defining them as

> services provided to families of handicapped infants and toddlers to assist them in gaining access to early intervention services and other services identified in the infant's or toddler's individualized family service plan; to ensure timely delivery of available services; and to coordinate the provision of early intervention services with other services (such as medical services for other than diagnostic and evaluation purposes) which the infant or toddler needs or is being provided. Specific case management services include: coordinating the performance of evaluations, assisting families in identifying available service providers; participating in the development of the IFSP, coordinating and monitoring the delivery of available services; informing families of the availability of advocacy services available to the family; coordinating with the medical and health providers, and facilitating the development of a transition plan to preschool services, where appropriate.

Another criterion in the law defining early intervention services is that services must be provided in conformity with an individualized family service plan (IFSP). This provision makes it clear that planning should not focus wholly on the young child but must consider the broader environment and family system within which the child lives. The IFSP must be in writing and must contain the following:

a statement of the infant's/toddler's present levels of physical development, cognitive development, language and speech development, psycho-social development, and self-help skills based on professional acceptable objective criteria.

a statement of the family's strengths and needs relating to enhancing the development of the family's handicapped infant or toddler.

a statement of major outcomes expected to be achieved for the infant/toddler and the family including the criteria, procedures, and timelines used to determine the degree to which progress toward those outcomes is being made and whether modifications or revisions of the outcomes or services are necessary.

a statement of the specific early intervention services to meet the unique needs of the infant/toddler and the family, including the frequency and intensity and the method of delivering services.

projected dates for initiation of services and the anticipated duration of services.

designation of the casemanager from that profession most immediately relevant to the infant's or toddler's or family's needs who will be responsible for the implementation of the plan and coordination with other agencies and persons.

steps to be taken to support the transition of the handicapped infant or toddler to other services and into preschool intervention programs.

Another section under Title I specifies that minimum components of a statewide system should consist of comprehensive, coordinated, multidisciplinary, interagency programs providing services for all handicapped infants and toddlers and their families. This statewide system must include the performance of a timely multidisciplinary evaluation of the child and the needs of the family to appropriately assist in the development of the handicapped infant and toddler.

Title II, the section of P.L. 99-457 concerning handicapped preschoolers ages 3–5, further stresses the parental role and parental needs in early childhood–special education service systems. Again Congress noted in the law that the family is the primary learning environment for children under age 6 and stressed the critical need for parents and professionals to function in a collaborative manner. In explaining provisions of the law, the Congressional Committee on Education and Labor (U.S. Congress, 1986) stated that "Whenever appropriate and to the extent desired by parents, the preschooler's IEP [individualized education program] will include instruction for parents so that they can be active and knowledgeable in assessing their child's progress'' (p. 20).

Alternative service delivery systems for preschool-aged children were noted in the law, including home-based programs (through which families will obviously be brought into major involvement with professionals as a part of the intervention). This acknowledgement of the home as an acceptable site for the delivery of services opens up a whole arena for bringing parents and professionals together for more continuous, direct interactions. It offers opportunities for cooperative teamwork never before applied so extensively or in similar forms in educational programs for older school-aged students.

Finally, P.L. 99-457 extended all rules and regulations provided under P.L. 94-142, applicable to children ages 6–17 in elementary or secondary special education programs, to handicapped preschoolers, ages 3–5, served in state approved and funded early intervention programs. This means that regulations concerning development of the IEP, due process procedures, notification and informed consent, and confidentiality and access to records that are standard procedures in special education for school-aged students must now be applied in early intervention programs. All of these regulations relate directly to roles parents can play in their child's education and rights they have under the law. Table 9.2 provides a review of those rules and regulations.

The Rationale for Parent Education and Involvement in Early Intervention

Special education services for school-aged students and most activities involving their parents have often been problem oriented and based on the remediation model. That is, special services are rendered after there is a clearly identified, diagnosed problem or disability evidenced by the student's inability to function adequately in the regular classroom or lack of academic or social skills commensurate with age or grade-level norms. Interaction between professionals and parents thus tends to be concerned with one or both of the following tasks.

1. Routine school matters such as parent–teacher conferences, IEP meetings, or placement conferences when a student's assignment to a particular special education classroom or service is decided

2. Situation-specific issues that arise when the student's behavior or performance is problematic, deviant, or there is concern about the student's welfare outside the classroom

Table 9.2   Rules and Regulations under P.L. 94-142[a]

The IEP
1. Parents must be contacted to set a mutually agreed-upon time and place for the conference.
2. Efforts to involve the parents through home visits, telephone calls, and letters (if they have not attended the IEP meeting) must be documented.
3. Efforts to use alternative methods to meet with parents in order to include them in the IEP planning should be made if they express a desire to be involved but cannot attend the meeting (e.g., a conference phone call).
4. Parental input at the IEP meeting should be encouraged. Parents are *not* to be presented with a prewritten IEP.
5. Parents have the right to bring other individuals to the meeting.
6. Parents must receive a written summary of the meeting and may request a copy of the IEP document.

Due Process Procedures
1. Parents may request a fair hearing in regard to any matter related to initiating or changing the identification, evaluation, or educational placement of their child, or the provision of an appropriate education for their child.
2. Parents should be informed of legal and other available services that are free or low cost.
3. Parents may be accompanied by counsel and advised during the hearing.
4. Parents or their counsel may give evidence as well as cross-examine witnesses and compel the attendance of a witness.
5. Parents many prohibit the introduction of new evidence that has not been disclosed prior to 5 days before the hearing.
6. Parents may obtain verbatim records of the hearing.
7. Parents are to receive a copy of the written facts and decision within 45 days after the hearing.
8. Parents may appeal the decision of a hearing conducted by a local agency to the state education agency.
9. Parents may bring action if they disagree with the decision.

Notification and Informed Consent
1. All communications to parents are to be in the parents' native language and in clear, understandable wording.
2. Parents must be notified and asked to give their consent by signing approval for an evaluation to determine whether the child needs special education.
3. Parents are to be notified of *all* meetings dealing with identification, evaluation, and placement of their child for educational services in *advance* of the meeting.
4. Interpreters are to be present at the meetings if the parents' native language is not to be used.
5. Parents are to be notified of their right to have an outside evaluator, paid for by the local agency, if they disagree with the agency's evaluation.
6. Parents are to be notified of their rights in regard to the due process procedures.

Confidentiality and Access to Records
1. Parents must be informed of policies related to storage of records, disclosure to third parties, retention of records, and destruction of any information regarding their child.
2. Parents may inspect and review any record of the agency that is related to their child; no more than 45 days can pass before an agency responds to a parent's request to examine records.

Table 9.2 (*Continued*)

---

3. Parents may request copies of the records. A reasonable fee can be charged.
4. Parent may request an explanation of the records.
5. Parents may select a representative to inspect their child's records.
6. Agencies must keep a record of third parties who obtain access to a child's records, which includes: (a) the person's name, (b) the date the records were inspected, and (c) the purpose for which authorization was given.
7. Parents may request a list of the types and locations of education records maintained by the agency.
8. Parental consent must be obtained before information is disclosed to anyone other than officials of the agency or if the information is to be used for purposes other than in regard to the child's education program (such as for research).
9. Transfer of the rights of privacy to children should take into consideration the age, type, and severity of the child's handicap.

---

[a] From Peterson (1987). Used by permission.

In essence, existence of a problem or concern is the catalyst that brings parents and professionals together. If the student is enrolled as a nonhandicapped student in regular education, parents and professionals usually come together to find a solution and resolve the problem. Hence the underlying expectation of professionals, at least, is to address the problem, "fix it," and move on to other tasks.

Parent consultation and involvement in the field of early intervention is approached from a different point of view. It is best understood when we consider the purposes of early intervention services. Peterson (1987) notes that such programs serve young children with handicapping or at-risk conditions and their parents with the intent of

1. Minimizing the effects of a handicapping condition upon a child's growth and development and maximizing that child's opportunities to engage in the normal activities deemed important during the early years

2. Preventing (if possible) at-risk conditions, early developmental irregularities, or congenital abnormalities from developing into more serious problems that become deviant to the extent they are labeled as significant disabilities

3. Preventing the development of secondary handicaps resulting from interference by a primary disability which may alter a child's ability to learn, to engage in normal experiences other children access, or to acquire certain developmental and foundation skills at the expected ages

4. Helping parents develop positive attitudes and constructive reciprocal relationships with their special child from the onset by providing

social and emotional support, giving parents pertinent information (through which they can better understand their child's condition, behavior, development, and special needs), and helping parents acquire special skills that enhance their chances for experiencing success, pleasure, and self-worth in caregiving activities with their child.

Early intervention programs thus are designed to take constructive action before problems become full blown. The goal is to provide help early in anticipation of the support parents will need and training their young child will require when a condition is present that is known to interfere with normal development. Given these objectives, professionals working with early intervention services must assume a new perspective, especially in their relationship with parents and the family.

1. The professional role is to provide support and ongoing assistance. Services are not necessarily "problem oriented." Services are not initiated from a perspective that the family is disfunctional, inadequate, or that a "problem" exists that must be alleviated. Instead, the task is to provide education, optimal care, and stimulation for the child and help parents to nurture and deal constructively with the child as he or she grows and moves on to each new developmental stage.

2. The professional role is not merely one of diagnosing and labeling disorders in young children. Rather, the intent of early intervention is to avoid premature diagnoses and instead to help these children progress as normally as possible to see what can be achieved by the time they reach kindergarten. With school-aged students, professionals are accustomed to applying their professional expertise in tasks of assessing, diagnosing, describing the nature of the problem and giving it a diagnostic label. This is perhaps one of the least important tasks for professionals who work with delayed or handicapped children during their infancy or preschool years. This is not to suggest assessment is unnecessary or unimportant. But constructive timely action in addressing a child's delays and in helping the child acquire critical developmental skills is far more crucial for the child and parent than spending precious time deriving a premature diagnosis and making a prognosis.

3. The professional role is one of preparing parents to assume new roles and responsibilities as caregivers and teachers of their handicapped infant or preschooler that may not be part of the usual parenting experience. This means helping parents learn skills they need for teaching and managing their child. With older children, professionals often become involved only when there is a dysfunctional family or a "problem" to be resolved. In early intervention, the family is not necessarily dysfunctional or inadequate. Rather, professionals are involved from the beginning to

help the family become or remain a stable, happy, functional unit. Professionals thus apply their expertise to assist parents in integrating the special child into their family system while addressing his or her special needs as constructively as possible within family routines.

Basic Premises Underlying Parent Education and Involvement in Early Intervention

Given these purposes of early intervention and the changing roles of professionals with parents within these programs, how do parent education and parent involvement fit into the overall scheme? Several empirical, economic, legal, humanistic, and simple common-sense reasons are cited in the professional literature explaining why the parent role is such a crucial part of early intervention services (Arnold, Rowe, & Tolbert, 1978; Bristol & Gallagher, 1982; Cartwright, 1981; Foster, Berger, & McLean, 1981; Goodson & Hess, 1975; Hayden, 1976; Peterson, 1982, 1987; Shearer & Shearer, 1972, 1977; Simpson, 1982; Turnbull & Turnbull, 1986; Welsh & Odum, 1981). Peterson (1987) summarizes 12 basic premises reflected in that literature:

1. Parents (or their substitute caregivers) are the most significant teachers, socializing agents, and caregivers for children during their years from birth to age 5. This parent figure is the key person who determines what opportunities, what stimulation, physical–emotional–social–nutrition care, and nurturance a child receives during those early years.

2. Parents are in a unique, strategic position to enhance or negate the potential benefits of an early intervention program. Who is in the best position to first note irregular behavior or development in a young child? Parents. Their perspective and knowledge about the child, given the fact that they have the greatest exposure to the child is very helpful in planning interventions. Furthermore, parents are more likely to respond to requests by professionals and to work on similar goals with the child if their input is included in the development of the intervention plan.

3. Parents can act as key intervention agents in their child's life and can be a primary teacher of the special skills their child needs to acquire. Parents gain a great deal when their child makes progress and becomes more independent and skilled through effective early intervention. They are in a good position to facilitate optimal learning in their own child. Including them as either the primary change agent or as a part of the intervention team gives them a constructive, active way to deal with their child. It also is an economical, practical strategy for dealing with the young handicapped child's needs in the context of the family.

4. Parent involvement and education offers a means for parents to build

a positive perspective about their child and their position as parents. Involvement helps curtail the isolation that parents often feel during these early years when their child is found to be handicapped or to have developmental irregularities. Emotional support and fellowship from others can be of utmost importance during this time as parents come to recognize, then understand, and gradually accept their child's condition or "differentness." The degree to which parents work through this trying, often painful time affects their attachment to the child. Attitudes toward the child and the child's potential are also formed during this time. When professional help can be more accessible and opportunities are created for parents to meet and share with others having similar experiences, more constructive parent–child and child–family relationships can be formed from the beginning.

5. Parents of infant, toddlers, and preschoolers with handicapping or at-risk conditions often face additional caregiving demands and stresses that demand new coping skills and parenting skills and may tax their emotional and coping systems.

It makes no sense to ignore the additional pressures and demands that a handicapped child can place upon the family and leave parents on their own to deal with these conditions if help can be offered. Services for parents and assistance to aid them in their parenting roles can only help parents respond more ably to their child's special needs.

6. The success of early intervention services and the duration of those benefits is directly related to the degree to which parents are part of the intervention process. Research suggests that the effects of early intervention are lessened and gains made by the child are more likely to be lost if parents are not a part of the intervention process. Parents are more likely to learn new strategies and methods of dealing constructively with the child in the home if they have been involved with professionals in their child's intervention program. They are more likely to apply those strategies if they have watched intervention teachers and other staff apply and model them.

7. Intervention works best when parents and professionals are collaborating and working together toward common goals for a child. The impact of any intervention is diminished notably if parents and professionals are working at cross-purposes with each other or if each is teaching and working with the child in very different ways. No matter how skilled professionals are, or how loving and helpful parents are, each cannot achieve alone what the two parties, working hand-in-hand, can accomplish together. But coordination does not occur magically. It means a deliberate effort is made and a mechanism is created for parents and professionals to truly work as a team.

8. Involving parents by educating them and helping them build new skills for dealing with their child's special needs from the onset has obvious economic benefits. Early intervention services can be costly because of the necessary small staff ratio. Furthermore, the cost of supporting a handicapped child outside of the home in foster care or in institutional placements when a family is unable to care for that child is a far more costly alternative. Parent education and involvement is thus cost efficient for two reasons: (a) their participation increases their own investment in the intervention and increases chances for achieving and sustaining the greatest child gains for the dollars spent, and (b) parents offer a practical means for implementing intervention programs with children in sparsely populated rural areas where distance and time limitations of professionals make center-based programs costly.

9. Involvement brings parents into contact with a variety of resources (caring people, agencies, materials, information, professionals) which they can draw upon to aid them in their parenting roles. Parents often describe their initial hesitancy to seek help or be assertive in working through the barriers they encounter in making contact with agencies or people who can provide assistance. When left to their own initiative to deal with the hurdles that make service access difficult, some parents simply give up. Involvement and education programs for parents can be a tremendous boost to help them connect with information sources, community services, parent support groups, child-sitting services or other resources.

10. Parent education and involvement is advantageous simply because a great many parents are particularly eager during their child's early life to be good parents, to nurture their child, and they are often not willing to relinquish control over a child so young to others. Most parents want a voice in how their child is managed, taught, and cared for, especially when the child is very young. While school-aged students are more independent and hence parents release more control to the older child or to those who work with him or her, infants and preschoolers are still dependent upon parents or primary caregivers. Given this dependency, few parents want to be told, "Stay away." Most want to know what others are doing with their child. Most wish to support the efforts of a program in ways that help their child make progress, at least to the extent possible given their own life demands and job responsibilities.

11. Parent education and involvement fosters parent and community support for early referral, early intervention programs. The reality is that early intervention services for 0–5 year olds are still in the formative stages. While a mandate now exists for services to 3–5 year olds by 1990–91, communities and state and local agencies still have the choice of

supporting or not supporting special services for handicapped infants and young children from birth through age 2. Parents, of course, are a program's best advocates, especially if they are knowledgeable about early intervention and the program in which their child is served. Public policy and state legislation is greatly influenced by parent advocate groups. While parent advocacy may be less crucial to services as children enter the public schools, it still remains a crucial factor as we look to the years ahead and formulate statewide systems of early childhood intervention services for infants and preschoolers.

Conditions Unique to Parents with Young Children

In this section we discuss several unique conditions that may affect parents and families when the child in question is very young and hence affect the professional–parent relationship when professionals first become involved in a helping role. These conditions influence what services and supports parents seek from professionals and others in their supportive network. They affect what professionals must do if they are to be responsive and constructive in the lives of these parents and families.

Parents may be in the initial steps of confronting their own disconcerting feelings and concerns that something is wrong with their child. They probably lack a clear diagnosis or answers about their child's status. It is possible that the only diagnosis is verification that the child is delayed and shows atypical behavior but with no known causes. At this stage, parents may be desperately seeking answers. They are undoubtedly worried, fearful, and frustrated by their child's behavior or delayed development. The vagueness of the situation makes it even more unclear as to what actions they should take to help the child.

Parents recently receiving a diagnosis of abnormality and disability for their child are right in the initial and most intense reactive stage to that information and their own initial emotional and personal feelings about it. At this stage, parents may be facing the realities (or deciding what they think these realities are) of the diagnosis and what impacts it will have upon their own personal lives, those of other family members, and the life of the child. Parents of older children with disabilities have been dealing with and adjusting to their feelings over a longer period of time when professionals encounter them for the first time. Professionals will be dealing with parents of young children at a time when they are going through the very initial stages of shock, grief, guilt, denial, anger, and other emotions that may come when an unwelcome diagnosis is made.

Parents may be anxiously seeking more information about their child's condition or merely existing in a fearful, uninformed state of confusion about what their child's condition actually involves. Parents may get the technical diagnostic terms from medical professionals at this stage. But they often do not get (or may be unable to absorb the information when the diagnosis is given) more specific information or understanding about what the condition entails and what impact it will have on their child's development and learning. They typically have many unanswered questions about the prognosis and what they can do to foster optimal learning and progress in the child. Or, they may have too much information with too many premature prognoses about how debilitating a condition will be for the child. Given this potential information deficiency or overload, parents often have no one to interpret, explain, and help them sort through conflicting reports and professional opinions and then translate it all into constructive actions they can take to help their own child. Some parents become frantic about what they should do at this stage. Others simply give up on the child and protect their own feelings by withdrawing emotionally from the child and any concerns about the child's condition or ultimate welfare.

Parents may be existing in a state of uncertainty, nebulousness, and suspended concern when their child is exhibiting unusual behavior or delayed, irregular development that cannot be explained; they may not know whether those "symptoms" are suggestive of a true problem or simply the child's unique but normal developmental characteristics. When children show subtle behaviors or irregularities that cause concern, the prognosis is not always apparent. Is there something wrong or is this normal variation among children? Is the child handicapped or not? Should one be alarmed and take immediate action? Or should one just give the child some time and wait to see what happens? The symptoms of a serious problem are not always clear, especially when a child is young. There is not a long developmental history from which predictions can be made about the child. Parents are thus suspended between an unwanted reality and a desire for a normal, healthy child, between a decision to seek help or not to worry. Parents may be in an exceedingly anxiety-ridden, fearful, worried state. Furthermore, the lack of clear, decisive answers and the risks associated with premature diagnoses and prognoses may prolong this state for parents.

Parents may be attempting to cope with and care for a child whose problems or behaviors tax their parenting skills and threaten their feelings of competence, success, and enjoyment as parents. Some parents find themselves dealing with a passive, unresponsive infant or preschooler. Or the child may be one who cries and screams constantly, presents frustrating feeding and management problems, and requires constant supervision that places more demands and stresses upon the parents and family members. These difficult-to-care-for children quickly produce parents who are tired and stretched to the limit of their emotional and financial resources. These additional demands on their lives give them limited time to deal with professionals. This invites more frustration for them if professionals offer nothing other than a listening ear and give no tangible help that deals with the daily realities of their family life.

Parents may be dealing with a child whose medical conditions or developmental disabilities significantly alter what they must do to provide adequate care and stimulation. These conditions can dramatically alter what it takes to teach their child skills that normally developing children acquire more easily and spontaneously. Parents usually need to acquire new specialized parenting skills in order to nurture and help their child develop optimally. For example, parents may need to learn to handle prosthetic devices or special medical equipment. They may need to learn sign language to communicate with a hearing impaired or deaf child. They may need to learn alternative ways of interacting with and teaching a blind child. They may have to learn special methods of positioning for a child with major motor-orthopedic problems. These are skills parents do not learn by osmosis. They are not instinctive caregiving behaviors or skills that parents learn by asking the next door neighbor. This is a stage when parents usually are eager for help, they are searching for answers. They have not given up—yet.

Parents may be attempting to find services for themselves and their child and encountering the confusion of where to go for help. They also are probably encountering the frustrations that come from the mounds of red tape, rules, and restrictive regulations that they must surmount if they gain access to services. Parents quickly discover that services for very young children are distributed across many agencies and administrative systems. Often they experience difficulty in getting the help they need at the very time they are most eager, possibly even desperate, for help. Parents' first contact with early intervention services is often the first contact they have (beyond the medical personnel) with professionals concerning their child's special needs. This means they have limited support systems established to help them with their child's problems or special needs or to help them make those first contacts with agencies, services, or resources that could be available to them.

Parents may already be stressed, tired, discouraged, and in need of caring, professional support because of the emergency conditions under which they have existed during the early months, even years, of their child's life. In cases where a young child is medically fragile or has conditions which require constant medical intervention, parents may be dealing with a child who has been constantly hospitalized or has required round-the-clock monitoring and care. One couple, who gave birth to a baby boy with Down's syndrome accompanied with major heart and intestinal abnormalities, spent the larger part of the first 9 months of their son's life in the hospital intensive care unit. Another couple experienced 35 hospitalizations and repeated major surgeries with their daughter by the time she reached age 3. These parents need immediate assistance that is helpful and constructive. They do not need professionals who will simply add more expectations, frustrations, and turmoil to an already overtaxed family system.

Parents are in the initial stages of developing a bond and personal relationship with their young child. They are at a vulnerable point when this evolving relationship can move in the direction of a nurturing-loving-committed one or rejecting-detached-indifferent regard for the child. Experts have pointed to the early months and years of a child's life as the time when bonding occurs between the child and the caregiver (Kennell, Voos, & Klaus, 1979; Lamb, 1976; Weinraub, Brooks, & Lewis, 1977). Many conditions can disrupt this process when a young child is handicapped or has some serious medical or developmental condition that is life threatening or potentially disabling. The degree to which parents can be helped to relate to the child instead of becoming wholly distracted by the negative aspects of the abnormality can help positive relationships be formed. The degree to which parents can be given hope in situations that have possibly shattered their dream of the normal child they wished for greatly affects how readily they can accept and embrace their baby as a wanted and accepted family member. Professionals who work with parents at this time are thus dealing with adults who are initially confronting those conflicting feelings of acceptance/rejection, hope/despair, out of which will evolve those attitudes and views that will permeate their continuing interactions with their child.

Special Needs of Parents of Young Children with Disabilities or Developmental Problems

So what do parents need during the time their handicapped child is an infant, toddler, or preschooler? What do they want from professionals who approach them in the role of helper or service provider? What can professionals offer to parents that will actually support and benefit them and other family members? Professionals are often quick to offer answers to these questions, drawing upon their own professional training, theory, and experience with other populations if they have had none with young children. But perhaps that is the first point of error—professionals making assumptions about what parents need and want. In their eagerness to be productive in their profession and to demonstrate their expertise, professionals often expect themselves to produce answers and solutions for parents. But perhaps the answers to such questions should come from parents themselves or from mutual problem solving and evaluation by professionals and parents working together. What constitutes this "assistance and support" is undoubtedly an individual matter for each parent and family based upon their unique circumstances, their personal and social resources, and their style of living, including their methods of coping with family stresses. The importance of individualized parent–family services has been a growing theme among early-intervention professionals (Bricker & Casuso, 1979; Karnes & Zehrbach, 1975; Turnbull & Turnbull, 1982). Here lies one of the unique aspects of early intervention services; services to parents concern home and life circumstances that vary greatly from family to family. Effective parent–family services must therefore be individualized and designed to match the needs of the family, in both content and method of delivery.

Since the primary-care environment for young children is the home, and the parents or their alternative caregivers are the major figures in the lives of children from birth to school age, professionals find themselves dealing with very personal aspects of family living. They are not simply dealing with children whose lives are spent primarily within an elementary school building. Many areas of need where parents of young children now ask for help from professionals concern the more private, intimate aspects of their relationships and interactions with immediate and extended family members, including activities that go on in the home and neighborhood. In early intervention service programs, professionals must therefore deal with a new set of issues and concerns that transcend the traditional school or center environment and focus upon parent–child relationships and care within the home arena. Professionals must not only offer consultation, instruction, information, and guidance for parents, they must deal with these needs in the context of the home. What is most significant here is that the nature of the home environment is greatly affected by the personal values, religious beliefs, cultural patterns, and individual styles of living of those parents. We run head on into questions of privacy, parents' freedom to choose their own life style and methods of child rearing, and the rights of parents to make decisions about their own lives and those of their children. Professionals, in their attempts to help parents and their handicapped young child, must recognize potential value conflicts and questions about the boundaries of their roles as interventionists and advisors. There is a risk of transforming "assistance'' into an imposition of one's own professional values and expectations upon parents. There is a risk of professionals reinterpreting parental responsibilities to conform to their own conceptions of what parents should do, how they must rear their children, and what family-living routines should be. There is a risk of professionals placing expectations upon parents that press for changes that are unrealistic, perhaps condescending and judgmental, and possibly unfair. Here lies the challenge for professionals and the thin line between assistance and services that are helping or hindering, supportive or infringing, sensitive or oppressive to parents and families.

Parents of young children with handicaps or developmental irregularities are in those first stages of seeking help and becoming acquainted with the professional community of service providers. If their child's handicap is identified early, they may come into contact with a great many professionals over a relatively short period of time. Parents often refer back to this period as a frustrating, stressful, and emotionally wrenching time. They quickly learn what helps and what hinders and which professionals are helpful and sensitive and which are not. Professional literature often describes this period as a time when many parents go through a lot of ''shopping'' for answers, a time when parents sift through the offices of one professional or service site after another. It is interesting to note that such behavior is often interpreted as ''symptomatic'' of the state of the parent and as evidence of a frantic parent. Perhaps another interpretation should be considered, however, based upon views parents share about their own shopping behavior. Some parents tell us that they shop because they find professionals vary in their ability to deal helpfully with the problems and questions presented.Parents usually learn through the trial and error of dealing with numerous professionals which ones have a true understanding of the issues and know what resources can be tapped, which ones understand the unique problems of parents in dealing with young handicapped children, and which ones can offer real help to parents in the day-to-day realities of caring for such a child.

One mother, who had worked as a professional parent consultant and educator in an early intervention program for several years before herself becoming a parent of a severely handicapped child, wrote the following candid statement about her feelings about professionals and her perceptions of parent needs:

> My attitudes about how professionals can help parents changed dramatically when I was no longer just the professional working in this area but was dumped abruptly on my head on the other side of the fence as one of ''those parents'' with a handicapped young child.

What an eye opener! Now I laugh at my overly narrow view of parent services. Sometimes I even stand aghast at some things I expected of parents. I understand now why they winced, seemed so discouraged and even passive at times, or balked at tasks I wanted them to do at home. As I have tackled the same problems in my home as they were dealing with then, I understand more clearly what real help is and what it's not. Now as a parent on the asking–receiving side of the fence, I see painfully how shallow, insensitive, and sometimes off-target our professional bag of skills, consultation methods, and services can be. I am surprised at myself when I find myself reacting like parents I used to work with, feeling hostile, angry, and cynical about professionals who think their degree and theory is enough to give them the know-how to tell me what to do. It isn't. Professionals with only theory, but no real experience with these kids, are ill prepared and presumptuous to suggest they can offer true under-standing and help.

How many professionals are coming into this field, claiming expertise, but have never really worked with one of these children? They have no idea of the day-to-day tasks involved in working with them or caring for them. Now I say to them, if you're going to enter into our lives suggesting you have something to offer, then have something concrete and real to offer, not just talk and a pseudo-professional listening ear!! We have an abundance of listening ears, more than we need! The bottom line for us is we need meaningful help, not people who consume precious time we no longer have and leave us empty-handed in the end still asking again for help. Our children require lots more attention and care than most normal infants and preschoolers require. They are demanding, often cannot be left along. They are dependent. There is no clear promise that situation will change or our child will grow out of it like others. I have learned that parents need more than a listening ear from a profes-sional who knows how to way "hm-m-m-m" at the right time or who will give you 30 minutes of time to vent frustrations. We need more than an interpreter who can reflect back to us that we are stressed, tired, maybe even angry. We need more than a diagnostician who puts the label on our child's disability, predicts (probably pre-maturely and presumptuously) what our child can and cannot do and then walks away. These things we already know. What we are asking for is help and support based upon those conditions. We don't need a professional to merely affirm those facts and then send us away with nothing more.

When our children are young, we are eager to do whatever we can. We still have hope we can help this little person. I hate professional rhetoric. I think we professionals dish out far too much of that, then refer parents on to somebody else to get the real nitty-gritty help. We end up still going home empty-handed, still asking how to control an uncontrollable, unresponsive child. We end up still asking how to communicate with a child who doesn't understand or communicate back like other children. We are still anxious for suggestions on how to help this kid learn what other kids do just through the course of everyday living. We're the ones who are left wondering how to deal with neighbors and relatives who don't understand or accept our child, who challenge our efforts saying we're uptight parents or that we're overreacting, or that our kid will grow out of it if we'd just leave him alone. This is the help we need and we need it desperately. This is where inexperienced professionals just don't have sufficient know-how. But how many will pretend they know the answers anyway.

Parents like me want skilled "friends" who'll work with us, think with us, problem-solve over daily issues of childcare and child rearing we encounter. We don't expect professionals automatically have the answers. We don't. We need an informed, educated professional partner who can help us find strategies that work for handling the tasks like feeding, dressing, communicating with our child, teaching our child, managing our child at home and minimizing disruptions in the lives of other family members. We need support services, someone to be there when we need help or just an extra hand. We need someone to talk to, someone to care about us and our child, not just one time here and there, but on a regular basis. This changes too from day to day or year to year. A pat formula for services that professionals apply to us year after year is not the answer. If professionals really expect to work with and involve parents in early intervention programs, they must first LISTEN to parents. HEAR what we have to say about our own needs! Professionals have got to remember they're not serving themselves or their own egos. They say they are there to assist and give services to families and parents and children when and where they need and want it most. So we'd all better practice what we preach.

Other parents were consulted in the writing of this chapter regarding their needs. Professional literature reflecting parental input also offers some new perspectives. Those parents were as candid and to the point as the parent whom we just quoted. Their words vividly described the realities of their lives and the kinds of assistance they believe professionals can offer that will be of greatest value to them. While parents expressed their suggestions in various ways, their responses tended to target six areas of need.

INFORMATION. Parents need information of many types to help them better understand their child's handicap or condition, how it will potentially affect the child's development, what special needs it creates, and how this may alter their role and interaction with the child as parents. Parents also need continuous opportunities to expand upon this information, review it with someone, reflect upon its implications and meaning, and ask questions. They need information about local resources where services and other forms of assistance can be obtained to support them in their parenting roles (e.g., babysitting, respite care, special activities that are appropriate for the child and family given the child's disabilities), as illustrated by the observations of two parents of handicapped children:

> It took months, even years for me to hear then absorb all the information about Jacob's diagnosis of Cornelia de Lange syndrome and what it meant for him. The 15 minutes our pediatrician spent attempting to explain this condition didn't educate me. They were only moments of pain, of hearing a diagnosis I didn't want to hear, of listening to facts that would alter the rest of my life. It was not a time for learning, it was a time for grief. The information I needed had to come slowly from people who could deal with my tears, give me time and a shoulder to cry one. That began with the person who worked with Jacob as an infant, later from his special preschool teacher. Each gave me information from day to day as questions came up, as I became able to accept and understand more information, and as I observed the affect of this condition upon my son's development. They were ready to teach me when teaching was needed. They were there to answer questions when I wanted an answer. I didn't need or want information in one big awesome dose. It's a continual need. I want professionals who have the information with the know-how and sensitivity to deliver it at the right times. I especially appreciate when they help us use the information constructively to deal with those daily issues that can come up with this kind of child.

When we learned Sarah had Downs' syndrome plus other congenital defects, the hardest thing for me was to face my family and friends to explain it all. My in-laws denied that anything was wrong. They stayed away and kept arguing that our daughter would be all right—that the doctors were just wrong. My parents were quiet, distant, They didn't even come to see their new granddaughter for months after she was born. I didn't know what to tell them. I couldn't even explain this condition to them without crying. How could I give them hope when I didn't even have it myself. The lady from the infant program at the University saved me in that aspect. When she started working with Sarah and me when Sarah was only 3 months old, she suggested I bring the grandparents to some of our therapy sessions. We tackled my hustand's parents first, then my own. Between the two of us, we explained what was different about Sarah, showed them what Sarah could do and what we were doing in our therapy sessions to help her. By the time we finished, they finally understood what Downs' syndrome meant. After a few more sessions they began to show interest in her achievements; they began to cheer for her. Most of all, I watched them begin to care about her and finally adopt her as their own. I couldn't have explained all those things on my own. That's one place sensitive professionals can help.

A PROFESSIONAL PARTNER. Parents need an informed professional partner and consultant to participate with them as needed in mutual problem solving relative to personal and family issues in caring for, managing, teaching, and integrating the child comfortably into the family routines.

While life with a handicapped preschooler definitely has similarities with rearing our other children, it definitely brings on lots of unpredictables, demands beyond the usual, problems you simply don't know how to handle. It's comforting to me to know the staff at the center (the early intervention program) are there to help when I need it. They're like a second family to me. We've sat there together many a day to discuss Stephanie's wierd behavior and to figure out what to do about it. They don't have all the answers. I'm glad they don't, or I'd feel really like a real dummy. They help me get over my frustrated state of inaction to see alternatives. We think out loud together. It makes it easier to laugh at our tribulations and go on to do our best. We work together to pick solutions and try them. It's a lonely road out there when you think you've got to deal with a child like this all by yourself. It's easier when you know you've got some professionals there who know you well, care about you and your child, and have the time and skill to help you. I feel more secure as a parent with them as my friend and partner.

When Michael was an infant and preschooler, we lived in a small town. He was seriously physically handicapped and who knows what else. The experts we contacted for help gave us three things: a diagnosis that Michael was severely handicapped, mentally retarded, and likely to be unable to walk, talk, or function independently in his life. One person said he'd probably be a "vegetable" and that there was really nothing much we could do. They gave us the sense of futility. The second professional we encountered was his pediatrician. When we asked him if there was anything, anything we could do to help our son, he said no. He gave us despair and when we asked him if there were any programs or services for children like him, he didn't know.

When we tried to get programs in our area to accept Michael, people generally explained his disabilities to us once again, conducted evaluations that produced long written reports on his low functioning levels. When we asked what to do next there was typically silence and usually not much more. Sometimes we got a suggestion to contact a different program or expert. No one seemed to know what to do; no one wanted to tackle this child's problems except us. How sadly we needed a helping hand. We felt like failures. These things gave us hopelessness and kept our reality as that of mere survival. The third thing we got was a new diagnosis when it came time for kindergarten round up. This time he was multiply handicapped and severely MR. But no one was forthcoming to help us do what we could, so we did the best we could. Those years took a toll on our family. It no longer exists. As I see professionals work with parents now, and I look back to Mike's early years, I grieve. How much I and my husband and kids needed help—someone to show us—teach us what Mike could learn to do. Michael is institutionalized now. I wonder what life might have been like if parent education and support had been available to us at those critical times. I envy families and professionals who work together as partners to help these children and their parents live more satisfying, successful lives together.

A SUPPORT NETWORK. Parents need a support network of caring, understanding persons with whom they can share their feelings, discuss their concerns, get constructive and empathetic responses, and enjoy a sense of friendship and camaraderie. Parents need someone who not only offers sensitive listening, but who has the experience and expertise to offer suggestions on actions parents can take.

I need people to care about me and my child, to show me that they can accept me as a person and accept my child, to love him and show us that we're both okay. You may not believe this, but the thing that starts my day out right is to bring Wendell to preschool and watch people be glad to see him, just talk for a minute with people who are so positive toward us. When I see you all work so hard with Wendell each day, it's inspiring to me. I try harder to do the same because of you. I see you (the teachers) get discouraged at times too, but that tells me that my moments of desperation aren't times I should feel so guilty for. They're feelings we all have. I do feel support from the people here, a lot of closeness, like people are rooting for me. I can't tell you how important that reassurance can be.

When Mitsy was an infant no one knew something was wrong, so life was pretty normal. But as she has grown bigger and her abnormalities more obvious, more and more people have backed off. Invitations to birthday parties and to neighborhood family gatherings have stopped. Friends come around less often. I find myself too tired to keep trying. It's a hastle trying to handle Mitsy around other people whose normal children are all obeying and responding to their parents' instructions and requests. Then there's Mitsy who will do anything at any unpredictable time. That leaves other children and adults staring, wondering what's wrong. I end up either pretending to be nonchalant about it all or feeling terrible because we disrupted everyone else's life. Even I stay away from them to avoid the hastle. What I'm saying is that my need for a support group has changed through the years. I need people around me, those who work with Mitsy at her preschool, people with children like her, who understand, who empathize, who don't stare. These people I have come to appreciate deeply. We help each other, we support each other, we can laugh and cry together, we can talk about the good things and we can be honest about the bad times and go on because there was someone there who could listen and really understand what I'm talking about. These are the things I need. These are the things I value.

TRAINING. Parents need special training and information on how to care for, stimulate, and teach their handicapped young child. They may need instruction to help them acquire special skills to meet the child's special needs and integrate the child successfully into the family system. They may need training on how to best manage the child or on how to engage the child in activities that will promote optimal development and learning.

Things professionals can do to help us parents is such an individual matter. I've attended parent meetings that were terrible—a waste of my time. I've sat in a planning meeting with professionals where I left asking myself what I gained and concluded it was nothing except feelings of frustration and incompetence. But then I've had some training and demonstrations from the professional staff at the center that have made life so much more tolerable. The teacher, speech therapist, occupational therapist, and psychologist have been showing me how I can work with Jamie—taught me things I couldn't have figured out alone: how to feed Jamie to simply get some food into her stomach instead on the floor. They've shown me how to have fun with her, to enjoy her even though she can't do things her brother and sister did at that age. They've taught me how to set her up in a relaxed position so she can use her arms and legs to play with a toy (Jamie has C.P.). They've taught me how to move Jamie, position her, help her move when she can on her own so that dressing isn't such a struggle. I've learned I can help my child! Life is so much happier for both of us. That's the kind of help us parents need, the practical stuff that you deal with every day when you've got a child like this.

A father of a hearing-impared preschooler who had worked through some training sessions for parents of deaf children remarked:

It's great to have people who say "Here's how you can communicate with your son. Here's how you can teach him to talk. Here's what you can do to help him understand what you are saying to him." My wife and I learned sign language and from the beginning learned to communicate with Jerry. The staff has helped our family in ways I can never repay. Initially, I had a hard time relating to this son of mine who couldn't hear and wasn't going to talk like other kids. The worst of all positions as a parent is to stand passively or to feel that you can do nothing. Training of us parents in communication with a deaf child and teaching us sign language has been a constructive, productive way of helping us be responsible parents and helping us to help our own child. We have people we can go to for advice when we need them. These people are ready with constructive "how to do it" suggestions that are practical methods for teaching our child. The time my wife and I have is tight, so help from these professionals needs to be good and to the point. I don't have tons of time to attend meeting after meeting. I need help that counts—something that'll make a difference.

TIME OFF. Parents need intermittent "personal relief" from the parenting demands that come when a young child is handicapped and needs 24-hour supervision and care. Professionals are in a position to help parents obtain services or create the support systems they need.

The years after Tammy was born were hard years, demanding years. I look back, I was chronically tired, worn out, badly needy of a break which I rarely got. When Tammy was an infant until she was about 3, my husband and I never went out for an evening or even went on a vacation. Our attentions focused on Tammy. Our other kids suffered too. But we didn't have much choice. It was nearly impossible to get a babysitter for her. She was hard to handle. We hesitated loading any responsibility for her care upon others. Friends and neighbors rarely offered to help, so we didn't pursue it with them. I honestly can't remember a time we left her with anybody else until she was about 3 or 3 1/2 years old. I would have paid millons for just a chance just to go to the store alone or go rest without worrying if she was okay. Here are the times parents need a break for our own mental health. We need time to regroup to rejuvenate ourselves. That's difficult when you have a kid like Tammy. Professionals can help us a lot if they understand that we not only need therapy or services for the child but that we need help with everyday survival. So when you think about services, include services that deal with the simple tasks of supporting families in daily living. If those go well, if we can still move smoothly through family routines each day, then we can be more responsive, loving parents. Then we will have time to do the home programs you want us to do to reinforce what you professionals are doing in the centers with our handicapped children.

Staff at Gerome's special education preschool are the best friends I have, and they're there when I need them. Maybe this goes beyond the normal call of duty for professionals, but the position they hold in my family's life has made a real difference for us. When we rushed Gerome to the hospital, it was the teacher I called to say, "What do I do?" It was the teacher who said, "Don't worry. I'll be there to take care of the other kids." And she organized other staff and parents from the preschool to take care of my other children during that emergency. The people who came to sit with me and the doctor to talk about Gerome's condition were two staff members from the preschool who knew Gerome well. Because of them we were able to give the brain surgeon the information he needed. It was they who arranged intermittent breaks for me at the hospital when I was staying in Gerome's room 24 hours a day to take care of him. If you ask me what professionals can do to help during the early years of life for these special children, I say we need professionals who can recognize what help is, who are willing to work with us to create

those help resources. In my case, I've met some wonderful professionals who are dedicated to doing just that.

INFORMAL CONTACT WITH STAFF.   Parents need opportunities for informal contact with professional staff who work with their children and
opportunities to be a part of the therapeutic and educational programming
that goes on with their handicapped child if they so desire.

Service providers may mistakedly assume responsibility for working
with the child with the message, "We'll take care of your child now, you
don't need to stay here." But many parents give us a different message,
especially when the child is young; they feel considerable responsibility
for the daily caregiving and education of their own child. Parents often
want to be involved as participants or at least observers in intervention
activities with their child.

If I had to choose between the opportunity to watch staff work
with my child or to attend a parent meeting, I'd take the observation
booth any day. I learn a lot watching staff work with Steffie. They get
things out of her that I never can. It's exciting and encouraging to see
that. Lots of us parents sit here in the observation booth and watch
what goes on. It's therapeutic for us; it's a pleasure to see others
working with and enjoying our child. It's good for me to see how
others deal with my child, how they handle the bad behavior and
draw out the good. Maybe you don't call this a type of service for us,
or maybe you don't see it as parent involvement, but I do. So many
programs ignore this as important and make no effort to allow us a
chance to simply watch others model good teaching with our child. I
think it ignores one of the most important ways we can be involved.
You'd be surprised at the discussions that go on among parents when
we watch our kids in an observation booth. You'd be impressed with
the friendships that evolve, even the babysitting pools, the transportation pools, the sharing. No one probably ever thought of an
observation booth and an invitation for parents to hang around as a
"service" for parents. Staff people come in and talk; they answer
questions. We become more appreciative and understanding of each
other. Maybe professionals need to think again about what parent
involvement and parent–professional cooperation really is. Maybe it
begins with an invitation for us to have the freedom to be here to see
what's going on with our child.

This program has become an important part of my life. The chance
to talk with staff regularly, to visit with other parents each day is one

of the things I appreciate most. I dread the day when my kid starts riding the school bus and I find myself viewed as a stranger who must explain herself if she enters the school building. Its a great feeling to join hands with a group of people whom you can regard as your friends, your advocates and helpers. The best times between us are not in formal meetings. It's the informal times, the brief conversations before and after therapy or preschool sessions. We trade information. We talk a lot so I know what staff are working on with Sadie so that I can carry on at home. I need this contact; I miss it if we don't get it. The staff let me ask stupid questions if I must; they give me suggestions. I don't have to guess what's going on with my child. I feel I still have control over her life and my own, that I'm a part of her program. When they need help, I pitch in, cook, classroom aide, playground helper. I like to do that and feel like I'm giving something back to those who are serving us.

Parent–Professional Teamwork in Early Intervention Programs: What Does It Really Mean?

If one listens to what parents of young children with handicaps or at-risk conditions are saying, including those persons quoted in this chapter, there is one clear message: These parents want something different from programs for older school-aged students, both in content or types of services and in the procedures through which professionals interact with parents and render services.

Some important values and expectations are being communicated by this population of parents about professional behavior. First, parents want open, two-way communication that can be initiated as readily and acceptably by parents as by professionals when there is a perceived need. Parents do not want to always be on the receiving end of the communication line where interactions are initiated primarily at the convenience of the professional when the professional sees the need. Second, parents want the choice of engaging in *frequent and face-to-face contact or communication,* allowing them to know what professionals are doing with their child and why. Formal meetings two or three times a year are not the kind of involvement most parents desire at this stage of their child's life. They want freedom to observe professionals working with the child. We emphasize *choice,* inasmuch as parents want the prerogative of making decisions about their own lives and those of their children and thus choosing a level of involvement (given their own life demands, time schedule, and needs). This means some parents will wish to be highly involved with their child's intervention services and with staff. Others will have limited time (particularly if both parents work) and thus may want only minimal involvement. Third, parents want the freedom to have informal contact with persons who deal with their child in early intervention programs. They do not wish to be restricted to formal, structured meetings where the agenda is set, time is limited, and formalities are followed. Parents are often at a disadvantage in those formal sessions where their skills for formal discourse are not necessarily a match for those of professionals, and where activities and the flow of dialogue are largely controlled by professionals (if for no other reason than they usually outnumber the parent). These meetings are more conducive to achieving the agendas of professionals than meeting parent needs. As needs or issues arise, parents want the opportunity to initiate informal person-to-person interactions where discussion can occur without strain, with more personal comfort and ease for them, and with a more equal balance of control between parties over what is said and done. Fourth, parents want to hold the power of decision making over their child's life and activities including, to some degree, what others do to and with their child. Furthermore, parents want to know what is happening to their child during their absence and how the child responds. They want information enabling them to monitor their child's well-being and to respond appropriately when they continue their own caregiving activities for the remainder of the day. After all, the early years of a child's life are when parental responsibility and good parenting are especially praised. Parents are usually anxious to be nurturing and good caregivers. They do not readily relinquish that responsibility during a time when it is so valued. It is no surprise that they want professionals to respect their desires to be responsive, conscientious parents and to receive their questions with openness. Parents do not wish to be told, directly or indirectly by professional staff, to "Go away," "We don't need you," "I will make decisions for you because I know more than you and I understand best what your child needs."

What are the implications of these parental values and expectations for professionals? Perhaps it means that professionals who view their own "preparedness" for dealing with parents as an agenda, a plan, and some recommendations or solutions prior to their encounters should pause, back off, and realize that parents do not have that same advantage when they deal with professionals. Parents are often at a disadvantage when dealing with knowledgeable, assertive professionals and easily are placed in a secondary, subordinate role. Professional preparedness for a particular parent interaction might be better viewed as coming into encounters with parents armed instead with those "process skills" (and an attitude) for facilitating open two-way communication, and mutual sharing–planning problem solving dialogue. This does not mean that parents will be equally skilled or ready to engage immediately in this free-flowing dialogue and joint problem solving. They may be ill at ease and unsure of their own footing. Parents may be no match for the fluency with which professionals can talk about ideas, conceptualize the issues, or identify potential solutions. This is no reason, however, to presume parents cannot or wish not to engage in the open kind of interaction we are suggesting. This is where the skills of the professional are more important. It takes a skilled, sensitive professional to set the stage, create the rapport, and facilitate the style of interaction that will lead to comfortable parent–professional collaboration and teamwork.

These values are already being integrated into early childhood intervention practices across the country. Professionals who are familiar with this population of children are usually tuned into these expectations and views of parents. Jargon used in the field of early childhood intervention reflects this orientation. Phrases like *parent involvement, parent participation,* or parent and professionals as team members, parent–professional collaboration, or *parent–professional teamwork,* are common in the professional literature and in written program descriptions. For those professionals who have not worked with this population, but who may now become involved as services expand, these notions and their applications may be less familiar. Such professionals may be less experienced within this working model for parent–professional teamwork and may not be comfortable with such close partnership relationships with parents in their own professional practices. But it is a new philosophy and orientation one needs to acquire.

A Philosophy about Parent–Professional Relationships

How then can professionals best engage in this new brand of parent–professional teamwork and facilitate constructive forms of parent involvement? To answer this question, it is helpful to first identify the potential types of involvement activites through which parents and professionals are brought together. Peterson (1987) noted that while parent involvement activities and parent–professional contacts typically encompass an extensive array of alternatives, all can be categorized under four broad kinds of involvement processes:

1. Things that professionals do for parents or give to them (e.g., information, services, advice, consultation, training, or emotional support)

2. Things that parents do for the intervention program, its staff, or the agency providing the services (e.g., fund raising, dissemination of information, advocacy, assistance to staff on various chores, financial contributions to the agency, or donated services to the center)

3. Things parents do with or for their own child as an extension of the intervention program carried out by professional staff members (e.g., teaching and tutoring the child on specific tasks at home or at the early childhood service center)

4. Things that parents and staff do together, where both work on a common activity or task relating to the child, the program, or the center (e.g., planning, evaluating the child or program, participating in social activities, making joint presentations on the program, working on a project together to make something for the classroom or a child, or determining policy for a program or center)

These four types of involvement processes represent parent roles that range from passive to very active. The first type of involvement, where professionals are the doers and parents are the receivers, places parents in the most passive role. The types of involvement described as items 2 and 3 bring parents into more active roles. The final type of involvement process brings parents not only into the active roles, but also into a joint or partnership role with professional staff. Because parents vary in what they need and want from professionals and because the needs of any single set of parents change over time, it would be presumptuous to suggest that any one type of parental involvement is more desirable than another. Family circumstances and many other variables affect how practical each form of involvement is for a given family at any given time (Bailey & Simeonson, 1987; Ehly, Conoley, & Rosenthal, 1985; Karnes & Zehrback, 1975). At the same time, the extent to which parents are encouraged to be passive or active participants in their child's intervention program and the extent to which professionals do for the parent or help parents do more for themselves projects a powerful message to parents. For example, if professionals over-assume the role of the active, more powerful decision maker and doer in the child's intervention program, if they replace the parent wholly and minimize their active participation with the child or program, then messages like these may be communicated to parents:

I (the professional) am best skilled and prepared to deal with your child and his or her special problems.
You don't know how to do this, I can do it better.
You don't need to do this, I'm supposed to do it for you.

I am the expert, you're not; you need me to do this for you and your child.

Given the fact that parents take their child home after professionals complete their services and that parents continue providing the care for the larger portion of the child's waking hours, it makes no sense for professionals to assume that what they can do in a few hours is more powerful or important than what parents do with the child for the remaining 20 or 21 hours of the day. On the other hand, if professionals work for a better balance in the forms of involvement available to parents and work for a more active involvement by parents in their child's intervention, they are likely to communicate messages to the parent like these:

> You can learn to be skillful in dealing with your child's special problems and needs.
>
> I need your help to identify alternatives and to decide what is best for your child.
>
> We both have information that's important as we plan how to best help your child and by working together we can help both here at the center and at home.
>
> I am here to help you do your best as John's parent and to help you help him.

Perhaps all too often professionals fail to consult parents as to their preferred forms of involvement and instead make arbitrary choices about what options are even offered. In a desire to be helpful, to serve, and to demonstrate their own expertise, professionals may be tempted to take over, to involve parents wholly in the first type of involvement as passive receivers and observers only. While this approach has its place and is usually well intended, its continual use to the exclusion of other more active forms of involvement encourage parents to become dependent, to release responsibility for functions we want them to maintain. It encourages frustration, feelings of incompetency, more isolation and failure as a parent. For parents who are struggling in their roles, who are discouraged already and somewhat psychologically removed from the child, this approach may only further encourage them to divorce themselves from the child and to abrogate responsibility for their child's needs. Professionals need to avoid tactics that leave little room for parents and communicate the message "I need to do this for your child; we don't need you here."

We suggest that professionals should work for a healthy balance of parent–professional activities across the four optional involvement processes described here. Professionals should avoid taking the stance that they are the ones to determine which alternatives are most acceptable for a given parent and hence which opportunities should even be offered. When parents are told "These are meetings we are going to hold for you," "These are the activities we offer parents," they are given little opportunity to call their own shots on how they are involved or on what assistance is given. Professionals should avoid communicating, "This is what is best for you and what I expect you to do. If you are a conscientious, cooperative parent in our program, you will support our parent program and be involved in the activities we set up for you." The best approach is to create alternative choices for parents. Then through mutual planning and discussion, options that are most attractive to the parent and targeted to their current needs, including those which are most feasible and practical for both parents and staff, can be selected.

Involving Parents in Intervention Programs

What are some of these alternative roles and activities for parents that could be developed with parents as alternative services or means for involvement? Briefly, some broad types of activities can be described in terms of various parent roles (Peterson, 1987):

Parents as observers (formal or informal observation of others working with a child who demonstrate management, caregiving, teaching, communication strategies)

Parents as audience (attendance at meetings, informative presentations, lectures by professionals, or special programs performed by the child and his or her preschool peers)

Parents as providers of services and information (transportation, food, carriers of information between agencies, or volunteer providers of professional assistance such as legal, therapeutic, business, or repair services)

Parents as decision makers and intervention team members (participation in staff meetings on their own child, IEP, and other planning–work sessions with staff)

Parents as policy makers and advisors (participation in center advisory boards, committees, or other groups that deal with program policy or management tasks)

Parents as liaisons or representatives (work as a representative of the center or program with outside groups for purposes of advocacy, coordination, or general public relations)

Parents as advocates, disseminators and fund raisers promotion of

interests and status of the program through connections with significant community or legislative leaders, agencies, or commercial
enterprises)

Parents as counselors, friends, and supporters (assuming leadership roles over parent support groups, special parent service networks such as respite care and day care, or for new parent consultation contacts when a needy family appears)

Parents as learners/trainees/advisees (participation in activities
designed to teach or educate parents such as courses, educational
meetings, workshops, therapy, or consultation sessions)

Parents as teacher and tutors of their own children (conducting
formal teaching and training sessions with one's own child at the
center or at home)

Parents as volunteers, aides, or assistants (work on tasks that
contribute to the overall operation of a center or a classroom or that
assist teachers and therapists in certain activities, e.g., field trips,
center construction or clean-up tasks, instructional tasks in the
classroom, administrative–clerical tasks, materials development, or
collections of items needed by a center or its staff)

These optional roles encompass a multitude of alternatives for individualizing parent services and involvement. To identify which are a best
match for parents and families calls for open, continual discussion and
planning between parents and professionals. Dunst (1985) uses the term
empowerment to describe what outcomes parent service and involvement
activities such as these should be designed to achieve. He suggests parent
education and involvement should be organized with the intent of
empowering individuals to make informed decisions and to assume
control over their lives. Empowerment is achieved through the generation
and allocation of power through decision making whereby parents can
gain access and control over certain aspects of their lives and certain
physical, emotional, educational, and service resources. Katz (1984)
notes that a "sense of control over [one's] life becomes a renewable,
expansively accessible resource, as does the process of empowerment
itself" (p. 202). Parent involvement activities of the types described here
not only help parents maintain control over their own lives, they can
foster a sense of intra- and interpersonal effectiveness. Dunst (1985)
suggests these also can enhance parents' understanding of their own
empowerment as a resource to themselves and others, as coping-
successful individuals, and as adaptive caregivers who are learning new
skills as parents. To the extent to which parents and families can be
helped to meet their own needs through increased intra- and interpersonal

effectiveness, the family is likely to be strengthened. This in turn is likely to decrease any unnecessary dependence upon educational or social service agencies.

Summary

So how can professionals work most effectively with parents of young children who are handicapped or at-risk for developmental disabilities? The answer cannot be provided in a set "recipe" for the successful parent involvement program nor in a prescribed set of procedures that professionals should apply systematically with all parents. To attempt to do this or even suggest it is appropriate ignores those values and concepts described in this chapter that lie at the heart of true parent–professional teamwork:

Active, sensitive listening to what parents say about their own needs and desires

Respectful acceptance of what parents say about their own values, needs, and desires concerning education and treatment of their handicapped child

An attitude of partnership manifest through joint sharing, planning, and decision making

Alternative options for parents

Equal importance given to roles played by each party

Individualization and flexibility of parent and family services and parent involvement

Respect for the parameters of parenting responsibilities and the prerogatives of parents to control their own lives

Respectful acceptance of what parents say about their own values, needs, and desires concerning education and treatment of their handicapped child

Open, reciprocal, and honest communication

Fair, appropriate distribution of decision-making powers among parents and professionals.

The question beyond this point are ones the reader or the professional service provider must answer. Now it is time to consider: How will I respond to the individual needs and requests of parents who will ask me to listen and hear what they believe is important. How will I translate the concepts presented in this chapter into actions that promote a genuine partnership between me and the parents I serve? How can I translate the concepts of equality and mutual collaboration described here in developing an Individualized Family Service Plan for each set of parents that will empower them, not usurp power, and that will render true support, not infringe upon their personal prerogative as parents and heads of their own family system? How will I translate these concepts into effective services both for parents who work and have minimal time for interaction or for parents who have abundant time available and wish to spend it helping their child and the program? How will I go about individualizing assistance to parents whose major concerns focus upon the at-home care of a medically fragile, severely handicapped young child whose care demands 24-hour-a-day monitoring? How will I apply my professional skills to listen to parents and respond to them in ways that are helpful and constructive?

The needs of parents with young handicapped infants or preschoolers are not all the same. The call is here for a new generation of professionals who can relate to and work with parents as equal partners as states expand and build comprehensive services for young handicapped children, birth through age 5, and their parents.

References

Arnold. E., Rowe M., & Tolbert, H. A. (1978). Parent groups. In E. Arnold (Ed.), *Helping parents help their children*. New York: Brunner/Mazel.

Bailey, D. B., & Simeonson, R. J. (1987). *Family assessment in early intervention*. Columbus, OH: Merrill Publishing Co.

Bricker, D., & Casuso, V. (1979). Family involvement: A critical component of early intervention. *Exceptional Children, 46,* 108–115.

Bristol, M. M., & Gallagher, J. J. (1982). A family focus for intervention. In E. T. Ramey & P. L. Trohanis (Eds.), *Finding and educating high-risk and handicapped infants* (pp. 137–161). Baltimore: University Park Press.

Cartwright, C. E. (1981). Effective programs for parents of young handicapped children. *Topics in Early Childhood Special Education, 3,* 1–9.

Dunst, C. J. (1985). Rethinking early intervention. *Analysis and Intervention in Developmentl Disabilities, 5,* 165–201.

Ehly, S. W., Conoley, J. C., & Rosenthal, D. (1985). *Working with parents of exceptional children*. St. Louis, MO: Times Mirror/Mosby College Publishing.

Foster, M., Berger, M., & McLean, M. (1981). Rethinking a good idea: A reassessment of parent involvement. *Topics in Early Childhood Special Education, 1*(3), 55–65.

Goodson, B. D., & Hess, R. D. (1975). *Parents as teachers of young children: An evaluative review of some contemporary concepts and programs*. Washington, DC: DHEW/OC, Bureau of Educational Personnel Development. (ERIC Document Reproduction Service No. ED 136 967)

Hayden, A. H. (1976). A center-based parent training model. In D. L. Lillie, P. L. Trohanis, & K. W. Goin (Eds.), *Teaching parents to teach*. New York: Walker.

Karnes, M. B., & Zehrbach, R. R. (1975). Matching families and services. *Exceptional Children, 41,* 545–549.

Katz, R. (1984). Empowering and synergy: Expanding the community's healing resources. *Prevention in Human Services, 3,* 201–226.

Kennell, J. H., Voos, D. K., & Klaus, M. H. (1979). Parent–infant bonding. In J. D. Osofsky (Ed.), *Handbook of infant development.* New York: Wiley.

Peterson, N. L. (1982). Preschool intervention with the handicapped. In E. L. Meyen (Ed), *Exceptional children and youth: An introduction* (2nd ed, pp. 96–143). Denver: Love.

Peterson, N. L. (1987). *Early intervention for handicapped and at-risk children: An introduction to early childhood-special education.* Denver: Love.

Shearer, M., & Shearer, D. E. (1972). *The Portage report: A model for early childhood education. Exceptional Children, 39,* 210–217.

Shearer, M., & Shearer, D. E. (1977). Parent involvement. In J. B. Jordan, A. H. Hayden, M. B. Karnes, & M. M. Woods (Eds.), *Early childhood education for exceptional children: A handbook of ideas and exemplary practices* (pp. 208–235). Reston, VA: Council for Exceptional Children.

Simpson, R. L. (1982). *Conferencing parents of exceptional children.* Rockville, MD: Aspen Systems.

Turnbull, A. P., & Turnbull, H. R. (1982). Parent involvement in the education of handicapped children: A critique. *Mental Retardation, 20*(3), 115–122.

Turnbull, A. P., & Turnbull, H. R. (1986). *Families and professionals: Creating an exceptional partnership.* Columbus, OH: Merrill.

U.S. Congress. House. Committee on Education and Labor. (1986). 99th Cong., 2d sess., 1986. H. R. Rept. 99–860.

U.S. Department of Education. (1985). *Seventh annual report to Congress on the implementation of the Education of the Handicapped Act: To assure the free appropriate education of all handicapped children.* Washington, DC: U.S. Government Printing Office.

Valentine, J., & Stark, E. (1979). The social context of parent involvement in head start. In E. Ziegler & J. Valentine (Eds.), *Project Head Start: A legacy of the war on poverty.* (pp. 291–314). New York: Free Press.

Weinraub, M., Brooks, J., & Lewis, M. (1977). The social network: A reconsideration of the concept of attachment. *Human Development, 20,* 31–47.

Welsh, M. M., & Odum, C. S. H. (1981). Parent involvement in the education of the handicapped child: A review of the literature. *Journal of the Division for Early Childhood, 3,* 15–23.

III

Training and Research

10

Measuring the Effectiveness of Parent Education

Frederic J. Medway

Introduction

Despite the attention given to the problems found among many families today, most married couples await the arrival of a child with great anticipation and excitement. As soon as the news is heard the planning begins. Husbands and wives begin discussing their feelings regarding the site and method of delivery, may attend classes to understand the birth process better and learn techniques to ease the delivery, start thinking about names for the baby, where to obtain needed furniture, supplies, and maternity clothes, think about the effect of the new child on any prior children, and, if both parents are employed, consider the availability of day care.

Despite planning and good intentions, many couples are not only unprepared to handle their child's physical needs, but, to an even greater degree, have difficulty dealing with the child's emotional, educational, and socialization needs. In short, while most young marrieds clearly are able to be parents in a biological sense, that is, produce offspring, far fewer are themselves psychologically mature enough or knowledgeable enough about child rearing to set the family on a course that satisfies both the child's and their own needs without some guidance.

Recognizing this fact, professionals from numerous disciplines, including medicine, mental health, religion, and education, long ago set out to systematically teach parenting skills. Books on the subject appeared and informal discussion groups were held in the early 1800s (Hess, 1980). Over the next 150 years, parent education grew in scope, popularity, and influence, but at the same time, changed its direction many times over. Early attempts to teach the inculcation of moral virtues were replaced with attempts to teach "philosophies of parenting" with initial philosophies stressing the need for parental control and later ones emphasizing egalitarian parent–child relations. Later attempts to teach general parenting styles and philosophies were themselves replaced by programs to train parents in specific skills such as when and how to praise and punish, how to set limits, how to encourage decision making, how to communicate openly, and how to understand the reasons behind the child behavior.

Today, parents are literally drowning in a sea of information and advice, some welcomed and some not, from professionals, the media, and numerous well-meaning friends and relatives telling how to be a proper parent. There are literally thousands of articles in the popular press (Clarke-Stewart, 1978) and hundreds more in the scientific literature addressing numerous aspects of child behavior and development. And this does not count a similarly extensive literature on child health, nutrition, and education.

It should be recognized, however, that most people who seek parenting advice are being reeducated, not educated for the first time. This is because parenting philosophies, attitudes, and skills are acquired throughout life as people observe the behavior of their own parents, grandparents, older siblings, other relatives, and friends. And once they become parents, adults turn to these sources for help. Erma Bombeck writes, "The other day I called Mother in desperation. 'I need help,' I said. 'I've used every threat on my kids that you ever used on me and I've run out. Do you have anything stronger that you held out on me?' " (Bombeck & Keane, 1971). Parent education is a process of attitude change. Like any other skill, parenting skills can be acquired, to a greater or lesser degree, if taught under the right circumstances (Jackson, 1980; S. M. Johnson & Katz, 1973; Moreland, Schwebel, Beck, & Wells, 1982).

This chapter reviews empirical research on the effectiveness of parent education. Because most of the controlled investigations of parent education have been done with groups of parents, this chapter focuses only on group interventions and only on those where parents alone (not their children) were seen. Research has indicated that groups which include only parents are not any less beneficial than groups which include both parents and children (Guzzetta, 1976). Further, because most parents who make use of parent education programs come from relatively normally functioning families and do not have children with severe mental or emotional disabilities, this review excludes studies where target children are in an institutional setting or have been clinically diagnosed as mentally retarded, emotionally disturbed, learning disabled, substance abusers, organically or neurologically impaired, or have developmental problems that may be traced to physical disorders. Typically, these are children who exhibit some kind of conduct or anxiety disorder with the degree of severity ranging from minimal to moderate. Finally, since the growth in the group parent education movement is only 20 years old and because most research in this area has been conducted since the mid-1970s, this review is restricted to studies published between 1973 and 1984.

Even after delimiting the research base in this way, one is faced with the unenviable task of defining the nature of parent education. This is a particularly difficult problem due to the tendency of writers to use the terms *parent education, parent training,* and *parent consultation* interchangeably. Fine (1980) attempted to delineate parent education from parent therapy or training by noting that the former is typically led by uncredentialed persons from a variety of disciplines, is conducted over a set number of sessions, deals almost exclusively with common problems faced by many parents, and avoids parental or therapist confrontation; the latter is typically led by a mental health professional, may go on for an indefinite number of sessions, often has groups of parents who share a common concern, may involve collateral treatment of the target children, and may involve the ultimate formation of close bonds among group members. For the most part, parent training and therapy are considered types of parent education, and parent education one form of parent consultation.

The research interventions in this area are typically some unspecified amalgam of parent training and education, with the emphasis on one or the other depending upon the philosophy of and materials used by those carrying out the program. On one hand, most studies have credentialed or experienced group leaders and do deal with uncommon problems; on the other hand, the number of sessions is usually set in advance and there is little concern with the group dynamics that arise. The goals of these programs are to improve parents' child-rearing skills and their children's behavior.

The chapter owes much to several earlier reviews of parent education (see, e.g., Dembo, Sweitzer, & Lauritzen, 1985; Moreland et al., 1982; Rinn & Markle, 1977; Tramontana, Sherrets, & Authier, 1980) which have described in depth the findings and procedures of the specific studies in this area. The aim of this chapter is twofold: to summarize the methodological issues involved in conducting research in this area and to quantitatively evaluate the effectiveness of these programs using meta-analysis (Glass, McGaw, & Smith, 1981), a procedure that allows one to compute the degree of change that parents (and children) show after participating in group education programs compared to control groups of parents who did not participate.

Methodological Problems and Issues

Misconceptions about Parent Education

When one attempts to provide an evaluation or critique of any type of therapeutic or educational intervention, a number of misconceptions may arise that may influence the manner in which the results are interpreted. One misconception involves the belief that parent education involves a unitary process. Although the title of this book and this chapter inadvertently serve to reinforce this belief, even a cursory reading of this and other chapters reveals that parent education encompasses a wide range of philosophies, programs, purposes, and materials. Simply stated, there is no one thing called *parent education* and no parents can be absolutely sure of what their training will involve until after they have gone through a particular program.

Most researchers and practitioners are sophisticated enough to realize that there are several types of parent education. There are three major models in contemporary usage: reflective, behavioral, and Adlerian. *Reflective* parent education "places a major emphasis on parental awareness, understanding, and acceptance of the child's feelings. . . . This model uses cognitively mediated variables (feelings) as a means of affecting the child's behavior and the parent–child interaction" (Tavormina, 1975, p. 22). Reflective parent education has its roots in Carl Rogers's client-centered therapy, and parents are trained to employ communication techniques used in that therapy. The best known and most widely used reflective program is Gordon's (1975) *Parent Effectiveness Training* (P.E.T.).

Behavioral parent education "places its emphasis on actual observable behavior and the environmental variables that maintain behavior patterns" (Tavormina, 1975, p. 22). Starting from the assumption that the parenting system to which the child is exposed is somehow dysfunctional, behaviorists seek to train parents to apply empirically validated procedures and techniques in order to control atypical child behavior. The *Adlerian* model is derived from theories initially forumuated by Alfred Adler and subsequently applied to child rearing by Dreikurs and Soltz (1964) and Dinkmeyer and McKay (1976). The model focuses on understanding the goals of misbehavior, establishment of cooperative family environments, and the use of logical consequences to control behavior.

Although parent education outcome studies have been criticized on the grounds that they do not provide enough detail about group leaders, their training, and the exact content of various sessions (Dembo et al., 1985), there is little difficulty judging which general model the investigators used. Some studies compare different models (see, e.g., Anchor & Thomason, 1977; Pinsker & Geoffrey, 1981). Even when models and procedures are specified, however, one needs to be careful of not falling prey to a second misconception, namely, that procedures were applied exactly as dictated by the model or that week-to-week sessions did not deviate from the intended format. In many group therapies the needs and wishes of participants determine the direction and pace of sessions. In few groups are participants so passive that they accept a prearranged schedule without modification. Knowing that an investigator used P.E.T. or Patterson and Gullion's (1971) behaviorally based *Living with Children* clearly tells the philosophy of the program but less clearly exactly what was taught and what occurred. Further, sometimes limitations in the number of sessions available make it necessary to present a systematic program in an abbreviated format.

Even when the specifics of a particular parent education program are reported, it may still be difficult to replicate it because of two final misconceptions. These involve the beliefs that the quality and competency of group leaders and the makeup of parent participants do not affect success rates. Such beliefs have been contradicted repeatedly by the research literature.

First, the personal styles and attitudes of therapists cannot be separated from the therapy they provide (see Fiske et al., 1970). Davidson and Schrag (1969) found that parents were more likely to implement the recommendations of more experienced psychiatric consultants than less experienced ones. Group leaders in research studies of P.E.T. are less likely to have backgrounds in clinical psychology than are group leaders of behavioral parent education.

Second, although for simplicity's sake most research articles speak of their parent subjects as if they were essentially homogeneous, clearly they are not. Parenting skills, values, and attitudes of those attending group training vary dramatically, even given the fact that the overwhelming majority of participants are middle class. Lower-class parents are less likely to sign up, attend, and finish group sessions than middleclass parents (Gabel, Graybill, Demott, Wood, & Johnston, 1977; D. L. Johnson & Breckenridge, 1982). Parents who successfully complete these sessions tend also to have more than one child, to have at least one child under 10 years of age, to attend alone as compared to with their spouse, and to be relatively active members of their communities (Powell, 1984). However, within these broad parameters there are numerous differences among participants. Unfortunately, little is known about the interactions of various training program properties and specific participant characteristics (Dembo et al., 1985).

Estimating the Effects of the Intervention

The main purpose of this chapter is to show the impact of group parent training efforts. If one wanted to experimentally study this issue one would, in the ideal case, take groups of similar parents with children with similar problems, randomly assign half of them to a treatment program and the other half to some kind of control group such as a different type of educational program (e.g., individual therapy, videotape) or wait-list control, institute the program over a period of time, and finally measure program effects on these families. Unfortunately, however, less than half of the studies of group parent education have employed adequate experimental procedures, leading some reviewers to conclude that "there are not enough well-designed studies to draw definitive conclusions and implications about the general effectiveness of parent education" (Dembo et al., 1985).

Some problems with these studies are methodological in nature. For example, Dembo et al. found that only 40% of behavioral, 28% of P.E.T., and 30% of the Adlerian studies they reviewed employed random assignment of families to experimental and control groups. Further, in some studies which did employ control groups, the control families were provided with interventions that did not deal with parent–child relations and the time given to these control interventions was less than the time given to experimental families.

While proper control groups have increasingly been used in studies conducted since 1980, other problems are less easily rectified. One of these is that other therapeutic interventions of both a formal and informal nature may be occurring at the same time as the group sessions. For example, coincident with the group, the children of the parents may be in therapy or counseling, or the parents may be soliciting or getting advice from friends, neighbors, and the media that reinforces or contradicts group training.

Another confound is the dropout rate in group parent education. Forehand, Middlebrook, Rogers, and Steffe (1983) reported that in 45 parent training studies conducted from 1972 to 1982, the average dropout rate was 28%. Although this rate is lower than that of adult group therapy (Baekeland & Laundwall, 1975), it is still substantial. Those parents who remain are likely to be more satisfied with the intervention and this will serve to bias reported results in a positive direction. Thus, even with random assignment of parents to treatment and control groups, the treatment group undergoes a change over time whereas the control group does not. Rarely would one expect subjects to drop out even from a wait-list control since, outside of completing dependent measures, there is nothing to be dissatisfied about.

Outcome Measurement

Nearly everyone who sets out to evaluate a parent education program attempts to answer one or more of the following questions: Does the program help? In what way? How much? At what cost? And, how much more did it help than other available educational and therapeutic interventions? Although on the surface these appear to be rather simple questions, the choice of measures and evaluation procedures is a complex matter.

First, before one can ask if a program is beneficial, one must specify its contents. Thus, it is not surprising that since the approaches to parent education are diverse so too are the ways used to evaluate effectiveness (Dembo et al., 1985).

Beyond this, however, it appears that many of the studies of group parent education have done a poor job of tying intervention goals to measurement strategies or have simply neglected measuring certain aspects. For example, regardless of whether a program is based on reflective, behavioral, Adlerian, or eclectic models, there do appear to be some shared general goals. At a minimum, most programs seek to (1) change the parents in some way (e.g., make them better problem solvers, better understanders of child development, or better appliers of behavior therapy), (2) change the children in some way, (3) improve parent–child communication and relationships, and (4) change the family social system. Yet most studies use outcome measures that address changes in parents or children rather than family interaction variables. A notable exception to this rule is a study by Pinsker and Geoffrey (1981).

Second, even if one has carefully specified program goals, one still must decide who to evaluate, what to evaluate, when to do it, and how often. In the vast majority of group parent education research the primary source of the information is the parents, whether parents state their own attitudes or chart changes in their children's actions. Few studies have employed independent observers or ratings from nonfamily members familiar with the child, such as teachers.

In deciding what to evaluate there has been a preference, most marked in the P.E.T. studies, to assess internal states (attitudes, values, and knowledge) rather than overt behaviors. One of the most popular attitude scales used in various types of programs is Hereford and Johnson's (1976)

Parent Attitude Survey on which parents rate their degree of child acceptance, understanding, and trust. Another scale that is used primarily in Adlerian programs is the Attitude toward Freedom of Children (Shaw & Wright, 1967). Whenever questionnaires are the only measures used, issues of reliability, validity, susceptibility to faking, and relation to actual behavior must be considered.

Finally, in deciding when and how often to evaluate, most studies in this area have taken measures before and after training. However, the actual period of training has been as little as 2 hours (see, e.g., Walter & Gilmore, 1973) to well over 20 hours (see, e.g., Frazier & Matthes, 1975). Rarely have data been collected on the ongoing training process. And although recent studies are increasingly using follow-up measures, few studies have checked on participants more than 6 months later.

In summary, the evaluation of group parent education programs has been based on a broad range of outcome measures. This variability of measurement has resulted in many studies which report success on some measures but not others and considerable variability across studies.

Approaches to Evaluating Parent Education Literature

Several writers have described the processes by which integrative reviews of literature are conducted (Cooper, 1982; Jackson, 1980). According to Jackson (1980) such reviews are valuable in that they summarize the existing state of knowledge in a field and the methodological limitations of the studies, assist in generalizing from the results, and aid in designing new and procedurally sounder studies.

Up until the late 1970s, most integrative reviews followed one of four different procedures (Light & Smith, 1971). Some reviewers merely made lists of any factor found to impact on a specific dependent variable in at least one study. Some reviewers only analyzed outcome studies conducted from a certain perspective. For example, there have been reviews of P.E.T. studies (Rinn & Markle, 1977) and behavioral parent training studies (Berkowitz & Graziano, 1972). Some reviewers have chosen to average findings across a series of studies. And finally, some reviewers have sought to estimate effectiveness by comparing the number of studies which find significant results on one or more measures with the number of studies which fail to find significant results. This latter method is known as the *voting* or *tallying procedure*. It has been widely used but also subject to the criticism that it is biased in favor of studies with large sample sizes (which few parent education studies have), that it does not take into account the strengths of statistical effects, and that it is not suited to determining the relative impact of different types of psychological interventions.

More recently researchers have begun to develop procedures of quantitative reviewing. These are explicit statistical procedures that serve to reduce the potential for subjectivity and bias found in traditional qualitative outcome reviews (Cooper, 1982).

One procedure that allows for data integration across a series of outcome studies is meta-analysis (Glass et al., 1981). Meta-analysis involves "transforming the findings of individual studies to some common metric, coding various characteristics of the studies, and then using conventional statistical procedures to determine whether there is an overall effect" (Jackson, 1980, p. 451). Thus, meta-analytics yield single sets of numbers describing an entire body of literature that shares a common conceptual hypothesis or independent variable treatment. When most of the studies reviewed include some type of control group, the standardized measure of the results is typically the *effect size*. This metric is usually calculated by taking the mean difference of the treatment and control groups and dividing this by the within-group standard deviation of the control group. Some of the advantages of effect size measures are

> (a) effect size measures are generally easy to calculate, and hence there is less work, time, and expense involved; (b) where pre- and post-treatment effect sizes are used, there is intrinsic control for the problem of poor reliability of individual raw gain scores because all change scores are pooled to yield one metric; there is general familiarity with and more advanced development of the concept of effect size as in Cohen's (1977) contributions; and (c) effect size statistics are unique in that they reflect both the number of individuals having changed and the average magnitude of change in these individuals. (E. R. Christensen & Reick, 1983, p. 49)

Numerous meta-analysis reviews have appeared in recent years in all areas of psychological research, but particularly in clinical, educational, and developmental areas. This trend continues to be on the rise (Slavin, 1984). Smith and Glass (1977), Landman and Dawes (1982), and Shapiro and Shapiro (1982) employed meta-analysis to study the effectiveness of therapy. The practice of combining many different types of therapy, therapists, clients, and dependent measures was defended on the grounds that consumers and funding agencies often ask questions about the general effectiveness of specific psychological techniques rather than making distinctions according to technique and setting. All three studies concluded that therapy was effective and that the average therapy client made desired improvements that exceeded 75% of those in control groups. Medway and Updyke (1985) applied meta-analysis to mental health consultation programs and found that consultees made improvements that were 66% greater than those in control groups.

Meta-analysis, however, is not without its critics. Researchers have argued over the relative merits of "combining apples and oranges" from different studies, whether to include poorly designed studies along with better-designed ones, and whether meta-analysis adequately accounts for interaction effects (Cook & Leviton, 1980; Cooper & Arkin, 1981; Slavin, 1984). However, there is general consensus that these same criticisms can and do apply to traditional reviews and that meta-analytic procedures have heuristic value provided that the biases of the studies are not overlooked.

Meta-Analysis of Group Parent Education Studies

The remainder of this chapter is devoted to a discussion of a meta-analysis of group parent education outcome studies. Taking into account the methodological limitations of studies in this area, this quantitative review was done to provide some preliminary answers to two questions: How effective are such programs in changing parental behavior and attitudes and how effective are they in changing child behavior and attitudes. For both these issues, study outcomes were examined for the different models of parent education.

Locating Studies and Quantifying Results

The first step in this meta-analysis was to locate appropriate outcome studies. A previous review by Dembo et al. (1985) helped provide an initial pool of studies from 1974 to 1983. *Psychological Abstracts* provided a second source. The bibliographies of each of these studies helped provide additional titles. And finally, to be sure no relevant studies were missed, the tables of contents of the journals most likely to publish these studies were examined.

For the most part the same study-inclusion criteria used by Dembo et al. were employed. Studies included had to (1) be empirical rather than descriptive and have at least one dependent measure reported in quantifiable terms, (2) be designed for relatively normal children, not those "who had severe developmental, behavioral, or learning problems (e.g., mental retardation, autism, psychoses)" (Dembo et al., 1985, p. 159), (3) train parents how to deal with present problems and how to handle future ones rather than attempt to teach narrow behavior-therapy skills, (4) use group procedures, and, unlike the Dembo et al. studies, (5) include a separate control group (not just a baseline or pre–post comparison) to allow for maturational and extraneous variable changes. Only published studies were included. While this restriction tends to exclude studies with negative or nonsignificant results, it does assure that those studies included have all met editorial standards of proper methodology and experimental design.

Guidelines were established to make sure that each study was treated equitably in the analysis. These were as follows. First, to quantify study outcomes, effect-size statistics were computed. This was done by either taking the difference in the means between the experimental and control groups and dividing this by the standard deviation of the control group or estimating the effect sizes from corresponding t, f, or proportion values (see Glass et al., 1981). "An 'effect size' of $+1$ indicates that a person at the mean of the control group would be expected to rise to the 84th percentile of the control group after treatment" (Smith & Glass, 1977, p. 753). If multivariate statistics were reported, the effect sizes were computed from them rather than from the univariate measures. Similarly, effect sizes were computed on total scores from questionnaires rather than scores on discrete subscales.

Second, some studies were included which had the necessary information to compute effect sizes on only certain measures. These studies reported that other measures yielded nonsignificant results but did not report the precise level of nonsignificance or means and standard deviations. Because the excluded measures were seldom central to the major treatment focus of the study, their exclusion only skews the average effect size per study slightly in a positive direction.

Third, some studies examined variations of different procedures, such as having mothers or fathers only in a group versus having both. In these cases only the group format initially hypothesized to be the best (rather than all the subvariations) was compared with its control. Similarly, if a study reported program effects at different time intervals, the only comparison for which effect sizes were computed was between control and experimental groups at program termination.

Final Study Pool

After eliminating studies that did not meet the criteria discussed above, a total of 27 outcome studies remained. Twenty-four of these studies were evaluation of one model of parent education: 12 studies of behavioral parent training, 7 studies of Adlerian training, and 5 studies of P.E.T. These are shown in Table 10.1. Three other studies were located that compared two different models. These are shown in Table 10.2.

Table 10.1 Group Parent Education Outcome Studies

Study	Outcome measure[a] Parent attitude	Parent behavior	Child attitude	Child behavior	Average study effect	Average follow-up effect
	Behavioral Group Programs					
Adesso & Lipson (1981)	X			1.04	1.04	1.04[b]
Bergan, Neumann, &		0.22				
Karp (1983)		0.65				
		0.23				
		3.20				
		0.39				
		0.27				
		−0.72				
		0.22			0.56	
A. Christensen,	0.71			0.60		
Johnson, Phillips, &	X			0.67	0.66	
Glasgow (1981)						
Eyberg & Matarazzo	0.68	X		0.49	0.58	
(1980)						
Karoly & Rosenthal	1.08					
(1977)	0.64			1.68	1.13	
Martin (1977)		0.74		0.60		
		0.54		0.37		
		0.81[c]		1.01[c]	0.68	
		1.01[c]		0.40		0.81[c]
Patterson, Chamberlain,	1.95			0.76	1.33	
& Reid (1983)						
Walter & Gilmore (1973)		0.55		0.58		
				1.07	0.73	
Webster-Stratton (1981)	0.09					
	X			0.88	0.48	
Webster-Stratton (1982)	0.19	0.79		0.60		No control
	0.16	0.79		0.55		
	−0.49	1.92		0.48		
	−0.24	1.20		0.79		
	−0.33	X		X	0.49	
Webster-Stratton (1984)	X	1.18		0.69	0.85	
		0.63		0.75		
		0.61		1.12		
		1.09		1.29		
		0.77		1.00		
				0.78		
				0.78		
				0.50		
				0.64		
Wiltz & Patterson (1974)				0.96	0.96	

Table 10.1 (*Continued*)

Study	Outcome measure[a] Parent attitude	Parent behavior	Child attitude	Child behavior	Average study effect	Average follow-up effect
	Communication/P.E.T. Programs					
Levant & Doyle (1983)	1.22		1.44			
	−1.06		1.41		1.89	
Mitchell & McManis (1977)	1.89				1.89	
Peed, Roberts, & Forehand (1977)	X	0.72		X	0.96	
		1.25				
		0.90				
Taylor & Swan (1982)	0.21[d]				0.21	
Therrein (1979)	0.88				0.88	
	0.88[e]					
	Adlerian Programs					
Berrett (1975)	0.78	1.57		1.21	1.18	
Croake & Burness (1976)	0.21	X		X	0.21	
Freeman (1975)	2.63	X		0.87	1.75	
Hinkle, Arnold, Croake, & Keller (1980)	1.65	0.89	1.11	0.23		
				0.01	0.78	
McKay & Hillman (1979)				0.80	0.80	
Moore & Dean-Zubritsky (1979)	1.07	0.75				
		0.92				
		0.76			0.87	
Summerlin & Ward (1981)		0.65			0.65	

[a] X indicates that measure was obtained but no statistics were presented.
[b] Followed up at 3 months.
[c] Followed up at 6 months.
[d] Parent knowledge.
[e] Followed up at 4 months.

The studies varied in terms of the type and variety of outcome measures employed. Every behavioral study located except one had a measure of child behavior, consisting of either a rating made by a parent or a direct observation. Many of the behavioral studies also collected measures of changes in parent's child-rearing attitudes. Changes in these attitudes were measured by every Adlerian program located. The Adlerian studies also examined parents' behavior and child's behavior. The

Table 10.2 Comparison Programs[a]

Study	Behavioral model				Other model[b]			
	Parent attitude	Parent behavior	Child attitude	Child behavior	Parent attitude	Parent behavior	Child attitude	Child behavior
Bernal, Klinnert, & Schultz (1980)	0.82			0.82 X	X		X X	
Haffey & Levant (1984)	-1.10^c -0.28 0.82^c			0.22	0.80^c -0.34 -1.22^c			0.18
Pinsker & Geoffrey (1981)	X 1.65^c		X	1.22 0.44 0.60	X 1.12		X	0.50 0.58 0.36

[a] X indicates that measure was obtained but no statistics were presented.
[b] For Bernal et al., P.E.T.; Haffey & Levant, Adlerian; Pinsker & Geoffrey, communication/reflective.
[c] Knowledge measure.

use of multiple measures was found less often in the P.E.T. studies than in the other two models. All P.E.T. studies in the analysis had a measure of parents' attitudes, but none examined whether there was any impact on the children of these parents. Only three of the studies included follow-up measures and these were studies of behavioral parent training. The studies differed also in terms of whether they reported statistics on nonsignificant measures. As the two tables show, several studies included at least one dependent measure that was reported to be nonsignificant, but the strength of the effect or associated means and standard deviations was omitted. This tends to partially bias the average effect sizes computed per study in a positive direction.

Parent Education Effectiveness

To examine the issue of program effectiveness, effect sizes were first computed for the 24 outcome studies listed in Table 10.1. As can be seen, all but a few of the effects were positive. An average effect size was computed for each study, and then a mean and standard deviation of these statistics were computed. By doing this, each study contributed equally even though the studies differed in terms of their total effect sizes. The mean average effect size for the 24 studies was 0.90 ($SD = 0.46$, $SE = 0.09$). The values for measures for those involved in parent education programs—both parents and children—evidenced gains in a positive direction that were approximately 62% greater than control populations who were not involved in these programs.

Since group parent education programs generally seek to help parents and improve the behavior or personality of their children, it is important to examine the data separately for parents and children. In doing this, the individual effects for each study rather than average effects were analyzed. The mean effect size for parent measures was 0.76 ($SD = 0.74$, $SE = 0.10$) and the mean effect size for child measures was 0.80 ($SD = 0.36$, $SE = 0.06$). Thus, the data indicate that these programs appear to have equally strong effects on parents and children.

A final question of interest was whether group parent education programs would have a differential impact on attitude measures versus behavior measures. In examining this issue, the individual effects for each study were again analyzed. The mean effect size for attitude measures was 0.70 ($SD = 0.83$, $SE = 0.17$), and the mean effect size for behavior measures was 0.79 ($SD = 0.50$, $SE = 0.06$). Thus, parent education programs appear, based on these studies, to be influencing attitudes and behavior to a similar extent.

Comparisons of Different Models

Although it is intuitively appealing to ask whether one type of parent-education model is any better than any other, outcome studies using one type of model cannot be compared to studies using another type of model since these studies differ not only in terms of the model treatment and the characteristics of group leaders but also in terms of the choice of outcome measure used. To deal with some of these problems, three studies, shown in Table 10.2, attempted to directly compare different models. Given the limited number of studies, any conclusions drawn must be highly tentative. However, it does appear that the behavioral model yields stronger effects on child behavior measures than the reflective or Adlerian model.

Summary

Psychologists and educators have long advocated that parents receive group training in parenting skills. However, only since the early 1970s have researchers asked if such practices result in any meaningful changes in the attitudes and behavior of parents and their children. In this review, 24 studies of behavioral, reflective or Parent Effectiveness Training, and Adlerian parent training were examined, all of which had some type of control group. It was found that these programs were highly effective in that participants and their children evidenced improvement on diverse measures that was 62% greater than similar populations who were not so trained. Whatever knowledge, skill, and change in parenting philosophy is communicated to these parents is directly carrying over to their children. The few studies which have used follow-up measures indicate that these gains are enduring. Still, some problems remain with the studies themselves, including the use of measures of questionable reliability and validity, the lack of follow-up assessment, noncomparability of treatment and control groups, and the failure of the investigators to report fully on procedures and to include the results from nonsignificant measures.

The parent faced with choosing among different types of programs can be comforted in the fact that all the models have empirical support even though there are only meager data for deciding the type of program to attend. Such a choice can only rest on the documented effectiveness of the different programs in relation to the parent's own goals. For example, if the goal is to improve parent or child attitudes, then the nonbehavioral programs would appear preferable; if the goal is to improve child behavior, then the behavioral, and to a lesser extent, Adlerian programs might be chosen; and, if the goal is simply to learn how to be a better parent, then any one of the three models might be chosen, depending on the exact nature of what the parent wants to learn and the child's presenting problems.

References

Adesso, V. S., & Lipson, J. W. (1981). Group training of parents as therapists for their children. *Behavior Therapy, 12,* 625–633.

Anchor, K., & Thomason, T. C. (1977). A comparison of two parent-training models with educated parents. *Journal of Community Psychology, 5,* 134–141.

Baekeland, F., & Laundwall, L. (1975). Dropping out of treatment: A critical review. *Psychological Bulletin, 82,* 738–783.

Bergan, J. R., Neumann, A. J., & Karp, C. L. (1983). Effects of parent training on parent instruction and child learning of intellectual skills. *Journal of School Psychology, 21,* 31–48.

Berkowitz, B., & Graziano, A. M. (1972). Training parents as behavior modifiers: A review. *Behaviour Research and Therapy, 10,* 297–317.

Bernal, M. E., Klinnert, M. D., & Schultz, L. A. (1980). Outcome evaluation of behavioral parent training and client-centered parent counseling for children with conduct problems. *Journal of Applied Behavior Analysis, 13,* 677–691.

Berrett, R. D. (1975). Adlerian mother study groups: An evaluation. *Journal of Individual Psychology, 31,* 179–182.

Bombeck, E., & Keane, B. (1971). *Just wait till you have children of your own.* New York: Fawcett/Crest.

Christensen, A., Johnson, S. M., Phillips, S., & Glasgow, R. E. (1981). Cost effectiveness in behavioral family therapy. *Behavior Therapy, 11,* 208–226.

Christensen, E. R., & Reick, D. T. (1983). Meta analysis in mental health treatment evaluation. In M. J. Lambert, E. R. Christensen, & S. S. DeJulio (Eds.), *The assessment of psychotherapy outcome* (pp. 33–55). New York: Wiley.

Clarke-Stewart, K. A. (1978). Popular primers for parents. *American Psychologist, 33,* 359–369.

Cohen, J. (1977). *Statistical power analysis for the behavioral sciences.* New York: Academic Press.

Cook, T., & Leviton, L. (1980). Reviewing the literature: A comparison of traditional methods with meta-analysis. *Journal of Personality, 48,* 449–472.

Cooper, H. (1982). Scientific guidelines for conducting integrative research reviews. *Review of Educational Research, 52,* 291–302.

Cooper, H., & Arkin, R., (1981). On quantitative reviewing. *Journal of Personality, 49,* 225–230.

Croake, J. W., & Burness, M. R. (1976). Parent study group effectiveness after four and after six weeks. *Journal of Individual Psychology, 32,* 108–111.

Davidson, P. O., & Schrag, A. R. (1969). Factors affecting the outcome of child psychiatric consultations. *American Journal of Orthopsychiatry, 39,* 774–778.

Dembo, M. H., Sweitzer, M., & Lauritzen, P. (1985). An evaluation of group parent education: Behavioral, PET, and Adlerian programs. *Review of Educational Research, 55,* 155–200.

Dinkmeyer, D., & McKay, G. (1976). *Systematic training for effective parenting.* Circle Pines, MN: American Guidance Service.

Dreikurs, R., & Soltz, V. (1964). *Children: The challenge.* New York: Hawthorn.

Eyberg, S. M., & Matarazzo, R. G. (1980). Training parents as therapists: A comparison between individual parent–child intervention training and parent group didactic training. *Journal of Clinical Psychology, 36,* 492–499.

Fine, M. J. (1980). The parent education movement: An introduction. In M. J. Fine (Ed.), *Handbook on parent education* (pp. 3–26). New York: Academic Press.

Fiske, D. W., Hunt, H. F., Luborsky, L., Orne, M. T., Parloff, M. B., Reiser, M. F., & Tuma, A. H. (1970). Planning of research on the effectiveness of psychotherapy. *Archives of General Psychiatry, 22,* 22–32.

Forehand, R., Middlebrook, J., Rogers, T., & Steffe, M. (1983). Dropping out of parent training. *Behaviour Research and Therapy, 21,* 663–668.

Frazier, F., & Matthes, W. A. (1975). Parent education: A comparison of Adlerian and behavioral approaches. *Elementary School Counseling and Guidance, 11,* 31–38.

Freeman, C. W. (1975). Adlerian mother study groups: Effects of attitudes and behavior. *Journal of Individual Psychology, 31,* 37–50.

Gabel, H., Graybill, D., Demott, S., Wood, L., & Johnston, L. E. (1977). Correlates of participation in parent group discussion among parents of learning disabled children. *Journal of Community Psychology, 5,* 275–277.

Glass, G. V., McGaw, B., & Smith, M. L. (1981). *Meta-analysis in social research.* Beverly Hills, CA: Sage.

Gordon, T. (1975). *P.E.T.: Parent effectiveness training.* New York: American Library.

Guzzetta, R. A. (1976). Acquisition and transfer of empathy by the parents of early adolescents through structured learning training. *Journal of Counseling Psychology, 23,* 449–453.

Haffey, N. A., & Levant, R. F. (1984). The differential effectiveness of two models of skill training for working class parents. *Family Relations, 33,* 209–216.

Hereford, C. R., & Johnson, O. G. (1976). Parent attitude survey. In O. G. Johnson (Ed.), *Tests and measurements in child development: A handbook II* (pp. 1113–1114). San Francisco: Jossey-Bass.

Hess, R. D. (1980). Experts and amateurs: Some unintended consequences of parent education. In M. Fantini & R. Cardenas (Eds.), *Parenting in multicultural society* (pp. 3–17). New York: Longman.

Hinkel, D. E., Arnold, C. F., Croake, J. W., & Keller, J. F. (1980). Adlerian parent education: Changes in parents' attitudes and behaviors, and children's self-esteem. *American Journal of Family Therapy, 8,* 32–43.

Jackson, G. B. (1980). Methods for integrative reviews. *Review of Educational Research, 50,* 438–460.

Johnson, D. L., & Breckenridge, J. N. (1982). The Houston Parent–Child Development Center and the primary prevention of behavior problems in young children. *American Journal of Community Psychology, 10,* 305–316.

Johnson, S. M., & Katz, R. C. (1973). Using parents as change agents for their children: A review. *Journal of Child Psychology and Psychiatry, 14,* 181–200.

Karoly, P., & Rosenthal, M. (1977). Training parents in behavior modification: Effects on perceptions and family interaction and deviant child behavior. *Behavior Therapy, 8,* 406–410.

Landman, J. T., & Dawes, R. M. (1982). Psychotherapy outcome: Smith and Glass' conclusions stand up under scrutiny. *American Psychologist, 37,* 504–516.

Levant, R. F., & Doyle, G. F. (1983). An evaluation of a parent education program for fathers of school-aged children. *Family Relations, 32,* 29–37.

Light, R., & Smith, P. (1971). Accumulating evidence: Procedures for resolving contradictions among different research studies. *Harvard Educational Review, 41,* 429–471.

Martin, B. (1977). Brief family intervention: Effectiveness and the importance of including the father. *Journal of Consulting and Clinical Psychology, 45,* 1002–1010.

McKay, G. D., & Hillman, B. W. (1979). An Adlerian multimedia approach to parent education. *Elementary School Guidance and Counseling, 14,* 23–25.

Medway, F. J., & Updyke, J. F. (1985). Meta-analysis of consultation outcome studies. *American Journal of Community Psychology, 13,* 485–501.

Mitchell, J., & McManis, D. L. (1977). Effects of P.E.T. on authoritarian attitudes toward child-rearing in parents and non-parents. *Psychological Reports, 41,* 215–218.

Moore, M. H., & Dean-Zubritsky, C. (1979). Adlerian parent study groups: An assessment of attitude and behavior change. *Journal of Individual Psychology, 35,* 225–234.

Moreland, J. R., Schwebel, A. I., Beck, S., & Wells, R. (1982). Parents as therapists: A review of the behavior therapy parent training literature—1975 to 1981. *Behavior Modification, 6,* 250–276.

Patterson, G. R., Chamberlain, P., & Reid, J. B. (1983). A comparative evaluation of a parent-training program. *Behavior Therapy, 13,* 638–650.

Patterson, G. R., & Gullion, M. E. (1971). *Living with children.* Champaign, IL: Research Press.

Peed, S., Roberts, M., & Forehand, R. (1977). Evaluation of the effectiveness of a standardized parent training program in altering the interaction of mothers and their noncompliant children. *Behavior Modification, 1,* 323–349.

Pinsker, M., & Geoffrey, K. (1981). Comparison of parent effectiveness training and behavior modification parent training. *Family Relations, 30,* 61–68.

Powell, D. R. (1984). Social network and demographic predictors of length of participation in a parent education program. *Journal of Community Psychology, 12,* 13–20.

Rinn, R. C., & Markle, A. (1977). Parent effectiveness training: A review. *Psychological Reports, 41,* 95–109.

Shapiro, D. A., & Shapiro, D. (1982). Meta-analysis of comparative therapy outcome studies: A replication and refinement. *Psychological Bulletin, 92,* 581–604.

Shaw, M. E., & Wright, J. M. (1967). *Scales for the measurement of attitudes.* New York: McGraw-Hill.

Slavin, R. E. (1984). Meta-analysis in education: How has it been used. *Educational Researcher, 13*(8), 6–15.

Smith, M. L., & Glass, G. V. (1977). Meta-analysis of psychotherapy outcome studies. *American Psychologist, 32,* 752–760.

Summerlin, M. L., & Ward, G. R. (1981). The effect of parent group participation on attitudes. *Elementary School Guidance and Counseling, 16,* 133–136.

Tavormina, J. B. (1975). Relative effectiveness of behavioral and reflective group counseling with parents of mentally retarded children. *Journal of Consulting and Clinical Psychology, 43,* 22–31.

Taylor, P. B., & Swan, R. W. (1982). Parent effectiveness training: Adolescents' responses. *Psychological Reports, 51,* 331–338.

Therrein, M. E. (1979). Evaluating empathy skill training for parents. *Social Work, 24,* 417–419.

Tramontana, M. G., Sherrets, S. D., & Authier, K. J. (1980). Evaluation of parent education programs. *Journal of Clinical Child Psychology, 9,* 40–43.

Walter, H. D., & Gilmore, S. K. (1973). Placebo versus social learning effects in parent training procedures designed to alter the behavior of aggressive boys. *Behavior Therapy, 4,* 361–377.

Webster-Stratton, C. (1981). Modification of mothers' behaviors and attitudes through a videotape modeling group discussion program. *Behavior Therapy, 12,* 634–642.

Webster-Stratton, C. (1982). The long term effects of a videotape modeling parent training program: Comparison of immediate and one year follow-up results. *Behavior Therapy, 13,* 702–714.

Webster-Stratton, D. (1984). Randomized trial of two parent-training programs for families with conduct-disordered chidren. *Journal of Consulting and Clinical Psychology, 52,* 666–678.

Wiltz, N. A., & Patterson, G. R. (1974). An evaluation of parent training procedures designed to alter inappropriate aggressive behavior of boys. *Behavior Therapy, 5,* 215–221.

11

Development and Validation of the Cleminshaw–Guidubaldi Parent-Satisfaction Scale

John Guidubaldi
Helen K. Cleminshaw

Introduction

Recent changes in American family life have alerted a diverse group of professionals to severe changes in socialization patterns of children and life satisfaction of adults. Articles relating to marital separation, divorce, maternal employment, and declining fertility are regularly found in a wide variety of professional and popular publications (see, e.g., Hetherington, 1979; Sawhill, 1977; U.S. Bureau of the Census, 1979), and it now seems clear that marital stability and parenting popularity have been severely diminished since the mid-1970s.

Cook, West, and Hamner (1982) compared attitudes toward parenting of samples of college women in 1972 and 1979. They found that the 1979 sample desired fewer children, were more accepting of the decision to remain childless, and were more uncertain with regard to parenting as a factor in mate selection. Thus, changing sex roles and fewer societal sanctions for nontraditional roles appear to influence attitudes and satisfactions related to the parent role.

Considering the fact that dependable birth control procedures and abortion are now widespread means of exercising control over fertility, commitment to child rearing has become a conscious, willful decision potentially subject to careful analysis of costs and benefits (Beckman, 1978; Bigner, 1979). An increasing number of adults are refusing or

Note: This research has been jointly supported by the William T. Grant Foundation, the National Association of School Psychologists, and Kent State University. Special gratitude is extended to 144 school psychologists who gathered data for this project and to Bonnie Nastasi, Jeanine Lightel, and Bonnie Heaton, who provided valuable assistance in data analysis and manuscript preparation.

257

postponing marriage or deciding to remain childless after marriage (Blake, 1979). Actual or projected satisfaction with parenting thus plays a more central role in determining whether a couple will become parents and how large their family will be. Parenting satisfaction assumes new salience as a central factor in determining life styles and general life satisfaction of adults.

Espenshade (1977) summarized the issue:

> Children are valued as sources of joy and happiness, companionship, and pride. In some circumstances, children may also be prized because they are a potential means of support and security once parents are no longer able to provide for themselves. At the same time, children are costly. They put added pressure on family resources, and they can in other ways curtail the activities and opportunities of parents. . . . An awareness of the variety of satisfactions parents gain from having children may lead to a better understanding of the parent–child relationship. (p. 3)

In an attempt to understand the psychological satisfactions associated with having children and the relationship of these satisfactions to fertility attitudes, a large cross-cultural study was carried out in six countries under the supervision of Fawcett (1972). Based upon data collected from the U.S. sample, Hoffman and Manis (1979) reported a number of advantages of having children. They identified seven major value categories, which were rank ordered as follows: (1) primary group ties and affection, (2) stimulation and fun, (3) expansion of the self, (4) adults' status and social identity, (5) achievement and creativity, (6) morality, and (7) economic utility. An interesting national survey by Yankelovich, Skelly, and White (1977) used a probability sample and included queries about satisfaction with family life. These findings supported the work of Hoffman and Manis, showing that 73% of the parents, both mothers and fathers, derived fun and enjoyment from their parenting role. If given the opportunity, 90% stated they would become parents again. Chillman (1980), in a study of Milwaukee parents, asked, "What do you find particularly satisfying about having children?" In response, 70% of parents felt that "watching children grow and develop" was satisfying; 40% reported "love" and 30% reported "companionship" as sources of satisfaction with the parent role. Although other reasons were cited such as children's achievements, self-fulfillment, a shared marital project, general enjoyment, hope for the future, reliving childhood, passing on values or family name, social conformity, only 15% or fewer of the parents reported these satisfactions.

While all these studies provide information regarding parents' stated reasons for valuing their children and feeling satisfied with being a parent, they generally utilized open-ended response modes lacking reliability and validity. They therefore do not permit normative comparisons of subjects or comparisons of one area of satisfaction with other areas, an approach which might prove more useful in research studies and clinical practice. Despite the rather obvious connection between parents' satisfaction toward child rearing and their actual child-rearing behaviors, little research has been devoted to the assessment of parent satisfaction. Much of the difficulty lies in the general lack of appropriate instrumentation for measuring affective areas of development (Gordon, Hanes, Lamme, & Schlenker, 1972).

Instruments constructed in the past for the study of child-rearing approaches often did not differentiate between attitudes and behaviors. For example, Hanes and Dunn (1978, p. 60) state, "Little information is available, however, about possible attitudinal bases which may explain variations in behavior and enduring behavior patterns. While attitudes undoubtedly influence maternal behavior, few studies of young children have examined the relationships between verbalized attitudes, maternal behavior and child behavior." Where instruments were designed to probe nonbehavioral aspects of parenting, the assessment focus has typically been on cognitive understanding about child rearing or on attitudes about specific child-rearing techniques such as authoritarian versus permissive approaches. Affective orientation toward the parenting process itself has not been emphasized in previous assessment devices.

Clearly, an instrument that measures the various components of satisfaction related to parenting is needed. The Cleminshaw–Guidubaldi Parent Satisfaction Scale (CGPSS) described in this study is a 50-item Likert-type instrument designed to meet this need. This chapter examines its development, concurrent and predictive relationships between CGPSS domains, and a very extensive set of child and family adjustment criteria employed in a nationwide study.

Research Procedures

Scale Development

PILOT STUDY SAMPLE SELECTION. The sample for the instrument development study was composed of 130 parents, 52 fathers and 78 mothers. They were selected from local educational, religious, and community groups. Additionally, spouses and friends were recruited using a sociological sampling technique referred to as a "snowball" sampling process, wherein volunteers themselves recruited additional subjects. This sample was intentionally quite heterogeneous. For example, ages of the subjects ranged from 21 to 71 years. Educational levels extended from Grade 11 to postdoctoral study, and income varied from less than $6,000 to more than $40,000 per year. The number of children in the family ranged from 1 to 11, while the ages of the children ranged from 6 weeks to 38 years. Of the participants, 122 were married, and 8 were single parents.

INSTRUMENT DESIGN. Two processes were employed to generate items. First, approximately 100 adults (21 to 54 years of age) were asked to respond to an open-ended questionnaire which asked two questions: (1) What three factors do you believe contribute to satisfaction in the parenting role? and (2) What three factors do you believe contribute to dissatisfaction in the parenting role? Responses fell into specific categories (e.g., spouse support) with high frequencies in certain areas. Second, the work of other researchers (see, e.g., Schaefer & Bell, 1958) was reviewed in order to determine if existing items on their attitude instruments were relevant to the instrument being developed. A total of 250 items was generated through the combined use of the above two approaches. The items were written in first-person format (Becker & Krug, 1965) with a four-point Likert-type scale for response (strongly agree, agree, disagree, strongly disagree). Items were phrased in either a negative or positive direction, although the entire test was balanced for directionality. Items pertaining to each domain were randomly ordered. A cover sheet which included directions and a background data sheet which asked for demographic data were also constructed and attached to the instrument.

This initial product was given to a pilot sample of 35 parents ranging in age from early 20s to late 60s. In addition to responding to the questions, they were asked to respond critically to the instrument in terms of relevance to the parent role. Additionally, they were asked to provide suggestions or comments with regard to readability or clarity.

This test was further submitted to three experts in the field of child and family development in order to assess the items for face validity. After a revision on the basis of the input derived from the above sources, a final pool of 211 items was selected for inclusion in the preliminary scale.

PILOT CRITERION INSTRUMENTS. In order to determine the construct validity of this instrument, four additional satisfaction measures were also administered. These other assessments of satisfaction were used as validity criteria based on the assumption that parenting satisfaction should relate to satisfaction in other areas. Unfortunately, at the time of scale construction, no other Parent Satisfaction Scales were found in a search of both published and unpublished literature. It was therefore not possible to employ an established parallel instrument as a criterion.

The Dyadic Adjustment Scale developed by Spanier (1976) was utilized as an overall measure of marital satisfaction. It is composed of 32 items and has four subscales which assess dyadic satisfaction, dyadic cohesion, dyadic consensus, and affectional expression. Measures of reliability and criterion-related validity were high, .96 and .86 respectively.

Two scales developed by Lee (1978) which measure marital and life satisfaction were also administered. The marital satisfaction measure was a five-item scale, scored on a five-point response set. The five items were shown to be highly intercorrelated, and the reliability of the scale using Cronbach's coefficient alpha was determined to be .90 for males and .94 for females; validity of these measures was not presented by the author.

The assessment of life satisfaction was also determined by the use of the Life Satisfaction Index (A) (Neugarten, Havighurst, & Tobin, 1961). This 20-item, five-point scale was derived and validated from the Life Satisfaction Ratings (LSR), a scale developed by Neugarten et al. (1961). The reliability of ratings was determined to be .78 with two judges independently reading the recorded interview material without interviewing the respondent.

PILOT STUDY DATA ANALYSIS.   Data were subjected to several analyses, including factor analyses, correlations with criterion measures, correlations between factor scores and unit weighted subscale scores, and reliability calculations for unit weighted scores. Principle Components and Equimax rotations were performed and yielded five factors. An Eigenvalue of one served as the cutoff for factor loadings, and items that loaded on more than one factor were placed on only the factor that yielded the highest loading. To balance the number of items on each factor, the 10 highest-loading items were used to construct each scale. The first factor, accounting for 14.81% of total variance, was labeled Spouse/Ex-Spouse Support and included items which clearly reflected respondents' satisfaction with the degree of assistance spouses provided for child rearing. The second factor accounted for 10.58% of total variance and was labeled Child–Parent Relationship. Content of this factor reflected a parent's satisfaction regarding his or her own relationship with the child. Factor 3 accounted for 9.16% of total variance and was labeled Parent Performance. Content of these items related to parents' satisfaction with the quality of their child-rearing skills. The fourth factor accounted for 8.18% of total variance and was labeled Family Discipline and Control; content of Factor 4 related to satisfaction with respondent's and spouse's performance as a parent, particularly in regard to disciplinary matters. Factor 5 accounted for 6.87% of the variance and was labeled General Satisfaction. Content related to feelings of overall parenting satisfaction.

The four criterion measures showed consistently significant relationships with the subscales, and the total unit scores for the five scales showed significant predictive relationships with criteria ranging from .46 to .56 ($p < .01$). Spouse/Ex-Spouse Support and Family Discipline and Control subscales showed higher relationships than the other subscales when marital satisfaction scales were used as criteria, while general satisfaction related more highly to life satisfaction than it did to marital satisfaction criteria. These results provide support for the construct validity of the subscale and total scores.

To determine whether unit-weighted scores could be appropriately used instead of the more laborious factor-scoring procedures, correlations between the two approaches were calculated. The following correlations illustrated a high degree of compatibility between the two scoring procedures: Spouse/Ex-Spouse Support, $r = .94$; Parent–Child Relationship, $r = .85$; Parent Performance, $r = .92$; Family Discipline and Control, $r = .82$; General Satisfaction, $r = .73$; total score, $r = .99$

Unit score subscale and total reliabilities were computed using Cronbach's alpha. Results indicated quite satisfactory reliabilities as follows: Spouse/Ex-Spouse Support, $r = .93$; Parent–Child Relationship, $r = .86$; Parent Performance, $r = .83$; Family Discipline and Control, $r = .82$; General Satisfaction, $r = .76$; and Total Parenting Satisfaction, $r = .93$.

Final Scale Revision and Norming

NORMING STUDY SAMPLE SELECTION. A total of 661 parents were utilized in the norming of the Parent Satisfaction Scale (PSS). They were the responding parents of school-aged children (first, third, and fifth graders) randomly selected from 38 states by 144 school psychologists participating in a large nationwide study sponsored by the National Association of School Psychologists (NASP) for the purpose of analyzing the impact of divorce on family adjustment. From the total national sample of 699 parents, 38 did not complete the scale. The parents represented both divorced ($n = 314$) and intact ($n = 347$) families. Although the majority of the parents were mothers ($n = 589$; 89.1%), a sample of fathers ($n = 72$; 10.9%) was also included. The median family income for the divorced sample ranged from $10,000 to $14,999, and for the intact sample, from $25,000 to $29,999. Further details about sample selection and general information regarding the NASP-KSU impact of divorce study can be found in earlier publications (see, e.g., Guidubaldi, Perry, & Cleminshaw, 1984).

NORMING STUDY CRITERION INSTRUMENTS. The Parent Satisfaction Scale (PSS) was only one among a large battery of instruments administered to the children, parents, and teachers. This battery was designed to predict child and family outcomes as related to parent satisfaction. It included assessments of intellectual and academic achievement, social competence, and family health, as well as home and school environment. The school psychologists gave the WISC-R IQ test (Wechsler, 1974) and WRAT (Wide Range Achievement Test: Jastak, Jastak, & Bijou, 1978) to each child individually and recorded standardized achievement test scores obtained from their student folders. Social competence measures were derived from seven sources including the Hahnemann Elementary School Behavior Rating Scale (HESB: Spivack & Swift, 1975), the Vineland Teacher Questionnaire (VTQ: Sparrow, Balla, & Chicchetti, 1981), the Sells and Roff Peer Acceptance–Rejection rating (PAR: Sells & Roff, 1967), a locus-of-control measure taken from the Harvard Project on Family Stress (LC), an optimism–pessimism scale abridged from Stipek, Lamb, and Zigler (OPTI: 1981), and selected items from child and parent interviews. The interviews were structured questionnaires designed to gather data on the following variables: home environment, marriage and employment information, daily routines, external and internal support systems, quality of life, child-rearing styles, and divorce arrangements.

NORMING STUDY DATA ANALYSES. Alpha Factor Analysis and Equimax Rotations were performed and yielded three major factors rather than the five previously derived. Analyses were conducted separately for divorced- and intact-family samples, and Tucker's Coefficient of Congruence (Harmon, 1967) was performed to determine equivalence between the factor structures for the two groups. All coefficients were .93 or above, enabling analyses to proceed on the basis of total group data. Using all subjects, the first factor, Spouse/Ex-Spouse Support, accounted for 26.1% of the total variance; the second factor, Parent–Child Relationship, 11.2%, and the third factor, Parent Performance, 5.1%. The final scale thus included three factors of 15 items each. Spouse/Ex-spouse Support included items relating to the amount of satisfaction with the parenting assistance provided by the other parent (e.g., "I am happy about the amount interest that my spouse or ex-spouse has shown in my children"). The second factor, Parent–Child Relationship, was derived from items that assessed satisfaction with the quality of the respondent's parent–child interaction (e.g., "My children are usually a joy and fun to be with"). The third factor, Parent Performance, related to satisfaction with the respondent's own child-rearing practices (e.g., "I am upset with the amount of yelling I direct towards the children").

Unit score reliabilities were computed for each factor using Cronbach's alpha. Again, results indicate high reliability as follows: CGPSS I, Spouse/Ex-Spouse Support, $r = .96$; CGPSS II, Parent–Child Relationship, $r = .86$; and CGPSS III, Parent Performance, $r = .82$. The means and standard deviations for each of the three factors are: Factor I, $m = 39.55$, $SD = 12.45$, $n = 581$; Factor II, $m = 50.48$, $SD = 5.42$, $n = 643$; and Factor III, $m = 40.13$, $SD = 6.35$, $n = 641$.

FOLLOW-UP STUDY SAMPLE SELECTION.   All 144 school psychologists who participated in the original norming study were requested to participate again in the 2-year follow-up study. As can be expected, a number of factors including residential and job mobility, and time constraints reduced the number of psychologists who were able to contribute to the Time 2 study. Thus, data were gathered on a sample of 137 children from the original group of 699. Chi square and Z-test comparisons were performed for the follow-up sample and the original norming study. In order to determine comparability between samples, analyses were performed separately for each marital-status group (i.e., divorced and intact). For both groups no significant differences were found on the following characteristics: grade, sex, race, respondent's and spouse's/ex-spouse's occupational rating and educational level, family income, or length of time in a single-parent household. Thus, the follow-up sample was judged to be a representative sample from the original population.

FOLLOW-UP STUDY CRITERION INSTRUMENTS.   The collection of instruments used for the follow-up project changed somewhat from the original study in that both the parent interview and the psychologist's rating form were expanded. Modifications also included the addition of the Achenbach Parent and Teacher Rating Scales (Achenbach & Edelbrock, 1983) and the elimination of the Vineland Teacher Questionnaire, the Optimism vs. Pessimism Scale, and the WISC-R. All other instruments employed at Time 1 such as the HESB, WRAT, and the locus-of-control scale were employed in this data-gathering period. As in the original study, all assessment was conducted or coordinated by the school psychologists.

FOLLOW-UP STUDY DATA ANALYSES.   Cronbach's alpha was again computed to examine reliability of the three domains: Spouse/Ex-Spouse Support, $r = .95$; Parent–Child Relationship, $r = .89$; and Parent Performance, $r = .82$. Correlational analyses were performed between Time 1 and Time 2 scores for each of the three domains. Results indicate test–retest stability of each of the three domains across two years: Factor I, $r = .81$; Factor II, $r = .59$; and Factor III, $r = .64$.

Validity information was determined by correlations of the three Time 1 Parent Satisfaction domains with adjustment criteria at the Time 1 period and across time with the Time 2 academic and social competencies of children. Correlations between Time 1 parent satisfaction domains and selected family criteria, including other indices of adult satisfaction (i.e., marital, job, and life satisfaction) at Time 2 were also computed. In addition, the means and standard deviations derived on the follow-up sample for the three factors were as follows: Factor I, m = 40.97, SD = 12.34, n = 118; Factor II, m = 51.53, SD = 4.64, n = 131; and Factor III, m = 40.80, SD = 6.44, n = 130.

Correlational Results

Correlational analyses indicate a strong relationship between level of parent satisfaction and children's social and academic performance, health ratings of the family members, and many family environmental and interactional variables. When parents scored higher on each of the three factors—Spouse/Ex-Spouse Support, Parent–Child Relations, and Parent Performance—their children scored higher on both academic and social performance criteria. The family health ratings were also higher as was the quality of the family environment and interaction. The positive relationship between parent satisfaction and child and family criteria was evident for both concurrent predictions of Time 1 criteria and cross-time predictions of Time 2 criteria.

RELATIONSHIPS OF TIME 1 CGPSS WITH TIME 1 CRITERIA. The Time 1 CGPSS was consistently related to many Time 1 criteria (see Table 11.1). Children whose parents rated their satisfaction on Factor I (Spouse/Ex-Spouse Support) as high achieved higher scores on social criteria as follows: 14 of the 15 HESB factors; Communication, Daily Living, and Social Scales of the VTQ; higher final grade in conduct, more internal locus of control, higher measures of peer acceptance and peer relations; and fewer number of days absent from school. The relationship of CGPSS scores to children's academic performance was supported by higher scores on the Reading, Spelling, and Math subtests of the WRAT, final grade in reading and math, and higher scores on the WISC-R and the academic achievement rating of the HESB. Children of satisfied parents were also less likely to have repeated a grade. With regard to health ratings, responding parents reported better health for themselves, their spouse/ex-spouse, target child, and other siblings. The school psychologist also rated the target child as being more healthy, attractive, better coordinated, and larger in size. When family variables were assessed,

Table 11.1 Correlations of Time 1 CGPSS with Time 1 Criteria

	Factor		
Variable	I	II	III
Social			
HESB			
Originality	.13***		
Independent learning	.24***	.12**	.10**
Involvement	.15***		
Productive with peers	.18***	.09*	.09*
Intellectual dependency	−.21***		
Failure anxiety	−.18***	−.11**	−.09*
Unreflectiveness	−.22***	−.11**	−.09*
Irrelevant talk	−.21***	−.11**	−.12**
Social overinvolvement	−.24***	−.15***	−.17***
Negative feelings	−.19***	−.13***	−.12**
Withdrawn	−.20***	−.08*	
Critical competitive	−.22***	−.13***	−.16***
Blaming	−.21***	−.13***	−.13**
Approach to teacher			
Inattention	−.26***	−.12**	−.12**
Vineland			
Communication	.19***		
Daily living	.10*		
Social	.24***	.13**	.12**
Locus of control	.09*		
Grade in conduct	.11*		.14**
Absence from school	−.14**		
Sells and Roff			
Peer acceptance			
(teacher rating)	.22***	.10*	.10*
Quality of peer relationships			
(parent rating)	.20***	.22***	.14***
Academic			
HESB			
Academic achievement	.23***		
WISC-R IQ	.12**	.08*	
WRAT			
Reading	.09*		
Spelling	.12**	.08*	
Math	.10*	.08*	
Final grade in reading	.13**	.10*	
Final grade in math	.14**		
Regular class placement		.11**	
Repeated school grade	−.12**	−.10**	
Health			
Psychologist's rating			
Attractiveness	.10*		
Physical size	.10*		
Physical coordination	.10*		
Physical health	.13***	.09*	

Table 11.1 (*Continued*)

Variable	Factor		
	I	II	III
Respondent's health	.20***	.12**	.17***
Spouse's/ex-spouse's health	.31***	.23***	.23***
Target child's health	.23***	.21***	.22***
Siblings' health	.26***	.27***	.24***
Family			
Mother's happiness (child rating)	.18***	.15***	.12**
Father's happiness (child rating)	.15***	.16***	.10*
Education			
Respondent	.14***		
Spouse/ex-spouse	.25***		.10*
Job satisfaction			
Respondent	.25***	.23***	.28***
Spouse/ex-spouse	.30***	.20***	.20***
Occupation level			
Respondent	.16***	.11*	.10*
Spouse/ex-spouse	.26***	.10*	.08*
Relationships			
Parent–child	.21***	.18***	.12**
Mother–child	.20***	.15***	.14***
Father–child	.48***	.11**	.15***
Family income	.48***		.13***

*$p < .05$; **$p < .01$; ***$p < .001$.

results indicated that both father and mother happiness were higher; parent–child, mother–child, and father–child relations were more positive. In addition, socioeconomic status indicators (i.e., education and occupation levels of both parents, family income) and parental job satisfaction were higher.

The findings related to Factor II (Parent–Child Relations) also illustrated significant relationships to Time 1 criteria. Considering social criteria, parents with high PSS scores had children who performed better on 11 of the 15 HESB ratings, the Vineland Social scale, and measures of peer acceptance and peer relations. In regard to academic criteria, both Spelling and Math subtests on the WRAT were higher, as were final grade in reading and IQ score on the WISC-R. The child was also more likely to be placed in a regular class and less likely to repeat a grade. On health criteria, health ratings for the responding parent, the spouse or ex-spouse, the target child, and the child's siblings were higher when the parent was more satisfied. Again, both father and mother happiness, and general

Table 11.2 Correlations of Time 1 PSS with Time 2 Criteria

Variable	Factor		
	I	II	III
Social			
HESB			
Independent learning	.22*		
Irrelevant talk	−.19*	−.19*	
Social overinvolvement	−.20*		
Negative feelings			.22**
Withdrawn	−.29**		
Critical/competitive		−.20*	−.21*
Blaming	−.19*		−.19*
Inattention	−.29**		
Achenbach (teacher rating)			
Child's happiness	.38***		
Appropriate behavior	.34***		
Work effort	.44***		
Total number of behavior problems	−.31***		−.20*
Achenbach (parent rating)			
Behavior with parents		.28***	
Plays/works alone		.24**	
Total number of behavior problems	−.30***	−.28**	−.41***
Peer relations			
Parent rating		.31***	.31***
Teacher rating	.19*		
School absence,			
1981–82 school year	−.22*		
School tardiness,			
1982–83 school year	−.27*		
Grade in conduct			
1982–83 school year			.30*
Fall 1983		.36**	.28*
Academic			
Final grade in reading			
1981–82 school year	.29**		
1982–83 school year	.26***		
Fall 1983	.30***		
Final grade in spelling			
1981–82 school year	.32**		
1982–83 school year	.24*		
Fall 1983	.32**		
Final grade in math			
1981–82 school year	.27*		
1982–83 school year			
Fall 1983	.30**		
Achenbach (teacher rating)			
Reading	.31**		

Table 11.2 (*Continued*)

Variable	Factor		
	I	II	III
Spelling	.25*		
Math	.20*		
Social studies	.32**		
Science	.28**		
Language	.33***		
Amount of learning	.37***		
Achenbach (parent rating)			
Reading	.36***	.19*	
Spelling	.27**		
Social studies	.37*		
Language	.29**		
Math	.21*		
Health			
Psychologist's rating			
Attractiveness	.27**		
Spouse/ex-spouse's health	.29**		
Target child's health	.25**	.23*	.23*
Siblings' health	.24*	.40***	.22*
Family			
Job satisfaction			
Respondent	.37***		
Spouse/ex-spouse	.25*		
Education			
Respondent	.26**		
Spouse/ex-spouse	.28**		.22*
Family income	.50***		
Relationships			
Parent–child			.18*
Father–child	.33***		.21*
Parent interview			
Stress (life changes)	−.32***		−.27**
Child interview			
Positive life changes	−.29**		−.22**
Negative life changes	−.22*		−.21*
Life satisfaction	.36***		.28**
Marital satisfaction			
Married same person	.56***		
Love/attention	.43***		.24**
Understanding	.42***		.27**
Companionship	.33***		.28**
Overall satisfaction	.50***		.26**
Frequency of arguments	.39***		.24*
Number of arguments			−.24*
Severity of arguments	.24*		
Child's exposure to arguments	.22*		.24**

*p < .05; **p < .01; ***p < .001.

parent–child, mother–child, and father–child relations were higher. Responding parent and spouse/ex-spouse's occupation and job satisfaction levels were also higher.

Factor III (Parent Performance) correlations again provided evidence for widespread relationships of the CGPSS with Time 1 criteria. Of the social variables, 10 of the 15 HESB items, the Social Scale of the VTQ, final grade in conduct, and measures of peer acceptance were higher. There were no significant relationships found for academic criteria. With regard to health criteria, all family members had higher reported health ratings when the CGPSS parent performance factor was higher. Mother and father happiness, parent–child, mother–child, and father–child relations; responding parent and spouse job satisfaction; and family income were related to higher parent satisfaction with parent performance.

RELATIONSHIPS OF TIME 1 CGPSS WITH TIME 2 CRITERIA. The results relative to the 2-year follow-up study illustrate the predictive value of the CGPSS with children's social and academic functioning as well as with family and environmental variables (see Table 11.2). For example, parents who rated their satisfaction on Factor I (Spouse/Ex-Spouse Support) as high were more apt to have children who were rated by their teacher as being happier, displaying appropriate behaviors, exerting better work effort, and having fewer behavior problems. They also achieved better scores on 6 of the 15 HESB scales, and their parents rated them as having fewer behavior problems. Children of more satisfied parents also achieved better peer relations as rated by their teachers and had fewer school absences and tardiness. With regard to academic criteria, teachers rated children as performing higher in reading, spelling, math, social studies, science, and language, and as learning more overall. On the parent ratings children achieved higher scores on reading, spelling, social studies, language, and math. Throughout the 2-year interval, school grades were also better.

Health measures were higher at Time 1 for family members when the responding parent rated satisfaction with spouse/ex-spouse support as high. In addition, several other family factors were related to high satisfaction, such as job satisfaction and educational level of both parents, family income, father–child relationship, life satisfaction, and marital satisfaction (based on 8 of 10 indices). Additionally, parental satisfaction with spouse support was related to fewer life changes as rated by the parent and child.

For Factor II (Parent–Child Relationship), higher scores on social and health criteria at Time 2 were again predicted by higher levels of parental satisfaction at Time 1. However, only one academic and no family criteria were related to Factor II. On the social criteria, the more-satisfied parents reported the child as having fewer behavior problems, better ability to work and play alone, better peer relations, and better behavior toward parents. Teachers rated these children as displaying less irrelevant talk and less critical-competitive behavior, and conduct grades were higher. Additionally, parents rated academic performance in reading as higher. Both the target child's and the siblings' health ratings were related to higher parent satisfaction.

Factor III (Parent Performance) was shown to relate to 3 of 15 HESB factors, better peer relations, and both teacher and parent rating of fewer child behavior problems. This factor also predicted better health ratings for both the target child and the siblings. Measures of general parent–child relations and father–child relations were more positive when satisfaction with parenting performance was higher. In addition, respondent's life satisfaction, spouse/ex-spouse's job satisfaction, and 7 of 10 marital-satisfaction items were predicted by satisfaction on this factor. Satisfaction was higher on Factor III when life-change ratings were lower, based on both parent and child ratings of life-change events.

The cross-time results thus illustrate that the relationships of parental satisfaction to social, academic, familial, and environmental criteria do persist over time. This was especially evident for children's social competence and health status, which were correlated with higher levels of parental satisfaction across all three factors. Measures of father–child relations, life and marital satisfaction were predicted by two factors.

Discussion

These results dramatically document the relationship of all three domains of parent satisfaction (spouse/ex-spouse support, parent–child relations, and parent performance) to the social and academic competence of school-aged children and to various family environmental and interactional variables both concurrently and across time. These findings thus verify the importance of assessing parent satisfaction levels. In the following discussion, results are treated separately by domain.

Findings in the area of spouse or ex-spouse support are consistent with the traditional notion that parenting is a two-person job. When responding parents (typically, mothers) report dissatisfaction with parenting support from spouses/ex-spouses by such statements as "My spouse or ex-spouse usually does not help enough with the children," children show poorer performance both socially and academically. One explanation for these findings is provided by Lewis and Weinraub (1976) in their discussion of *tension introduction.* The term refers to contrasts in behavior as two people perform similar tasks, such as in co-parenting. Weinraub (1978, p. 125) argued that

> The presence of two adult authority figures with similar but different opinions and expectations regarding the child's behavior forces the child to learn to deal with differences of opinion and to consider more than one side of an argument or issue. In this way, the presence of two social objects can be expected to increase the child's analytic skills.

This may partially explain the differences in the child's social and academic functioning when the mother does not perceive the father as providing parental support.

Additionally, one parent can counterbalance the other's interaction with the child. For example, if one parent is being too critical, the other can be more accepting, or if one has a problem expressing warmth or affection, the other can attempt to help the child understand or compensate in some ways for this deficiency. Thus, a relationship with two cooperating parents is important.

Previous work has suggested that the mother's perception of spouse support in parenting has an impact on the child's relationship with both parents. Feiring (1975), for example, reported that the mother's perception of support from the father was related to her sensitivity and responsivity to her infant. Park and O'Leary (1975) found that the father's presence during mother–child interaction was associated with the mother's increased interest and positive affect toward her infant. There is also evidence that the mother's relationship to the father has an effect on the father–child relationship (Pederson, Anderson, & Cain, 1977). The current research reinforces this notion, in that children whose mothers were more satisfied with spouse/ex-spouse support reported better relations with both parents.

The demonstrated relationships between satisfaction with spouse/ex-spouse support and measures of marital and life satisfaction are consistent with earlier reports on this CGPSS instrument (Cleminshaw & Guidubaldi, 1981; Guidubaldi & Cleminshaw, 1985) as well as by studies linking marital and life satisfaction (see, e.g., Andrews & Withey, 1974; Campbell, Converse, & Rogers, 1976; Glenn & Weaver, 1981). Satir (1964, p. 1) suggested that "the parents are architects of the family and the marriage relationship is the key to all other family relationships. When there is difficulty with the marital pair there are more than likely problems in parenting." This study supports Satir's predictions in that marital satisfaction and parenting were found to be strongly related.

In view of the changing characteristics of American families, the results have even greater implications for life and marital happiness. The dual-provider family is rapidly becoming the most prevalent family pattern. Demographic statistics report that 59% of mothers with school-aged children are working outside the home (Kamerman & Hayes, 1982), and role overload or strain is often cited as a major problem for the dual-provider family. Rapoport and Rapoport (1976) suggest that four conditions could account for this feeling of overload or role strain. One of these conditions was the degree to which there was a satisfactory reapportionment of tasks, or in other words, assistance in role demands such as required in parenting. It has further been suggested that satisfactory reapportionment of tasks is a coping strategy that helps alleviate strain. Clearly, role strain related to parenting may contribute to a decline in marital satisfaction (Glenn & McLanahan, 1982; Rollins & Galligan, 1978; Spanier & Lewis, 1980; Waldron & Routh, 1981), and most parents would benefit from the parenting support of the other spouse as a means of diminishing this level of strain. These problems become more pronounced today due to changing family conditions, such as the increasing number of mothers entering the work force. The relationship of parent satisfaction with spouse support to marital and life satisfaction in general thus has important implications, especially for dual-provider families.

Results pertaining to the relationship of Factor II (Parent–Child Relationship) to children's social and academic functioning support the work of Yarrow (1963), which indicates that a mother's positive emotional involvement with her infant is related to the infant's social initiative. Additionally, Gordon (1977) found that when mutual gazing during mother–infant interaction was high, levels of infant development were high.

Reciprocity is an important consideration in parent–child relationships. The parent who expects and anticipates a negative relationship (or a positive one) may in fact be either initiating, maintain, or accelerating it. A parent may communicate how he or she expects the child to respond and thereby get what he or she expects. As Dreikurs stated, "We are moving ourselves in line with what we anticipate" (Soltz, 1967, p. 10). Therefore, it may be that the quality of the parent–child relationship predicts the quality of a child's social interactions outside the home with both peers and teachers. That is, the child's perceptions of the parent–child relationship set up expectations about relationships in general and thus affect how the child interacts with others. Modeling and lack of adequate teaching of social skills are possible explanations for this phenomenon. In any case, children whose parent–child relationships were poor were rated as having poorer peer relations and less acceptance from their peers, and conversely those whose parent–child relationships were good were rated as having good peer relations and better acceptance from peers.

Terner and Pew (1978, p. 5) have stated that "the attitudes, values, and relationships within the immediate family . . . provide the initial critical medium through which the child's personality takes shape." Thus, parent–child interaction patterns may affect later personality development which will have impact on the child's interpersonal relations. As current results suggest, satisfaction with parent–child relationships was related concurrently and across time to the child's social competence and, additionally, to concurrent academic performance.

The results associated with Factor III (Parent Performance) illustrate the critical need for parents to feel competent in the role of parent. Zigler (1966) has observed that families with incompetent parents seem to provide ineffectual models for problem-solving skills, and this pattern appears to be transmitted from one generation to the next. The relationship of satisfaction with parent performance and child competence is comsistent with Zigler's findings. In addition, Blechman (1984) demonstrated that parental incompetence was associated with physical illness and financial difficulties. On the CGPSS, families in which the parent was less satisfied with his or her parent performance experienced lower family incomes and poorer health for all family members.

In general, the overall findings confirm the need to improve parent satisfaction. Parent education programming may facilitate this objective. Over 30 years ago, Ginott (1957) recommended the training of parents; he contended that poor parenting was a reflection of lack of experience, misinformation, or exposure to poor parental models rather than to poor mental health or personal problems. Thus, improvement of parent satisfaction might well be accomplished through parent education programs that stress mutual responsibility of both parents (whether in divorced or intact families), realistic expectation levels for both parent and child performance, and identification of positive parent–child relationship elements that can serve as objectives of good parenting. When coupled with traditional parent program content concerning such issues as reinforcement practices and communication skills, these additional emphases should enhance both parenting skills and parent satisfaction.

Concurrent relationships of all three factors with job satisfaction suggests that enhancing satisfaction with one area of life may result in commensurate improvement in other areas as well. The long-term predictive relationships of two of the CGPSS factors with life and marital satisfactions suggest further that interventions which enhance parent satisfaction at a given time may enhance future satisfactions with other areas of life roles.

Based on the empirical support described in this chapter, the CGPSS is recommended for research and clinical applications. The extensive correlations with adjustment criteria merit attention. For example, if children's performance levels affect parent satisfaction, as might be expected, the CGPSS could serve as one indicator of success for child intervention strategies. If parent satisfaction affects child adjustment, as might also be expected—particularly in light of the demonstrated long-term predictive validity—parent education and other supportive interventions may result in improved child development. The CGPSS provides a valid assessment tool for determining current parent satisfaction status and for assessing intervention effects. Moreover, the factor structure of the CGPSS permits analysis of three discrete areas of satisfaction, thus enabling clinicians to identify more focused intervention strategies. In an era of family disruption, changing adult sex roles, and extremely high frequencies of child and adolescent adjustment problems, such improved assessment devices are prerequisites to effective parent education programs.

References

Achenbach, T. M., & Edelbrock, C. S. (1983). *Manual for the Child Behavior Checklist and Revised Child Behavior Profile.* Burlington: University of Vermont, Child Psychiatry.

Andrews, F. M., & Witney, S. B. (1974). Developing measures of perceived life quality: Results from several national averages. *Journal of Social Indicators Research, 1.*

Becker, W. C., & Krug, R. S. (1965). Parent Attitude Research Instrument: A research review. *Child Development, 36*(3), 29–265.

Beckman, L. J. (1978, Spring). The relative rewards and costs of parenthood and employment for employed women. *Psychology of Women, 2*(3).

Bigner, J. J. (1979). *Parent–child relationships.* New York: Macmillan.

Blake, J. (1979). Is zero preferred? American attitude toward childlessness in the 1970s. *Journal of Marriage and the Family, 41,* 245–257.

Blechman, E. A. (1984). Competent parents, competent children: Behavioral objectives of parent training. In R. F. Dangel & R. A. Polster (Eds.), *Parent training foundations of research and practice* (pp. 34–63). New York: Guilford Press.

Campbell, A., Converse, P. E., & Rogers, W. L. (1976). *The quality of life: Perceptions, evaluations, and satisfactions.* New York: Russell Sage Foundation.

Chillman, C. S. (1980). Parent satisfactions, concerns, and goals for the children. *Family Relations, 29,* 339–345.

Cleminshaw, H. K., & Guidubaldi, J. (1981). Assessing parent satisfaction. In *Resources in education.* (ERIC Document Reproduction Service No. ED 200 858)

Cook, A. S., West, J. B., & Hamner, T. J. (1982). Changes in attitudes toward parenting among college women, 1972 and 1979 samples. *Family Relations, 31*(1), 109–113.

Espenshade, T. J. (1977). The value and cost of children. *Population Bulletin, 32*(1).

Fawcett, J. T. (1972). *The satisfactions and cost of children: Theories, concepts, methods.* Honolulu: East–West Population Institute.

Feiring, C. (1975). *The influence of the child and secondary parent on maternal behavior: Toward a social systems view of early infant–mother attachment.* Doctoral dissertation, University of Pittsburgh, Pittsburgh.

Ginott, H. G. (1957). Differential treatment groups in guidance: Counseling, psychotherapy, and psychoanalysis. *International Journal of Social Psychiatry, 3,* 231–235.

Glenn, N. D., & McLanahan, S. (1982). Children and marital happiness: A further specification of the relationship. *Journal of Marriage and the Family, 1,* 63–72.

Glenn, N. D., & Weaver, C. N. (1981). The contribution of marital happiness to global happiness. *Journal of Marriage and the Family, 43,* 161–168.

Gordon, I. J. (1977, March–April). *Significant factors in effective parenting.* Paper presented at the Effective Parenting Conference sponsored by Bilingual Children's Television, New Orleans.

Gordon, I. J., Hanes, M. L., Lamme, L. L., & Schlenker, P. (1972, May). *Research report of parent-oriented home-based early childhood education programs.* Atlanta, GA: South Carolina Department of Education as fiscal agent for USOE, Region IV.

Guidubaldi, J., & Cleminshaw, H. K. (1985). The Development of the Cleminshaw–Guidubaldi Parent Satisfaction Scale. *Journal of Clinical Child Psychology, 14*(4), 293–298.

Guidubaldi, J., Perry, J., & Cleminshaw, H. K. (1984). The legacy of parental divorce. In B. B. Lahey & A. E. Kazdin (Eds.), *Advances in clinical child psychology* (Vol. 7) (pp. 109–147). New York: Plenum Press.

Hanes, M. L., & Dunn, S. K. (1978). Maternal attitudes and the development of mothers and children. In J. H. Stevens, Jr. & M. Matthews (Eds.), *Mother/child father/child relationships.* Washington, DC: National Association for the Education of Young Children.

Harmon, H. H. (1967). *Modern factor analysis.* Chicago: University of Chicago Press.

Hetherington, E. M. (1979). Divorce, a child's perspective. *American Psychologist, 34,* 851–858.

Hoffman, L. W., & Manis, J. D. (1979). The value of children in the United States: A new approach to the study of fertility. *Journal of Marriage and the Family, 41,* 583–596.

Jastak, J. K., Jastak, S. R., & Bijou, S. W. (1978). *Wide Range Achievement Test.* Washington, DC: Jastak Associates.

Kamerman, S. B., & Hayes, C. D. (1982). *Families that work: Children in a changing world.* Washington, DC: National Academy Press.

Lee, G. R. (1978). Marriage and morale in later life. *Journal of Marriage and the Family, 40,* 131–139.

Lewis, M., & Weinraub, M. (1976). The father's role in the child's social network. In M. Lamb (Ed.), *The role of the father in child development.* New York: Wiley.

Neugarten, B. L., Havighurst, R. J., & Tobin, S. S. (1961). The measurement of life satisfaction. *Journal of Gerontology, 16,* 134–143.

Park, R. D., & O'Leary, S. (1975). Father–mother–infant interaction in the newborn period: Some findings, some observations and some unresolved issues. In K. Riegel & J. Meacham (Eds.), *The developing individual in a changing world: Vol. II. Social and environmental issues.* The Hague: Mouton.

Pederson, F. A., Anderson, B. J., & Cain, R. L. (1977). *An approach to understanding link ups between the parent, infant and spouse relationship.* Paper presented at the convention of the Society for Research in Child Development, New Orleans.

Rapoport, R., & Rapoport, R. N. (1976). *Dual-career families reexamined.* New York: Harper & Row.

Rollins, B. C., & Galligan, R. (1978). The developing child and marital satisfaction of parents. In R. M. Lerner & G. B. Spanier (Eds.), *Child influences on marital and family interaction: A life span perspective.* New York: Academic Press.

Satir, U. (1964). *Conjoint family therapy.* Palo Alto, CA: Science & Behavior Books.

Sawhill, I. V. (1977). Economic perspectives on the family. *Daedalus, 106,* 115–125.

Schaefer, E. S., & Bell, R. Q. (1958). Development of a parent attitude research instrument. *Child Development, 29,* 339–361.

Sells, S. B., & Roff, M. (1967). *Peer acceptance–rejection and personality development.* Washington, DC: U.S. Department of Health, Education and Welfare.

Soltz, U. (1967). Study group leaders' manual for *Children: The challenge.* Chicago: Alfred Adler Institute.

Spanier, G. B. (1976). Measuring dyadic adjustment: New scales for assessing the quality of marriage and similar dyads. *Journal of Marriage and the Family, 38,* 15–28.

Spanier, G. B., & Lewis, R. A. (1980). Marital quality: A review of the seventies. *Journal of Marriage and the Family, 42,* 96–110.

Sparrow, S., Balla, D. A., & Chicchetti, D. F. (1981). *Vineland Adaptive Behavior Scales: Classroom edition* (Research ed.). Circle Pines, MN: American Guidance Association.

Spivack, G., & Swift, M. (1975). *Hahnemann Elementary School Behavior Rating Scale: Manual.* Philadelphia: Hahnemann Medical College and Hospital, Department of Mental Health Services.

Stipek, D., Lamb, M., & Zigler, E. (1981). OPTI: A measure of children's optimism. *Educational and Psychological Measurement, 41*(1), 131–150.

Terner, J., & Pew, W. L. (1978). *The courage to be imperfect: The life and work of Rudolf Dreikurs.* New York: Hawthorn Books.

U.S. Bureau of the Census. (1979). *Divorce, child custody, and child support* (Current Population Reports, Series P-23, No. 84). Washington, DC: U.S. Government Printing Office.

Waldron, H., & Routh, D. K. (1981). The effect of the first child on the marital relationship. *Journal of Marriage and the Family, 43,* 785–788.

Wechsler, D. (1974). *Wechsler Intelligence Scale for Children—Revised.* New York: Psychological Corporation.

Weinraub, M. (1978). Fatherhood: The myth of the second-class parent. In J. H. Stevens & M. Mathews (Eds.), *Mother–child father–child relations.* Washington, DC: National Association for the Education of Young Children.

Yankelovich, Skelly, & White, Inc. (1977). *Raising children in a changing American society.* Minneapolis: General Mills.

Yarrow, L. J. (1963). Research in dimensions of early maternal care. *Merrill-Palmer Quarterly, 9,* 101–119.

Zigler, E. (1966). Mental retardation: Current issues and approaches. In L. W. Hoffman & M. L. Hoffman (Eds.), *Review of child development research* (Vol. 2). New York: Russell Sage Foundation.

Adler–Dreikurs Parent Study Group Leadership Training

Bryna Gamson
Hope Hornstein
Barbara Borden

Introduction

In this age of professionalism, credentials are respected in all fields and required in most cases. The demand for professionalism extends to those who would teach parents. Thus, there has arisen a demand to train even volunteer parent educators in as professional a program as possible.

History of the Adlerian Parent Education Groups

Dr. Rudolf Dreikurs, an acknowledged pioneer in the field of child rearing, introduced the Adlerian concept of parent education in the United States through the Community Child Guidance Centers, which he began in Chicago in 1939. At these Centers, parents were given the opportunity to experience public family counseling with a professional, in a group setting where other parents in addition to teachers and other professionals observed. Through these Centers, parents were also given the opportunity to participate in parent education groups, called "parent study groups." The study groups, later led by lay people, discussed parenting techniques presented at first orally by Dr. Dreikurs, then through books (Dreikurs, 1948, 1968; Dreikurs & Soltz, 1964). The most popular, *Children: The Challenge* (Dreikurs & Soltz, 1964), served both as adult educational reading and as a course of study for parents.

It was Dreikurs' belief that the concepts he articulated should be presented in a form easily understood by mothers and fathers. Like Adler, his writing was not complicated by technical or professional jargon;

rather, his ideas were simply stated. Parents could identify both with the examples of children's misbehavior that he cited in his text and those that parents brought to the Community Child Guidance Centers.

Those who attended the Centers were encouraged to participate with comments, questions, and discussion when an individual family was being counseled. Parents and other lay people were encouraged by Dr. Dreikurs to lead parent study groups. These lay leaders were instructed by Dreikurs and his colleagues, who professionally counseled families, not to assume the role of expert in the study group setting, but instead to refer to *Children: The Challenge* as the guide.

The emphasis in the Centers, as well as in the separately conducted parent study groups, was on parent and family education rather than psychotherapy. In fact, as more counseling centers developed and more parents began attending the additional study group sessions in the Chicago area, the child guidance movement adopted (in 1964) the name "Family Education Association" (FEA) to replace Community Child Guidance Centers. This new name provided for the inclusion of the parent study groups as an integral part of the parent education program. Nationally, Adlerian organizations with programs similar to these described have also commonly adopted names like Family Education Center.

Family counseling was conducted in community settings such as churches and schools—places familiar, comfortable, and easy to reach. Parent study groups were also conducted in these settings as well as in parents' homes. Membership in a group was free, although generally participants were asked to join FEA, the nonprofit organization supporting the Centers. Groups of 6 to 12 parents convened with leaders on a weekly basis for a period of about 10 weeks to discuss *Children: The Challenge* and how to apply the various precepts to their specific situations.

Early Training for Leaders through FEA

At first, there was no specific training for volunteer study group leaders. Anyone who had attended child guidance counseling sessions or participated in a group as a member was encouraged to become a group leader. The only prerequisite for group leadership was that one had been a group member.

The Child Guidance, and later, Family Education Centers and parent study groups developed rapidly in the metropolitan Chicago area as well as nationally in the 1950s and 1960s. A *Study Group Leader's Manual* (Soltz, 1967), prompted by requests nationally, was prepared, following the Dreikurs–Soltz text *Children: The Challenge* chapter by chapter, posing discussion questions for leaders to use in their parent study groups. It also contains information supplementary to the text and articles on the philosophy of the groups, for example, the role of the leader as facilitator.

The grassroots nature of parents becoming involved in their own study group leadership was repeated in many parts of the country under the guidance of those influenced by Dreikurs and Adler (Christensen & Thomas, 1980). These traditional FEA study groups were provided free of charge. Volunteer leaders formed a network under FEA and ran groups in their own neighborhoods, in Chicago, and, within similar organizations, around the country.

However, some individuals ran groups independently of any organization. There were groups that went on for months, demonstrating the leader's inability to focus discussion, with no clear idea of the original time frame suggested by the pioneers. Others took too forceful a role by expanding the leader's function to include giving advice and counsel. Another very damaging problem arose when in some instances leaders misinterpreted the principles themselves.

Thus, while the majority of leaders essentially followed the model prescribed by Dreikurs and outlined by Soltz in the manual, it became apparent that the volunteer organization, FEA, would have to initiate training and monitoring of leaders.

In 1975, the FEA established volunteer training. They authorized certain qualified leaders to conduct 1-day training sessions for new leaders. Those who expected to lead under the auspices of FEA were required to take part in the training session, participate in one group as a member, and colead at least once with an experienced leader. The leadership training emphasized the importance of the leader's role as facilitator and emphasized the need to understand the material so that group members did not miss or misinterpret key concepts.

In the 1970s, as with many large volunteer organizations, FEA found itself diminished by the career-oriented woman's liberation movement. Since commitment to the ideas studied in the "Dreikurs groups" (as they were commonly called) was still high, arrangements were made to turn over FEA's activities to the Alfred Adler Institute. In 1981, the Institute formally accepted FEA as a division (the *A* then became *Activities* rather than *Association*), to be administered by a paid worker.

With the Alfred Adler Institute of Chicago's evolution from informal workshop and training institution to fully accredited graduate school in 1977, there had arisen a need for more formalized instruction for its students in Adlerian parent education and family counseling. With the coming of the new FEA division, practicum opportunities for students of Adlerian counseling could be provided in both the family counseling and parent education study group fields. The training program for leaders was designed with graduate students in mind; however, it has applied equally well to lay leaders and other professionals interested in leading groups. Its design also addresses the lessons learned from FEA's experiences. (For a thorough discussion of principles covered in an Adlerian parent study group, see Christensen & Thomas, 1980).

Types of Adlerian Parent Study Groups

Typically, as mentioned, groups did and still do meet in neighborhood locations familiar to their participants. They are also most frequently organized by individuals within a neighborhood: an interested parent, administrator of a church or synagogue, school administrator or guidance counselor, social service agency worker serving families, youth committees, anti-substance abuse organizations, and the like.

The length of time a group is willing to commit to a class also varies. Sometimes the leader prefers a shorter sequence, and then doubles up on individual class times. Typically, a class is $1\frac{1}{2}$ hours each week for 8 weeks. Some are 6 sessions for 2 or more hours each. Professionals have been known to condense materials into two full-day workshops (theory of democratic child rearing, the use of consequences, and a minimum amount of experiential time). Some have had great success in meeting evenings, others do well during the daytime or weekend.

Special interest groups seek out Adlerian parent study materials to supplement therapy with education. For example, social workers in the Illinois Department of Children and Family Services assign clients whose children have been removed from the home due to suspected or proven abusive treatment to FEA parent study groups. Therapists, privately and in hospital and teenage treatment centers, often recommend that parents of children in their care participate in such groups with FEA. Special training has been provided by FEA to Parents Anonymous volunteers, a group working via hotline and self-help discussion groups for abusive or potentially abusive parents, to incorporate parent education into their agenda.

Other types of special interest groups for whom classes might be tailored include the single parent, adoptive parents, parents of handicapped children, "remarried" families, and those touched by alcoholism and drug abuse. While it is our conviction that parents of all ages, backgrounds, and beliefs can participate together in a single study group situation, many parents often prefer to meet with those whose backgrounds are similar to theirs.

Books have been developed to meet the needs of some of these specialized groups, for example, parents of teenage children or youngsters under age 10 or 11, although *Children: The Challenge* led by a flexible, understanding leader could address any group needs with the exception of perhaps parents of teenagers. Dreikurs pointed out that while no two mothers (or fathers) are alike, they all make the same mistakes. Thus, parents are taught, among other things, not to pity children and to "downgrade 'bad' habits," (Dreikurs & Soltz, 1964), meaning not to draw further attention to any problem behavior or condition, but instead to encourage positive behavior.

Materials Used by Study Group Leaders

Children: The Challenge has received criticism for its somewhat haphazard structure, but leaders over the years have simply reorganized its design by assigning chapters out of sequence, perhaps adding to group discussion by collecting comic strips, articles, and other materials suggested in newer literature (Zuckerman, Zuckerman, Costa, & Yura, 1978). Here and there some examples need updating, as life in 1964 was in many respects less complicated than it is now. While it has remained as one of the 12 all-time best-selling books on child rearing, it has been eclipsed in the public consciousness by other textbooks, some of which are also Adlerian.

Among the more prominent child-rearing guidebooks written expressly for group studies is the S.T.E.P. program: *Systematic Training for Effective Parenting* (Dinkmeyer & McKay, 1976). These students of Dreikurs translated the concepts taught in Dreikurs' books and demonstration family counseling into an appealing, modern format. Whereas Dreikurs may have only implied certain ideas, for example, communications techniques, the authors of S.T.E.P. were able to make use of his ideas as well as incorporate modern communications theories, like those developed by semanticists and found in *Parent Effectiveness Training* (Gordon, 1970).

Another modernized presentation of the Dreikurs principles, likewise well packaged and professionally produced and promoted, is the newer video-enhanced *Active Parenting* (Popkin, 1983, see also this volume, Chapter 4). Popkin's ideas, like those found in S.T.E.P., are clearly stated, sequentially arranged, relevant to modern life, and an improvement upon the less organized *Children: The Challenge*.

Another useful example of such self-contained programs for parent groups is that of Marlin (1973). His *Basics of Practical Parenting* is far less costly than the two programs mentioned above and assumes that the leader is an unpaid volunteer.

These examples of entire programs written specifically as self-contained study group programs are directly in line with the leader-as-facilitator model Dreikurs first espoused. They have, because of modern formats and excellent marketing, found their utilitarian way into multiple agencies, schools, and church organizations all over the country. These groups recognize the material as practical and know that it works.

Other specialization areas have also been addressed: Books for parents of teens, single parents, and "remarried" families, even books with a religious orientation, are available from Adlerian authors. There is also a variety of books in the traditional format of *Children: The Challenge,* not really intended so much for study group use per se as for general reading or enrichment.

At the workshop for training parent education group leaders, as wide an assortment of these books as possible is available for browsing and some critique. Leaders are encouraged to maintain a personal library of Adlerian parent education materials to add depth to whatever text they select. Many groups request follow up in the form of personal reading or a second course; it is useful to have other books for this reason. The various texts make the Adler–Dreikurs principles available on a variety of reading levels, in a variety of formats and appeal, translated into various languages. The leader needs to be in a position to see the various options and judge what text will suit his or her and the target population's needs (see Appendix A).

Training at the Alfred Adler Institute

An Overview

Training at the Aldred Adler Institute of Chicago represents a generic Adlerian parent educator model useful to anyone interested in leading a group. Because one textbook is not favored over another, and because the traditional model has had time to evolve and be critiqued, the present system is practical and reasonably without bias.

Replicability of a standard model is one of the tasks of the training workshop, in order to promote a degree of consistency in teaching these techniques to both leaders and parents. At the same time, training provides for a broad range of styles and needs.

The model used by the Alfred Adler Institute stresses leadership skills in group dynamics and communications. Without these skills, dissemination of concepts and materials would most likely be ineffective. Knowledge of concepts to be mastered by parents and of the breadth of materials available to leaders and parents, as well as methods of organizing parent education classes, are also components of the training.

The program consists of three interrelated parts, any of which could be taken separately if the situation warranted it. These are an all-day workshop emphasizing group leadership skills; a seminar series meeting three more times over a period of several weeks on a variety of leadership topics; and a supervised internship as a leader or coleader of a parent group.

Accepted into the training program are counseling psychology graduate students of the Institute; parents who have participated in other study groups and wish to become leaders; other lay people generally affiliated with agencies and organizations ready to begin a parent-education group led by a volunteer; or school and other professional personnel who feel underprepared to begin a parent study group without some training.

A key point emphasized to anyone applying for training is that the basic child rearing principles themselves are not taught in the Leadership Training Program. We assume and emphasize in advance that anyone planning to lead a group should have become familiar with Dreikurs' basic principles before arriving at the workshop. Those who have not had the background are assigned to a study group or to read *Children: The Challenge* before attending the workshop.

Students in the workshop are, however, given a handout with a listing of the essential points to be stressed in their future groups. We strive to maintain the focus of this training: While it emphasizes group dynamics and facilitation in general, it has the goal of helping parents learn Adlerian–Dreikursian child-rearing principles in particular.

The Workshop

INTRODUCTION

The optimum number of participants in the workshop, led by two trainers, is between 15 and 30 people. Enrollment is limited to maintain a favorable trainer–participant ratio.

For purposes of this discussion, our reference to "coleader" within the workshop refers to two co-equal trainers. In a parent study group situation, one parent educator may instead operate as a subordinate.

The workshop day is divided essentially into two large segments, the morning didactic, the afternoon experiential. While the morning is largely lecture, many opportunities are provided for participants to give feedback, ask questions, or explore in more detail points which interest them.

As participants arrive, they are given a name tag and a syllabus consisting of the outline of material to be covered in the workshop as well as pertinent supplementary information. Coffee and refreshments are provided. The class begins within a minute or two of the designated time. In this way, the first lesson is modeled: The trainer points out such things as how the room has been prearranged in a circle and the materials set out, that the group begins on time, and the cooperative efforts of coleaders. (The philosophy of the training is that though an individual's needs and personality must be considered, coleadership in some form is favored over single leadership. This is modeled continually during the day.)

The group trainer begins by giving a personal introduction, including educational background, perhaps the children he or she has or works with, and asks the members of the group to introduce themselves as well. Two things are accomplished. Both the leaders and group members now know with whom they are training—their goals and backgrounds. Additionally, the trainer can also point out that most participants followed the first speaker's lead in the information they offered about themselves. The trainer has in this way modeled how one begins to set the tone in a study group.

To assist trainers in the development of parent education programs, an outline is utilized for program planning. The following is a discussion of that outline. Depending upon size and needs of the group in a particular workshop, this outline is either discussed in detail, or used as supplementary material and referred to for quick reference.

Outline for a Parent Education Program

The first section of the outline (see Appendix B) suggests that group leaders develop objectives for their own parent-education programs. Included in these are the identification of the audience that program is intended to reach and various aspects of the content. It is helpful in planning to establish measures for assessing the increased awareness and knowledge to be acquired during the course of the program, as well as observable changes that occur in the behavior of study group participants.

It is also important for trained leaders to be able to identify specific skills parents will learn during the course of the parent study group, as well as attitudinal changes that are expected to occur during the course of the program; for example, parents will employ natural and logical consequences rather than punishment as a means of disciplining their children and parents will implement weekly family council meetings after the *x*th session of the study group program.

The second aspect in the program development outline for trainees in the workshop is the program design. It is important that, in developing the program design, new leaders elaborate on goals and objectives for each of the group sessions, planning specific topics for each study group session, and determining what methods will be employed as part of the format, for example, presentations and group discussion. Session 1 may cover a discussion of democratic versus autocratic methods of child rearing. Session 2 may address understanding the development and impact of the family constellation in approaching effective child rearing. Session 3 may cover the goals of children's misbehavior, and so on.

Emphasis is also directed towards planning for group sessions that will ensure mutual support among study group participants so that they feel a shared experience in their efforts at parenting and have their feelings validated by others. While there is not individual problem solving in parent study groups, the sharing of personal experiences as they relate to the educative material being discussed is encouraged. Mutual respect and support are also built into the group sessions with the establishment of rules such as no advice giving or confrontation and no interrupting while the others are speaking. Methods for learning new skills need to be developed and can include a variety of techniques, such as reading and discussion of material, homework assignments, and role playing of specific child–parent interactions.

The final section of the outline for trainees discusses program evaluation. This component, based on program objectives, helps group leaders determine the effectiveness of their groups and allows for changes in specific aspects of subsequent programs leaders will conduct. In the evaluation, leaders are encouraged to examine whether the parent education program met the specific needs of the audience. For example, were the designated skills and knowledge acquired by group participants? What behavioral changes occurred in parents relating to their children? Were the materials utilized geared to the audience's experience and level of understanding? Questions or issues could be posed to the group members of parent education group (pre and post) that might more clearly indicate what new skills and awareness have been acquired. For example, a parent might respond to the following: I use encouragement as a parenting technique daily ____, 3 times per week ____, 1 time per week ____, never ____. Also, open-ended questions can be utilized for evaluation throughout the course of the program; for example, describe one incident where you implemented a logical consequence this week. How did you handle it?

It should be emphasized with prospective leaders that in attempting to measure the learning of group participants, the evaluation materials should be geared to the level of the group members. Also, program evaluation should not be implemented at the expense of the program itself; it is useful only as a tool in developing more effective programming.

Trainees are encouraged to utilize an outline (like that provided in Appendix B) for parent education programs for each of the groups they lead. It is designed to set guidelines and give specific direction in charting the course and meeting the needs of each individual group.

Other Didactic Training in the Workshop

COURSE GOALS AND REVIEW OF BASIC PRINCIPLES

Summarized in the syllabus training leaders receive are basic principles parents should be expected to understand upon completion of an Adler–Dreikurs study group. These include understanding the child (democratic versus autocratic society, role of family constellation, the four goals of misbehavior); social equality and mutual respect; encouragement and use of natural and logical consequences as substitutes for reward and punishment (including separation of doer from deed); and effective communication (less talk, more listening and action). As noted previously, trainees in the workshop are expected to understand these principles before taking this training. The principles are noted as minimum goals for leaders. (For further explanation, see any of the texts in Appendix A or Christensen & Thomas, 1980).

ROLE OF THE LEADER(S)

Also included in the didactic portion of the training is information on the role of the leader. The leader is trained as group facilitator rather than expert, regardless of professional background, thus preserving the original parent study group model initiated by Dreikurs. Trainees are taught to refrain from individual problem solving, pointing to the training materials that explain the Adlerian concepts. Leaders are encouraged to turn discussion back to the group rather than maintain a lecture type of format. This is not to say that group members do not learn and receive help with specific problems: They learn from relating the principles to their own specific situations and from hearing each other's experiences. They gain problem-solving skills and receive mutual support and encouragement from one another, utilizing an Adlerian–Dreikursian model.

In addition, learning to refer problem situations back to the group fosters several useful areas of growth for parents in the program. The burden of being "expert" is taken off the leader's shoulders, and parents truly learn because they must think about the concepts and use them creatively in application to real-life situations. Since people remember more of what they have thought out and contributed than what they have inactively listened to, more learning takes place. Also, training leaders are exposed to a model of technique, as trainers utilize group problem-solving experiences as part of the workshop. The role of coleader in this training aspect (and in a study group) is quite valuable; for example, one leader may be seduced by an issue presented, but the coleader or assistant leader can tune in and deflect the problem-solving situation back into the hands of the group participants.

Establishing a Group

The workshop attempts to address all aspects of organizing and conducting an effective parent study group. Suggestions made to trainees include using homework assignments; using parents in the group as coleader–assistant leader, perhaps on a rotating basis; assigning leadership from within the group for each different chapter to be covered, prepared as a homework assignment; and the possibility of having a group member act as secretary or recorder, reporting in summary form from week to week what was studied, who volunteered to lead discussion on which chapter, and so on.

At the first session, much must be covered. Among other items, group business needs to be settled. Agenda items such as where to meet, under what circumstances (e.g., hours and duration; babysitting arrangements; children present in same facility or not), and whether or not refreshments will be provided and by whom must be attended to. Ground rules are covered. Areas to be agreed upon by members of the group include confidentiality within the group and policy on member tardiness.

Workshop participants are also cautioned not to include new members in their study groups after the second of the planned 8 to 10 sessions of the course, because the foundations for new disciplinary behavior have already been established. The group either loses time explaining to a new member how things function, or, worse, the new member may implement the new techniques being learned without first gaining the appropriate frame of reference. Through utilization of group processes, the leader demonstrates that the group will operate as a unit, by consensus. The democratic process is both demonstrated and utilized.

Additionally, in the first session, leaders may wish to engage in a warm-up exercise to stimulate cohesiveness and interest in the class as well as provide an orientation to the sort of insight a parent may gain from the study group.

In one such exercise, the role of birth order is described briefly to the group by the leader. Parents consider personality traits of their children and usually discover great similarities between like-positioned children from family to family, for example, first-born, youngest, or middle children. In fact, Adler observed that first borns from different families frequently have more traits in common with one another than they do with their own closest sibling. Discussion of this interesting psychological phenomenon gets a study group off to an enthusiastic start. For the uninitiated, it also serves as an excellent warm-up exercise at the workshop for new leaders.

In an additional get-acquainted exercise, each parent study group member anonymously lists on a 3 × 5 card some personal family concerns. For example, group parents may be asked to list the most pressing problem in parenting in their households at the moment, or what they most wish to learn about or accomplish during the course of the class. The cards may be kept by the parents for future reference and progress notation, or passed to the leader, who reads them aloud (anonymously) so participants can see how many concerns they share.

Another topic for the first session, once group business and warm up have been established, is discussion of the chosen text itself. In some instances, it is possible for the class members to receive reading assignments before the first session, so the leader may shorten the warm-up period and move directly into chapter discussion. In most cases, however, the first reading assignment is made as homework following the first session. In the latter case, the get-acquainted period may be lengthened, or the group can do oral reading of the introductory chapter and begin discussion in this way.

Group Process

The training program also covers material on group process. The trainers present information on the various stages in group life, based upon an adaptation of the work of Yallom (1975).

The initial period might include anxiety, testing, and attempts at connecting on the part of participants. Another group state is the honeymoon, in which group members seem enchanted with the material. Training leaders are taught that participants might at some point challenge the material, express disagreement with it, the leader, or each other. Participants may also question at this posthoneymoon point whether the course is beneficial to them. Leaders are taught that this need not represent a poor job on their part as leader, but may instead merely be the result of process in the life of any group.

It is important for group leaders to anticipate that, at some point when the book examples begin to be implemented in the homes of participants, there will be many success stories, and some frustration. The leaders should be aware of how they might capitalize on stories of successful implementation, while remaining encouraging to those not yet able to succeed in using the suggestions. The hidden agendas of some group members (such as the need for therapy) may be interfering with their ability to implement the text ideas. Part of the workshop trainers' task is to make new leaders aware of these possibilities and give them tools to deal with them successfully.

After the stage of risk taking and growth, wherein group members take important steps in the implementation of their learning, some effective growth work is usually accomplished. As the group reaches termination, effective closure is required.

In microcosm, each individual session of a parent study group (and likewise a workshop modeling the format) requires a definite beginning, room for testing, allowance for frustration, reports of success and encouragement, trust and risk taking, and closure, a definite conclusion to the session.

COPING WITH PROBLEM MEMBERS

Leaders are also trained to recognize typologies of problem members. Soltz (1967) describes these in the *Study Group Leader's Manual.* Common types are the challenger, the resister, the chatterbox, the debater, the bored one, the breezy parent, the discouraged parent, the reluctant spouse, and two who fight. Sensitivity to these types of participants and preparation for handling their behavior in the group are explored intensively in both the didactic and experiential portions of the workshop training.

AVOIDING COMMUNICATIONS PITFALLS

Communication is covered in the didactic portion through a brief introduction to communications theories. Background is provided in the syllabus. Participants cover Gordon's (1970) Twelve Roadblocks to Communication and various substitutions for these roadblocks, such as I messages, reflective listening, and other helpful skills found both in P.E.T. and S.T.E.P. Communications skills of parents as well as of leaders are stressed as being essential to better interpersonal relationships. A great deal of emphasis is placed upon learning successful styles of communication.

MATERIALS

As mentioned, time is allotted in the workshop day, generally in the half hour before the lunch break, for an examination of materials available to study group leaders, both as supplements for themselves and their group members and as main texts for their future groups. Critiques are presented in order to assist leaders in determining the best materials available for their anticipated populations. The books, pamphlets, and related materials are displayed over the lunch period, enabling trainees to examine them further. They are also available for purchase.

MARKETING

Some time is spent in the workshop upon methods of marketing a parent study group. A sample of one or two effective, simple flyers is included in the handout materials. Flyers may be distributed through doctors' offices, supermarkets, schools, or religious institutions. Local newspapers are frequently helpful in announcing the formation of a parent study group, particularly one offered as a public service under the auspices of a recognized local organization. More on marketing strategies is covered in the follow-up seminars for study group leaders.

EVALUATION

The training materials also contain several samples of evaluation forms which leaders may ask participants to fill out at the conclusion of their sessions. Their use is required for those enrolled in our complete training program and they form part of the evaluation made of leaders. Other trained leaders may use these or modify them, or take them as a guide for their own purposes. One sample form, the midsession evaluation, is taken from Soltz's (1967) *Manual.* Many experienced leaders like to conduct midsession evaluations to assess and correct unsatisfactory group situations.

An evaluation form in reference to the workshop is also utilized to provide feedback on the workshop itself. From comments made over the years on these forms, the workshop format has been restructured and refined.

Experiential Training

After the didactic portion of the training, the afternoon agenda turns to experiential work, applications of what was studied earlier. One such exercise is referred to as "Problem Solving Situations."

Participants are divided into four groups of three to six members (based upon enrollment in the workshop). Each group is given a Problem Solving Situation card with one of the following dilemmas:

1. If you were conducting a group and felt that you were being sabotaged or were not receiving cooperation from your group, how would you handle it? Discuss.

2. If you had a husband-and-wife couple in the group and found that

they openly disagreed with one another about the principles being discussed, how would you deal with it? Discuss.

3. Discuss how you would handle a group in which one member was obviously in need of therapy, perhaps was abusive to her or his children or suicidal.
4. As a group leader, how would you keep on task should your group want to change focus from principle-centered sessions to problem-centered sessions, or, in other words, from a study group to a therapy group? Discuss.

Each small group is given 10 minutes to work on its alloted problem. At the end of that time, the group reconvenes and a person chosen from each group presents the problem and the proposed solution(s). Discussion then may include suggestions from other trainees and comments from the workshop trainers.

Dyad Encounters

Another experiential opportunity is a set of exercises involving as many of the workshop participants as possible. If the group is very large, one half become an outer ring of observers, arranged around an inner circle of trainees who for this exercise comprise a simulated parent study group. After the inner circle has had an opportunity to role play in the Dyad Encounters, they switch places with the remaining trainees and become the outer circle of observers.

In these exercises, trainees role play leadership and group Problem Member roles. Those portraying leaders are identified; Problem Members are enacted, not pointed out. A focus topic is randomly assigned so each leader has a topic to address within the simulated parent study group exercise. Each trainee, time permitting, has an opportunity to experience, in a timed exercise, a challenging situation both as leader and as a group member. Critique and discussion led by the workshop trainers follow each Dyad Encounter.

The experiential exercises are very time consuming but useful on many levels. All who participate can "try on" the various roles and develop an appreciation for both the distracted leader and troubled problem member. Attempts to concentrate on the focus topic are challenged and frequently effectively sabotaged by Problem Members, which is exactly what training leaders need to experience. That which has been theoretically discussed can be implemented in this exercise, emphasizing the need for mastery of text material by the new leader.

The workshop day ends with this activity. Evaluation sheets are filled in and opportunities for follow-up training made clear to participants. In addition, a Certificate of Workshop Attendance is made available, as are press releases which announce that training has been taken. Participants are encouraged to mail the press releases to local media, one way of publicizing their availability.

As this chapter demonstrates, so much can be taught to new group leaders that a 2-day workshop can easily be the first choice of trainers. However, techniques like the above and the provision of a full syllabus and other materials do enable a 1-day workshop to function adequately. Thus, while training is perceived as packed into the day, it also may be offered at a reasonable price and at a minimal time commitment on the part of trainees, realistic factors that are sometimes very important.

Completing the Program

INTERNSHIP AND SEMINAR SERIES

The complete leader-training program follows up the workshop with approximately 3 months more of supervised training. Most leaders who do go on opt for the entire internship and seminar series; however, it is possible to take them each independently.

The Seminar Series consists of three seminars of 2 hours each offered over a 2- or 3-month period at the majority's schedule convenience. Trainers and participants include former leadership trainees now involved in the Registration/Referral System (see below). These registered leaders add their experiences to the group's discussions and refresh their own group activities through their participation in the seminars.

Topics discussed in the Seminar Series include problem solving and successful strategies employed in the interning leaders' concurrently functioning groups. The Institute Director of Family Education Activities oversees the discussion of problem solving. Emphasis is placed on the group leader's ability to gain group confidence, establish an atmosphere of acceptance, and move his group along the assigned sequence. Not getting caught up in therapy and problem solving within the intern's study group are often topics of discussion at the seminars.

Each seminar also revolves around a main focus topic. These topics include marketing strategies, close examination of more resource materials and alternative texts, and enrichment topics like role playing and exercises not already introduced at the workshop. Experienced leaders return to share what they have learned at NASAP conventions, psychodrama workshops, or other reading.

The internship component provides new leaders with an opportunity to lead or, preferably, colead, a parent study group under supervision. The intern selects the text most comfortable for him or her, most likely *Children: The Challenge* or *STEP* or *STEP/TEEN*. An on-site visit is made halfway through a course by the FEA Supervisor or his delegate to see firsthand how the leader functions. A full written summary of the session is provided to the leader and filed for future reference on his observed skills. The training leader is invited to discuss this report or his concerns privately with the supervisor as well as within the seminar. Further, interns provide a means for the Institute to offer low-cost parent study groups.

At the conclusion of the complete Parent Study Group Leadership Training Program, an Institute candidate for the Master of Arts in Counseling Psychology degree program has earned the credit equivalent of one client (10 hours of counseling). In addition, the candidate, qualified lay person, or professional completing this course of study has earned the Certificate of Training in the Parent Study Group Leadership Program and gained a great deal of practical experience. The workshop condenses 2 days into one commitment of $6\frac{1}{2}$ hours. The Internship/Seminar Series adds 6 hours of coursework and eight $1\frac{1}{2}$- to 2-hour study group sessions (12–16 hours) of supervised leadership experience, including an additional hour conference with the supervisor in relation to the observed class session and report.

Feedback on this training program terms it an excellent one, valuable to all concerned: those trained, those served, and the future network of trained leaders. The variety of experiences offered, combined with the variety of presenter-trainers, ensures that while quality control of new leaders is high, no one leaves the training as a clone of the trainers. Extensive training combined with evaluation by parents and professional trainers helps to ensure that subsequent Referral Service memberships reflect very high standards.

Registration/Referral System Service Network

Those completing training in the entire course of study are invited to become part of the FEA's Registration/Referral System. For a single yearly fee, they are entitled to costfree return to any portion of the training program as participants or assistant trainers, as are any of those who have completed the entire training. The network established on their behalf functions as a service referral system for the metropolitan Chicago area: Members of the public know, due to extensive publicity efforts, that the Institute can supply parent study group leaders when called for referrals. When there is a need for low-cost group membership, individuals are placed in an intern's class. Interns may also be assigned to agency classes, where an agency organizes a low-cost class for its clients. Otherwise, those who inquire are given two to three names of Registered

Leaders operating groups in the inquirer's geographic area whenever possible. It is then up to the client to contact and make arrangements for group enrollment. No fees other than the single yearly registration fee are required by FEA for the networking service.

Registered Leaders, as noted, are entitled to participate in the training program as frequently as they desire to refresh themselves and update their information. They also must perform one voluntary activity on behalf of the Institute's FEA Division. The volunteer activity may include coleading a seminar for trainees, taking on an intern as coleader, lecturing at a Family Education Center program (see below), or participating at FEA request in a speakers bureau capacity.

Follow-Up for Leaders and Parents in Study Groups

Parents involved in study groups may become inspired to lead groups themselves in their own neighborhoods. These individuals are of course welcomed into the Parent Study Group Leadership Training Program. Other parents find that they simply want to keep up their lay training and maintain their family's progress. They discover further opportunities to join study groups that use different texts, as described, or several other Institute-sponsored activities. These include the public family counseling demonstrations offered free of charge on a regular basis, once a month, at the Institute. A volunteer family is counseled by a professional counselor before a live audience of parents, teachers, and students who likewise attend free of charge.

In the metropolitan Chicago area, the local Family Education Centers also provide parents with an opportunity to hone and refine their study group skills. In these community centers, Adlerian counselors, Institute staff, and graduate students lecture and provide panel discussions of basic Dreikurs' principles of child rearing. Past Center lectures have been videotaped and are available for rent to organizations around the country.[1]

Summary

The Parent Study Group Leadership Training Program of the Alfred Adler Institute of Chicago reflects the lessons learned from the initial development of such programs. The experiences of the Family Education

---

[1]Write to Alfred Adler Institute of Chicago, 618 S. Michigan Avenue, Chicago, IL 60605 for rental list.

Association and development and extension of the parent education movement begun under Dr. Rudolf Dreikurs in Chicago have resulted in professionalization of training procedures.

In the democratic society of the 1980s, there is no longer a need to exhort parents to take training in parenting. Parent educators must be professionals; the volunteer leader has nearly vanished. Certainly, anyone who would offer services as a parent educator must demonstrate professional competence.

Those seeking competence are trained in the Adlerian-Dreikursian mode in the discipline of group leadership. They include graduate students of the Alfred Adler Institute of Chicago, practicing social workers, psychologists, nurses, school counselors and teachers, and parents committed to the system. The 1-day workshop, subsequent hours of small-group supervision in seminars with fellow interns, the internship experience itself, and opportunities for constant update and refresher periods all combine to provide thorough preparation of parent study group leaders.

As they are taught to pass on democratic techniques of child rearing, so do they experience the format within the context of their training as leaders. By modeling, through exposure to many publications which give examples in detail, lecture, demonstration, and experiential exercises, trainees are introduced to useful techniques to insure that a consistent level of learning is provided to members of parent study groups. In Chicago, the Registration/Referral System keeps these standards functional. In Chicago and many other parts of the United States, Canada, and other nations, Family Education Centers alert and educate parents, teachers, and counselors to the possibilities of democratic child rearing methods based upon the observations and teachings of Alfred Adler and Rudolf Dreikurs.

Appendix A: Adler–Dreikurs Parent Study Group Program Materials

Introductory-Level Texts

General (Parents with Children Ages 0–10)

Dinkmeyer, D., & McKay, G. (1976). *Systematic training for effective parenting (STEP): Parent's handbook* (including STEP kit and Leader's manual, audio cassettes, posters). Circle Pines, MN: American Guidance Service.

Dinkmeyer, D., McKay, G., Dinkmeyer, Jr., D., Dinkmeyer, J., &

McKay, J. (1987). *The next STEP.* Circle Pines, MN: American Guidance Service.

Dreikurs, R., & Soltz, V. (1964). *Children: The challenge.* New York: Hawthorn Books.

Marlin, K. (1973). *The basics of practical parenting.* Columbia, MO: Practical Parenting Publications.

Popkin, M. (1983). *Active parenting handbook.* Atlanta, GA: Active Parenting.

Soltz, V. (1967). *Study group leader's manual for "Children: The challenge."* Chicago: Alfred Adler Institute.

Zuckerman, L., Zuckerman, V., Costa, R., & Yura, M. (1978). *Parent's guide to "Children: The challenge."* New York: Dutton.

SPECIALIZED

Albert, L., & Einstein, E. (1986). *Strengthening stepfamilies.* Circle Pines, MN: American Guidance Service.

Baruth, L. (1979). *A single parent's survival guide; How to raise the children.* Dubuque, IA: Kendall/Hunt.

Brusko, M. (1986). *Living with your teenager.* New York: McGraw-Hill.

Dinkmeyer, D., & McKay, G. (1983). *Systematic training for effective parenting of teens (STEP/TEEN): Parent's handbook, Leader's guide.* Circle Pines, MN: American Guidance Service.

Einstein, E., & Albert, L. (1983). *Stepfamily living series.* (Available from E. Einstein, P.O. Box 6760, Ithaca, NY)

Gould, S. (1977). *Teenagers: The continuing challenge.* New York: Hawthorn Books.

King, L. (1979). *Study group leader's manual to accompany "Teenagers: The continuing challenge."* Maple Ridge, British Columbia, Canada: Maple Ridge Family Education Centre.

Weinhouse, E., & Friedman, K. (1986). *Stop struggling with your teen.* St. Louis: JB Speck Press.

Wood, P., & Wood, M. (1979). *Living with teens and surviving.* Toronto: Wood Associates.

Zuckerman, L., & Yura, M. (1979). *Raising the exceptional child: Meeting the everyday challenges of the handicapped or retarded.* New York: Hawthorn Books.

Books for Follow-Up Parent Study Groups

Albert, L. (1982). *Coping with kids.* New York: Dutton.

Corsini, R., & Painter, G. (1975). *The practical parent: ABCs of child discipline.* New York: Harper & Row.

Dinkemeyer, D., & McKay, G. (1973). *Raising a responsible child*. New York: Simon & Schuster.

Dreikurs, R. (1948). *Coping with children's misbehavior*. New York: Hawthorn Books.

Dreikurs, R. (1948). *Challenge of parenthood*. New York: Duell, Sloan, & Pearce.

Dreikurs, R., & Grey, L. (1968). *A parent's guide to child discipline*. New York: Dutton.

Glenn, S. H., with Jane Nelson (1987). *Raising children for success: Blueprints and building blocks for developing capable people*. Fairoaks, CA: Sunrise Press.

Gould, S. (1979). *How to raise a responsible child*. New York: St. Martin's Press.

Grey, L. (1974). *Discipline without fear: Child training in the early school years*. New York: Hawthorne Books.

Kvols-Riedler, B., & Kvols-Riedler, K. (1978). *Parenting guidelines*. Boulder, CO: RDIC Publications.

Kvols-Riedler, B., & Kvols-Riedler, K. (1979). *Redirecting children's misbehavior*. Boulder, CO: RDIC Publications.

Nelson, J. (1981). *Positive discipline: Teaching children self-discipline, responsibility, cooperation, and problem solving skills*. Fair Oaks, CA: Adlerian Consulting & Counseling Center.

Supplementary Publications for Leaders and Parents

Allred, H. (1977). *How to strengthen your marriage and family*. Provo, UT: Brigham Young University Press.

Cassel, P. (1980). *Why kids jump over the moon*. Toronto: Cassel Consultants.

Christensen, O., & Schramski, T. (1983). *Adlerian family counseling*. St. Paul, MN: Educational Media.

Dinkmeyer, D., & Losoncy, L. (1980). *The encouragement book*. Englewood Cliffs, NJ: Prentice-Hall.

Dreikurs, R. (1967). *Adult–child relations*. Chicago: Alfred Adler Institute.

Grunwald, B., & McAbee, H. (1985). *Guiding the family: Practical counseling techniques*. Muncie, IN: Accelerated Development.

Mosak, H. (1980). *A child's guide to parent rearing*. Chicago: Alfred Adler Institute.

Supplementary Pamphlets for Leaders and Parents

Carlson, J. (1978). *The basics of discipline*. Coral Springs, FL: CMTI Press.

Dinkmeyer, D. (1976). *Basics of adult–teen relationships.* Coral Springs, FL: CMTI Press.

Dinkmeyer, D., & Dinkmeyer, J. (1980). *Basics of parenting.* Coral Springs, FL: CMTI Press.

Dreikurs, R., & Goldman, M. (1959). *ABC's of guiding the child.* Chicago: Alfred Adler Institute.

McKay, G. D. (1976). *The basics of encouragement.* Coral Springs, FL: CMTI Press.

Pielet, B. (1988). *Dear parents of young teens . . . : A guide to understanding the challenges of young adolescence.* Chicago: Alfred Adler Institute.

Rigney, K. B., & Corsini, R. (1970). *The family council.* Chicago: Alfred Adler Institute.

Soltz, V. (1970). *Articles of supplementary reading for teachers and counselors.* Chicago: Alfred Adler Institute.

Sonstegard, M., & Sonnenshein, M. F. (1977). *Allowance: Wages for wee folks.* Chicago: Adams Press.

Walton, F. (1980). *Winning teenagers over.* Columbia, SC: Adlerian Child Care Books.

Walton, F., & Powers, R. (1974). *Winning children over.* Chicago: Practical Psychology Associates.

Zuckerman, L., & Gladish, F. J. (1979). *A practical approach to dealing with children's misbehavior.* Chicago: Alfred Adler Institute.

Audio–Video Supplements

Dreikurs, R. (prior to 1972). Audio cassette recordings. Chicago: Alfred Adler Institute.

Dreikurs, R., et al. (prior to 1972). *Family counseling live sessions* ($\frac{3}{4}$-inch videotapes and VHS). Others available from 1973. Chicago: Alfred Adler Institute.

Family Education Center of Northern Illinois video tape lectures. (Write to Alfred Adler Institute of Chicago, 618 S. Michigan Avenue, Chicago, IL 60605). Includes the following VHS half-inch video tapes, most 60 min long:

Parenting after Report Cards
Childrearing in a Competitive Society: What's a Parent to Do?
Fostering Responsibility through the Use of Consequences
Positive Parenting Techniques
Dual Crises: Midlife Parents, Adolescent Children
Teaching Responsibility to Adolescents
Understanding Children's Misbehavior

Motivating Children to Learn
Encouraging Responsible Family Behavior
Harmony and Cooperation Between Parents and Children
Introduction to the "SEED" Program

Appendix B: Outline for Parent Education Program

I. Program objectives
    A. Intended audience
    B. Content
        1. Awareness
        2. Knowledge
        3. Observable behavior change
        4. Development of new skills
        5. Change in attitude
II. Program design
    A. Goals for each study group session
    B. Topics for each session
    C. Methods
        1. Presentations
        2. Group discussion
            a. Support
            b. Skill building
            c. Sharing of resources
        3. Experiential learning
            a. Role playing
            b. Exercises
        4. Instructional aid
            a. Books
            b. Handouts
            c. Tapes
            d. Other
III. Evaluation of program
    A. Are specific goals and objectives met?
    B. Does program meet specific needs of audience?
        1. Level and type of program materials
        2. Teaching methods
        3. Leadership style
    C. Does program reach intended audience?
    D. Does program offer potential for new knowledge and skill
        building

    1. Is there growth in knowledge, skills?
    2. Is growth measurable?
E. Can program be replicated?
F. Would pre- and posttests indicate increases in awareness and skills?

References

Christensen, O., & Thomas, C. R. (1980). Dreikurs and the search for equality. In M. Fine (Ed.), *Handbook on parent education*. New York: Academic Press.

Dinkmeyer, D., & McKay, G. (1976). *Systematic training for effective parenting (STEP)*. Circle Pines, MN: American Guidance Service.

Dreikurs, R. (1948). *The challenge of parenthood*. New York: Duell, Sloan, & Pearce.

Dreikurs, R. (1968). *Logical consequences: A handbook of discipline*. New York: Meredith Press.

Dreikurs, R., & Soltz, V. (1964). *Children: The Challenge*. New York: Hawthorn Books.

Gordon, T. (1970). *Parent effectiveness training*. New York: Wyden.

Marlin, K. (1973). *The basics of practical parenting*. Columbia, MO: Practical Parenting Publications.

Popkin, M. (1983). *Active parenting*. Atlanta, GA: Active Parenting.

Soltz, V. (1967). *Study group leader's manual for "Children: The challenge."* Chicago: Alfred Adler Institute.

Yallom, I. P. (1975). *The theory and practice of group psychotherapy*. New York: Basic Books.

Zuckerman, L., Zuckerman, V., Costa, R., & Yura, M. (1978). *Parent's guide to "Children: The Challenge."* New York: Dutton.

IV

Trends and Directions

13

Adult Children and Their Aging Parents

Sally Van Zandt
Bridget Cannon-Nifoussi

Listening, sharing, touching, laughing, celebration,
can create a loving atmosphere for
your parents and
for you.
As you meet their needs,
your own needs may be met.

As you give them your hands,
you may find your own heart.

As you help them end their days,
you may find new beginnings in yourself.
Grollman & Grollman, 1978, p. 145

Introduction

There comes a time in the lives of most middle-aged persons when the major problems of parenting their children begin to diminish and they become more aware of the health and welfare of their parents. They become concerned with understanding the aging process, its effect upon their parents and, indirectly, upon themselves.

The intent of this chapter is to assist adult children in learning about the aging process, personality in old age, and the needs of older persons. With this background, they can then examine their own feelings, evaluate support networks that are available in their communities, and move toward finding the optimum situations for their elders.

It is hard to accept the fact that the persons who have raised us, fed us, clothed us, and healed our hurts may eventually need that same kind of care themselves. It is also hard to accept the fact that a by-product of their aging is the fact that we, too, are aging. We are reminded that life is finite and that death is an important part of life, that death is a reality we cannot deny.

Accepting our future and working toward a positive outlook for both ourselves and our aging parents is important. When questioning middle-aged and older persons about their concerns and worries about the future, Gingles (1979) found "becoming a burden to others" consistently ranked highest. The high value our society places on independence makes it difficult for anyone to become dependent upon another person, no matter what the age.

Even though adult children may worry about their parents' future, the majority of our older persons never lose their independence. They live out their lives in their own homes. They die of heart disease, cancer, or accidents, the same diseases that cause death at any age.

Older parents may not be as concerned about their problems as their children are (Gingles, 1979). The parents have faced many other problems in life and have learned to cope with adversity. The parents may be in Erikson's last stage of life, "Ego Integrity versus Despair and Disgust" (Erikson, 1980). Despair is evidenced by the feeling that time is too short to do anything for self or society. It may be accompanied by a fear of death. Disgust may be shown by the person's contempt of himself. Ego integrity, on the other hand, is "acceptance of one's own and only life cycle and of the people who have become significant to it" (p. 104). People who have reached this stage feel a sense of fulfillment, a feeling that life has been worth while. They come to terms with death.

Several years ago, the American Association of Retired Persons and the National Retired Teachers Association asked their members to write on their experiences and concerns as elderly parents. Their message was

1. We want—and need—emotional more than financial support.
2. We want involvement, participation, communication.
3. We want to continue sharing our lives with you, and we would like you to share your lives with us.
4. We want—so long as it is financially and physically possible—to maintain our independence. (Briley, 1978 p. 19)

Understanding Aging

The realization that our parents are growing older often brings out negative expectations in us, their adult children. We realize there are many aspects of the aging process over which we have no control; we become aware that we, too, are aging; and we recognize that death must come to those we love.

When our children were young, we may have overlooked some of the negative aspects of their behavior because we were looking toward the future, focusing on growth. In contrast, with our parents we have a greater tendency to focus on those characteristics of the aging person that support the negative stereotypes of aging. According to Schwartz (1977), clinicians have done such a good job describing the pathologies and losses of older persons they have given aging a bad name. The belittling protrayals of sick older people on TV has added to the negative focus.

Although only a small proportion of older persons live in nursing homes, we seem to be more aware of them than of those living in their own homes. Only 5% of men and women age 65 and over are in nursing homes, but that number becomes 9% of men and women over age 75, and 27% of white single women over age 85 (Schaie & Geiwitz, 1982).

The majority (67%) of older persons (over age 65) who are not institutionalized live in family settings, either with their spouses or with their children (Fowles, 1987). This total includes 83% of older men and 57% of older women. Fourteen percent of the elderly lived with children, siblings, or other relatives; 66% lived within 30 minutes of at least one child; 62% of the old people had seen a child within the previous week; and 76% talked on the phone at least weekly. Middle-class adult children keep in touch by telephone and letter. Many families maintain strong ties even though they may not actually see each other very often.

Children may also worry about their parents becoming senile. Senility, however, is a "wastebasket" term which can include anything from occasional forgetfulness to severe memory loss due to chronic brain damage or Alzheimer's disease. Many forms of so-called senility are caused by ailments that are treatable, such as anemia, high blood pressure, excessive medication, depression, vitamin deficiency, or a heart attack.

Personality and Patterns of Aging

Not all older people are alike. In fact, as most people grow older, each individual's pattern of behavior tends to be unique to his or her own needs and desires. Hopefully, one can be more appreciative of others by recognizing the variety of personality types in older persons. Based on data from following people aged 70 to 79 for 6 years, Neugarten, Havighurst, and Tobin (1968) describe eight different patterns of aging based on personality types, extent of social role activity, and degree of life satisfaction.

The four main personality types were described as *integrated,*

armored–defended, passive–dependent and *disorganized*. These personality types were divided according to role activity and life satisfaction.
(See Table 13.1.)

First, the integrated personalities are well-functioning individuals who
maintain control over their lives, are flexible, motivated, and highly
satisfied with life. These integrated people can be further divided into
three types based on role activity. The reorganizers are competent and
active. They substitute new activities when old ones are lost and
reorganize their remaining activities. The focused group are integrated
persons whose life satisfaction is high, but they have medium levels of
activity and are more selective in the activities in which they choose to be
involved. The disengaged persons are also integrated persons who have
high life satisfaction but low activity. These "rocking chair" persons have
high feelings of self-regard but are more content to "watch the world
go by."

The second personality type is armored–defended. These people are
ambitious and achievement oriented and need to maintain control. These
can be further divided into two patterns of aging. The holding-on persons
respond to the threat of aging by holding on as long as they can or working
till they drop. The constricted are defending themselves against aging by
their activities and choosing low role activity. However, they have
high-to-medium life satisfaction.

The third personality type, passive–dependent, is less actively involved. The succorance seeking are very dependent on others. They have

Table 13.1 Personality Types of Older People by Role Activity and Life Satisfaction[a]

Personality type	Role activity	Life satisfaction
Integrated		
Reorganizer	High	High
Focused	Medium	High
Disengaged	Low	High
Armored–defended		
Holding-on	Medium to high	High
Constricted	Low	Medium to high
Passive–dependent		
Succorance-seeking	Medium	Medium
Apathetic	Low	Low to medium
Unintegrated		
Disorganized	Low	Low to medium

[a] Adapted from Neugarten (1968, p. 174).

medium life satisfaction and role activity and maintain themselves as long as they have other people who will meet their emotional needs. The apathetic persons are medium or low in life satisfaction and low in role activity. These rocking-chair people are much more dependent upon others than the ones described in the first group.

Those in the fourth personality type maintain themselves in the community but are much less integrated. These disorganized persons show deterioration of thought process, less emotional control, and defects in psychological functions. They are low in life satisfaction and in role activity.

A larger study of older persons might identify more personality types, but the major purpose for including these data is to illustrate the various ways in which people adapt to their environments as they age. Instead of becoming more like each other, people age according to their own long-established needs, exercising choices and selecting from the environment that which will enhance their own styles of adaptation. The sexy 20-year-old is likely to still be sexy at 80. The attitudes of society will need to change to recognize the continuation of personality attributes and activities throughout life.

Psychological Needs of Older Persons

Although physical health is certainly important, and perhaps a major factor in adult children's concern over their aging parents, the psychological well-being of their parents is even more critical. Based on the characteristics of people over the age of 100, Stinnett, Walters, and Kaye (1984) list five important psychological needs of elderly persons:

1. The need to feel important to someone. We are all social beings. Everyone needs to feel loved, valued, and respected. Older persons have the same need to feel necessary as their adult children do. When they are included in the decision-making process, they feel their input is necessary and they are important.

2. The need for a clear, respected social role. Many younger persons think older people have little to contribute to society. Once they have retired, they have no clear social role. However, about 12% of the elderly are in the labor force (Fowles, 1986), and a much larger number is involved in volunteer work. They say it is doing things for others that makes them feel needed and worthwhile.

3. The need for self-esteem. Perhaps the most important need of all is to be able to look at oneself and one's life as being worthwhile. In a society

which values work and titles, older persons need to be valued and respected for their own worth as persons.

4. The need for companionship. We all need to be with others who respect us and enjoy our company. We need to be able to call others or to have them call us in times of need. The widowed person has just as great a need for companionship as an individual whose mate is still alive. Many late-life marriages are the result of the desire to share life with another person.

5. The need to continue to grow. No matter how long they live, older persons who continue to look forward to the future and have plans for tomorrow are the happiest and best adjusted. Such an attitude toward life can keep a person young in spirit and in mind.

Dealing with Our Own Feelings

Unexpected reactions generally come to the surface when we realize our parents are growing older and need our help. The strength upon which we relied as children seems to be lessened. We may feel it is unfair. According to Grollman and Grollman (1978), we must understand our own disbelief, anger, guilt, panic, and physical reactions before we can be of much help to our parents.

1. Disbelief. It is easy to pretend that what is happening to our parents is not true. If we don't think about it, it will go way. We can pretend lapses of memory and hearing and urinary problems do not occur. But denying powerful events will not make them go away, and instead prevents us from finding help and seeking adquate solution to the problems.

2. Anger. We may be angry with our brothers and sisters for their lack of understanding of the situation, their inability to see things from our point of view, their lack of empathy for our parents, and their unjustified criticism of us and the way we are trying to help our parents. We may feel even more anger if we feel our parents favored our brothers and sisters or punished us as children.

3. Guilt. If we have neglected our parents and not visited them as often as we would have liked, we may feel guilty. We may have shouted at them or treated them as if they were ignorant or childish. We may be embarrassed about the way they are acting now. We may even have thought things would be better if they were dead. These are typical reactions adult children face as they see their parents, who were once infallible, unable to solve their own problems.

4. Panic. Many people feel hopeless and overburdened when they see their parents begin to lose control. They play the game with themselves called "Horribilizing." If mother forgets to turn off the oven today, tomorrow she may forget to turn off a burner and burn the house down. With our children, we think things will get better; with our parents, we may think that things will only get worse.

5. Physical reactions. The stress caused by our worry can cause headaches, sleeplessness, exhaustion, even ulcers. Our feelings of helplessness can intensify these physical reactions.

The feelings we have are natural and normal. We can seek the answers together with our parents, but it will not be easy.

Gerontologist James Peterson (1984) said when his mother died he wanted to get extra help for his father, age 95. His father, however, rejected the help. He was old enough to do it himself. Four years later the father said, "Son, I'm incontinent and my pump isn't so good and I don't hear at all and it may be that we have to think about me going to an institution. You know more about that sort of stuff than I do, so you pick it out." Dr. Peterson, who had learned something in the ensuing 4 years, said, "No, Father, what I will do is take you to visit five or six facilities. Then we will talk and together we will make the decision" (p. 10). His father nodded and a smile came on his face. That was what he wanted.

Parents and children working together makes this life transition easier for all concerned and can make our parents' last stage of life a growing stage of life for adult children and their families as well.

The Helping Relationship

The helping relationship between parents and children is one which remains strong throughout life. Certainly, parents help their children a great deal when they are young, but they continue to help their children as they grow into adulthood. In fact, parents continue to help their children even into old age. Shanas (1980) reported that in 1975, 70% of the people over age 65 said they gave help to their children and their grandchildren, and 50% reportedly gave help to their great-grandchildren. Help to children included caring for grandchildren or great-grandchildren and giving money or other gifts. These same people also reported receiving help from their children. Such help from children was in terms of home repairs, housework, care when ill, and various gifts. As older parents become ill and less able to live independently, the parents turn more often to their children for help. Sharing of a home is sometimes accomplished in the older parents' home and sometimes in the homes of the children.

Some adult children are motivated to help their parents by a sense of duty, while others are motivated by affection or by a combination of the two (Adams, 1986). In spite of the large number of community programs, adult children increase their help to their parents "at the first sign of decline due to aging, and at a point before actual help may be needed" (Cicirelli, 1983, p. 38). The children help when they perceive their parents have unmet needs. Even when some children are providing little or no support, they still feel the stress. Cicirelli terms these feelings *filial anxiety*, "the experience of anxiety when contemplating or anticipating the possibility of providing help to parents" (p. 41).

A problem arises in the helping relationship when the adult children go beyond giving help and assistance. They may take over and do more than necessary. The outcome of trying to manage the older person's life is infantalizing the older adult (Schwartz, 1977).

Being treated like a baby damages the older person's self-esteem. Even though older people may take a long time to accomplish a task or not do it as effectively, other psychological needs cannot be met if everything is done for them. If the older person's dignity and self-respect are lost because of the inability to complete a task, then children can give help without infantalizing. Children who try to take over and "parent their parents" end up demeaning the parents. It is much better if the children will remove some of the barriers that prohibit parents from doing things for themselves and then allow their parents that feeling of competence that comes from being able to do things for themselves.

If there are hard feelings or resentments which have built up in the family over the years, the family members can work to eliminate or reduce some of the problems. Ginny Snow (in Gingles, 1979) suggests making lists of the strengths and the weaknesses of parents, in-laws, and self. Generally, the adult child finds the strengths outweigh the weaknesses. She recommends focusing on the strengths of self and parents "while aknowledging and trying to be acceptant of the weaknesses" (p. 423). Such a technique is helpful to children who are working to strengthen intergenerational relationships. When a strong basis of friendship and trust has been established, it is easier to help parents with the decisions which must be made about finances, housing, and health.

A student of the first author of this chapter reported:

This summer my husband's mother had two falls within a week which resulted in crushed vertebra in her back, a broken wrist, and a broken finger in her other hand. This offered my husband and me the opportunity to return some of the helping they had given us in the past with child care and farm work. It was definitely extra work on my part to make special visits, take meals to their home at least twice a week or invite them to our home to eat, help with the cleaning and washing and setting her hair each week, but they were so appreciative that it makes me just wish I could have done more. It definitely strengthened an already good relationship. (Erickson, personal communication, December 14, 1985)

Support Networks

As parents age, it is important for adult-child caregivers to develop for themselves a means of social support as defined by Lin (cited in Wan, 1982): "support accessible to an individual through social ties to other individuals, groups and the larger community" (p. 67).

Different types of support help to meet changing needs as parents grow older, so it is important for families to develop a supportive network with many different people, agencies, or groups to allow for changing needs. Springer and Brubaker (1984) describe four different levels of support: ongoing support, to help deal with particular long term burdens; intermittent support, short-term support to help in acute-need crisis; instrumental support, actual physical assistance with necessary tasks; and expressive support, companionship and caring (pp. 104–105).

This support is developed with many different people, most often through and preferentially with family menbers, close neighbors, and friends. In addition, informal supports may be found within communities.

Family Support

As families try to be supportive of their elderly parents, they must also look for supportive networks for themselves. Developing support networks involves the conscious effort of all family members in seeking what they need for themselves and their elders.

The most often-cited support network for elderly family members is the extended family itself (Shanas, 1979). Assessing what needs to be done, how it is going to be done, and who is going to do it takes time and the concerted effort of all family members. The first task at hand is the family conference to talk with an elderly parent, to determine what the needs are and who in the family can best meet those needs. With many families spread out across the country, having a family conference during a holiday or family gathering allows all family members to have input into decisions and helps to eliminate unnecessary disagreements as emergencies arise. Having tasks designated to several family members (for example, Aunt Mary makes doctor's appointments, Uncle John takes care of finances, and Granddaughter Sue cheers up Grandma) helps to prevent all responsibilities falling to one person. Leaving the responsibility to one person leads to anger, guilt, family quarrels, and disintegration of family relationships later on.

The first step in the development of a social-support network in helping parents as they age can be taken at the family conference using a worksheet (see Table 13.2). At that meeting the family should list all needs that the elder individual has to have addressed, what kind of support (instrumental, expressive, intermittent and ongoing) each need requires, who in the family is best suited and most accessible to help and community agencies that may be able to help. Developing support networks requires a cooperative effort, and the person best suited to a job or task may not be the person who is most accessible.

After the family has developed a network of support for aged family members and there remain needs which family members cannot meet, the next step is to look to informal support networks within the community. Neighbors or friends very often provide the link between older adults and their adult child when the child is not accessible or appropriate for the task. Having friends share a meal, a ride, or a phone call can help to ease caregiving responsibilities. A group of older friends supporting each other provides socializing, sharing, and independence that caregiving children may not so freely provide.

Informal Community Support

In implementing appropriate supports for elderly parents, there may be help in the community. Many community services have been established with independent elders (or with maintenance of independence) in mind.

Table 13.2 Sample Worksheet for Grandpa Jones, 85, Living Alone

Need/task	Type of support required	Caregiver/ supporter	Agency support
Doctor's appointments every 3 months	Instrumental	Aunt Mary	Volunteer transportation services
Financial bookkeeping tasks	Ongoing support	Son George	Volunteers in Equity
Transportation to dental appointments	Intermittent support	Granddaughter/ grandson	Volunteer transportation service
Daily "check-in" phone calls	Expressive support	Daughter-in-law Wilma	Church group lifeline

Church groups will often provide transportation, meals on wheels, phone calling to shut-ins, educational training, and emotional support. Such programs not presently being provided in a church can be developed to address issues of concern for many caregivers needing help. Often neglected when developing a support network is the need for spiritual support, for the aged as well as the caregiver. A program such as the Stephen Ministry series, an interdenominational system of a lay caring ministry, can provide spiritual support throughout the life cycle (Haugk, 1984).

Formal Community Supports: Large Communities

When the need for supportive services is more than the family, friends, or neighbors can provide, looking to community agencies for a more formal support network may be necessary.

1. Visiting nurse services provide services for the maintenance tasks of chronic illness (e.g., blood-pressure checks, medication administration, injections) and for help in recovery from acute illness episodes, wound and bandage care, and physical therapy if needed.

2. Home health aides provide homemaker services, hygienic care, and information for emotional support or appropriate referrals. Home health aides can become the counted-on friend and contact from the outside world for a disabled elderly shut-in.

3. Meals on Wheels delivers nutritious meals daily, providing not only nourishment but a visit from an interested volunteer.

4. Lifeline emergency response programs provide electronic devices for summoning help in medical emergencies.

5. Telephone reassurance programs provide a call at a prearranged time each day to check the well-being of the older person and relieve fears.

6. Home handyman services provide minor home repairs and maintenance for homeowners age 60 and older who can care for themselves but may need help in maintaining their home.

7. Nutrition sites provide low-cost nutritional noontime meals for older adults, giving an opportunity for socializing as well.

8. Job opportunities bureaus provide help to find jobs for those over age 55 who need to work.

9. Senior centers provide social, recreational, and educational opportunities for people 60 and older.

10. The Retired Senior Volunteer Program provides volunteers to help more frail elderly through transportation services, friendly visiting, keeping appointments, as well as volunteering with other agencies.

11. Adult day services provide day care for the frail elderly, thus providing basic opportunities for socializing, meaningful activity, and one to two meals each day. As needed, services may also include personal care, health maintenance, and rehabilitation services. Adult day care allows for functionally impaired adults to remain in the community while receiving the support services needed.

12. Departments of social service provide information about community resources and services available at state and local levels. Local health care facilities' social service departments may help in accessing home nurse aides, 24-hour nursing care, or respite nursing care to relieve family caregivers.

13. Area agencies on aging provide access to numerous personal, financial, and legal services, make referrals, and develop resources for the independent and semi-independent older adult.

Formal Community Supports: Small Communities

In smaller communities which may lack the financial resources to maintain formalized agencies, individuals with specialized knowledge may be able to provide information:

1. The local pharmacist may be able to explain drug reactions, interactions, and the diminished effect of drugs with aging.

2. The local attorney can give basic information on what is power of attorney, who needs a conservator, and when to draw up guardianship papers.

3. The general physician can provide an overview of the normal aging process and discuss an overview of chronic illnesses which affect older adults.

4. The local dietician, minister, and school nurse are all resources which are often neglected when looking for support networks in small communities.

Innovation and flexibility are the best approaches to solving problems which seem insurmountable.

Support Groups

Short-term Support Groups

To help provide emotional support when family members are unavailable or unable to help, several programs have been described in the literature: An 8-week counseling session for families of elders in a day care program helps families make decisions as to the extent of responsibility these adult children could comfortably assume (Hausman, 1979). This informal, limited support-group format was found to be helpful to adult children in making decisions and acting upon them.

In California, a support group, respite care, and education project was developed for older women who were the sole caregivers for elderly husbands (Crossman, London, & Barry, 1981). The wives gained self-esteem in sharing with each other. Such groups address needs which cannot be met by friends, family, and other formal support services.

Sancier (1984) describes a family support group model done in four 2-hour sessions. Each session dealt with a specific topic area: helping alleviate feelings of guilt, learning to link family elders with ongoing family life, teaching families to talk about problems with their situation, and asking family members to describe their own problems.

Another short-term intervention program was developed by Johnson and Spence (1982), who conducted a 1-day workshop and workshop meetings for 2 hours a week over a 4-week period. The results were generally positive, in that the workshop information helped the adult children have better relationships with their parents. The most important aspect of the study was revelation of the need for a supportive milieu.

Hartford and Parsons (1982) identified several themes within a group setting of adult children of frail elderly: actions taken, feelings, relationships, and knowledge. These repeated themes give some idea as to what kind of programs could be provided to help these families with frail elderly. The University of Michigan Gerontology Center developed a program model, As Parents Grow Older, which provides a format, references, and discussion topics for a 6-week workshop for adult children (Brahce, Silverman, Zielinski, & Leon, 1981). Another model, Aging Parents: Whose Responsibility? was developed as part of the Family Life Education Series of the Family Service Association. This model is also a 6-week workshop providing suggested topics, discussion guidelines, and several experiential exercises for use with adult children (Goodman, 1980).

All of these programs have some basic commonalities: All were started to provide services to families with elders, all provide knowledge about specific issues, and all try to deal with the emotions inherent in the situation.

Such programs provide a supportive milieu for family caregivers. In the instance of adult-child caregivers, supportive workshops can help the adult children achieve filial maturity, which is the recognition that both they and their parents are interdependent. Such knowledge can assist children in coping with stressful situations as their parents age (Hayes & Truglio-Londrigan, 1985).

Institutionalization after Hospitalization

In this day of more stringent Medicare guidelines concerning hospitalization, older persons are often released from the hospital before they can function adequately in their own homes. In such an instance, a nursing home which has a good rehabilitation unit is the best choice. For example, the older person who has broken a hip needs therapy and exercise under the supervision of a physical therapist. Such nursing home placement should be seen as temporary. The family will need to support and encourage the older person in this period of transition and will need to continue to assist the older person in the move back into his or her own home. More and more families in the future will use this type of nursing home care.

Ongoing Caregiving Support

When long-term institutionalization becomes necessary, it is important for caregivers to take care of their own needs and responsibilities, to realize that making the decision to institutionalize an aged loved one is truly in the best interest of all concerned. Preplanning and decision making by the whole family together can help in alleviating difficulties as physical infirmities progress. Ross (1976) gives a general guide for families as they look for nursing home placement:

1. List the special needs of your loved one, for example, intermediate or skilled nursing care; open country settings; close to medical facilities, doctor's office, hospitals; affordable.

2. List your own special needs, for example, easy driving distance from work or home, philosophy conducive to maintaining family relationships.

3. List those nursing homes which meet your needs.

4. Visit each facility first thing in the morning, at meal time, and in the early afternoon to assess the care being given, the food being served, and the interactions between staff and residents.
5. Talk to staff, other residents, their families, and volunteers. Are they pleased with the care being given?
6. Determine the costs. Do residents pay for medication? Laundry services? Beauty shop?
7. Investigate what services are available to help the resident and family through this life transition.
8. Obtain a copy of the brochure *Thinking about a Nursing Home, Revised.*[1]

When decisions can be made with the elder loved one involved, much anxiety, anger, and other negative feelings can be resolved or eliminated.

A Model Family Support Program

With the awareness that families do indeed maintain their caring relationships with elders after institutionalization, more nursing homes are offering support services for families. A family support group provided by the nursing home for families as they bring their loved one to long-term care can help to strengthen family ties while offering information to family members. A three-component program of emotional support, education, and liaison with the facility can offer an appropriate forum to meet the changing needs of families (Cannon-Nifoussi, 1984).

Emotional Support

Long-term care is never considered a possibility by many persons for their aged family member, yet through uncontrollable circumstances or changed medical needs, it may become a reality. By participating in a supportive atmosphere with others in similar situations, families are able to talk about and work through their problems or discomforts. As families become more accepting of their situations they become the support for incoming families. A supportive network among families naturally occurs and can provide benefits, for example, talk about issues of concern, answers to problems through the experiences of others, a listening ear and

[1] Available from American Health Care Association, 1200 Fifteenth St, N.W., Washington, DC 20005.

safe shoulder to lean on, open communication with people who have the same situation and often the same feelings, and help in transition to institutionalization. Families benefit from a supportive atmosphere in which common frustrations and problems can be shared (Hartford & Parsons, 1982; Johnson & Spence, 1982).

Educational Support

The educational aspect of a family support group helps families learn what their elder's changing needs are and contributes to each individual's awareness of his or her own aging process. By providing topics which are fuel for thought, family members have the information to adjust their attitudes and ways of living so they can understand their own last stages of life. This information is also passed along into the community through the group members visiting with friends and their own children.

Programs on legal issues, insurance issues, community resources, drug interactions, and family relationships can contribute to the knowledge and successful aging of adult children, as well as help these adult children plan for their own future with their children.

Liaison with Facility

The family support group can act as a forum for the facility to talk about issues of concern and policies of the facility. Some families may not understand policies and how these policies affect each individual elder; sharing misunderstandings allows families to learn from the process of working through problems successfully. As an open forum for families who have requests or special needs, it allows families to speak to the facility administrator without a person-to-person confrontation.

The family support group serves as a link between families and the facility administration. With the addition of the family support group to long-term care facilities, the administration can become aware of problems before they reach an unsolvable state.

The liaison component of the family support group serves a dual function for the administration. It provides a place to inform families of policy changes in the facility and gives the administration the opportunity to present topics which may be of concern to families at a future time. In this way the administration maintains open communication with families before, during, and after problems or changes arise.

Working with families in a long-term care facility takes the cooperation and commitment of all staff and requires a thorough assessment of what needs families value, balanced with what resources each facility can provide. In a survey of nursing home administrators across Nebraska, 77% considered family input to be high after institutionalization, with 97% of the administrators agreeing that emotional support was needed by families (Cannon-Nifoussi, 1984). George (1984) found that the relatives of Alzheimer's patients spent nearly as much time with the patient after institutionalization as they did when they were caring for the patient at home.

Linking the Components

The system of long-term care for our parents can be divided into three different components with linkages between the components (J. Robinson, personal communication, June 14, 1985).

The first component includes informal care and support systems that exist naturally in our communities. This system includes the older person, his or her family, friends, neighbors, church or synagogue, and service organizations.

The second component includes more formal care and support systems such as public and private agencies. Structured volunteer programs, access services, social services, and medical services are included in this component whether in a person's own home or in an institution.

The third conponent includes client-centered case management and should include the family as well as the older person. Information, referral, outreach, comprehensive assessment, service planning, and plan monitoring should be used to provide for the optimum care of the older person.

Between each of these components should be a system of interaction that maximizes the potential of the older person. Affiliate agreements between agencies, shared information, and common language will all be helpful in keeping channels of communication open.

Families have an important role in seeing to it that community agencies function for the betterment of their older family members. We can relieve future stressful situations by knowing what resources are available in our own families, our neighborhoods, and our communities.

Summary

As stated earlier in this chapter, most older persons live active and involved lives in their own homes. Death for them is likely to occur in the same ways it occurs to younger persons: by accident or by disease.

Some will have massive strokes or heart attacks and die in their sleep. Most older persons do not become senile or need nursing home care. However, there are always some older persons who need special assistance and services to remain in their own home.

This chapter has examined the psychological needs of the elderly and described various personality styles of older persons. It has also examined the concerns of adult children as their parents age; their place in the aging process, the left-over baggage from their own childhood, and possible ways of working out problems which arise.

Adult-child caregivers need support when they are trying to meet the needs of their parents as well as meet their own needs as individuals. Within the family, responsibilities can be shared and both emotional and physical support given by the adult children to each other and reciprocally between parents and children. Several models of support were described including family support, informal community support, and formal community support.

Even when institutionalization of the parent occurs, adult children need support. Some of this support can come from within the family and some from outside sources. This support can be divided into three components: emotional, educational, and some form of liaison with the nursing home. Formal groups based upon these three components can help family members face their own feelings about legal issues, drug interactions, community services and family relationships, and provide an arena for dealing with the nursing home administrator in a positive client-centered atmosphere.

Both adult children and their parents can benefit from a knowledge-based approach and appreciation of each other in their family relationships.

References

Adams, B. (1986). *The family: A sociological interpretation* (4th ed.). New York: Harcourt, Brace, Jovanovich.

Brahce, C., Silverman, A., Zielinski, C., & Leon, J. (1981). *As parents grow older: A manual for program replication.* Ann Arbor: University of Michigan, Institute of Gerontology.

Briley, M. (1978, September/October). You and your aging parent. *Dynamic Years,* pp. 19–21.

Cannon-Nifoussi, B. (1984). *A family support group for family of institutionalized elders.* Unpublished master's thesis, University of Nebraska, Lincoln.

Cicirelli, V. (1983). Adult children and their elderly parents. In T. Brubaker (Ed.), *Family relationships in later life* (pp. 31–46). Beverly Hills, CA: Sage.

Crossman, L., London, C., & Barry, C. (1981). Older women caring for disabled spouses: A model for supportive services. *Gerontologist, 21*(5), 464–470.

Erikson, E. (1980). *Identity and the life cycle.* New York: Norton.

Fowles, D. (1987). *A profile of older Americans: 1987.* Washington, DC: American Association of Retired Persons.

George, L. (1984). The burden of caregiving: How much? What kinds? For whom? *Center Reports on Advances in Research, 8*(2). Durham, NC: Duke University Center for Aging for Human Development.

Gingles, R. (1979). Enjoying your aging parents. In N. Stinnett, B. Chesser, & J. DeFrain, (Eds.), *Building family strengths: Blueprints for action* (pp. 415–426). Lincoln: University of Nebraska Press.

Goodman, J. (1980). *Aging parents: Whose responsibility?* New York: Family Service Association of America.

Grollman, E., & Grollman, S. (1978). *Caring for your aged parents.* Boston: Beacon Press.

Hartford, M., & Parsons, R. (1982). Groups with relatives of dependent older adults. *Gerontologist, 22*(3), 394–398.

Haugk, K. (1984). *Christian caregiving, a way of life.* Minneapolis: Augsburg Press.

Hausman, C. (1979). Short term counseling groups for people with elderly parents. *Gerontologist, 19*(1), 102–107.

Hayes, P., & Truglio-Londrigan, M. (1985). Helping children of aged parents achieve filial maturity. *Journal of Community Health Nursing, 2*(2), 93–98.

Johnson, E., & Spence, D. (1982). Adult children and their aging parents: An intervention program. *Family Relations, 31*(1), 115–121.

Neugarten, B., Havighurst, R., & Tobin, S. (1968). Personality and patters of aging. In B. Neugarten (Ed.), *Middle age and aging: A reader in social psychology* (pp. 173–177). Chicago: University of Chicago Press.

Peterson, J. (1984). The contemporary family: Confusion, collapse, and recovery. In G. Rowe, J. DeFrain, H. Lingren, R. MacDonald, N. Stinnett, S. Van Zandt, & R. Williams (Eds.), *Family strengths: Vol. 5. Continuity and diversity* (pp. 3–17). Newton, MA: Education Development Center.

Ross, W. (1976, March). How to find a good nursing home. *Reader's Digest.*

Sancier, B. (1984). A model for linking families to their institutionalized relatives. *Social Work, 29*(1), 63–65.

Schaie, K., & Geiwitz, J. (1982). *Adult development aging.* Boston: Little, Brown.

Schwartz, A. (1977). *Survival handbook for children of aging parents.* Chicago: Follett.

Shanas, E. (1979). The family as a social support system in old age. *Gerontologist, 19*(2), 169–174.

Shanas, E. (1980). Older people and their families: The new pioneers. *Journal of Marriage and the Family, 42,* 9–15.

Springer, D., & Brubaker, R. (1984). *Family caregivers and dependent elderly.* Beverly Hills, CA: Sage.

Stinnett, N., Walters, J., & Kaye, E. (1984). *Relationships in marriage and the family.* New York: Macmillan.

Wan, T. (1982). *Stressful life events, social support networks and gerontological health.* Lexington, MA: Lexington Books.

14

Effective Parent Education and Involvement Models and Programs: Contemporary Strategies for School Implementation

Barbara A. Nye

Glad to have you aboard. . . .
For the next 18 years, you will be
personally responsible for the
care and well-being of another
human being. You're on your
own. Good luck.

Popkin, 1986

Introduction

The role of and responsibility for effective parenting has become more ambiguous throughout the years within the United States. Unlike many jobs, parenting has not become less mentally or physically demanding as society has progressed technologically. In 1976, an Atlanta newspaper reported that 70% of parents in America wanted parenting help.

Based upon the consistency of need expressed by parents and the positive research data from quality parent education and parent involvement programs, an important question is, What mechanism should be mobilized to assist parents? As parents face structural changes in family status, what is the best or most pervasive strategy our society can employ?

This question could be answered in a variety of ways in terms of social system responses. Various institutions can support and educate parents and enlist their participation as partners promoting successful child rearing. One institution, the public schools, however, has maximum accessibility to children and parents. Furthermore, this institution should have a relationship with families that is mutually beneficial to the family and to the primary mission of the schools to educate the populace in the United States.

Many school systems have fostered parent–school partnerships. Joint nurturance of children by parents and schools has decreased in focus, however, as other school reforms have gained momentum and then been incorporated into or eliminated from school practice. Parents have maintained their position as the primary agent responsible for the care and success of the child. The parental partnership with schools has been put on the shelf to some degree. This has occurred due to decreased parent involvement in the schools for a variety of reasons.

This chapter focuses on (1) the change in family structure that has produced a need for changes in parent education and involvement, (2) contemporary strategies for parent education and involvement, (3) research on the benefits of parent education and involvement in school-sponsored settings, (4) parent education and involvement strategies for local school systems and state departments or agencies of education, (5) important components in effective parent education or involvement program implementation and evaluation, and (6) evaluation criteria for parent education and involvement programs.

The Changing Family

Demographic studies report that the family is undergoing rapid structural changes. These changes in how we live together are most dramatic in terms of families' structural characteristics and economic factors that impact on families.

An increase in the number of working parents, primarily mothers, is a dramatic change influencing families and schools. As reported by the National Center for Education Statistics (Grant & Snyder, 1983), the number of mothers of children under age 6 who work outside the home has increased 34% from 1970 to 1980. The National Commission on Working Women (1985) reported that, in 1984, 48% of children under age 6 had mothers in the labor force. Census data report the female workforce with children under age 6 at 50–52% in 1986—with more than 50% of all women in the workforce. Of these women, 90% will bear one or more children while employed. The percentage of working mothers continues to increase.

Other major changes have taken place which dramatically affect traditional parenting and the traditional role of schools. In 1955, 60% of U.S. households had a working father, housewife, and two children. In

1980, that unit represented only 11% of U.S. families and in 1985 only 7%. Of children born in 1983, 59% will live with only one parent before reaching the age of 18. Of every 100 children born today, 12 will be born out of wedlock, 40 will be born to parents who divorce before the child is 18, and 5 will be born to parents who separate. Teen births are reported in epidemic proportions. Teen mothers account for 50% of births out of wedlock. Each day in America 40 teen mothers give birth to their third child ("Briefing," 1984).

Herman (1984) and others state that the majority of 5 year olds in the United States are accustomed to being away from home much of the day. They are more aware of the world around them and more likely to spend a large part of the day with peers than children of previous generations. The demand for corporate child care and full-day kindergarten is being expressed in most economically stable communities.

Contemporary Strategies

Changing family patterns and economic status factors are coupled with the current dilemmas being faced in particular by public education. Schools have embarked on a national course to improve student test scores in an effort to simultaneously raise basic skill performance and public confidence in public educational institutions. These two monumental goals have left schools feeling inadequate to solve the advanced literacy and community support problems alone.

A renewed interest in engaging parents as partners has resulted. Some local school systems have recognized the mutual benefits of sustained appropriate parent education and involvement. They have been trying local models to effect the partnership and confronting the reality of scarce resources along with limited state policy support for their efforts.

Early education research, such as the longitudinal studies conducted by High Scope Educational Research Foundation (Weikart, 1985), provides conclusive support for the impact of sustained parent education and parent involvement during and following quality early education programs. Both decreasing specific social concerns and increasing academic achievement were significant positive outcomes.

High-quality early childhood education enables families and communities to improve the quality of life opportunity for children. According to 19 years of research conducted on the Perry Preschool Project, children who attended the high-quality preschool program made greater gains in education, employment, and selected social factors when compared with those who did not attend preschool (Weikart, 1985). Sustained parental involvement and education is an essential factor when considering positive findings of this study.

In summary, fewer of those in high quality preschool were classified as mentally retarded (15% vs. 35%). More completed high school (67% vs. 49%), and more attended job training programs (38% vs. 21%).

Among students from the high-quality preschool, more hold jobs (50% vs. 32%), more support themselves on their own (or spouse's) earnings (45% vs. 25%), and more are satisfied with work (42% vs. 26%) when compared with their peers who did not attend preschool. Community quality data showed that the high-quality preschool enrollees exhibited important social responsibility characteristics when compared with their non-preschool peers. Fewer were arrested for criminal acts (31% vs. 51%). Fewer were arrested for crimes involving property or violence (24% vs. 38%). The data showed a higher birth rate per 100 women (64 vs. 117) for the non-preschool group. Fewer high-quality preschool enrollees received public assistance (18% vs. 32%).

These levels of gains in the education, work, and community sectors represent substantial economic benefits. According to the data, an investment in high quality preschool programs with a strong parent education and involvement component results in returns of $7 for every $1 invested (figures are based on "one year of preschool after adjusting for inflation and discounting at 3% to estimate present value" [Weikart, 1985]).

Prevention of problems among high-risk children is an excellent community investment. Reduction of major social and economic problems among the low-income group enrolled in the Perry Preschool Project is an example of the degree to which sustained parent involvement and education could potentially effect all groups of preschool enrollees. Also, the greater availability of resources due to the results of the preschool investment would benefit the entire community.

The Institute for Responsive Education has cited six ways that quality parent education and involvement programs can have a positive impact on parent–school partnerships: (1) contribution to the student's academic success, (2) contribution to the child's social and emotional well-being, (3) enrichment of the school climate and programs for learning, (4) encouragement of positive parenting techniques, (5) encouragement of the growth and development of teachers, and (6) serving as a link to the larger community to stimulate interest and support in education. A variety of parent involvement and parent education programs are available which reflect positive research outcomes. The programs have multiple goals, but the six goals listed above have dominated the quality programs.

Other chapters in this book discuss in detail several parent education and involvement programs. Appendix A briefly summarizes the content and evaluation data on a group of programs categorized as classic parent education programs. These programs focus on training parents through lecture, discussion, simulations, and at-home activities. The content generally concerns giving parents insight to raise more responsible children in terms of family values and to foster more satisfying family relations. The program goals are accomplished through providing new or enhanced parent skills in communication, discipline, and conflict resolution.

Based upon two primary references (Dembo, Sweitzer, & Lauritzen, 1985; Hamner & Turner, 1985) together with evaluation data from an examination of over 50 studies (Nye, 1986), the following general statements on group parent education programs can be made.

1. Research in the 1970s focused on parent education programs aimed toward cognitive intervention in early childhood programs. Most national follow-through studies document that parent involvement and parent education are crucial to producing positive long-term effects of quality preschool programs.

2. Research and evaluation in the 1980s have been less systematic in terms of evaluating popular parent education programs which primarily aim toward improving child-rearing methods. The primary goals listed by the 1980 programs include

> the formal attempt to increase parents' awareness and facility with the skills of parenting (Lamb & Lamb, 1978, p. 14).

> purposive training activity of parents who are attempting to change their method of interaction with their children for the purpose of encouraging positive behavior in their children (Croake & Glover, 1977, p. 151).

> a systematic and conceptually based program intended to impart information, awareness, or skills to the participants on aspects of parenting (Fine, 1980, pp. 5–6).

3. The changes in parent skills and attitudes which the major group parent education models claim to bring about do not always occur consistently. This is due somewhat to faulty research design, some variables that cannot be controlled, and the lack of a volume of good extensive research.

4. Follow-up studies on each model and comparison studies between models are very sparse.

5. Evaluation of the effectiveness of a program often depends on the type of assessment and educational approach.

6. The parent education leader as a variable was not controlled for in

most studies. Leader training, qualifications, and characteristics, are probably very important in terms of evaluation results.

7. P.E.T. and Adlerian (S.T.E.P. and Active Parenting) studies often measured parent attitude. The studies yielded more positive outcomes than data from children's reports of change in their parent's behavior or parents' records of behavior changes in themselves.

8. Some studies showed the Adlerian approaches to be more consistent than P.E.T. programs in producing attitude changes.

9. There will be a continuing need for parent education in the future because of (a) a limited number of individuals experienced with children, (b) smaller family size, (c) a huge increase in out-of-home care (9 million preschoolers in 1985), (d) isolation from extended family during child-rearing years, (e) changes in family structure, and (f) changes in social structure effecting children's and families' functional environment in terms of options, stress, and obstacles.

10. Parent-educational readiness and involvement programs in general have been shown to produce positive relationships between home and school and they have some immediate and long-range significantly positive effect on children's attitude toward school and academic achievement scores. The parent program, in concert with a high-quality early education program, produces positive long-term results.

Appendix B summarizes a group of programs classified as parent-involvement programs for academic readiness or success. Research data are not available for each of the programs profiled. Where evaluation data are available, they are included.

The parent involvement programs focus on obtaining parents' active assistance in the area of academic improvement. Parents focus their efforts on assisting their own child and/or improving the overall support for the instructional environment in terms of resources or climate. Research shows that these programs on the whole are successful. Parents who participate rank the programs positively. The objectives for each of the programs included are met by schools, according to the developers.

Strategies for Local and State Implementation

Parent education and involvement programs offer a solution to schools which are struggling to reform key aspects of the educational process, while improving public confidence. Education, unlike business, has to expose its lack of productivity in certain areas to gain resources.

Corporations market their products based upon user appeal and performance.

Schools do not receive additional revenue in general for successful products, but for continued improvement through broad-based reform. Support for parent education and involvement as a public school policy will have to undergo the same legislative scrutiny as the basic skills movement, transition classrooms, special education, and so on to gain financial support. Unlike these other reforms, parent education and involvement cannot be mandated. State and local systems can mandate program availability, but it is unlikely that parent participation can be required by public schools.

What strategies, therefore, hold the most potential to form the crucial partnership between parents and schools and between parents and their children in relation to education? And what are the policy and implementation barriers?

Local Control

Most successful educational reforms require local control and impetus for the reform to endure. Parent partnership as a reform movement will certainly need to meet this criterion. Some of the initial problems which must be overcome for local initiation of programs to succeed include the areas discussed below.

Total commitment of school leadership, especially the principal, is needed. The establishment of an expectation among staff that parent involvement is a priority of the school and school system must occur. When commitment and information about a unified parent involvement policy and the types of available programs are absent, the administration and teachers do not consider parent programs as priorities. Lack of support and understanding results in resistance or tertiary emphasis on the programs. Principals with strong programs cite their role as key.

Teacher load relative to the ability and time to interact with parents, including training in parent communication skills, cannot appear to decrease the teacher's instructional control, classroom time, or sense of power as an instructional expert. This has implications for teacher education program requirements as well as school policy. Teachers must be the primary link between children and their parents' desire to improve communication, involvement, and skills.

Overcoming parent apathy or lack of motivation to become more involved must be planned for by schools. This is often especially necessary when attempting to engage parents with students' school experiences beyond the lower grade levels. Often schools offer several parent opportunities for routine, in-depth conferences during the kindergarten year. Many schools establish an evening parenting-skill development program. The program may include child development, basic communication skills, and curriculum content.

After the kindergarten year, fewer structured parent programs are offered. A compendium of programs titled "Methods for Achieving Parent Partnership" (MAPP) (Frymier, 1985) is presented in Appendix C and provides concrete examples of how to keep parents involved as partners in the educational process. For example, one of the programs enables parents to obtain help on students' homework at night. School personnel continually look to parents to increase students' learning time on task. Yet parents are as busy as teachers, and they need assistance in balancing quality time with their children while promoting academic success.

Promoting a positive perception of parents in terms of school expectations and the communication system is important. The value placed on parent education and involvement and the types of programs available and supported must be evident. A school handbook should reflect specific programs for parents for each grade level. Structured parent education and involvement program innovations in the kindergarten, third, sixth, ninth, and twelfth grades are recommended.

State-level expectations and requirements for parent partnership efforts should be an ongoing priority, not just a one-year, one-shot approach. As state departments or agencies plan how they will support local parent education program innovation, they should consider recognition, modeling, partnerships, and training within their leadership roles. Policy making must reflect the fact that parent involvement and education are desirable at all levels but cannot be mandated. Program availability can be mandated and supported through various research and demonstration efforts.

Perceptions of legal problems by superintendents and local board members must be addressed by state and district policy to avoid misunderstandings and road blocks to parent education and involvement. Legal problems of a greater magnitude may exist for schools when they ignore the parent role. Public schools need to consider how parent involvement can best elicit public confidence. For example, using parents as homework tutors or to support an attendance program may be handled within appropriate confidentiality policies.

Local school systems should be provided training as well as resources to select various partnership programs which emphasize their local parents' and system's interests and schedules, and their parents' economic and educational characteristics. The types of partnership programs provided by schools offer the greatest prospect of success when they vary by grade level, family economic status focus, and are supported by an organized unit of the school and school system.

Components of Effective Programs

Several criteria for implementing parent education and parent involvement programs have been identified by principals, superintendents, teachers, state agency personnel, parents, and researchers. An immediate consideration is cost and measurable returns. The cost of the program should be in line with returns and available resources. (Program evaluation is dealt with later in this chapter.) Return is somewhat different from the cost factor. How do we know a program is worthwhile? Should the return on investment be fewer high school drop-outs, improved parent communication, improved math scores, or other criteria? If we do not accept parent education and involvement as inherently good, then specific returns should be even more clearly defined and programs selected even more carefully. A program chosen on the basis of a superficial consideration of objectives may not produce the desired results.

Minimal intrusion is important in terms of teacher and principal time not being consumed beyond normal parent education and involvement programs. Intrusion on facilities has also been identified as a local concern. Principals' and teachers' knowledge of parent partnership returns, maintenance of instructional leadership power, and program orientation usually ameliorates the intrusion concern.

Equal in importance to the school staff sense of instructional power is the parents' sense of power. Parents have to feel the programs are in their interest with regard to developing parenting skills or academic understanding. They have to sense their cooperation and assistance is vital to student emotional and academic well-being.

Ease of partnership program implementation is a final criterion. Such questions as who will work with parents and when are the key issues. Low-cost, nonintrusive, power-producing, effective programs can be identified. Even when the above criteria are met, parent education or involvement programs can fail to attract parents or produce the desired results if certain components of effective implementation are not present:

1. Trained leaders
2. Some local investment in planning, resources, and selection of evaluation criteria

3. Extra pay for leaders if the parent education and involvement program is beyond normal job responsibilities (pay may be based on number of parents trained or group meetings held)

4. Positive regard and recognition of local systems for parent education and involvement programs

5. Selection of appropriate parent education or academic readiness involvement models based on cost, time commitment, training of leader, parent socioeconomic characteristics, and age of the children of the parents involved in the group sessions

6. Evaluation of parent attitudes toward the training and the school at the end of training and 6 months after training by means of a brief questionnaire

7. Provision of materials to parents who cannot afford them, but requirement that parents in general purchase materials. Some model developers believe if parents buy materials they drop out of programs less often. Community partnerships (Adopt-a-School, etc.) can help with materials and perhaps with the fee for trained leaders.

8. Local options for selecting models

9. Consistent training on the model selection process and implementation at the state and district level by the developer of the model or program, if possible, along with training by an experienced parent educator

10. Durable materials

11. Continuity of parent education and involvement across grade levels

12. Preparation of school administrative and teaching personnel to implement parent education and involvement programs.

Evaluating Partnerships

Parent partnerships can be as simple as parent–child joint effort on homework or parents attending school events. These beginning levels of partnership are very important. The six major contributions of parent education and involvement programs, as identified earlier, require a further investment of time and energy by parents and schools.

The more advanced levels of partnerships include parents' active participation in and organization of events which contribute directly to the instructional climate, such as focused sequential parent–teacher conferences with jointly evaluated objectives or homework hotlines which improve individualization of instruction and parent–child support systems to help students successfully complete the additional time-on-task necessary for learning. Parents can also serve as community members in instructional policy planning and evaluation. Implementation of policies and evaluation should be managed by teachers and principals with defined mechanisms for parents to serve as key resources.

Adopting criteria for success or evaluation of parent education and involvement should focus on some or all of the areas discussed below.

Clear objectives for the specific program or model selected need to be identified. These should be matched to school and parent subgroup needs.

Percentage increase at each level in the program participation rate by parents and teachers is important and should be quantitatively measured. For certain grades, however, a small group of parents may enable an entire grade level to have cohesive representation.

Increase in satisfaction and positive attitude of parents, teachers, and principals toward parent partnership programs as well as the general levels of involvement of parents in the schools is an important variable. School staff should feel positive results from the programs they develop. The objectives should reflect the desires of staff as well as parents.

Variety of opportunities for parents to be involved in and with school efforts across all grade levels is the best approach. If one grade level of teachers carry the parent-program load, they will regard this as extra work. As children move to a new grade level, parents will experience a letdown and may assume certain teachers do not care about them or their concerns. As children change schools, parents may feel certain principals, even within the same school system, do not want their involvement.

Improvement in school climate and school–community relations is an important goal. Only through strong parent programs has school climate or community relations been continually enhanced. Sustaining improvement and continuing to build parent–community regard is essential.

Case Study

In Tennessee, several steps have been taken to develop parent education and involvement as a state and local priority. Individual school systems and state departments or agencies could follow some of these strategies and enhance others.

In 1984, a newly created nine-member, noneducator body of business and lay representatives recognized that schools could not by themselves produce more healthy, literate, well-socialized students. The State Board of Education, the policy-making branch for public education in Tennessee, recognized the value of parent partnerships in its Master Plan (Tennessee State Board of Education, 1986) to effect better schools. The Master Plan represents a goal-directed policy document to improve public instruction in Tennessee.

The Board and the State Department of Education, the administrative and programmatic branch for public education, convened a discussion group of individuals interested in the issue of parent–school partnerships. The author provided training for this group. The training consisted of an overview of 6 parent education and 17 parent involvement partnership programs. The discussion group included representatives of the state school boards association; the superintendents' associations; teachers; principals; the superintendents', principals', and teachers' study council representatives; the Tennessee PTA; parents; higher education faculty; state agency personnel; and others.

Following the discussion group meetings, a task force was convened to give serious consideration to the criteria for successful partnership efforts and to select programs which fit the interest and needs of Tennessee schools and parents. The task force studied how to begin to create a "slow-moving train," with local passengers (school systems) boarding the partnership effort at different times, for different reasons, and with different options in mind.

The task force conducted a state survey, asking superintendents to indicate current local parent education and involvement programs and current funds budgeted for coordination and implementation aside from PTA activities. The survey allowed districts to call or write the State Department if they were interested in becoming a pilot demonstration program during 1985–86 and continuing in 1986–87.

Approximately 23% of the districts responded by identifying their local efforts and/or interest in parent partnership program demonstration. The task force reviewed all the local system responses. In keeping with the criteria for effective programs and reform developed by the author, they determined that local systems would be chosen as demonstration sites only if they wanted to be and that local school(s) and systems would choose their own parent education or parent involvement model to implement. This meant that some districts would receive funds to enhance and formally develop and evaluate their own partnership programs. Other districts would receive an orientation to the programs selected by the task force. These districts would choose the partnership program they wished to implement either through a defined short proposal process or training session.

Phase I of the parent–teacher partnership in Tennessee had as priority allocating the state's limited resources for local district planning in 1986 to encouraging thorough orientation to the selected partnership program, obtaining willing leaders, assessing parent interests, and formalizing any local model being enhanced. Phase I involved in some manner all of the 33 local systems that responded to the survey. The State Board of Education requested $1 million from the legislature to implement the enhancement process and the selected program pilots within the 33 districts. These were evaluated following implementation.

Phase II included plans for a recognition–award system by the business community and state education professional organizations and other appropriate groups. The local school systems were showcased at a parent education and involvement conference for other interested school systems. The slow-movin train will add passengers based upon local interest, local selection of program options, and the availability of local and/or state funding.

The task force considered an affiliate status whereby school systems could visit demonstration sites and receive technical assistance from the system implementing the parent partnership model they wished to replicate. The new systems would become affiliates of the pilot systems. Technical assistance models are also being planned for Phase II.

Summary and Conclusions

Parent partnership programs which can benefit students, parents, teachers, administrators, and the community require careful selection. Commitment to the parents' relationship to school success is a policy-planning and implementation value which must be accepted in part on its face value as well as its documented merit.

It has been said that children are the last group demanding to be a part of democrary and participate on a level equal with others. Children of today are faced with so many more choices—50 kinds of cereal, cars, drugs, pregnancy. Likewise, parents are faced with choices, changes in immediate family structure, loss of extended family support, as well as helping their children confront more decisions at earlier ages. Parent education and parent involvement programs offer an opportunity to decrease the ambiguity of the parental role. Helping parents attain role success, in conjunction with parents assisting schools to meet their goals, is very important.

How to mobilize parent partnerships will be addressed by schools in the coming decades. There will be a continuing need for public education to mobilize in assisting and involving parents because of young parents who have limited experience with children; smaller family size and isolation from the extended family; huge increases in out-of-home care (9 million preschoolers in 1985 and up to 20 million in 1990); and changes in family and social structure affecting children's and adults' functional environment in terms of options, stress, and obstacles.

Parent education and involvement programs in general have been shown to produce positive relationships between home and school. Giving parents and the community a stake in identifying parent programs, testing models, and sharing results is one of the best ways to bring about change. Resource support is required with any change effort. Lasting reform is accompanied by the redistibution of current resources based on priorities or upon new dollars to support a particular priority.

Evaluation criteria for parent programs have to be matched to various groups. Each stake holder—schools, parents, and students—needs to identify program objectives. This allows the results to be more easily measured. Cost–benefit analysis should only be considered in terms of which program to choose. Parent education and involvement is necessary and cannot be regarded as something to be scrapped if the first program does not work. We will always need reading programs, science curricula, parent programs, and so forth. The main question is which ones, not at which grade levels or for which students.

> The most dedicated teachers and administrators, the most stringent curricula requirements, the highest standards and expectations cannot hope to accomplish the goals of improving our education system without active support and encouragement of the parents.
>
> (Rudolph, 1986, p. 7)

Appendix A: Classic Parent Education Programs

ACTIVE PARENTING, developed by Dr. Michael Popkin in 1982–84, is a video-based parent education program that builds on the Adlerian philosophy and work of Rudolph Dreikurs and Don Dinkmeyer and Gary McKay, who published Systematic Training for Effective Parenting (S.T.E.P.) in 1976.
Purpose: to enable parents to improve a broad range of parenting skills and to support parents in raising "cooperative, responsible, courageous children."
Basic Features:
Length: 12–18 hours; includes 40 video vignettes

Schedule: Six 2-hour sessions; meetings once a week
Intended audience: parents or prospective parents
Class size: Not stated
Evaluation:
Developers claim
1. helps parents gain skills to facilitate their child's development of courage, responsibility and cooperation
2. fosters agency– or school–community support
3. contributes to supporting parents in dealing with substance abuse, single parenting, school problems, etc.
Available from Active Parenting, 4669 Roswell Road, N.E., Atlanta, GA 30342, (404) 843-2723, (800) 235-7755

PARENT EFFECTIVENESS is the updated version of the original Parent Effectiveness Training (P.E.T.) first developed by Dr. Thomas Gordon in 1962.
Purpose: to give parents insights and skills needed to raise more responsible children and to foster more satisfying family relationships.
Basic Features:
Length: 24 hours
Schedule: 3 hours ideally over an 8-week period
Intended audience: parents or prospective parents
Class size: 10–25
Evaluation:
Developers claim
1. fosters community support
2. decreases student behavior problems
3. improves classroom performance
4. parents more cooperative with schools
5. parents gain confidence, fewer problems with children, show increased understanding of children's behavior
6. underachievers improve academic achievement, decrease disruptive behavior, increase self-esteem
Available from Effectiveness Training, Inc., 531 Stevens Avenue, Solana Beach, CA 92075, (619) 481-8121

YOUTH EFFECTIVENESS
Purpose: to help young people develop communication and problem-solving skills to help them function more effectively in their relationships with peers, parents, teachers and other adults

Basic Features:
   Length: 28 hours
   Schedule: fourteen 2-hour sessions (1 per week)
Evaluation:
   Developers claim
   1. stronger leadership potential for children
   2. increased internal control
   3. more positive attitude toward parents
   4. higher self-esteem
   5. improved interpersonal relationships
Available from Effectiveness Training, Inc., 531 Stevens Avenue, Solana Beach, CA 92075, (619) 481-8121

SYSTEMATIC TRAINING FOR ACTIVE PARENTING (S.T.E.P.) was published in 1976. Written by Don Dinkmeyer and Gary McKay, students of Rudolph Dreikurs, who wrote *The Challenge of Parenthood* and *Children: The Challenge,* it is based on the work of Alfred Adler, a psychologist who conducted open family counseling sessions in Vienna. Dreikurs was Adler's student prior to his establishment of child guidance and Family Education Association centers in Chicago.
Purpose: encouragement, mutual respect, discipline that is consistent with behavior, firm limits, choices, making suggestions, and joint decision making by parents and children. A key element is the democratic family atmosphere.
Basic Features:
   Length: 18 hours
   Schedule: 1 1/2 to 2 hours per week
   Intended audience: parents and future parents
   Class Size: 12
   Available in English and Spanish
Evaluation:
   1. Mothers who participate in S.T.E.P. perceive their child's behavior as significantly more positive than no treatment control group based on mother ratings on Adlerian Parent Assessment of Child Behavior Scale (Dinkmeyer, 1979)
   2. Parents in S.T.E.P. showed more positive attitude than control group. In a 2-month follow-up study, parents in S.T.E.P. showed higher self-concept than control group (26 subjects) (Summerland & Ward, 1978)
   3. S.T.E.P. parents demonstrated more democratic attitudes, increased self-esteem (Hinkle, 1980)
Available from Systematic Training for Effective Parenting, American

Guidance Service, Publishers' Building, P. O. Box 190, Circle Pines, MN 55014-1796, (612)786-4343

Appendix B: Parent Involvement Programs for Academic Readiness or Success

THE BOWDOIN METHOD
Purpose: to improve the child's self concept and develop the skills necessary for school success.
Basic Features:
Length: 6–10 group sessions
Schedule: Weekly
Intended audience: all parents
Class size: not stated
Evaluation:
1. Pilot group (1970s): Found to be helpful for remediation or enrichment, USOE study shows Bowdoin reduces risks of children's low achievement upon first grade entry.
2. Metro School data, 20 schools, 48 Kindergarten classes, 6 parent sessions, 1 leader session (teachers). 94% said better parent, 100% enjoyed program
3. Pilot Murfreesboro City Schools. Academic achievement increase after Bowdoin. Used *MRT* and *Peabody* tests.
Available from The Bowdoin Method, Webster International, Inc., P. O. Box 110338, Nashville, TN 37211, (615)373-1723

HOME IS A LEARNING PLACE was developed by Eugene Rutland, the retired Director of Education Services for the *Commercial Appeal* newspaper in Memphis. He originated the use of the newspaper as a classroom (preschool through post secondary) and home-learning tool in Tennessee. The program has been used in Memphis City Schools during one parent session for Title I parents.
Purpose: to help parents realize how important they are in the learning of their children, and to teach parents ways and activities to help their children at home in reading, language arts, and mathematics, using materials normally found in the home.
Basic Features
Length: one 1-hour session (demonstration)
Schedule: all parents given their level of the book
Intended audience: K, first, second grade parents
Class size: not stated (large)

Evaluation Title I study, 49 schools, questionnaire, percentage of "yes" responses)
1. meeting worthwhile, 98.8%
2. Learn ways help child, 99.6%
3. Help parent see his or her importance to child's learning, 99.6%
4. Help feel more confident at home helping child, 99.6%
5. Willing to attend more sessions, 99.2%
Available from Educational Consultants, Inc., Suite 531, 4646 Poplar Ave., Memphis, TN 38117, (901) 682-3830

EXPLORING PARENTING is a federally developed program based upon the improvement of parent skills and attitudes with regard to child rearing. It was first issued by Health and Human Services–ACYF in 1978 and reprinted in 1978 and 1980. Original Exploring Parenting work was developed from the high school home economics program, Exploring Childhood.
Purpose: to increase the meaningful role of parents as the primary and first educators of their children and to bring parents into partnership with the institution sponsoring Head Start (public schools, private and public agencies). The model deals with personal and social values.
Basic Features:
Length: 10–20 weeks (2–4 hour sessions)
Schedule: 10–20 "sequential" sessions (1 per week); 20 recommended
Intended audience: parents of children 0–6
Class Size: 15–20
Evaluation:
Developers, Health and Human Services, and parents say Exploring Parenting has a very positive effect on parent child-rearing attitudes and skills and self-esteem. Also, most parents want more training and a closer relationship with the sponsoring school or agency.
Available from Head Start Bureau, ACYF/OHDS, Dept. of Health and Human Services, P. O. Box 1182, Washington, DC 20013, (202) 755-7700

FAMILY MATH
Purpose: to encourage parents and children to enjoy doing mathematics together.
Basic Features: Courses are usually taught by grade level (K–2, 3–4, 5–6, 7–9), although variations occur. The courses meet for about 2 hours a week for 6 to 8 weeks. Topics included in most classes are

arithmetic, geometry, probability and statistics, measurement, estimation, and logical thinking—concepts covered throughout the K–8 mathematics curriculum.

Available from Family Math, Lawrence Hall of Science, University of California, Berkeley, CA 94720, (415) 642-1823

NEW PARENTS AS TEACHERS was developed from a public–private sector forum on issues related to early childhood and parent education. Research evidence presented at the forum by Dr. Burton White emphasized that learning experiences during the first 3 years of life are too consequential to be ignored by schools and families.

Purpose: to demonstrate the value of early, high-quality parent education. The project provided training and support services which would enable parents to enhance their children's intellectual, language, physical, and social development from birth to age 3.

Basic Features:

Length: 1 school year

Schedule: periodic screening, monthly home visits, monthly group meeting (Parent Resource Center at school)

Intended audience: in each school district, 10% of families with children 0–3 years in first year; increases each year

Class size: 380 families in four school districts, pilot 1981–82; 1 : 60 educator to family ratio (high if recruitment has to be done also

Evaluation: Conducted through a Missouri Department of Education contract with Research and Training Associates (Overland Park, Kansas)

Design: Treatment comparison groups, using posttests of children's abilities and assessments of parents' knowledge and perceptions. (Random selection 75 NPAT children and 75 non-NPAT children from the same communities). Kufman Assessment Battery for Children (KABC) for intelligence measurement.

Outcomes:

1. NPAT children demonstrated advanced intellectual and language development.

2. NPAT children demonstrated significantly more aspects of positive social development than did comparison children.

3. NPAT parents were more knowledgeable about child-rearing practices and child development than were comparison parents.

4. Traditional characteristics of ''risk'' were not related to a child's development at age 3.

5. NPAT staff were successful in identifying and intervening in ''at-risk'' situations.

6. NPAT participation positively influenced parents' perceptions of school districts.

7. NPAT families had positive feelings about the program's usefulness.

Available from New Parents as Teachers Project, Missouri Department of Education, P. O. Box 480, Jefferson City, MO 65102, (314) 751-2095

Appendix C: Methods for Achieving Parent Partnerships

Program	Development
Parents-in-Touch	Indianapolis Public Schools
Dial-a-Teacher	Indianapolis Public Schools
School Improvement Councils	Developed for the State of South Carolina
Family Oriented Structured Preschool Activity	Saint Cloud Public Schools, Saint Cloud, Minnesota
Teacher–Parent Partnership Project	Lakewood Public Schools, Lakewood, Colorado
APPLE Corps, Inc.	Developed for Atlanta Public Schools
Parent-to-Parent: Attention on Attendance	Washington, DC Public Schools
Parent Education Partnerships	Elementary School District 159, Public Schools, Matteson, Illinois
SKIP: Special Kids, Improved Parents	Nutley Public Schools, Nutley New Jersey
Operation Fail-Safe	Houston Public Schools

References

Briefing on major demographic trends. (1984). *Report on Education of the Disadvantaged, 18*, 13.

Croake, J., & Glover, K. (1977). A history and evaluation of parent education. *Family Coordinator, 26,* 151–158. Cited in Dembo et al. (1985).

Dembo, M., Sweitzer, M., & Lauritzen, P. (1985). An evaluation of group parent education: Behavioral, PET, and Adlerian programs. *Review in Educational Research, 55,* 155–200.

Fine, M. J. (Ed.). (1980). *Handbook on parent education.* New York: Academic Press.

Frymier, J. (Ed.). (1985). *Methods for achieving parent partnership (Project MAPP).* Indianapolis, IN: Indianapolis Public Schools.

Grant, V., & Snyder, T. (1983). *Digest of education statistics.* Washington, DC: National Center for Educational Statistics.

Hamner, T., & Turner, P. (1985). *Parenting in contemporary society.* Englewood Cliffs, NJ: Prentice-Hall.

Herman, B. (1984). *The case for the all-day kindergarten* (Fastback 205). Bloomington, IN: Phi Delta Kappa Educational Foundation. (ERIC Document Reproduction Service No. ED 243 592)

Kagan, S. (1985). *Parent involvement research: A field in search of itself* (Report No. 9). Boston: Institute for Responsive Education.

Lamb, J., & Lamb, W. A. (1978). *Parent education and elementary counseling.* New York: Human Sciences Press. Cited in Denbo et al. (1985).

National Commission on Working Women. (1985). *Working mothers and their families: A fact sheet—Women and work: News about the 80%* (Report No. 5). Washington, DC: Author.

Nye, B. A. (1986). *Effective parent education and involvement models and programs.* Nashville: Tennessee Department and Board of Education Parent Education Task Force.

Popkin, M. (1986). *Active Parenting Newsletter.* Atlanta, GA: Active Parenting.

Rudolph, L. (1986, October 5). Parents play a major role in their children's education. *The Nashville Banner,* p. 7.

Tennessee State Board of Education. (1986). *Master plan.* Nashville: Author.

Weikart, D. P. (1985). *Changed lives.* Ypsilanti, MI: High Scope Educational Research Foundation.

15

Family Life Education and Research: Toward a More Positive Approach

Paul A. Lee
Diane G. Brage

Introduction

The 1980s are the decade of the strong, healthy family. In sharp contrast to the 1970s when the future and viability of the family was openly debated by family "experts," recent years have seen an increasing emphasis on positive aspects of family life and ways to build family strengths and improve family relationships.

In the past, family studies research and literature have tended to focus almost exclusively on the problems and pathology in family life. We have tended to accentuate the negative. Too little of our research has sought to identify positive family models. Consequently, families have had inadequate data-based guidance in developing a successful family life.

Fortunately, a shift in emphasis in much of our family life materials and research is now discernible. Increasingly, family research seems to focus on positive aspects of family life. Family life education materials provide help in developing a successful family life without assuming that every family has a mountain of problems and pathology to work through before growth can occur. Important shifts in emphasis have occurred in six areas: (1) strong, healthy families; (2) parent education; (3) building self-esteem in family members; (4) marriage enrichment; (5) the family life cycle; and (6) military family support.

Strong, Healthy Families

Stinnett and DeFrain (1985) report "Good, strong families aren't born, they are *made*. And what makes them has absolutely nothing to do with money, careers, or material possessions" (p. 108). Over the past two decades, family professionals have been studying strong families to determine how they differ from problem families. At first, only a few isolated studies were being conducted. Gradually, the number of family professionals interested in this approach to understanding families has grown to be a major force in the family studies field.

Most researchers seem to have had less difficulty in identifying healthy families than they have had in defining what *healthy* means. Beavers (1977) suggested that the simplest way to define a healthy family is negatively: "Health is the absence of emotional illness in family members" (p. 124). However, he opted for a more proactive definition which included optimal functioning and a dynamic process of acceptance and growth for all family members. Lewis (1979, p. 85) defined a healthy family as one that is "highly competent in raising autonomous children and maintaining the sanity of the parents."

FACTORS IN FAMILY STRENGTH (OTTO)

One of the pioneers in healthy family research, Otto studied the types of personal interaction which family members felt contributed to the strength of their family (Otto, 1962). Family strength was seen as the result of many factors, some of which tend to change over the lifespan. Important factors identified included (1) nurture, (2) support, (3) parental discipline, (4) encouragement of growth and maturation of all family members, (5) spiritual well-being of members, (6) good communication, (7) problem-solving skills, and (8) meaningful participation of family members in activities outside the home.

BIPOLAR DIMENSIONS OF A HEALTHY FAMILY (BARNHILL)

Barnhill (1979) identified eight bipolar dimensions of healthy family functioning, grouped into four interrelated functional themes (see Table 15.1).

IDENTITY PROCESSES. The first theme, identity processes, included the continuum of "individuation versus enmeshment" and the continuum of "mutuality versus isolation." Individuation is the process by which family members become differentiated from each other. It includes a firm sense of autonomy. On the other hand, enmeshment refers to dependency on others and poorly delineated boundaries of self. Mutuality or the sense of emotional closeness and intimacy contrasts with the feeling of isolation or withdrawal from others.

Table 15.1 Healthy Family Functioning[a]

Theme	Bipolar deminsion	
Identity	1. Individuation	Enmeshment
	2. Mutuality	Isolation
Change	3. Flexibility	Rigidity
	4. Stability	Disorganization
Information processing	5. Clear perception	Unclear perception
	6. Clear communication	Unclear communication
Role structure	7. Clear roles	Unclear roles
	8. Clear generational boundaries	Diffuse generational boundaries

[a] From Barnhill (1979).

CHANGE. The second theme was identified as change. This theme assessed the continua of "flexibility versus rigidity" and "stability versus disorganization." Flexibility is the capability of responding or conforming to changing or new situations. Rigidity is being unyielding. Stability refers to consistency and dependability in family relations. In contrast, disorganization refers to lack of clear responsibility and guidance in family interactions. According to Barnhill (1979, p. 95), "flexibility and stability are necessary in preference to rigid responses which deny the need for change, or disorganization responses to an unstable situation which prevents a clear view of real change."

INFORMATION PROCESSING. The third theme, information processing, was assessed on the continua of "clear perception versus unclear perception" and "clear communication versus unclear communication." "Clear perception refers to undistorted awareness of self and others. As a shared phenomenon, it refers to clear joint perceptions and consensual validation of shared events" (Barnhill, 1979, p. 95). The lack of clear perception means that the perception is vague or confusing. The dimension of communication refers to the degree of clear and successful exchange of information between family members. It may require "feedback" or "checking out" in order to clarify a message.

ROLE STRUCTURE. The final theme, role structure, pertained to the dimensions of "clear role reciprocity versus unclear roles or role conflict" and "clear generational boundaries versus diffused or breached generational boundaries." Role reciprocity referred to behavior patterns which complement the role of a partner and are mutually agreed upon. Unclear roles, in contrast, refer to confusing role behaviors between family members. The dimension of generational boundaries refers to the degree of clarity of role differences among family members of different generations.

According to Barnhill, these eight dimensions can be integrated as a mutually causal system, the family health cycle. For example, individuation facilitates mutuality and clear perception of self and others. Clear communication promotes clear role reciprocity and clear perception. Likewise, clear generational boundaries facilitate stability within the family. Thus, the eight dimensions of healthy family functioning are highly interrelated.

CHARACTERISTICS OF HEALTHY FAMILIES (LEWIS)

Lewis (1979, p. 85) defined healthy families as being "highly competent in raising autonomous children and maintaining the sanity of the parents." He identified 10 salient characteristics of healthy families.

STRONG MARRIAGE.   A family is more likely to be healthy if the parents have a "good" marriage, where both spouses feel competent and share power. They achieve deep levels of intimacy. Neither feels highly vulnerable or competitive. Their individual differences are enjoyed and supported.

PARENTAL POWER.   Parental power is another important characteristic of healthy families. The leadership of the parents in strong families is generally democratic. The children respect their parents' power. This respect and acceptance results from the parents' consideration of the children's opinions and feelings. The roles of the parents and children are clearly differentiated. The generation gap is considered appropriate by children and parents alike.

FAMILY CLOSENESS.   Strong, healthy families are closely knit. They share opinions and feelings with each other. However, a great deal of autonomy and individuality are evident in each family member.

COMMUNICATION.   Another important characteristic of healthy families is effective communication. These families communicate with a great deal of shorthand, are very spontaneous, and tend to interrupt each other frequently. Being good listeners, each person is confident of being heard and understood. Individuals take responsibility for their own thoughts and feelings. Children in these families speak their minds freely. Differences of opinion or feelings are taken for granted. Lewis (1979, p. 89) concluded that "this pattern of family communication is a factor in the development of children with high levels of individuality and autonomy."

EFFECTIVE PROBLEM-SOLVING SKILLS. Healthy families are able to deal with problems effectively. They seem to identify problems sooner than dysfunctional families. They also rarely place blame on family members. In order to find a solution to the problem, they use negotiation and problem-solving approaches in the search for consensus.

FEELINGS. Healthy families are able to share their feelings openly and freely. Thus, the needs expressed by these feelings are more easily met by other family members. Empathy and a nonjudgmental attitude play a major role in the sharing of feelings. Most families have a basic mood. "This is the general feeling tone within the family when there is no crisis. The basic mood of healthy families contains elements of warmth, humor, and concern for each other" (Lewis, 1979, p. 90). When the general mood of the family is positive, the expression of all kinds of feelings is encouraged and rewarded. The expression of feelings usually receives an empathic response. This reinforcement convinces children at an early age that feelings are normal and can be shared in a supportive environment. This openness has profound positive consequences for all interpersonal relationships.

DEALING WITH LOSS. Healthy families are also more likely to openly express their feelings about life's inevitable losses. Family members do not feel uncomfortable about feeling sad and sharing that sadness with others.

VALUES AND BELIEFS. Another characteristic of healthy family members is that they believe that although people are fallible, they are primarily good. Their approach to others is open and affiliative. They tend to view their own mistakes and those of others as simply part of being human.

INTIMACY AND AUTONOMY. Healthy families encourage intimacy and individual autonomy. Each person in the family is viewed as a separate, unique individual. Trust, empathy, openness of feelings, and acceptance of individual differences facilitate intimacy and autonomy.

FAMILY STYLES. Finally, all healthy families have similarities and differences. According to Lewis (1979, p. 93), "Healthy families do not look like they were all pressed out of the same mold. It is only when studying how they relate and communicate that the similarities are discovered." Their differences are evident in their widely varying interests, activity level, and involvements outside the home.

OPTIMAL FAMILIES (BEAVERS)

Beavers (1977, 1981, 1982, 1984, 1985) has been an important contributor to the growing body of literature defining characteristics of healthy families. He emphasized "optimal" families as the healthiest and most functional, in contrast with adequate, midrange, and severely dysfunctional families. According to Beavers (1977, 1982) optimal families exhibit unique characteristics across eight variables: a systems orientation, boundary issues, contextual clarity, power issues, encouragement of autonomy, affective issues, task efficiency, and transcendent values.

SYSTEMS ORIENTATION. Beavers noted that optimal healthy families have an open systems view of the world. This view is based on four assumptions relevant to the family (Beavers, 1982):

1. An individual needs a group, a human system, for identity and satisfaction.
2. Causes and effects are interchangeable.
3. Any human behavior is the result of many variables rather than one "cause"; therefore, simplistic solutions are questioned.
4. Human beings are limited and finite.[1]

These assumptions would suggest that

1. Family members do not grow and mature in isolation. Rather, their needs "are satisfied in an interpersonal matrix. As a child develops and matures, he leaves one system—the primary family—not for isolated independence, but for other human systems" (Beavers, 1977, p. 135).
2. Behavior by one family member always results in behavior by other family members in a circular fashion and not in a linear cause-and-effect manner. Family behaviors are at one and the same time both cause and effect of other behaviors. All family members are players on the family stage. There are no villains, victims, or victors.
3. Power and trust are relative. The development of healthy self-esteem and a feeling of adequacy in family members "lies in relative competence

---

[1] From "Healthy, Midrange, and Severely Dysfunctional Families" (p. 47) by W. R. Beavers, 1982. In F. Walsh (Ed.), *Normal Family Processes*. New York: Guilford Press. Copyright 1982 by Guilford Press. Reprinted by permission.

rather than in omnipotence'' (Beavers, 1977, p. 137). No one member of the family can accept final responsibility for the behavior or development of another family member. This attitude seems to provide the right atmosphere for the healthiest family and individual functioning.

CLEAR BOUNDARIES. Optimal families have very clear boundaries among individual members. It is easy to distinguish each family member's feelings. Individuals are assertive and share their concerns. Family members usually succeed in achieving mutual goals without any members feeling they have to compromise what they really wanted. Clear generational boundaries are present. The parents have the ultimate power and authority. Although there is a high level of interaction within the family, interaction outside the family is necessary for growth. Families are open to and respectful of different viewpoints and opinions. This facilitates greater intimacy.

CONTEXTUAL CLARITY. Contextual clarity is present in optimal families. There is good communication, with consistency between actions and the spoken word. It is generally clear to whom comments are addressed and what the relationship is between the speaker and the listener. Social roles are flexible, but distinct. According to Beavers (1982, p. 49), "in optimal families, children have assistance in accepting limitations from parents who present clear role definitions and a solid parental coalition."

EQUAL POWER. Beavers (1982, p. 49) reported that in optimal families, "there is a clear hierarchy of power, with leadership in the hands of the parents who form an egalitarian coalition." Even though the parents seemed to have relatively equal overt power, their complementary roles enabled them to avoid competitive conflict. Each parent seemed to have his or her own area of responsibility and authority. Beavers (1982) concluded that a balance of equal overt power is beneficial and not damaging when parents have nonstereotyped complementary roles.

ENCOURAGEMENT OF AUTONOMY. The optimal family also encouraged the development of autonomy within individual members. According to Beavers (1982), members of optimal families assume responsibility for their thoughts, feelings, and actions. They are receptive to the communication and uniqueness of other people.

JOY AND COMFORT IN RELATING. Optimal families experience joy and comfort in relating. Beavers (1977, p. 148) reported that "the optimal families had both an engaging warm, optimistic feeling tone and a striking emotional intensity.'' Family members had a high involvement with each other and showed a keen interest in what each other had to say. Interaction was characterized by caring, warmth, empathy, and hope for the future. There was a reciprocal affirmation and validation of feelings of personal worth. This affiliative orientation toward family members is to some degree projected to individuals outside the family. These families assume that all individuals are basically good, or at least benign in their intent toward others. It is assumed that people are doing the best they can considering their circumstances (Beavers, 1982).

SKILLED NEGOTIATION.   In shared duties and responsibilities, optimal families are able to accept instructions, organize themselves, negotiate differences of opinion and utilize problem-solving skills effectively (Beavers, 1982). The parents act as leaders and encourage the expression of the other family members' ideas.

SIGNIFICANT TRANSCENDENT VALUES.   Optimal families also experience significant transcendent values which are necessary for enjoyable, hopeful, and optimistic living. Family members are able to cope with the inevitable losses from growth and development, aging, and death. They are also willing to take risks despite the fact that losses might occur (Beavers, 1982).

TRAITS OF HEALTHY FAMILIES (CURRAN)

Curran's (1983) approach to determining traits of a healthy family was to ask professionals to list characteristics of healthy families they worked with. She summarized the results in 15 attributes. Healthy families communicate and listen, affirm and support one another, teach respect for others, develop a sense of trust, have a sense of play and humor, exhibit a sense of shared responsibility, teach a sense of right and wrong, have a strong sense of family in which rituals and traditions abound, have a balance of interaction among the members, have a shared religious core, respect the privacy of one another, value services to others, foster family table time and conversation, share leisure time, and admit and seek help with problems (Curran, 1983, p. 23).

FAMILY STRENGTHS RESEARCH PROJECT (STINNETT)

Stinnett (1979, see also Chapter 3, this volume) studied the characteristics of strong families through the Family Strengths Research Project in Oklahoma and concluded that most strong families exhibit six basic qualities.

APPRECIATION. Stinnett reported that strong families express a great deal of appreciation for each other. They build each other up psychologically. They give each other many positive psychological strokes, and make each other feel good about themselves. Stinnett stated that this is one of the most important qualities found among strong families and it seems to permeate all their interactions.

QUALITY TIME. Strong families spend quality time together. They sincerely enjoy being with each other. Each individual family member makes a commitment to be with the others and seems to enjoy doing so.

COMMUNICATION. Stinnett also emphasized the importance of communication in families. Effective communication is possible in these families because the individual family members spend a lot of time together and are good listeners. Good listening skills communicate respect and reciprocity. When conflict occurs, family members are able to discuss their problems openly and "share their feelings about alternative ways to deal with the problems and select a solution that is best for everybody" (Stinnett, 1979, p. 27).

COMMITMENT. An essential characteristic of strong, healthy families is commitment. These family members care deeply for one another. They are very concerned about promoting each other's happiness and welfare. These individuals are willing to give of themselves for the benefit of the family as a whole and for the well-being and growth of each individual member.

RELIGIOUS ORIENTATION. Many strong families have a strong religious orientation that seems to serve as a guideline for living. Many of the values and beliefs emphasized by religion, when implemented, can greatly enhance the quality of caring in human relationships.

ABILITY TO DEAL WITH CRISES IN AN EFFECTIVE MANNER. According to Stinnett (1979), strong families "manage, even in the darkest of situations, to look at the situation and see some positive element. They are also able to unite in dealing with the crisis instead of being fragmented by it" (p. 29).

SUMMARY

Tables 15.1 and 15.2 list the characteristics and dimensions of healthy families reported by each researcher. Table 15.3 lists the eight dimensions

Table 15.2 Dimensions and Characteristics of Healthy Families

Researcher[a]	Characteristic
Beavers (1977, 1982)	1. Systems orientation 2. Clear boundaries 3. Contextual clarity 4. Equal overt power 5. Encouragement of autonomy 6. Joy and comfort in relating 7. Skilled negotiation 8. Transcendent values
Lewis (1979)	1. Strong marriage 2. Parental power 3. Family closeness 4. Clear communication 5. Problem resolution 6. Empathic feelings 7. Dealing with loss 8. Affiliative values 9. Intimacy and autonomy 10. Distinct family style
Stinnett (1979)	1. Appreciation 2. Spend time together 3. Good communication 4. Commitment 5. Religious orientation 6. Positive crisis management
Curran (1983)	1. Communicate and listen 2. Affirm and support 3. Respect 4. Sense of trust 5. Sense of play and humor 6. Shared responsibility 7. Sense of right and wrong 8. Strong sense of family 9. Balance of interaction 10. Shared religious core 11. Respect of privacy 12. Service to others 13. Table time conversation 14. Shared leisure time 15. Seek help with problems
Otto (1962)	1. Nurture 2. Support 3. Parental discipline 4. Encourage growth 5. Spiritual well-being 6. Good communication 7. Problem-solving skills 8. Community involvement

[a] For Barnhill (1979), see Table 15.1.

Table 15.3   Dimensions and Characteristics of Healthy Families Reported Most Frequently

	Researcher					
Dimension	Beavers (1977, 1982)	Lewis (1979)	Barnhill (1979)	Stinnett (1979)	Curran (1983)	Otto (1962)
Good communication	3	4	6	3	1	6
Affection, appreciation	6	3	2	1	2	1
Commitment to growth	5	8	1	4	4	4
Problem-solving skills	7	5	3[a]	6	15	7
Systems orientation	1	1[a]	[b]	—	12	8
Parental authority	4	2	7	—	—	3
Clear boundaries	2	2[a]	8	—	8[a]	—
Transcendent values	8	—	—	5	10	5

[a] Implied.
[b] Barnhill stated that all eight dimensions can be integrated as a mutually causal system, the "family health cycle."

reported most frequently (the number under the author's name in Table 15.3 refers to the number in the author's list in Tables 15.1 and 15.2). Clearly, there is remarkable agreement among the various researchers and there are more similarities than differences.

Parent Education

All parents have significant responsibilities throughout the years their children are growing up. Parents are usually the child's only continuous source of guidance throughout the child's developmental years. Thus, parents need a broad understanding of human growth and development from birth to late adolescence.

According to Fine (1980, p. 5), parent education refers to "a systematic and conceptually based program, intended to impart information, awareness, or skills to the participants on aspects of parenting." Croake and Glover (1977, p. 151) suggest that the objective of parent education is to assist "parents who are attempting to change their method of interaction with their children for the purpose of encouraging positive behavior in their children."

The content of various parent education programs includes topics such as growth and development, appropriate play activities, discipline, first aid, safety, and nutrition (Robertson, 1984). "Parent education classes have also been initiated to improve communication, to enhance children's

cognitive functioning, and to promote parental self-understanding''
(Cooney, 1981, p. 100).

The format usually involves the presentation of specific content, group
discussion, sharing of experiences, and some skill development activities
(Fine, 1980). There are educational programs in which parents develop
their own agendas and goals and others in which a didactic teaching
methodology is combined with discussion. Still others offer highly
structured educational lessons (Robertson, 1984).

Principles of Adult Learning

Parent education can be carried out more effectively with an understanding and application of significant principles of adult learning. Miller
(1964) discussed six principles of learning important for adult learners.
These are adapted for the parent education process: The parent must be
adequately motivated to change behavior, be aware of the inadequacy of
his or her present behavior, have a clear picture of the behavior he or she
is required to adopt, have opportunities to practice the appropriate
behavior, get reinforcement of the correct behavior, and have available a
sequence of appropriate materials. Programs that are available seem to be
aware of these learning principles, as evidenced by their learning goals,
content, format, and reinforcement exercises.

Parent Education Programs

A wide variety of parent education programs have become available to
the public. The programs differ greatly in theoretical base, content,
instructional methods, and the degree to which their effectiveness is
documented by research. The following is an overview of several popular
approaches in parent education.

THE BEHAVIORAL APPROACH

In behavior modification, parents are taught how to use antecedent and
consequent stimuli effectively to alter the behavioral responses of their
children. ''The basic principles involve operationally defining a behavior,
observing its occurrence, then modifying or introducing reinforcement
procedures and continuing to observe them, so as to determine if the
behavior has been affected by the reinforcement'' (Fine, 1980, p. 8).

All behavior modification programs focus on positive reinforcement.
An assumption of these programs is that parents often utilize negative
reinforcement techniques which may actually lead to continuation of the
undesirable behaviors.

Many behavioral modification programs are available for parents. For example, Project READ (Baker, Brightman, Heifetz, & Murphy, 1973) assists parents with teaching their mentally retarded children self help, social, and language skills. *Parents Are Teachers* (Becker, 1971) is a programmed text designed to train parents in systematically applying consequences based on behavioral principles. The Responsive Parenting Program by Hall (1976) trains parents in basic behavior management techniques and implementation of these techniques to modify children's behavior.

A number of researchers have demonstrated that parents can effectively manage the behavior of their children through the use of behavior management programs. Pinsker and Geoffroy (1981) compared the effectiveness of Becker's (1971) behavior modification program with Gordon's (1970) Parent Effectiveness Training (P.E.T.). The behavior modification program was found to effectively reduce deviant child behaviors and parental perceptions of problem child behaviors. P.E.T. was found to increase positive parental consequences and family cohesion and decrease family conflict. The authors concluded that parenting programs accomplish different goals according to the nature of the materials and skills being emphasized. This finding highlights the need for a program to specifically include learning activities that are designed for different aspects of parenting.

ADLERIAN APPROACH

Much of the work that has been done in the field of parenting education is based on the contribution of Alfred Adler and Rudolf Dreikurs (see Chapter 12, this volume). The Adlerian approach focuses on a democratic lifestyle based on social equality of parents and children. Our society has evolved from autocratic family relationships to more democratic relationships (Fine, 1980).

Rudolf Dreikurs (a student and colleague of Adler) emphasized the importance of the socialization process that takes place in the family. Children are thought to adopt a lifestyle which is similar to the competitive strivings of the family and their unique position in the family constellation (Fine, 1980). Misbehavior is viewed as being directed toward gaining attention, obtaining power, or seeking revenge. According to Fine (1980, p. 12), Dreikurs viewed misbehavior as the "function of the child whose goals are misdirected. The goal of parenting is to help a child become an adequate person who uses constructive means to obtain his or her own sense of significance and status. *Children: The Challenge* (Dreikurs & Soltz, 1964) has been used by many parent education and study groups.

360 Paul A. Lee and Diane G. Brage

The concepts of Adler and Dreikurs are the focus of Dinkmeyer and McKay's (1976) Systematic Training for Effective Parenting (S.T.E.P.) program. S.T.E.P. begins with the assumption that all behavior is purposive. Therefore, if parents are to effectively guide the child's behavior, they need to identify the goal sought by the child's behavior, including the child's misbehavior. The four goals of misbehavior include gaining attention, power, revenge, and displays of inadequacy.

Natural and logical consequences are emphasized instead of reward and punishment discipline techniques. The S.T.E.P. program also stresses that encouragement will develop positive behavior in children. In addition, motivation is important for the child to develop self control and self sufficiency.

S.T.E.P. utilizes strategies for reflective listening, problem solving techniques, and the use of I messages. Parents are taught to state how they feel as a result of a child's specific behavior. An underlying emphasis of the program is on encouragement and building positive family relationships (Fine, 1980). S.T.E.P./T.E.E.N. (Dinkmeyer & McKay, 1983) is a parenting program for parents of adolescents and is based on the same Adlerian principles.

ACTIVE PARENTING

Active Parenting (Popkin, 1983, see also Chapter 4, this volume) brings the educational advantage of video to parent education. Popkin noted that the program recognizes that in today's society, parenting well is both extremely important and extremely difficult. The program is based on three assumptions: (1) Most parents have sufficient love and commitment to parent well, but (2) have not been given sufficient information, skills, or support. (3) This can be disastrous in our modern society where children openly reject traditional parenting methods.

The purpose of Active Parenting is to "streamline the democratic parenting model into a systematic and easily handled presentation that will encourage the active participation of the parent" (Popkin, 1983, p. 1). Active Parenting combines video segments, group discussion, reading and writing assignments, group and individual activities, and practice in developing parenting skills that complement the principles of S.T.E.P. and S.T.E.P./T.E.E.N.

PARENT EFFECTIVENESS TRAINING (P.E.T.)

This highly developed program by Gordon (1970) has been very popular. The program is derived from the client-centered therapy contributions of Carl Rogers. He emphasized certain necessary and sufficient conditions for client growth: empathy, congruence/genuineness and unconditional positive regard, along with an accepting, supportive, and nonjudgmental attitude. Rogers believed that clients would experience growth if therapists were able to provide this kind of therapeutic atmosphere.

Gordon based the P.E.T. program on the assumption that the parent–child relationship is analogous to the therapist–client relationship. Therefore, to help children grow and develop "naturally," parents need to provide a growth-inducing atmosphere of empathy, genuineness, and unconditional positive regard. Parents need to be accepting, supportive, and nonjudgmental of their children.

Gordon believed that parents frequently have difficulty communicating with their children. They often utilize 12 nonproductive verbal responses known as the "dirty dozen": ordering, threatening, moralizing, advising, arguing, criticizing, praising, ridiculing, diagnosing, sympathizing, probing, and withdrawing (Gordon, 1972, pp. 3–5).

Gordon (1980) advocates that parents use communication skills such as silence, open-ended questions, active listening, and I messages. Parents are encouraged to be honest with their children about their feelings. P.E.T. teaches parents problem-solving techniques for resolving conflicts. The program also teaches the parents the disadvantages of being too permissive or authoritarian.

Gordon's program seems to be very popular because of its humanistic approach and its clear presentation of effective communication techniques. P.E.T. is also appealing to parents because of the well-tested group activities and instructor training program (Fine, 1980).

The effects of P.E.T. have been evaluted in many research studies, the quality of which varies greatly in regard to methodology. Gordon (1980) reports significant improvement in the behavior of both parents and children.

TRANSACTIONAL ANALYSIS

"Transactional Analysis (TA) is the complex analysis or study of transactions and how these social interchanges shape an individual's personality and determine an overall pattern or style of life" (Fine, 1980, p. 124). All individuals seek the company of other people because they need social stimulation.

The concept of *strokes* is basic to the understanding of Transactional Analysis. A stroke is a unit of recognition such as positive and negative words, gestures, or actions. Strokes are based on "doing" (conditional) or "being" (unconditional). A being stroke is based on an individual as a person. A doing stroke is based on the individual's performance. A balance of both types of strokes is necessary for the child to feel good about himself or herself (Sirridge, 1980).

A person uses the ego states of Parent, Adult, and Child to transact with other people when giving strokes. Transactions can involve "games" which occur because of ulterior motives. Games are a non-straightforward way to relate to people. Excitement, stimulation, and recognition are some of the rewards of games.

"Script" is every person's life theme. Scripts tend to be either positive or negative. The way parents stroke their children greatly influences their children's life themes.

Popular transactional analysis books include *Games People Play* (Berne, 1964) and *I'm O.K.—You're O.K.* (Harris, 1969). *Becoming the Way We Are* (Levin, 1974) and *Raising Kids OK* (Babcock & Keepers, 1976) represent the TA approach to parent education.

The major goals of TA parent education are for parents to learn about themselves and to solve immediate family problems. TA also provides a model for identifying personal needs and needs of others.

POPULAR PUBLICATIONS

One of the early writers of popular books on parenting was Ginott (1965, 1969), who believed that many parents are misinformed about parenting and have poor role models. He advocated parent education for the majority of parents and believed that advances in parenting research should be shared with the public. His best-selling books, *Between Parent and Child* (1965) and *Between Parent and Teenager* (1969), discussed the problems and techniques of parenting and encouraged parents to express their feelings (Fine, 1980).

Ginott suggested that parents should adopt a democratic parenting style. Children should be given choices and encouraged to think and make decisions for themselves. Children's self-esteem would be higher if they encountered successful experiences. Ginott's approach could be summarized by stating that "he believed healthy child rearing practices would emerge from a self-aware parent who was able to accept the child, including the child's feelings and actions, and who was able to offer the child the experience of a parent as a 'real' person" (Fine, 1980, p. 7).

Ginott's technique is described in four phases: (1) recitation, (2) sensitization, (3) concept formation, and (4) skill learning. The recitation phase encourages parents to describe the problems they have encountered with their children. Problem-solving techniques which they have used are also discussed. In the second phase, sensitization, the leader helps the parents to understand why their children are behaving in a particular way. Concept formation provides the parents with a conceptual framework for analyzing and improving parent behavior. The final phase, skill learning, teaches parents about effective discipline techniques (Orgel, 1980). Several experimental studies suggest that Ginott's approach to parent education is effective.

How to Talk So Kids Will Listen and Listen So Kids Will Talk (Faber & Mazlish, 1980) is a "how to" book on communication skills for parents. It includes exercises to help parents improve their communication skills and provides examples of helpful dialogues so that parents can adapt this new language to their own personal style. *The One Minute Mother* and *The One Minute Father* (Johnson, 1983a, 1983b) describe how parents can use communication techniques with their children to help them quickly learn how to like themselves and behave appropriately. *How to Talk to Children about Really Important Things* (Schaefer, 1984) discusses the when, why, and how of talking with children and recommends being an approachable parent. Schaefer addresses both stressful life events and the day-to-day concerns of growing up.

Many other books on parenting continue to be published each year. Evidently, parents feel a great need for "expert" help with what most parents feel to be an important, difficult, and demanding task. Parents are able to select from a wide range of books to be studied on an individual basis, as well as program materials for group use. Increasingly, these materials seem to emphasize the positive possibilities in the parent–child relationship. Parenting is presented as an opportunity for the parent's continued growth and the child's growing level of competence and responsibility rather than just child management and discipline. This trend toward a more positive approach to parenting can be expected to continue.

Self-Esteem

A challenging task of personal development is building and maintaining a competent sense of self. A person needs to feel whole, worthwhile, and valued in the face of life's experiences. Self-esteem is essential to this task. According to Clarke (1978, p. 4), "Self-esteem is one of the greatest attributes a child can develop because learning, life, health, and even humanness itself are all functions of self-esteem."

Self-esteem has been defined in several ways. Rosenberg (1965, p. 30) states that self-esteem is a "positive or negative attitude toward a particular object, namely, the self.'' Coopersmith (1967) defines self-esteem as

> the evaluation which the individual makes and customarily maintains with regard to himself: it expresses an attitude of approval or disapproval and indicates the extent to which the individual believes himself to be capable, significant, successful and worthy. Self-esteem is a personal judgment of worthiness that is expressed in the attitudes the individual holds toward himself. (p. 4)

Elder (1968, p. 258) suggests that self-esteem includes ''feelings of personal worth influenced by performance, abilities, appearance, and judgments of significant others.'' Branden (1980, p. 124) states that self-esteem has two interrelated aspects: ''a sense of personal efficacy [effectiveness] and a sense of personal worth. It is the integrated sum of self-confidence and self-respect. It is the conviction—or more precisely, the experience—that we are competent to live and worthy of living.''

Characteristics of High Self-Esteem

According to Coopersmith (1968), individuals who possess high self-esteem tend to be

1. Active, expressive individuals who are successful academically, socially, and vocationally
2. Leaders and participants in discussion groups
3. Able to face disagreements and not particularly sensitive to criticism
4. Highly interested in civic matters
5. Secure and in control of their feelings
6. Trustful, confident, and able to act independently and decisively
7. Expectant of acceptance by other people
8. Optimistic and willing to face new challenges with eagerness
9. Not self-conscious or preoccupied with personal difficulties
10. Physically healthy
11. Creative and original
12. Achievers of higher goals than those of low self-esteem
13. Achievement oriented and expectant of success.

Battle (1982) concluded that individuals with high self-esteem tend to

1. Be more active, assertive, and effective in meeting life's challenges
2. Be proud of personal accomplishments
3. Be independent and not conforming to social pressure
4. Be popular with peers
5. Protect themselves from the threats of other people
6. Enjoy and participate in activities independently as well as with other people
7. Be confident in their abilities and less anxious than persons with low self-esteem.

Characteristics of Low Self-Esteem

According to Coopersmith (1968) individuals with low self-esteem tend to be

1. Depressed, discouraged, anxious. They worry a lot about failures and make little effort to overcome problems. They are pessimistic about the future and sometimes exhibit psychosomatic symptoms.
2. Isolated, feel unlovable, and incapable of expressing or defining themselves. They feel that they are different from other people and thus have greater difficulty forming friendships. They often have feelings of social alienation and persecution.
3. Fearful of angering others. They may withdraw from others. They remain quiet and do not express contrary opinion even when they know they are correct.
4. Sensitive to criticism. Individuals with low self-esteem become defensive if errors are pointed out. They remain defeated and exposed in their real or imagined deficiencies.
5. Lacking in confidence and indecisive. They are easily distracted by anxieties and obstacles and tend to procrastinate frequently.
6. Unwilling to set and achieve high goals. They have lower hopes, expectations, and ambitions. They may live vicariously through others' accomplishments.

Battle's (1982) additions to Coopersmith's (1968) list of characteristics include a tendency for individuals with low self-esteem to be:

1. Low in initiative and basically nonassertive in their interactions with others

2. More anxious than individuals who possess high self-esteem, tending to worry and be pessimistic in their views concerning the future
3. More prone to employing defenses of projection and repression
4. More susceptible to developing obsessive–compulsive reactions
5. More timid and predisposed to withdrawal
6. Indecisive and usually vacillating when confronted with obstacles
7. More prone to emitting self-defeating responses and developing self-punishing modes of behavior
8. More readily conforming to social pressure and exhibiting a greater degree of dependence.

Ways to Improve Adult Self-Esteem

Hamacheck (1971) developed guidelines and concepts useful in understanding and improving adult self-esteem. Adults are advised to pursue satisfying and enjoyable occupations that reflect their strengths. Individuals need to learn to be proud of their accomplishments and more accepting of their mistakes. They are encouraged to examine the criteria by which they have learned to think of themselves as inadequate and not impose unrealistic standards on themselves. People need to focus on developing the skills and interests they have rather than focusing on their weaknesses. They are urged to communicate more openly and honestly with others and are encouraged to continue to work hard even when they become discouraged.

McCrane (1982, p. 33) asserts that "lack of sound self-esteem is the fundamental reason people don't feel good about themselves and life in general. Lack of sound self-esteem is the root cause of practically every personal problem. Lack of self-esteem destroys natural confidence and exuberance, it makes people feel guilty, inferior, inadequate, unworthy and anxious."

In order to build sound self-esteem, McCrane suggests that adults need to accept themselves totally and unconditionally. He encouraged adults to accept weaknesses and failures without feeling inferior or ashamed, follow their personal authority and take responsibility for their own actions, and avoid comparing themselves with other people. McCrane asserted that if adults follow these guidelines, they will achieve their maximum potential for personal development and happiness, experience fulfilling and loving relationships, be confident about their capabilities, happy and experience less stress, and joyfully meet life's challenges.

Briggs (1977, p. 4) states that

You will do unto others as you do unto yourself. We are told to love others as ourselves. Most of us do precisely that. We do not affirm ourselves and we bombard others with the same treatment. If you do not value your own being you cannot cherish others. Improving your relationship to yourself is where enhancing adult self-esteem begins.

Briggs (1977) gives several guidelines for improving adult self-esteem

1. Adults must realize that they are responsible for their own happiness and feelings of self-worth.
2. Adults need to love themselves. They need to realize that self-love is not being selfish or conceited.
3. People need to develop a firm belief in themselves and be willing to take risks and accept new challenges.
4. Personal belief systems need to be examined.
5. Thoughts and statements should be positive rather than negative. Parents' statements to their children should be nurturing, affirming, and empathic. The nurturing parent utilizes words such as *wish, prefer, want, feel,* and *desire.*
6. Adults as well as children need to say *won't* instead of *can't.* People need to take responsibility for their choices.
7. Adults need to be patient with themselves. They must realize that learning and personal growth occur in small steps.
8. The criticism of others must be interpreted. Judgments by other people should not become self-judgments.
9. Adults should be honest with themselves about all of their feelings. However, they should not act on those feelings that could be harmful to themselves or other people.
10. Adults should be free to be themselves and not display a phony front, even though this involves risk taking.
11. Adults should be kind to themselves.

Clarke (1978) focuses on the way self-esteem can be nourished in parents and their children. She offers creative ways to develop high self-esteem utilizing TA techniques. The specific objectives of the course focus on three areas: self-esteem, family togetherness and flexibility, and conflict resolution.

These resources on self-esteem recognize that self-esteem grows out of all the significant relationships an individual has. Priority is placed on the home because it is there that an individual has his or her first and most influential relationships. Using these resources, parents have the materials to help their child develop a strong, positive sense of self-worth. Furthermore, the level of self-esteem developed early in the home tends to remain stable. If parents help a child develop a positive sense of self-worth, the child is likely to maintain a lifelong high sense of self-worth. However, for those individuals who lack high self-esteem, these resources offer hope and specific suggestions on how they can increase the level of their own self-esteem regardless of their age and early deficits.

Marriage Enrichment

Marriage enrichment activities have shown significant growth since the first marriage enrichment groups were conducted in the 1960s. Marriage enrichment classes are available on most college campuses, in mental health centers and other human service systems, and religious groups.

Otto (1975, p. 13) stated that marriage enrichment programs "are for couples who have what they perceive to be a fairly well functioning marriage and who wish to make their marriage even more mutually satisfying. The programs are not designed for people whose marriage is at a point of crisis, or who are seeking counseling help for marital problems." Marriage enrichment programs usually maintain a primary focus on the couple's relationship. Topics covered include improving the couple's communication, enhancing the sexual relationship, and ways to promote their growth as individuals and as a couple. In short, marriage enrichment seeks to enrich the couple's marriage, help them to focus on their strengths, and fully realize the potential inherent in their marriage.

Marriage enrichment programs are generally led by team couples who provide guidance and encouragement. Most programs are characterized by a considerable amount of structure. Important considerations for developing marriage enrichment programs include a focus on the identified needs of the couples, assistance with developing communication skills, awareness of each other's strengths, developing problem-solving skills and conflict resolution techniques, strengthening the couple's sexual functioning, and working together privately as well as in the total group in order to maximize growth and learning (Otto, 1976).

ASSOCIATION OF COUPLES FOR MARRIAGE ENRICHMENT

David and Vera Mace, pioneers in the area of marriage enrichment, are the originators of the Association of Couples for Marriage Enrichment (ACME), which has local chapters in many communities. The purpose of the organization is to foster marriage enrichment of couples on an ongoing basis, utilizing local chapters as support groups (Koch & Koch, 1976). The four objectives of ACME are (1) to work for the enrichment of one's own· marriage; (2) to unite with other couples for mutual support, by planning programs together for marriage enrichment; (3) to initiate and support more adequate community services designed to help marriages; and (4) to improve the public image of marriage as a relationship capable of promoting both individual development and individual fulfillment (Mace, 1976).

COUPLES COMMUNICATION PROGRAM

The Couples Communication Program (CCP) offers an educational program for assisting couples to improve their sense of awareness of self and others and to develop better communication skills (Nunnally, Miller, & Wackman, 1976). The program focuses on helping couples to become "active agents" in strengthening their relationship and to anticipate life changes. CCP recognizes that couples and families move through specific stages in their relationship and that critical role transitions tend to occur at different stages.

MARRIAGE ENCOUNTER

Marriage Encounter is a marriage enrichment program that focuses on spiritual values important in the marriage and improving the couple's communication. Couples are encouraged to talk about the strengths of the marriage, money, health, time, work, rest, sexual relations, children, relatives, atmosphere in the home, relationship to God, and death (Tengbom, 1976). The encounter groups are led by trained individuals who assist the couples with various communication techniques.

Most Marriage Encounter groups use questions and writing to increase the couple's awareness of their feelings and expectations for their relationship and to promote positive changes in their attitudes and interaction. Some questions that facilitate intimate sharing include "Why have I come here? What do I intend to get from it? What have been the happiest moments in our relationship? What three times have I felt most united with you?" (Sell, 1981, p. 139).

Marriage Encounter is not a group encounter experience. Group interaction is usually limited to shared meals, listening to lectures, and fairly casual conversation. The expression of intimate feelings takes place privately between husband and wife. As with other marriage enrichment programs, Marriage Encounter is not intended to be a therapy experience. Programs are designed for those couples who want to improve an already healthy marriage. Leaders make no attempt to provide therapy for couples attending.

EVALUATING AND NURTURING RELATIONSHIP ISSUES, COMMUNICATION, AND HAPPINESS (ENRICH)

ENRICH is a 125-item inventory designed to help spouses learn more about self, partner, and their relationship. It is a highly tested diagnostic tool that can be used in either marriage therapy or marriage enrichment. It helps a couple identify some of the strengths in their relationship as well as problematic issues for them to discuss. Couples complete the inventory individually and under the guidance of a trained counselor. After scoring, the couple can discuss their areas of agreement and disagreement in private and/or with the counselor administering the inventory (Olson & Cooper, 1982).

Marriage enrichment programs and materials continue to increase in availability and influence. Committed couples have a wide range of resources that can be used in enriching and enhancing their relationship. A growing number of couples are utilizing these positive growth-oriented resources.

The Family Life Cycle

As a theoretical framework, the family life cycle approach to the study of the family considers a wide range of marital and family data. It focuses on the dynamic change in the nuclear family from its establishment at marriage to its dissolution in death or divorce.

Although no two families are exactly alike, there is a predictability about family development based on the concept of the "family developmental task." These tasks are growth opportunities and requirements that tend to arise and require successful achievement at predictable times in the life of each family. The birth of the first child, the child's entering school, the empty nest, and retirement are major transition points for most families and can be expected to require new ways of adjusting and relating within the family.

As Duvall (1977, p. 141) noted, the family life cycle approach to studying the family recognizes "the successful phases and patterns as they occur within the continuity of family living over the years. Families that expanded to accommodate the arrival of new members at birth and the requirements of growing children later contract as they release the children as young adults into independent lives and families of their own.

And after all children have been launched, the spouses are once again members of a two-person family.

The family life cycle can be divided into eight stages. These divisions permit the study of the family at various points in time while still maintaining an awareness of the family's life as a continuous process. Duvall (1977, p. 148) cites the following eight stages:

    I Beginning families (married couple without children)
   II Families with infant(s) (oldest child, birth to 30 months)
  III Families with preschool children (oldest child, 2½ to 6 years)
  IV Families with school children (oldest child, 6 to 13 years)
   V Families with teenagers (oldest child, 13 to 20 years)
  VI Families as launching centers (first child gone to last child's leaving home)
 VII Postparental families (all children launched)
VIII Retired families (husband retired to death of one spouse)

Historically, there has been a strong emphasis on families in the child-rearing stages. Most of this literature has focused on parenting issues, for example, appropriate ways to discipline and child-management skills. Although these issues receive no less attention in the literature today, there has been a growing interest in later stages of the family life cycle as well. This interest indicates a more optimistic attitude toward family interaction, particularly during the child's adolescent years and during the "empty nest" stages.

Parent–Adolescent Relationship

Considerable literature has been published concerning the "generation gap" between parents and adolescents. The most frequent message has been that there tends to be an ever-widening gap between the two generations.

More recent research has illustrated a significant harmony between generations within the family. Coleman, George, and Holt (1979) investigated the ways in which adolescents and parents perceive each other. The results indicated that adults saw themselves as much the same as adolescents, while the adolescents evaluated adults much more positively than they did themselves.

An assumption sometimes noted in early studies was that adolescents orient their views with the culture of their peers and resist the culture of their parents. Among the supporters of this opinion, Coleman (1963) felt that adolescents separate themselves from the adult society and form their own culture and a value system that is different from adults.

Another assumption sometimes found in the literature is that adolescents are basically aligned with parental values on the most important issues. A proponent of this view, Bandura (1980) believed that in middle-class families, cooperative and mutually rewarding relationships between parents and adolescents are more in evidence than conflict and hostility.

According to Sebald (1986), teenagers do not orient themselves to either parents or peers as exclusive reference groups. Changes that have occurred in the orientation of adolescents toward parents and peers over the past two decades were examined. Identical questionnaires were administered to similar samples of teenagers in 1963, 1976, and 1982 to investigate whose advice they sought regarding social issues. Major findings suggested that there is a consistency as to which kind of issue prompts peer orientation and which questions result in parent consultation. Financial, educational, and career concerns were parent oriented, and social activities were peer oriented. One important finding indicated the decline of parent orientation between 1960 and 1970 and its partial recovery during the 1980s. Thus, on the "really important" issues in the adolescent's life and future, parents are regarded as a valued and trusted resource. Furthermore, their influence on the adolescent seems to be greater today than in the 1960s and 1970s.

The Empty Nest

The "empty nest" refers to the family life cycle stage after all the children have left home. For many years, it was believed that this was a problematic time for many couples, particularly in those families where the wife and mother was not employed but had devoted herself full-time to the care of her children and husband. After the children were launched, it was believed that she would experience feelings of no longer being needed and a dramatic loss of self-esteem.

Kennedy (1978, p. 281) states that as women grow older after their children have left home, "they begin a clear movement toward modification in self-concept and behavior. Whereas younger women describe themselves as vulnerable, dependent on husbands, and weighed down by heavy responsibilities of family life, women of maturity begin to express many of the dominant attitudes and aggressive/achievement behavior of men in middle age."

After the children leave the parent's home, the couple may need to readjust their relationship and roles. Many middle-aged women feel happier and more fulfilled if they are involved with other meaningful activities such as work, school, or volunteer organizations. Many couples look forward to their children leaving home because they will have more time to be together.

Many middle-aged couples experience increased intimacy and personal sharing because of freedom from child-rearing responsibilities. "Many a woman develops renewed interest in her husband and in maintenance of her own person and has described a 'second honeymoon' during her early fifties" (Kennedy, 1978, p. 282). This improved marital relationship is seen in the tendency for the level of marital satisfaction to show a dramatic increase during the empty nest stage and to continue higher during the retirement stages (Rollins & Cannon, 1974).

Military Families

In recent years, the U.S. military services have recognized the important link between the success of the military mission and the support which military personnel receive from their families. This important linkage is seen in higher morale, improved job performance, and increased retention rates.

The military has changed from a largely unmarried force to one consisting mainly of members with families. Today, over 80% of military career personnel are married (O'Keefe, 1986). Like their civilian counterparts, the modern military family has changed from a working father and mother who remains at home to care for the children. More than 50% of military spouses are employed. Many of these families make career decisions based not only on what is good for Dad's career, but on how the career affects the total family's needs and desires. Automatic support for a military career can no longer be assumed. In addition, military families now include a high number of single parents and couples in which both spouses are members of the military.

Families have become a vital support system on which the military relies. An appropriate and supportive response to the changing needs of the modern military family is vital to the effectiveness of the military mission.

The military services depend on an all-volunteer force. This requires members who are satisfied and committed to the military. The service member's satisfaction and commitment are influenced by his or her family having a comparable level of satisfaction and commitment. A focal point for building that commitment and satisfaction has been the development of Family Centers on major military installations. In the Air Force, these centers are called "Family Support Centers," in the Army, "Army Community Service Centers," and in the Navy and Marines, "Family Service Centers" (O'Keefe, 1986).

These family centers are staffed by military and civilian professionals trained in the fields of family studies, life-span development, and other human services skills. They provide a wide range of substantive programs designed to positively affect military family life. All the programs are based on the premise that effective family relationships do not just happen. They are the result of deliberate efforts on the part of all family members. The immediate objective is to help families realize an optimum quality of family life. The ultimate goal for the military is to increase military readiness and retention of highly trained career personnel.

With variation among the military services and depending on local needs, family centers generally provide programs and services in eight functional categories:

1. Information, referral, and coordination. This is an effort to link military families and their needs with appropriate military or civilian service providers.

2. Spouse employment training, consultation, and information. With over 50% of military spouses employed, assistance in this area represents a significant need among military families.

3. Family development education. These are proactive programs that focus on the normal developmental processes of growth and change over the family life cycle.

4. Services for families with special needs. This may include services for families with exceptional children, language classes for non-English speaking family members, or a cultural orientation class for families moving to a foreign country.

5. Family financial management education and consultation. Classes may be offered to help families determine financial priorities and to make sounder long-range financial decisions as a family.

6. Relocation assistance. Military families are highly mobile. Moving to new assignments every 2 to 4 years, they have a great need for information on other installations and suggestions for ways to make each move smooth and troublefree.

7. Aid for families in crisis. Family centers usually do not provide long-term, intensive family therapy. However, the professional staff will help families identify and prioritize their needs and if necessary, make appropriate referrals and follow-up.

8. Support during separation. Family centers act as a support system to help families cope with the special circumstances occasioned by family separations.

With family centers at most U.S. military installations, O'Keefe (1986) declared that "the newest and largest frontier in family support programs is the military" (p. 429). Centers are designed to meet the needs of the families assigned. There is considerable variation from one installation to another. However, centers are expected to provide programs and services in the above eight functional categories. Both military families and the military sevices are the beneficiaries.

Conclusion

This is the decade of the strong, healthy family. Although much of the research on families continues to have a problem orientation, an emphasis is increasingly being placed on family strengths and health. This is an exciting trend and can be expected to continue to grow and flourish.

Family life education materials are increasingly positive in nature. A wide range of positive, growth-oriented resources are available on all aspects of family life and interaction. Resources on parenting (structured programs and individual publications) have proliferated. Most of these materials have a strong positive approach to the responsibilities of parenting. Fortunately, a large number of parents are utilizing these resources in group and individual settings. In other areas of family life as well, there is a growing array of resources available which focus on positive ways of developing and nurturing a successful family life.

This chapter has highlighted the developments in six important areas of family life that have experienced a shift to a more positive approach: (1) strong, healthy families, (2) parent education, (3) building self-esteem in family members, (4) marriage enrichment, (5) the family life cycle, and (6) military family support.

References

Babcock, D., & Keepers, T. (1976). *Raising kids O.K*. New York: Grove Press.
Baker, B., Brightman, A., Heifetz, L., & Murphy, D. (1973). *The READ project series*. Cambridge, MA: Behavioral Education Projects.
Bandura, A. (1980). The stormy decade: Fact or fiction? In R. E. Muuss (Ed.), *Adolescent behavior and society: A book of readings* (pp. 22–31). New York: Random House.

Barnhill, L. (1979). Healthy family systems. *Family Coordinator, 28,* 94–100.

Battle, J. (1982). *Enhancing self-esteem and achievement: A handbook for professionals.* Seattle: Special Child Publications.

Beavers, W. R. (1977). *Psycotherapy and growth: A family systems perspective.* New York: Brunner/Mazel.

Beavers, W. R. (1981). A systems model for family therapists. *Journal of Marital and Family Therapy, 1,* 299–307.

Beavers, W. R. (1982). Healthy, midrange, and severely dysfunctional families. In F. Walsh (Ed.), *Normal family processes* (pp. 45–66). New York: Guilford Press.

Beavers, W. R. (1984). Attributes of the healthy couple. In R. F. Stahmann & W. J. Hiebert (Eds.), *Counseling in marital and sexual problems* (pp. 35–47). Lexington, MA: Lexington Books.

Beavers, W. R. (1985). *Successful marriage: A family systems approach to couples therapy.* New York: Norton.

Becker, W. (1971). *Parents are teachers.* Champaign, IL: Research Press.

Berne, E. (1964). *Games people play.* New York: Grove Press.

Branden, N. (1980). *The psychology of romantic love.* New York: Bantam Books.

Briggs, D. (1977). *Celebrate yourself.* Garden City, NY: Doubleday.

Clarke, J. (1978). *Self-esteem: A family affair.* Minneapolis: Winston Press.

Coleman, J. (1963). *The adolescent society.* New York: Free Press.

Coleman, J., George, R., & Holt, G. (1979). Adolescents and their parents: A study of attitudes. *Journal of Genetic Psychology, 130,* 239–245.

Cooney, J. (1981). Parent education: A focus on the issues. *School Counselor, 29,* 97–102.

Coopersmith, S. (1967). *The antecedents of self-esteem.* San Francisco: Freeman.

Coopersmith, S. (1968, February). Studies in self-esteem. *Scientific American,* pp. 96–106.

Croake, J., & Glover, K. (1977). A history and evaluation of parent education. *Family Coordinator, 26,* 151–158.

Curran, D. (1983). *Traits of a healthy family.* Minneapolis: Winston Press.

Dinkmeyer, D., & McKay, G. (1976). *Systematic training for effective parenting.* Circle Pines, MN: American Guidance Services.

Dinkmeyer, D., & McKay, G. (1983). *Systematic training for effective parenting of teens (STEP/TEEN).* Circle Pines, MN: American Guidance Service.

Dreikurs, R., & Soltz, V. (1964). *Children: The challenge.* New York: Duell, Sloan, & Pearce.

Duvall, E. (1977). *Marriage and family development* (5th ed.). Philadelphia: Lippincott.

Elder, G. H. (1968). Adolescent socialization and development. In E. F. Borgatta & W. Lambert (Eds.), *Handbook of personality theory and research.* Chicago: Rand McNally.

Faber, A., & Mazlish, E. (1980). *How to talk so kids will listen and listen so kids will talk.* New York: Rawson, Wade.

Fine, M. (1980). The parent education movement: An introduction. In M. Fine (Ed.), *Handbook on parent education* (pp. 3–26). New York: Academic Press.

Ginott, H. (1965). *Between parent and child.* New York: Macmillan.

Ginott, H. (1969). *Between parent and teenager.* New York: Macmillan.

Gordon, T. (1970). *Parent effectiveness training.* New York: Van Rees Press.

Gordon, T. (1972). *Parent effectiveness training: Parent handbook.* Pasadena, CA: Effectiveness Training Associates.

Gordon, T. (1980). Parent effectiveness training: A preventive program and its effects on families. In M. Fine (Ed.), *Handbook on parent education* (pp. 101–121). New York: Academic Press.

Hall, R. (1976). *Parent training: A preventive mental health program.* University of Kansas, National Institute of Mental Health Grant.

Hamacheck, D. E. (1971). *Encounters with the self.* New York: Holt, Rinehart & Winston.

Harris, T. (1969). *I'm O.K.—You're O.K.* New York: Harper & Row.

Johnson, S. (1983a). *The one minute father.* New York: William Morrow.

Johnson, S. (1983b). *The one minute mother.* New York: William Morrow.

Kennedy, C. (1978). *Human development: The adult years and aging.* New York: Macmillan.

Kock, J., & Koch, L. (1976). The urgent drive to make good marriages better. *Psychology Today, 10,* 33–34, 83–84, 95.

Levin, P. (1974). *Becoming the way we are.* Berkeley, CA: Transactional Publications.

Lewis, J. (1979). *How's your family? A guide to identifying your family's strengths and weaknesses.* New York: Brunner/Mazel.

Mace, D. (1976). We call it ACME. In H. Otto (Ed.), *Marriage and family enrichment: New perspectives and programs* (pp. 170–179). Nashville, TN: Parthenon Press.

McCrane, W. (1982). Total unconditional acceptance of yourself is vital to your success as a public speaker. *Creative Child and Adult Quarterly, 7*(1), 33–38.

Miller, H. (1964). *Teaching and learning in adult education.* London: Macmillan.

Nunnally, E., Miller, S., & Wackman, D. (1976). The Minnesota Couples Communication Program. In H. Otto (Ed.), *Marriage and family enrichment: New perspectives and programs* (pp. 180–192). Nashville, TN: Parthenon Press.

O'Keefe, A. (1986). Family focus in the military: Creating new linkages between civilian and military family support groups. In S. Van Zandt, H. Lingren, G. Rowe, P. Zeece, L. Kimmons, P. Lee, D. Shell, & N. Stinnett (Eds.). *Family strengths 7: Vital connections* (pp. 429–438). Lincoln, NE: Center for Family Strengths.

Olson, D. H., & Cooper, D. M. (1982). *Prepare enrich: Seminar director's manual.* Minneapolis: Prepare-Enrich.

Orgel, A. (1980). Haim Ginott's approach to parent education. In M. Fine (Ed.), *Handbook on parent education* (pp. 75–100). New York: Academic Press.

Otto, H. (1962). What is a strong family? *Marriage and Family Living, 10,* 481–485.

Otto, H. (1975). Marriage and family enrichment programs in North America. *Family Coordinator, 24,* 137–143.

Otto, H. (1976). Marriage and family enrichment programs: An overview of a movement. In H. Otto (Ed.), *Marriage and family enrichment: New perspectives and programs* (pp. 11–27). Nashville, TN: Parthenon Press.

Pinsker, M., & Geoffroy, K. (1981). A comparison of parent effectiveness training and behavior modification parent training. *Family Relations, 30,* 61–68.

Popkin, M. (1983). *Active parenting.* Atlanta, GA: Active Parenting.

Robertson, S. (1984). Parent education: Currrent status. *Canadian Counsellor, 18,* 100–105.

Rollins, B. C., & Cannon, K. (1974). Marital satisfaction over the family life cycle. *Journal of Marriage and the Family, 36,* 271–282.

Rosenberg, M. (1965). *Society and the adolescent self-image.* Princeton, NJ: Princeton University Press.

Schaefer, C. (1984). *How to talk to children about really important things.* New York: Harper & Row.

Sebald, H. (1986). Adolescents' shifting orientation toward parents and peers: A curvilinear trend over recent decades. *Journal of Marriage and the Family, 48,* 5–13.

Sell, C. (1981). *The enrichment of family life through the church.* Grand Rapids, MI: Zondervan.

Sirridge, S. (1980). Transactional analysis: Promoting Ok'ness. In M. Fine (Ed.), *Handbook on parent education* (pp. 123–152). New York: Academic Press.

Stinnett, N. (1979). In search of strong families. In N. Stinnett, B. Chesser, & J. DeFrain (Eds.), *Building family strengths: Blueprints for actoin* (pp. 23–30). Lincoln: University of Nebraska Press.

Stinnett, N., & DeFrain, J. (1985, November). Secrets of happy families. *Good Housekeeping,* pp. 108, 110, 112, 117.

Tengbom, M. (1976, December). When good marriages get better. Lutheran, pp. 10–12.

Index